FORGOTTEN
VOICES

Also available in the Forgotten Voices series:

Forgotten Voices of the Great War
Forgotten Voices of the Great War (illustrated)
Forgotten Voices of the Somme

Lest We Forget: Forgotten Voices from 1914–1945

Forgotten Voices of the Second World War
Forgotten Voices of the Second World War (illustrated)
Forgotten Voices of the Blitz and the Battle for Britain
Forgotten Voices of the Holocaust
Forgotten Voices of the Secret War
Forgotten Voices of D-Day

Forgotten Voices of the Falklands

FORGOTTEN VOICES OF BURMA

IN ASSOCIATION WITH
THE IMPERIAL WAR MUSEUM

JULIAN THOMPSON

EBURY
PRESS

Contents

Maps   vi

Author's Preface   vii

Acknowledgements   xii

Introduction by Lord Slim   xiii

Retreat   1

Striking Back   43
The Arakan – Round One

Striking Back   61
The First Chindit Expedition

Struggle for the Arakan   109
Round Two

Operation Thursday   149
The Second Chindit Expedition

Crisis Point   205
Kohima

The Turning Point   249
Imphal

On to Rangoon   305

Final Words   359

Glossary   369

Index of Contributors   384

General Index   387

Maps

Burma   2

The Arakan Campaigns   44

The Chindit Expeditions   62

Northern Burma   150

The Kohima Battle   206

The Imphal Battle   250

Southern Burma   306

Author's Preface

The war in Burma was the largest land campaign fought by the Western Allies against the Japanese in the Second World War. For the British, it was the longest of any fought on land in that war.

Initially, the Japanese invaded southern Burma to protect the flank of their invasion of Malaya. They subsequently occupied the rest of Burma because they viewed it as the western bastion of the Greater East Asia Co-Prosperity Sphere, their name for their conquered territories. But, in addition, by holding Burma the Japanese were able to cut the only land route by which the Chinese could be supplied: the Burma Road that ran from Rangoon north-east into China. As an added bonus, Burmese oil would be a welcome addition to the Japanese economy.

The entry of Japan into the Second World War found the defence of Burma unprepared. No invasion threat from the east was anticipated; the British deemed the jungle and mountain terrain to be impassable by any invader. Although, strategically, the British colony was an outpost for the defence of India, no railways and only one underdeveloped road connected the two countries; the section from Imphal to Kalewa, some 185 miles, was a mixture of cart track and bridleway.

Since August 1940, Burma had been under command of the Commander-in-Chief Far East, based in Singapore. The Far East was, in the British Government's view, low on the priority list for all manner of warfighting equipment. Burma, as an adjunct to that theatre, was almost off the list altogether. Only on 12 December 1941, four days after the Japanese attack on Pearl Harbor, did General Sir Archibald Wavell, Commander-in-Chief India, finally persuade Winston Churchill that Burma should be part of his area of responsibility.

Once Burma had fallen to the Japanese, it took about two years for the British – in the persons of Winston Churchill and the Chiefs of Staff – to decide on strategy in the region. There were four courses open to them: one, to invade overland; two, to invade from the sea; three, a combination of the first two; four, to bypass Burma altogether and head straight to retake Malaya by seaborne assault. The British were not entirely free agents in the matter, for not only were the Americans the dominant partner in the war against Japan, but they also supplied most of the transport aircraft to the RAF and USAAF supporting the British effort in Burma. The Americans were not in the least interested in helping the British regain a lost part of their empire. Their sole motive for supporting the British was to maintain their supply route to Chiang Kai-shek's Nationalist Chinese, initially by air, but by road after north Burma was liberated.

Contrary to popular belief, the Japanese had no experience in fighting in the jungle before the invasion of Malaya in December 1941. They owed their success to the high standard of training and toughness of their soldiers. Long marches and demanding field exercises had transformed them into superb light infantry, able to cover long distances on foot over rough terrain, carrying heavy loads. Rugged, pitiless and redoubtable, they were a formidable foe. Surrender was inconceivable. Death – either at the hands of the enemy or by one's own – was the only honourable exit from the fight. Prisoners were regarded with contempt, as expendable, and treated accordingly. When the British met the Japanese in battle, their prejudiced opinions of the enemy as inferior suffered a severe shock. They found that, man for man, the Japanese were better soldiers than the Germans.

By the end of the campaign in Burma in August 1945, about 106,000 Japanese had been killed and wounded, and some 1,700 taken prisoner, of whom only four hundred were physically fit – the remainder being wounded or desperately ill. No regular officers surrendered, and none senior to major. Once captured, for the first week most prisoners tried to commit suicide, using whatever means they had to hand. A British officer reported seeing a Japanese prisoner who had cut his own throat with the jagged edge of a bully-beef tin. He was a soldier, not an officer. If prisoners survived, they cooperated with their interrogators, not through cowardice, but merely because no one had ever instructed them what to do in these circumstances, because it had never occurred to their senior commanders that any Japanese soldier would allow himself to be taken alive.

Desmond Whyte, a doctor with the Chindits, remarked:

We underestimated the Japanese to begin with. They worshipped the Emperor as a God. They wished to die in his service. They had utter disregard of danger, and devious tactics; one could not help but admire them. In the early days they really were an invincible force until we learnt jungle craft and battle craft and realised we were superior. They were utterly ruthless and without compassion. I found a friend pinioned to a teak tree with a bayonet through both left and right wrist, and the lower limbs missing, eaten by jackals. The aim was to make us so terrified that we wouldn't wish to continue fighting. It had the opposite effect.

Until the British acquired the necessary jungle and battle craft, the Japanese were regarded as invincible. This was to change, but the process took time and cost many lives.

Burma is a large country, and if superimposed on a map of Europe, Fort Hertz in the extreme north would be in the middle of the North Sea, Mandalay near Paris, Rangoon where the Pyrenees meet the Mediterranean, and Moulmein on Marseilles. Victoria Point, at the southern end of the long isthmus of Tenassarim, would be three-quarters of the way across the Mediterranean.

The country is surrounded on three sides by mountain ranges covered in thick jungle. Four great rivers flow south into the Bay of Bengal. The Irrawaddy and its major tributary the Chindwin rise in the Himalayas to the north; to the east flow two more large rivers, the Sittang and the Salween. All have numerous tributaries, most of which are a serious obstacle to movement. The valleys in central Burma open out into thickly wooded plains, dotted with low hills. In the flatter areas rice is cultivated in paddy fields. South of Mandalay and Shwebo the country is arid with sparse vegetation.

In the cold weather, from mid-October to March, the climate is perfect, warm and dry by day and cool at night, but temperatures rise in April and May, and the heat strikes like an open oven with high humidity. The monsoon arrives in mid-May and lasts until about mid-September, enveloping the whole of Burma and Assam, except for the dry zone around Mandalay and Meiktila. During the monsoon malaria and dysentery flourish; the rivers swell; valleys and flat areas flood; thick cloud, thunderstorms and turbulence make flying extremely hazardous.

In one year, 1943–44, British and other Allied troops recorded 250,000 cases of malaria and dysentery. The rate of men falling sick in Burma equals those in earlier wars, before the introduction of modern medicine. For example, in 1943, for every man admitted to hospital with wounds, there were 120 from tropical diseases. By 1945 the rate dropped to ten men sick for one wounded, and in the last six months of the war, to six for one.

The Burmans, the indigenous Burmese, lived mainly in the centre of the country. They resented British rule, and disliked the thousands of Indians imported by the British to work on the railways and other public projects. They had no love for the Chinese, who, along with the Indians, had monopolised sections of the economy, including the rice trade, enriching themselves in the process. Before the British arrived, the Burmese had persecuted the Karens, Shans, Kachins and Chins, tribespeople living in the hills and mountains to the east, north and west of central Burma, and have continued to do so since independence in 1948.

In this book I use the term British to refer to forces from the then British Empire and Commonwealth. In Burma this included 340,000 Indians of many races: Sikhs, Rajputs, Baluchis, Punjabis and Gurkhas, to name but some. The Indians outnumbered the forces from all the other allies added together. Some 100,000 British fought in Burma, as did 90,000 Africans and about 66,000 Chinese. Around 60,000 Americans took part, most of them from the forty-seven United States Army Air Force (USAAF) squadrons (there were fifty-one British and Commonwealth squadrons). The overwhelming majority of accounts in my book are by soldiers from Britain – perfectly understandable in the archives of a national museum. It also reflects the fact that by the time the project was taken in hand by the Imperial War Museum, most soldiers of the old British Indian Army were difficult or even impossible to trace. Of those that have been interviewed, even fewer were translated, but some have now been transcribed and translated specifically for this book. The same constraint applies to the Africans and the Japanese.

The Indians who fought in Burma were part of the largest all-volunteer army in history. John Randle, whose testimony appears in this book, explains the ethos of that army:

The Indian soldier wasn't fighting for the defence of India against Hitler [or Japan]. He fought because in northern India, especially, there was a strong tradition of serving the British; and because of the culture of honour, *izzat*. Because of the land system, a small property was able to support only one son, so there was a culture of younger sons joining government service, the army or police. They got two square meals a day, pay, pensions, and were honoured and respected members of their community. Their whole history was one of service, for the Moguls and so forth, and was not anything to be ashamed of.

Following the outbreak of the Second World War in 1939, the Indian Army expanded thirteen-fold from its peacetime strength of 185,000 to nearly 2,500,000. This soon resulted in the 'milking' of experienced officers and NCOs from existing units to provide replacements in the Indian units fighting in the Middle East (from 1940 onwards), and in training centres to train the hugely expanded Indian Army. Thousands of Indian soldiers, along with their British officers, were captured by the Japanese in Malaya, and so were not available to fight in Burma. For this reason many Indian units in the early years of the campaign in Burma were not well trained or led; hence the censure levelled at these units by some of the voices in this book

Readers familiar with the 1957 film *Bridge on the River Kwai* will not find accounts of experiences on the Burma–Thailand Railway in this book, which focuses on the fighting in the Burma campaign. The 61,000 Allied prisoners of war who formed part of the workforce on the railway were captured in the earlier Malaya and Netherlands East Indies campaigns. They were hugely outnumbered by around 270,000 impressed labourers from Malaya, Thailand and the Netherlands East Indies. Prisoners of war taken by the Japanese in Burma were sent to Rangoon Jail.

What this book does capture is what it was like to fight in the demanding terrain and climate of Burma; and, from the British perspective, to be confronted by the most formidable soldiers encountered by anyone in the Second World War – the Japanese.

Julian Thompson, June 2009

Acknowledgements

Writing this book would not have been possible without the witnesses whose oral testimony was recorded by the Sound Archive of the Imperial War Museum. It is these witnesses that I must mention first. The expertise and painstaking attention to detail of the staff of the Sound Archive have ensured that the experiences of the witnesses have been recorded for posterity and assembled in such a way that researchers can access them readily. As so often in the past in my career as an author, Margaret Brooks, the Keeper of the Sound Archive, has been a great supporter, and for this I thank her, along with Terry Charman, Elizabeth Bowers, Abigail Ratcliffe and Madeleine James. I would particularly like to thank Richard McDonough, who has been a source of wise guidance and assistance.

I must also thank the Photographic Archive at the Imperial War Museum, especially Hilary Roberts and David Parry, for their help in this project. I am grateful to Barbara Levy, the Imperial War Museum's literary agent, for introducing me to the concept. I must also say thank you to my own agent, Jane Gregory, whose encouragement over many years has been invaluable.

Thanks to Liz Marvin and to Charlotte Cole, my editor at Ebury, who has been both patient and understanding in keeping me on track. I am most grateful to Hikari Nishimoto of King's College London, who translated and transcribed the Japanese interviews.

Last, but most certainly not least, my love and gratitude to Jane Thompson who has been my unwavering supporter and adviser.

Julian Thompson, June 2009

Introduction

Those who fought in Burma have never denigrated the courage of the Japanese soldier, airman or sailor. It can be argued that our nation has never fought such a tenacious, vicious and brave foe.

The 14th Army, the largest Allied Army of World War II, was built of many races and religions. It produced the leadership, spirit and courage to win and delivered the greatest defeat on land in the history of the Japanese nation.

I am a supporter of oral history as it brings the past to life and alerts the senses to the action of the moment. *Forgotten Voices of Burma* does just that. Julian Thompson, a proven battle commander himself, demonstrates in the cross section of those talking to us what it was like to fight, live and die in Burma. Duty, valour, selflessness, endurance, improvisation and above all comradeship capture the reader.

During the campaign I know my father met and spoke with many we hear from. He was so proud of these men and women of Burma. Some have since died but those who survive today, together with many from the Common-wealth and other Allies in that great army with its air forces and navies, still meet to continue their unique comradeship, and give help to those in need, through the Burma Star Association. Let us not forget there are also over 30,000 who still lie in Burma and very many more in Assam in the war cemeteries of Imphal and Kohima.

I wish Julian Thompson success with *Forgotten Voices of Burma*, and trust that our young men and women read, learn and realise that they owe much in their daily life to the generation who ensured their freedom today.

The Rt Hon The Viscount Slim
August 2009

Retreat

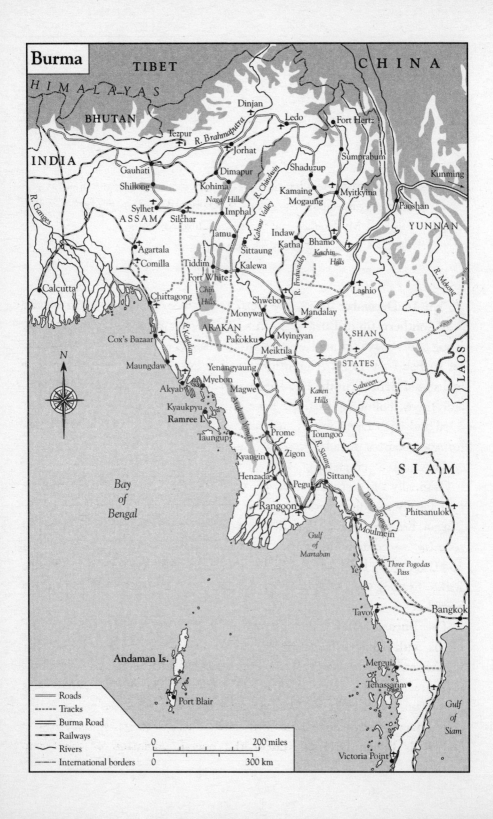

Burma

TIBET

C H I N A

H I M A L A Y A S

BHUTAN

Dinjan

Ledo

Fort Hertz

INDIA

Tezpur

R. Brahmaputra

Jorhat

Sumprabum

Kunming

Gauhati

Dimapur

Shaduzup

Shillong

Kohima

Kamaing

Myitkyina

Paoshan

Naga Hills

Mogaung

YUNNAN

Sylhet

ASSAM

Silchar

Imphal

R. Chindwin

Kabaw Valley

Indaw

Bhamo

Agartala

Tamu

Katha

Kachin
Hills

Comilla

Sittaung

R. Irrawaddy

Lashio

Tiddim

Kalewa

Fort White

Chin
Hills

Shwebo

Calcutta

Chittagong

Monywa

Mandalay

ARAKAN

Pakokku

Myingyan

SHAN

Cox's Bazaar

Meiktila

STATES

R. Salween

N

Maungdaw

Yenangyaung

R. Mekong

R. Kaladan

Myebon

Magwe

Karen
Hills

Akyab

Kyaukpyu

Ramree I.

Arakan Yomas

Prome

Toungoo

LAOS

Taungup

Kyangin

Zigon

R. Sittang

Bay
of
Bengal

Henzada

Pegu

Sittang

S I A M

Rangoon

Gulf
of
Martaban

Phitsanulok

Dawna Range

Moulmein

Three Pogodas
Pass

Ye

Andaman Is.

Tavoy

Bangkok

Port Blair

Mergui

Tenasserim

Gulf
of
Siam

Victoria Point

Roads
Tracks
Burma Road
Railways
Rivers
International borders

0	200 miles
0	300 km

The Japs fought with great ferocity and courage. We were arrogant about the
Japs, we regarded them as coolies. We thought of them as third rate.
My goodness me, we soon changed our tune.

On 14 December 1941, the Japanese captured Victoria Point on the southern tip of Burma. By this time the Japanese had invaded Hong Kong and Malaya. Hong Kong fell on Christmas Day 1941, and Singapore on 15 February 1942. A month before the fall of Singapore, the Japanese had seized airfields in the Kra Isthmus of Burma, at Mergui, Victoria Point and Tavoy. Following this, the Japanese Fifteenth Army, consisting of the 33rd and 55th Divisions, deployed in Siam (now Thailand), were waiting for the moment to advance to seize Rangoon when their campaign in Malaya neared completion.

Originally the garrison of Burma had consisted of two British battalions, four locally recruited battalions of Burma Rifles, and six battalions of the Burma Frontier Force. The first priority of these troops was internal security, to contain dissent among the Burmese (or Burmans). During 1941, the troop level was increased by raising more battalions of the Burma Rifles, forming the 1st Burma Division, and shipping in two Indian infantry brigades.

The Burma Rifles had consisted exclusively of Karens, Kachins and Chins, with British officers; the Burmans were considered unfit for military service, as being neither loyal nor martial enough. Although, under political pressure, some were recruited when the Burma Rifles was expanded, most proved unreliable and even treacherous when subjected to the test of battle.

The Japanese invasion found Burma defended by the 1st Burma Division and 17th Indian Division, under the overall command of Lieutenant

General J. T. Hutton. He sent the 1st Burma Division to central Burma to cover the routes in from the east from the Mekong Valley, along the Burma–Indo–China border. Major General 'Jackie' Smyth's 17th Indian Division was ordered to hold the line of the Salween River and cover Rangoon.

The battle for Burma was lost on 23 February 1942, early in the campaign, at the disaster at the Sittang River, when the British demolished the only bridge too early, leaving half their soldiers on the wrong side. This was followed by the longest fighting retreat in the history of the British Army, 1,100 miles, ending on 10 May when the British withdrew into Assam over the Chindwin River in north-east Burma. If properly defended, the Sittang position would have provided a good chance to impose a serious delay on the Japanese, and buy time for more British reinforcements to arrive in Burma. The battle was lost by attempting to hold too far forward, and underestimating the enemy. The confusion was made worse by pitting inexperienced troops against some of the best soldiers in the world.

INVASION AND DISASTER

Major General John 'Jackie' Smyth
GOC, 17th Indian Division
Hutton was out of his element as a battlefield commander in Burma. When Alexander arrived to take over, it was too late. Had he been there earlier, the Prime Minister of Australia might not have refused to send the two Australian divisions to Burma. Also, the Sittang disaster might not have occurred.

In early December, I was told by Wavell, then C-in-C India, that two of my brigades were being sent to Singapore, which came as a great shock to me. I was to go to Burma with my one remaining brigade plus two new ones. Wavell did not give the impression that he thought there was any threat to Burma at all.

Lieutenant Anthony Dillon
1st Battalion, Gloucestershire Regiment
My battalion was stationed on Mingaladon airfield, near Rangoon. There was no threat as far as we could tell. The war was a long way away, and there was a

The Japanese enter Tavoy in southern Burma on 19 January 1942, greeted by Burmese inhabitants who saw the invasion as an opportunity to gain independence from Britiish rule.

feeling of apathy. The amount of training we did before the Japanese invaded Burma was minimal, we were an Internal Security battalion; and there was a considerable amount of unrest in Burma.

We were badly equipped, signalling by heliograph or line. We had few vehicles, our mortars and machine-guns were carried on mules. We were unfit for modern war. In the days just before the Japanese attack on Pearl Harbor, a lot of US aid came in by sea to Rangoon and was taken up to China up the Burma Road. When the Japs bombed Rangoon, the Chinese abandoned the vehicles and equipment in the docks and we helped ourselves to all this stuff.

Private Neville Hogan
2nd Battalion, Burma Rifles Armoured Car Section
I am a Karen and lived in Rangoon, where my father worked as a shipping manager. Before the war I joined the Burma Auxiliary Force, Rangoon Battalion. In order to join, I lied about my age, showing the recruiting sergeant my elder brother's birth certificate.

Most Burmese civilians were anti-British. They wanted independence. The Karens, the Chins and Shans liked the British. The Burma army pre-war was mostly Karen.

In December 1941 I was a private soldier at Mingaladon Airfield with the Armoured Car Section of the 2nd Burma Rifles. The Japanese bombed us on Christmas Day. No one was killed or wounded, but two out of four of our so-called armoured cars had shrapnel holes in them. We then witnessed Rangoon being drained of the civilian population. The people, mainly Indians, walked past Mingaladon, which was about twelve miles out of Rangoon; the City was a ghost town. My mother and sister left at this time and went to north Burma and eventually into India.

Corporal William Norman
Mortar Platoon, 2nd Battalion, Duke of Wellington's Regiment
My battalion was in Peshawar training for operations on the North-West Frontier when the Japanese invaded Malaya. I was a bandsman. I remember saying to the RSM that we ought to be training for jungle warfare to fight the Japs in Malaya. In January 1942, all sorts of equipment started to arrive; we were still equipped as the British army had been in 1918. We got Bren guns, mortars. We had never fired a mortar. I was in the mortar platoon, formed

Neville Hogan, as a lieutenant later in the war.

from the band. We got radios, which no one knew how to work.

In late January we went by train to Madras. We were all excited and glad to be getting into the war at last. We embarked on a ship, and noticed that the ship was going east so we thought we were going to Malaya. We started to train on our new weapons, we all fired two rounds from the Boyes anti-tank rifle. We arrived at Rangoon to be greeted with the news that Singapore had fallen. We were amazed to see that the Burmese were not Indian, but Asiatic. We knew nothing about the place.

Mrs Margaret ('Beth') Bootland
Wife of RSM 1st Battalion, King's Own Yorkshire Light Infantry

Alan and I, with our five-year-old son Ian, lived in the sergeant major's house at Maymyo, where the battalion was stationed. Although the war against Germany had been going on for a couple of years, to begin with we never thought the war would affect us. But one day Alan said that the Americans were getting worried about the Japanese. We listened to the news on the wireless, and when we heard about Pearl Harbor, we knew we were in for it.

One Sunday morning after an early game of tennis I was in the bath. I heard a roar of planes, stood up in the bath, peeped through the net curtains. I saw the palm trees waving, thought it's only a strong wind, and sat back in the bath. I heard Alan running up the path shouting, 'Where are you, Beth?'

I replied, 'I'm in the bath.'

He told me, 'Get out quick, it is an air raid.'

He pounded upstairs shouting, 'Get out, get out.'

I jumped out of the bath, had a quick rub with the towel and tried to pull my panties on, and the Celanese material stuck to my wet legs. Try as I could I couldn't get them on.

He asked me what I was doing, and I said, 'I can't get my panties on.'

He said, 'Come out, put on my big army greatcoat which I have got here, grab your clothes off the chair.'

As soon as I was out, he asked where Ian was, and I told him that he was away somewhere on his cycle with his friends. Alan went off to find him. The gravel hurt my bare feet as I ran down the drive in Alan's greatcoat, holding my clothes, making for the slit trench in the garden. Each slit trench in the married quarters area had an armed soldier in it. I told the one in mine to turn his back while I dressed. To my relief, Ian eventually arrived.

The quarters were full because the Gloucestershire families had been evacuated from Rangoon, which had not been captured yet, but had been bombed. I had to go round all the families to find out how many pregnant women there were, so the army knew how many would require evacuation by air.

Major Charles MacFetridge
Officer Commanding 3rd Indian Light Anti-Aircraft Battery
On arrival at Rangoon we found the docks deserted because the Japs had bombed the docks on Christmas Day. We found a good assembly area about fifteen miles outside Rangoon near Mingaladon airfield. I deployed two troops to defend the airfield, and one troop moved by rail and boat over the river Salween to Moulmein.

On the last day of January I decided to pay the troop at Moulmein a visit, as a boost to morale. I thought Japs were still well to the south in Tenassarim. While I was travelling in a Tiger Moth with the soldiers' pay in a bag, the pilot indicated that he had been recalled to base at Rangoon, telling me that the Japs had overrun Moulmein. So I had four guns on the wrong side of the mighty Salween River. In the confused fighting there I lost all four guns.

Private Neville Hogan
2nd Battalion, Burma Rifles Armoured Car Section
At the end of January, the armoured car section was ordered to go to the south of Burma on the road to Martaban and Moulmein. On 19 February 1942 (my brother's birthday, which is why I can remember the date) we were ambushed in a roadblock nine miles north of Martaban. The leading car crashed through the roadblock. I was in the second car. We came around the bend in the road to see the enemy, who had been sitting on the trees forming the roadblock, shoot to their feet in surprise. They turned out to be Thai soldiers, forced by Japs to fight us. We opened fire as did they. They were using small calibre armour-piercing bullets, which came straight through our armour. I was wounded in the right thigh. We were not expecting to be ambushed, as far as we were concerned the war was on the other side of the bay, twelve miles away. Our armoured cars were First World War vintage, and the bullets jammed the turret preventing it from training round. We backed up the road, round the bend out of sight, and the Thais did not follow up.

We then fought a rearguard action all the way to the Sittang Bridge. We were bombed three times by Blenheim bombers of the RAF, despite standing in the paddy fields waving to them.

Second Lieutenant John Randle
Officer Commanding B Company, 7th/10th Baluch Regiment

I was a newly commissioned second lieutenant commanding a company. We arrived in the middle of an air raid at Rangoon, and moved by train to lower Burma in the general area east of the Sittang and west of the Salween. The part we went to was rubber, not jungle, and we were used to the vast open plains of our training area in India. I like trees, but, in rubber plantations, with no horizon, it is a bit depressing and confining.

The Japs had barely started their offensive; we guarded bridges, then deployed on the west bank of the Salween, before pulling back to Kuzeik on the River Salween opposite Pa-an. The Salween is broader than the Rhine at this point. The brigade was dispersed. Our role was to hold the waterfront at Kuzeik, and we established company patrol bases to try to identify if and when the Japanese crossed the river, at which point the brigade reserve battalion would come up from Thaton and drive the Japanese back into the Salween. The positions had been dug by 1st/7th Gurkhas, concentrating on holding the river front and hadn't been developed as a perimeter to face an attack from the west. Because we had two companies out in bases, and one holding the front, the perimeter facing west was practically non-existent. Because the perimeter was so shallow our own mortars and the two mountain guns in support could not fire on our own front.

The 1st/7th Gurkhas had already given the 215th Regiment a bloody nose at Pa-an, before being relieved by 7th/10th Baluch, but this did not deter this very battle-experienced Japanese Regiment, experts in night attacks.

Corporal William Norman
Mortar Platoon, 2nd Battalion, Duke of Wellington's Regiment

We were deployed near the coast east of Rangoon, in case of a landing across the Gulf of Martaban. We were not there long, but did fire our mortars. A despatch rider came up and we were on the move again. The mortars and ammunition, 150 rounds per mortar, were on fifteen-hundredweight trucks, but we had to march. As we marched we got covered from head to foot in dust and were continually thirsty. Whenever I think of Burma I think of dust and thirst, not jungle, we were not in that part of Burma. Although there was some jungle, it was not continuous.

The motor transport sergeant came along and shouted 'anyone who can drive over here'. The motor transport had been issued and there weren't enough drivers. Some who volunteered couldn't even drive, they volunteered to get out of the marching and the dust. We were entrained at Pegu and went across the Sittang River and to a place called Kyaikto. From there we travelled in trucks and took up a position in the village, where the villagers greeted us and gave us tea.

Second Lieutenant John Randle
Officer Commanding B Company, 7th/10th Baluch Regiment
A Company were in a patrol base at Myainggale, seven miles south of the battalion position. I was told to take over from A Company, and my Subedar, Mehr Khan, went off with one platoon as advance party. During the night the Japanese attacked and, as we learned subsequently, wiped out my platoon with Subedar Mehr Khan, and a platoon of A Company, the remainder of the company having already left. As I was moving to Myainggale with my remaining two platoons, I ran into the middle of 215 Regiment just getting across and taking up positions on the west bank of the Salween. I had a hairy old night, lost a few chaps, but managed to get my two platoons out back to the main position. The visibility was quite good, in banana plantations, and, with the full moon you could see about fifty yards, it was so light you threw a moon shadow. The CO had not laid down routes for my company and A company to move on, in order to avoid a clash, and I was worried about having a shoot-out with them. A Company were to move, leaving one platoon under Subedar Mehr Khan of B Company as soon as he arrived. We were in single file one platoon leading, followed by Company HQ, and the other platoon, when a man charged in to our column. I thought it was one of my soldiers running away, and shouted at him. It was a Jap who ran off into the bush. A couple of Japs were shot by my men, the first dead Jap I had seen. There was quite a lot of firing, and I realised there were quite a lot of Japs about. I tried to get through on my radio, which didn't work. So I sent my runner, the company bugler, back with a message to my CO to tell him there were a lot of Japs about. They cut in behind us and we could hear the runner

11

screaming as they killed him with swords and bayonets. This was followed by an enormous lot of firing a couple of miles away from the base we were going to relieve. The Japs were running about, in a fair state of confusion too, having just come across the river. We had no idea what tactics we should adopt. I just formed a circle which, looking back, was the best thing to do: river on one side, Japs on two sides. It was pure luck, not cleverness. It was clear to me there were a considerable number of Japs to the south of me, so I decided to return to the battalion position. I only lost a couple of chaps. Luckily I picked a route where there were no Japs and got back OK.

Corporal William Norman
Mortar Platoon, 2nd Battalion, Duke of Wellington's Regiment
In the morning a lot of fire came from our right flank, and we heard that a Burma Rifle battalion had all pushed off in a panic. We were ordered to withdraw. We didn't think much of this, we had not seen the Japs yet. As we were marching through high elephant grass a lot of aircraft came over and there was an argument about which type they were. The fellows just out from England who were 'experts', said they were Hurricanes. The planes circled and started diving down. We thought they were going to give the Japs hell. They weren't Hurricanes and they started to give us hell. We withdrew into a rubber plantation. All the trees were in lines. As we heard the planes diving in, the men tried to hide behind the trees in a long line. Actually the aircraft were RAF attacking our transport on the road.

Second Lieutenant John Randle
Officer Commanding B Company, 7th/10th Baluch Regiment
The next day they dive-bombed us. We weren't far from a major airfield at Cheng Mai across the Thai border. Slit trenches saved us losing many chaps although we had no overhead cover. Morale was OK, and the chaps were not too upset.

That night at about midnight, we were attacked by 215 Regiment and pinned against the Salween. The CO had sent one of my platoons and a platoon from another company out on a patrol, God knows what for, so I was down to one platoon, and a section of two Vickers medium machine guns. At about twelve o'clock (midnight) the Japs came in and we had hand-to-hand fighting. They overran us and C Company, whose commander got an immediate DSO.

John Randle as a captain.

The Japs came in with no artillery support in what started as a silent night attack. When they got close, they screamed *banzai* and came charging in shoulder-to-shoulder. The Vickers fired across my front and caused heavy casualties to the Japs. They surged into Company HQ, I killed the chap coming for me. I was standing up firing my revolver, and missed first time. My CSM was grappling with a Jap. My batman was killed by a grenade. Just before dawn, realising if we stayed we would get taken prisoner, we charged out and then lay up about 150 yards away, and after first light heard a second assault going in, on battalion HQ. Then we had a pause, then at about seven o'clock the next morning they finished us off. We lost 289 killed, and 229 taken prisoner in our first engagement.

I had fever and a temperature of 102. It took me two days to get back to our lines. I had two soldiers with me. We had no map, no compass. A whole Jap battalion, the 111th/215th passed me as I lay up. We got back to the Donthami river, where I heard a shout, and thought oh Christ, after all this. They were waving, it was the 1st/7th Gurkhas and they sent a boat over.

I rejoined the battalion. We were staked out there like a goat for the Jap tiger and sacrificed for no reason. The CO was killed and we lost over sixty per cent of our officers. Only about fifty of the battalion got away, but we had quite a big B Echelon, who were not involved, and the two platoons sent out on patrol got away. With the exception of one officer, the Japs butchered all our wounded. News of this got back to us and this conditioned my, and the whole battalion's, attitude towards the Japs. We were not merciful to them for the rest of the war. We didn't take any prisoners.

Private Neville Hogan
2nd Battalion, Burma Rifles Armoured Car Section
On arrival at the Sittang Bridge we dug slit trenches at the foot of the bridge. The next morning all hell broke loose as the Japs attacked our position, a settlement round a pagoda. Came down the hill straight at us at first light, with a crackle of fire. Our officer Keith Laurie had gone over the bridge to get orders from HQ. Our other officer was wounded.

We had no telephone, no radios, it was chaos. A private soldier, George Hyde, took command, when we were all about to run back across the bridge. We fired at the Japs with our .45 pistols and they were effective, and drove the enemy back. We all said 'this is good', and jumped back into our trenches.

Major General John 'Jackie' Smyth
GOC, 17th Indian Division

During operations around Sittang, Wavell came to visit us and instead of congratulating us on holding off two Jap divisions with one division, he spent the whole time saying that the Japs were useless, and therefore by implication we were worse.

The Sittang disaster was the cause of the loss of Rangoon and Burma; totally unnecessarily. We had been withdrawing towards the Sittang with its single-track railway bridge. I made it clear to Hutton that we must not be caught on the enemy side of the river with this one narrow way across behind us. On 12 February, I sent Brigadier 'Punch' Cowan, my Chief of Staff, to Hutton and told him that it was the opinion of all of us that if we were to get everyone across, I must start immediately that day. Hutton was under great pressure from Wavell and the Prime Minister not to withdraw at all. At the time he was trying to get the Australian Prime Minister to allow the two Australian Divisions, who were at sea on their way to Australia, to divert to Burma. It was thought that the Australian Prime Minister would not agree if the British were retreating.

On 19 February Hutton came forward and said that saving 17 Division intact was now the most important priority. We were faced by two divisions and a superior air force; it was going to be a desperate race to get anyone back over the Sittang.

Second Lieutenant John Randle
Officer Commanding B Company, 7th/10th Baluch Regiment

We assembled, pretty demoralised after an appalling baptism of fire, then moved east of the Sittang River and got involved in the early stages of the Sittang bridge debacle. All the Punjabi Mussulmen were put into one company of two platoons, which I commanded. We were at Mokpalin on the day of the opening part of the Sittang battle and ordered to move up the railway line and cross the bridge to the west side. The Battalion was formed into two companies. The 2i/c was in command, Pat Dunn. As we were moving to the bridge still on the east side, my company was the first to come under fire from Pagoda Hill, from Jap MMG, and took casualties. One of my platoons panicked and ran back and joined the rest of the battalion. I arrived at the bridge and reported to the CO of the 4th/12th Frontier Force Regiment who were holding the bridge. He told me to go up and give Sam Manekshaw of C Company a hand.

I went up and gave Sam the best help I could. Certain amount of firing, Jap probing attacks. Then the rest of the battalion came up, and we were ordered across the bridge. We came under desultory fire as we crossed the bridge.

'Jackie' Smyth took no proper steps to defend the bridge. There was no close bridge garrison, no proper fire plan, no proper defence. This bridge was the jugular of the division. We didn't see much of the Jap attack. They were just probing at the first stage. They used to take a commanding bit of ground and sit to see what we would do about it. We would attack and take heavy casualties. By holding Pagoda Hill they had a key feature overlooking the bridge and approaches to it. Smyth lacked moral courage, he should have pushed the 1st/4th Gurkha Rifles across and dug in a proper position in depth. I didn't know all this at the time. I didn't know what the hell was going on in my own little world.

Corporal William Norman
Mortar Platoon, 2nd Battalion, Duke of Wellington's Regiment
Arriving at Mokpalin we took up positions in the paddy, wet with sweat, and dying of thirst. During the night we fired in a panic like the Burmese. Somebody would see something, fire a shot, then another and in no time all the platoon was firing at nothing. All units did this until they learned better. The Japs were there shouting out to us. Things like 'all NCOs to me', and 'all KOYLIs come here'.

During the night there had been a tremendous explosion. Everybody said the bridge had been blown up and we were cut off.

Second Lieutenant John Randle
Officer Commanding B Company, 7th/10th Baluch Regiment
After crossing the bridge we took up position in the middle of bamboo thickets, and heard a loud bang and realised the bridge was blown. My CO and I went down to the bank to see what we could do. It was chaos with Gurkha and Indian and British soldiers swimming across, some wounded. We went into the water and helped them out, and brewed up tea for some of them. When I was with Sam Manekshaw I had seen the 2nd Battalion, Duke of Wellington's Regiment moving up across the bridge, very cheerfully going

in to battle. Now some of them were swimming back. The river is wide and we could not fire back at the Japs.

Corporal William Norman
Mortar Platoon, 2nd Battalion, Duke of Wellington's Regiment
We came to the Sittang, a huge river, and we were on our own. I thought what are we going to do? Along came another fellow from the band, and he said that he had tried swimming, but had turned back. Upriver I could see the two spans of the bridge hanging in the water.

Jack found a bamboo pole. I stripped the Bren, threw it into the water, stripped to shorts and started swimming. We swam and swam, I have no idea for how long. The bamboo pole was getting waterlogged and would only support one person. There was someone swimming along behind, and I said, 'If you want to rest on this pole, you can't.' This chap said, 'I am a good swimmer, I am Anglo–Burmese.'

He swam ahead and told us that he could touch the bottom. I expected to see masses of troops on the other side, but to begin with not a soul.

Private Neville Hogan
2nd Battalion, Burma Rifles Armoured Car Section
When the bridge was blown with us still on the enemy bank, I felt devastated and lost. My first thought was where am I going to get my next meal from. Chaos reigned all that day.

On our right was a Gurkha battalion. We came under the CO's command. To get across we followed the riverbank for about two miles up the river, we met some villagers who suggested that a good swimmer would get swept down but not so far as to end up in the estuary. We started to make rafts out of bamboo and big earthenware jars, because the Gurkhas could not swim. We were organised into parties of twenty or thirty to swim the river. I had my boots round my neck, my pistol on its belt, and a pair of shorts. About three-quarters of the way across I felt a blow on my thigh, and thought I had collided with a Gurkha, but it turned out that I had been hit by shrapnel. I got to the other bank about three hundred yards from the bridge, along with about ten out of our party of about thirty.

We made our way along the railway line to Pegu. It was a long arduous walk, forty-two miles, which took two days. There we found a hospital train, where my shrapnel was removed. Ten minutes later the RAMC colonel doctor said only seriously wounded could stay on the train, remainder walk. The two nurses who had removed the shrapnel tried to hide me under a bunk, but I could not fit.

I was very stiff and in pain. I left the station and found a lot of ambulances there, which we were told we were not allowed to use; not for walking wounded again. But we were told, 'When we move off, if you stand on the step at the back you can come with us.' There were two of us on the back of each ambulance, and the drive was a nightmare, with nothing to hold on to, and the step was about nine inches wide. The driver drove at about fifty miles an hour, swerving every time a plane came over. We found out later that he had not even passed his test. After a while we got to Pyinmana and the ambulances were due to leave next morning at six am. But they left at four, and we were left without any form of transport.

Corporal William Norman
Mortar Platoon, 2nd Battalion, Duke of Wellington's Regiment
Eventually I saw a Burmese soldier who told us to go to Waw. The Anglo–Burmese said, 'Don't trust him. Come with me to Rangoon, I live there.' We fell in with another chap from the regiment with a Dogra soldier. We came to a village and the villagers all turned out with dahs and shouted at us. Nearby there was pile of bamboo poles that had been sharpened at one end, probably to make a fence. I told the chaps, 'Grab one of these, and when I say "charge", charge forward at the high port.' But this Burmese fellow ran ahead and said, 'It is all right, I speak the language. They think we are escaped convicts.' They were kind to us, and told us to cover our bodies in mud, so that we wouldn't get burned by the sun, and to wear coolie hats which they gave us, saying that if a Japanese plane came over we were to wave to it, and they would think we were Burmese. They gave us a guide to the next village. There was a penal settlement nearby, whose inmates had been let out. Our Colonel, Owen, had been killed by some people who might have been escaped convicts.

In one village, the people crowded round and shouted at us. It was frightening. They calmed down when the Anglo–Burmese officer told them that they would be rewarded if they looked after us.

Private Neville Hogan
2nd Battalion, Burma Rifles Armoured Car Section
We started walking north towards Mandalay, about five of us, all friends who had stuck together. We got a lift from a lorry, and reported to the Upper Burma Battalion who did not want to know us. We had no means of identifying ourselves, the only proof that we were soldiers were our .45-inch pistols. We persisted, they gave us shelter, food, and a few days later uniforms. They asked us if we could drive, and being armoured car chaps we said 'yes'. They sent us to a transport company, in which my brother-in-law was a lieutenant.

Corporal William Norman
Mortar Platoon, 2nd Battalion, Duke of Wellington's Regiment
We kept going, eventually meeting a brigadier who asked us why we weren't in uniform, and if we were deserters. He handed us over to some RASC soldiers making tea. They told us they were part of the 7th Armoured Brigade, which meant nothing to us. But they looked at us very suspiciously. We were handed over to a military policeman who established our identity and returned us to the battalion. We joined them at Pegu, where they were amalgamated with the King's Own Yorkshire Light Infantry. That was a wrong decision. We didn't like the KOYLIs and they didn't like us. Eventually the decision was rescinded.

We were reformed into a mortar platoon with two mortars. We set off on foot towards Hlegu, near Rangoon. I had no boots, just a pair of sandals. We had one rifle in the platoon, an Italian carbine.

Second Lieutenant John Randle
Officer Commanding B Company, 7th/10th Baluch Regiment
After leaving the Sittang, the battalion was ordered to dig in round Pegu. We lost another hundred men at Sittang, all our transport and B Echelon were on the wrong side of the river. We had about five officers. The battalion was not in good fettle. We did practically no more fighting for the rest of that part of the campaign.

Anthony Dillon, as a major after the war.

RANGOON TO MANDALAY

Trooper Robert Morris
C Squadron, 7th Queen's Own Hussars

The regiment was on a ship bound for Singapore when we heard that it had fallen, we could hardly believe it, the place was so strongly held and defended. This made us afraid of meeting the Jap navy and being sunk. We were told that we would be diverted to Rangoon. What would we find there and how would we cope?

All we saw were blazing fires and oil dumps set alight. Mounds of equipment such as aircraft marked 'lease lend to China from USA' lay in crates awaiting assembly. The number of lorries lined up ready for shipment to China amazed us. The port had been deserted and ransacked.

With no dockers we had to use the ship's crew to help and to show us how to use the ship's cranes to unload, and we became good at it. Unloading took two days. As soon as ships were unloaded they sailed. Occasionally Jap fighters would fly over and we imagined would strafe any troops they could see, but they did not really affect us.

I was given an American Dodge three-ton truck commandeered from the Rangoon police. I had a co-driver, Trooper Robinson. I drove stores from the docks to the regimental assembly area. Going into some of the warehouses was like walking into a large London store that had been laid waste. The gunners found cleaning material for their guns: huge rolls of beautiful white silk, destined to make clothes for the rich locals. I managed to put on my vehicle large numbers of expensive tinned cigarettes, and some beer and spirits. Eventually the remaining stores were set alight.

In Rangoon, all law and order had ceased; the prisoners of the jails had been released as had the inmates of the lunatic asylum. The zoo had released all the harmless animals and the dangerous animals were put down. Gangs of Burmese looters roamed the streets fuelled by easy access to alcohol.

We found tinned peaches, pineapples and things we had not seen for years. I got a wonderful canvas bedroll. I had misgivings about stealing this, but knew that if I didn't take it it would be destroyed. I also got a fridge, although an electrical fridge, and I had no electricity, I used it to store my food to keep it clean of dust.

From the time we docked to getting away took about three days. I took on

Japanese troops enter Rangoon railway station on 7 March 1942.

board some forty-gallon drums of petrol and some oil to support the regiment. We were all fully laden. My squadron was C, my brother's squadron. We kept to the main roads or mud tracks, the rest of the terrain was mainly paddy field and we could not cross them in our tanks or trucks. Our movement, especially on the dusty tracks, would draw Jap fighter-bombers, so the majority of our resupply work was done towards evening and at night.

It was quite a strain, because as well as the physical effort involved in resupply, there was always the threat of Japanese encirclement and roadblocks. We had continual fear of being cut off by the Japanese; although we slept and worked, we had a continual fear of being captured.

Lieutenant Anthony Dillon
1st Battalion, Gloucestershire Regiment
Taukkyan was a key road junction north of Rangoon, and we were told to defend it, abandoning our unnecessary kit at Mingaladon, with Rangoon burning behind us and all our families having been evacuated. The whole of 17 Division and 7 Armoured Brigade were held up on the road by a Jap division that had hooked in to attack Rangoon from the north, not realising that we would not fight at Rangoon. The Jap division set up a flank guard consisting of a battalion-size roadblock at Taukkyan. The scene at Taukkyan was chaotic. We were attacked by Zeros, the road was jammed with transport, tanks, fuel tankers, mules, ambulances etc. We were ordered to attack this roadblock to allow the army to get north towards Mandalay.

One of our carriers went up the road, the driver killed the crew of a Jap anti-tank gun with his Bren, but the next carrier was hit and destroyed. It was the first real fighting I had seen. Some way back from the block I saw some Japanese crossing the road, setting up a machine gun, and for a second thinking 'for God's sake, you'll kill someone'; stupid of me really.

The CO sent the Adjutant up the road in his jeep to report on the situation. His jeep returned with some wounded and he himself mortally wounded and he died soon afterwards. The CO turned to me and said you are the Adjutant; at the ripe old age of twenty-one.

Eventually, with help of other troops, we got through. This was partly because the Japs withdrew the roadblock.

Captain Peter Varwell
Officer Commanding A Company 1st Battalion, Gloucestershire Regiment

I was second-in-command of A Company. The Company Commander was sick and sent home, so I took over. After the Jap war started my company was sent to guard an oil refinery at Syriam across the river near Rangoon. In the middle of the night we drove up to rejoin the main body of the battalion, who had already been in action at Taukkyan. We drove up during the night from Rangoon, and when we arrived we found that the battalion had already put in one attack and it had not been successful. We were told to put in an attack at first light next morning. We did, but during the night the Japs withdrew. We discovered that a whole Jap division had been walking down the railway into Rangoon parallel to the road up which we had been driving with headlights blazing. Having arrived at Rangoon, the Japs deemed the roadblock no longer necessary.

Major Michael Calvert
Officer Commanding Bush Warfare School, Maymyo

I was head of Mission 204 based at the Bush Warfare School at Maymyo preparing people to operate in China. After the fall of Rangoon, I was given orders to take some of my instructors and keep any Jap forces on the western bank of the Irrawaddy occupied. I got hold of a paddle steamer, which had a Goanese crew and a British Army captain in charge. To support us there was one launch with a Vickers medium machine gun, manned by Major Johnson and some of his Royal Marines Force Viper people. We were ordered to raid down the Irrawaddy, destroy the railway in places, and anything that would be useful to the Japanese. We finished up at Henzada.

I went in to town leaving two layback positions behind me. In the dry season the banks of the river were forty or so feet high, so the boat was out of sight. I began to give a speech in the town square. I had three or so men with me, including Corporal Dermott, all armed with Thompson sub-machine guns. As I was talking, someone said, 'You are surrounded, lay down your arms.'

It was a party of Japanese plus Burmese dissidents. I am a slow thinker. But Corporal Dermott shouted out 'Bollocks', and opened up with his tommy gun, as we all did. We jumped off the dais, and ran down the street to my first layback position. We fought a withdrawal battle across the paddy fields. Major

Johnson told his Vickers machine gunner to give us some covering fire. As we started to cast off, we fired a few rounds from a mortar we had on the deck, but after a few rounds the recoil drove the base plate through the deck, and we had to stop firing.

I discovered that I had left a party behind, so we had to circle round, beach with the boat pointing upstream, and land again. While we were recovering the party, my batman and I climbed up the bank and saw about thirty Japs all looking down on the ground, I don't know what they were looking at; a corpse perhaps. They were about twenty yards away. We opened up with our tommy guns into this bunch, each using the full thirty-eight rounds. I think we killed most of them. We then slid down into the sticky mud of the bank, got into the boat, and with the Royal Marine fast launch giving us covering fire, we steamed upstream.

Lieutenant Anthony Dillon
1st Battalion, Gloucestershire Regiment

Our battalion provided the rearguard for 17 Division as we withdrew north. Our first set-piece battle was at one of the villages on our route. We heard that the Japanese intended taking over the village and that the Burmese would be providing a civic reception. We told the GOC, who told us that we too were to arrange a reception. It was quite a tricky operation. The plan was to attack the enemy as they arrived. They arrived late. We sent one platoon down the main road to draw attention to themselves and at the same time we sent a company, supported by mortars and machine guns in scout cars pinched from the Chinese, in on another road to attack the village from a flank. They caught the Japanese completely by surprise in houses, and as they jumped from upper windows, our soldiers caught them on their bayonets, a new way of bayonet fighting.

The Japs were routed. The CO then ordered the company to withdraw, but the other platoon got entangled with the Japs and one section was cut off and attacked by about fifty Japs who fought to the end. After the war we found out what had happened from chaps who had been taken prisoner.

Our next operation was at Paungde; the Japs were on their way to occupy the place, and the plan was similar to the previous one. This time the CO decided to take a risk and move the assaulting companies close to the objective in transport. The assault went very well, but the CO decided not to stay too long in Paungde and withdrew the two companies. We had no radios, so the withdrawal was signalled by a bugle call.

Captain Peter Varwell
Officer Commanding B Company 1st Battalion, Gloucestershire Regiment

At Paungde, I commanded B Company, having been transferred from A Company. We got into the village without any trouble, but as soon as we arrived the Japs opened fire. I and one of my subalterns climbed over a fence between two houses, and seeing some Japs in the front room of one of the houses, I threw in a grenade. The Japs rushed back through the house, but as I walked past the door, I was fired on, hitting my shoulder and taking a chunk out of my back. I thought I had had it, but managed to stagger back to the company HQ, where some stretcher-bearers took me back to the RAP. I was evacuated to Prome by ambulance, and from there by steamer up the Irrawaddy to Mandalay, then to Maymyo, and finally by train to Myitkyina, the railhead in the north of Burma. After a couple of days, the cry went up 'The Japs are coming'. All the people who could walk were sent off on foot. I had plaster all over the top half of my body, had malaria, and was not capable of walking.

There was a nasty silence about what was going to happen to those who couldn't walk. The next afternoon two American Dakotas dropped in at Myitkyina airfield on their way back from flying supplies to China from India. They took all the stretcher cases to Assam. We were incredibly lucky, if they had not taken us, the Japs would have found us when they arrived a couple of days later.

Lieutenant Anthony Dillon
1st Battalion, Gloucestershire Regiment

The divisional commander decided after the first attack to send more troops to take Paungde again. Meanwhile the Japanese outflanked us and set up a big roadblock at Shwedaung. They planned to let our armour through and then close the roadblock. Some of the armour went through, and the roadblock was closed behind them. The roads were not wide and on each side there were steep-sided, deep monsoon ditches, so the vehicles could not get off the road, and were machine-gunned by Zeros. I saw an ambulance full of wounded attacked by a Zero, killing the driver. The doors opened and chaps, some with

26

bandages over their eyes, stumbled all over the road, and were killed soon after by another Zero.

I drove off the road in a carrier down into a monsoon ditch and was not able to drive it out. We then started taking fire from our own tanks, and only by standing up and waving to them managed to stop them.

Corporal William Norman
Mortar Platoon, 2nd Battalion, Duke of Wellington's Regiment
The operation at Paungde was very confused. Two of our companies were involved. We were cut off by a Jap roadblock at Shwedaung. One of our companies got mixed up with the Gloucesters. Our CO, Lieutenant Colonel Faithfull, gave the mortars our targets, and a sergeant said that our own troops were in the danger area. Our CO told him to obey orders, either that or our chaps would be captured. So we fired, knowing that a lot of our bombs would fall among our men. But our chaps got out.

On the way up to Shwedaung, I came across a burnt-out tank, with the men inside all roasted. I found a tin of peaches, they were still warm and made me feel a bit sick. I saw a Sikh with his bottom jaw shot off, gurgling, running about, bouncing off trees. People shouted to shoot him, and put him out of his misery. No one did, including those shouting 'shoot him'.

Eventually I joined a group of men who were going to rush the roadblock in a truck. I fired my Bren over the side. At the roadblock we came under machine-gun fire from a house, I fired long bursts back, someone else was changing magazines for me. Once through, we all got off. Next I got a lift from a gunner on a 25-pounder quad, and had to ride on the gun being towed by the quad, holding one of our chaps who had been wounded by pinning him down on the gun. After getting through, I was being taken along riding on a tank, and was thrown off when our tank hit another vehicle. I lay in the road, paralysed, and was lifted off the road by a passing refugee, just in time to prevent me from being run over by the next tank along. It crushed my pith helmet, which was lying in the road.

Major Michael Calvert
Officer Commanding Bush Warfare School, Maymyo
I got a message telling me to go back to Maymyo to hand over my mission to Colonel Musgrave, and that he would carry out some deception operations

locally, which he duly did with some of the Bush Warfare School staff. I would never allow my troops to stay in one position for more than four hours. But Musgrave, who had been brought up on more rigid lines, parked his force in a village; something that I would always avoid. He gave them positions to guard at night, and went to sleep. The Japanese attacked and wiped out most of them. One lot got away under Musgrave on to his boat, but about twelve were lined up, stripped naked to be bayoneted. The Japs were taught neither to expend ammunition on killing prisoners, nor waste men guarding them. Two men ran for it: Private Williams and a sergeant major. They swam the Irrawaddy, which was about a thousand yards wide at that point, and made their way up to Prome, where, still naked, they reported. I was annoyed with Musgrave.

FROM CENTRAL BURMA TO INDIA

Mrs Margaret ('Beth') Bootland
Wife of Lieutenant, commissioned from RSM, 1st Battalion, King's Own Yorkshire Light Infantry
I got a telegram to say Alan was on the hospital train. The train came up every evening from where the fighting was. He was commissioned by then. He had malaria and looked awful, but as he had a quarter and a bed, he was not taken into hospital, which was packed, with wounded even in the corridors. I had faith in the army, I knew they would look after us. It was a blessing that Alan was in Mandalay when he was. Every day he went to the hospital for a check up.

I and my friend Lotte, the wife of an NCO who was now sharing the quarter, went to the Durzi, the tailor, and ordered two sets of khaki bush jackets and trousers which we thought would be more comfortable to travel in than dresses. He measured me and was about to measure Lotte, when Alan arrived and asked us what we were doing, and when we told him, he told us we had two hours to get out. He spoke to the tailor, cancelled the order and we returned to pack.

Alan transferred some brandy into three small bottles. Anything of use to the hospital was put out in the hall, and collected by two band boys. We had a bedroll each. We were allowed no more than sixty pounds, including blankets, mosquito nets and food for fourteen days. When I started to pack a pillow, Alan told me to get two clean pillowcases, one for me and one for Lotte, and pack the pillowcase with our clothes. We took tinned fruit, rusks, anything that would keep. It was a godsend that Alan got malaria, and organised our evacuation and organised us. On the day of the evacuation, he gave me a small revolver wrapped in a piece of flannel, saying, 'I want you to promise me that if you do fall into the hands of the Japs you'll shoot yourself. They raped the nurses in Hong Kong and Singapore, and killed them afterwards. You might as well kill yourself straight away. Shoot Ian first, then Keith, Lotte and yourself.'

I would have done. I didn't fancy being raped by the Japanese.

He took me over the road into where there was some jungle and gave me some practice with the revolver. He put a target on to a tree, and then measured out some paces, and told me to see if I could hit the target. My dad taught me to shoot when I was thirteen. I had never touched a rifle since then. Dad taught me to look at the 'bull' and fire above it because the bullet drops. When Alan went to get the target, he said, 'How the hell did you learn to shoot?'

I said, 'My dad taught me.'

He said, 'I feel a lot happier now.'

He reloaded the revolver, and he told me to keep it in my pack, and that pack came to bed with me, even in the shower that pack came with me, because things were stolen out of bedrolls.

At ten o'clock that evening the gharries came to take us to the station. The train did not pull out until six o'clock next morning, arriving at Mandalay at nine o'clock. The station was crowded, and I saw Alan go and speak to the police commissioner and two tall Sikh policemen. He then came and said goodbye to me, Ian, Lotte and Keith. It was terrible. I did not break down until he moved off, then I had a weep. That was it.

The train went over the Ava Bridge and up to Monywa where we embarked on a steamer, which took us up the Chindwin River to Sittaung, where we started walking. A lot of people got off at Kalewa and took another route, which did not turn out so well. I was a bit nervous and fluttery but it had to be done. What has to be will be, fate. Our journey was from Maymyo to Mandalay, thirty miles; Mandalay to Monywa, sixty miles; Monywa to Kalewa, one hundred and ten miles; Kalewa to Sittaung, eighty miles;

Sittaung to Tamu, forty miles; Tamu to Imphal, eighty miles; Imphal to Dimapur, one hundred miles; Dimapur to Calcutta, four hundred and fifty miles.

The bedrolls were carried by elephants as far as Tamu, and after that by coolies. For several days, having set off at six am we would be in the next camp by eleven am, children carried in doolies by coolies. Started on flat paddy ground, then started climbing the hills.

In each stopping place we normally had a bamboo hut with two beds, which we put our bedrolls on. We were woken at five-thirty to put out our bedrolls and leave them, and not to let any children out as the elephants were half-trained and might stampede. So we had to go back and shut our doors, when the bell sounded we could go to wash, and after breakfast we set off walking, the elephants went ahead. We had a guide, and in the rear there were two Sikh policemen, and Ian often walked with them because he could speak Hindi. We were a party of about sixty. There were very few men, just retired civilians, mostly women and children. We had no idea what was going on in Burma. We did hear the wireless in one camp, and heard that Rangoon had fallen.

Major Michael Calvert
Officer Commanding Bush Warfare School, Maymyo
As our forces retreated up Burma, I was told to form a battalion from my Bush Warfare School for deception and delaying operations. The only troops I had were five officers and seventeen men of the Bush Warfare School staff. I had sent the majority of the administrative people back to India. I recruited men from Maymyo, including men convalescing and people under arrest in detention. Some were fine soldiers, some with bullets still inside them. We were told to protect the Gokteik viaduct bridge. We were deployed on the viaduct, with some Gurkhas from the Burma Rifles, but without their British officers. The bridge was about one thousand feet above the water, the greatest drop of any bridge in the world. I longed to blow it up. At first the Gurkhas said we could not lay explosives, but in the end we did.

The Japanese pushed up through the Shan States, with the Chinese retreating, and their one route to China was via the Gokteik Viaduct. I kept asking Alexander's HQ for permission to blow the bridge, but kept being told, 'No, to leave it to the Chinese, hand it over, and withdraw.'

The next time I saw Alexander, he asked, 'Did you blow the bridge up?'

'No,' I said, 'I longed to blow it up, but you gave me direct orders not to do it.'

He replied, 'I chose you because I was told that you were likely to disobey orders.'

That was a sad mistake on my part, I should have disobeyed orders.

Private Neville Hogan
2nd Battalion, Burma Rifles Armoured Car Section
In the transport company in which we now found ourselves, we drove American Fords from Mandalay to Maymyo, loaded up with ammunition, petrol and vegetables, and returned to Mandalay. Here we loaded again with huge drums of aviation spirit, and drove to Meiktila. On these trips we were sometimes strafed by Jap Zeros. We had no lookout because there weren't any spare men who could do this. If we saw or heard the planes coming, or the strike of bullets on the road, we got out of the trucks and ran like hell into such cover as there was nearby, but in Central Burma there is very little jungle or thick woods.

From Meiktila we took wounded to Mandalay. The wounded were laid in blankets in the back of the truck – and then off again on our round trip, Mandalay–Maymyo–Mandalay–Meiktila–Mandalay: forty-two miles from Mandalay to Maymyo, and seventy miles from Mandalay to Meiktila.

Then we started taking Chinese troops from Mandalay to Meiktila. They were a menace. If you left your rifle or rations unattended they took them. We dared not leave the truck in case they took the truck. They had no discipline. The junior officers were just bandits. There were hundreds of them, and a handful of us. They had no rations, poor uniforms, and were totally disorganised.

The Burmese helped the Japs to find routes around us, and took advantage of stragglers and killed them. I encountered some Indian Army soldiers who robbed Indian evacuee civilians and behaved badly, there were parties of these civilians on the road all the way back to India.

Major Michael Calvert
Officer Commanding Bush Warfare School, Maymyo
The Bush Warfare Battalion, or Calvert's Commando as some people called it, was depleting all the time, because so many of the men had been sick or

wounded. We fought some minor engagements near Mandalay. Here I encountered Peter Fleming, who I had met before. He had been sent to see me, to help in a deception operation, planned by Wavell. He would pretend to land at Mandalay airfield, and drive off in his staff car. It would crash, he would escape, but leave his attaché case behind, full of documents and letters to his wife. But in there were also letters to the War Office asking for more armour and aircraft to be sent to India, as well as giving fictitious numbers of our armoured vehicles, to deceive the Japs into thinking we had more equipment in India than we actually had. We took my jeep, with Private Williams my driver, and Fleming said I should drive the staff car with the Union Jack on it. We took Captain Coates, one of Wavell's ADCs, with us. There was still fighting south of Mandalay. We had to wait until the Japs were near enough to ensure that they found the vehicle. After a tense time of waiting, we set off. I was told by Fleming to drive the car in such a way that it left the road, went over the top of the embankment on which the road was built. I had to leave skid marks. I put on the brakes rather heavily, it left some skid marks, but the car did not reach the edge of the embankment. So I had to start again, and this time it toppled slowly over the edge, but without causing any damage. So Coates and Williams broke the windscreen. Coates had brought with him a supply of blood of the same group as Wavell's, and spilt it over everything.

We had to leave the area quickly, Coates and Fleming made for the bridge over the Irrawaddy, Williams and I headed for Mandalay. We found Mandalay had been bombed very heavily and there were thousands of Indians on the waterfront, bodies in the river, and many wounded. It was ghastly. We gave them some of our morphia, and some water, but as good Hindus they wouldn't let our mugs touch their lips, so we had to pour the water into their mouths.

Mrs Margaret ('Beth') Bootland
Wife of Captain commissioned from RSM, 1st Battalion, King's Own Yorkshire Light Infantry
One day, all of a sudden an army officer appeared on the path, and said, 'I am sorry to stop you but you can't go on this path any longer. They are dropping like flies with cholera in the camp you were due to go to. We daren't let you go any further. Have you got anything for the natives?'

All we had was brandy, no aspirin. We handed over the Dettol bottle that

Alan had filled with brandy back in Maymyo, to the officer. A guide came for us, it was the worst day of the whole trek, we walked on and on, the children were getting exhausted. My feet were OK, some people were wearing tennis shoes. They had no one to advise them. I was very lucky that Lotte and I had Alan to advise us. We arrived at the next camp absolutely bushed. We took the boys to a stream nearby and gave them a bath. Then Lotte and I went upstream and kept cave while we each had a bath. There was no food because we had arrived at the camp a day early, having passed the original camp we were intended for. Then it began to spit with rain, and then pour, the bashas were eight-people bashas. The heavens opened, and filled the pots in which our food was being cooked. Miss Baker, an army school teacher, poured the water out, tipped the rice out on to a plate, and from her pack took a small tin of Nestle's milk, and made a rice pudding for the children. We had nothing. The storm came back, and the rain dripped on to Ian's bed. He said, 'If Daddy knew what was happening to us, he would be awfully cross with God.'

Next morning we could not have any tea because the wood was all wet. We had to climb a big hill. Ian said he had a tummy ache, and he was flushed. I put some water in his mug and a good splash of brandy. Soon he was giggling and running around. At some time that morning we got to the top of this hill, and as we started down, we saw two big stalls dispensing bananas and hard-boiled eggs. They charged outrageous prices but we did not care. A colonel's wife said she would give a month's pay to dip her egg in some salt. About a mile further on there were some very old buses waiting, which took us to Imphal. We felt we were back in civilisation after twenty-seven days on the move.

Eventually we arrived at the railhead at Dimapur. We put the children to bed, and got some water from the railway refreshment room. It was full of soldiers and tea planters, all men. One said, 'Where in God's name have you ladies come from?'

When we told them we were refugees from Burma, they filled our bottles with clean water, and we returned to the train. We told them that there were many more refugees to follow. We were the first to be evacuated from Maymyo. The train took us to the Brahmaputra, which we crossed on a steamer. Then came the first snag. The Bengalis didn't like the British and tried to charge us for our fares. But Mrs Mansfield, an army schoolmistress who spoke Hindi, refused, and told them to get clean carriages as the ones on the train were filthy. We refused to pay and signed chits to say who we were. I was worried sick about my husband. I didn't know he had been badly wounded. The army met us on the platform at Calcutta. We went to Fort William in buses, and were interviewed. Apparently they had lost all trace of the 'walking party'.

Corporal William Norman
Mortar Platoon, 2nd Battalion, Duke of Wellington's Regiment

After falling off the tank, north of Shwedaung, my leg was broken and bruised. I was put on an ambulance, and taken to Allanmyo. Here I was robbed by an Indian soldier. I was put on a paddle steamer and taken up the Irrawaddy to Mandalay. Lying on a stretcher on deck, people would trip up over the handle of my stretcher, and this jolted me and was agony.

At Mandalay station the dogs were eating the bodies of the dead killed in an air raid. We were loaded on a train to Maymyo, a British hospital and run on army lines. I still had no treatment, but had a nice bed. There was no X-ray machine. After a while I was put on a train to Myitkyina. It was a very unpleasant trip, lots of people had dysentery and were not being cleaned up.

We were flown out by American Dakotas to Assam, dumped on the ground, and the plane left. An officer came up and said, 'Who are you, why are you so dirty?'

Someone said we had just come out of Burma and asked if we could be fed. The officer said, 'I can't feed you, you are not on our ration strength.'

He then changed his mind and did his best to help. They had no idea what we had been through. We were dumped on a train to India, and given twenty rupees. The tea planters' wives fed us at the stations at which we stopped in Assam. I ended up at Bareilly. The attitude of the army to those of us back from Burma was appalling; they blamed us for the defeat.

Trooper Robert Morris
C Squadron, 7th Queen's Own Hussars

When Mandalay was abandoned, the big beer brewery was going to be demolished. Each regiment was told to send in a lorry to collect a load of beer for their troops. It was a huge place and beer was gushing from tanks and pipes all over the place. I loaded crates of bottled beer. About twenty to thirty miles along the road, Robinson yelled, 'Planes planes, stop, stop.' There was nowhere to hide, we were on a raised road. I slammed on the brakes, and we jumped out into the recently harvested paddy field alongside the road. There was little cover, just eighteen-inch-long paddy stubble and thick black mud. The Jap planes swooped down and machine-gunned the lorry, hitting it several times. The bullets were so close that the stalks were being cut by the rounds covering us with chaff, which stuck to the ooze with which we were covered. After what seemed like ten minutes, the pilots probably thought they had killed the occupants, and flew off.

We dragged ourselves out of the paddy. Both rear tyres on the truck had been punctured, there was beer dripping over the road, but the engine and most of the beer was untouched. After recovering from the shock, we limped back about ten miles to the squadron with two flat tyres and the beer.

Major Michael Calvert
Officer Commanding Bush Warfare School, Maymyo
Having left Mandalay, I crossed the Irrawaddy, and joined up with the rest of my troops; we were still responsible for rearguard actions. I kept meeting up with Burma HQ. Alexander had no means of influencing the retreat except by his own attitude. He was very good, his uniform was always immaculate. He would visit and chat to the troops about cricket matches and army cup matches in Aldershot. He was unflappable. He didn't have any reserves so he couldn't influence the battle.

My force was depleting fast. I sent some of my lorries to evacuate some women and children, and I never saw the drivers again. I had an armed man with each driver after that. A retreat is not a pretty thing. There were masses of refugees, and people were dying of cholera by the side of the track. I was told to go to the Chindwin and to do what I could to delay the Japanese. I took an anti-tank rifle with me and a couple of the remaining men and hid in a cave.

Eventually a Gurkha company reached me in my cave, having been told they would come under my command. The Gurkha officer wanted to get back to his battalion. We set off to march to the Chindwin. On arrival we found the Japanese were in the process of landing on a large mud bank, it was dark, and they had lit fires to mark the place. I had only two men with me. I quickly went to the Gurkhas who had mortars and machine guns with them and told the officer. It was a marvellous target, the Japanese shouting and rushing about. We were about two hundred yards from them. The Gurkha officer merely said, 'My orders are to rejoin the battalion,' and he pushed off. Unfortunately he died on the way back to India. I was left with two men and no rations.

Major Charles MacFetridge
Officer Commanding 3rd Indian Light Anti-Aircraft Battery
We were ordered to move to Shwegyin on the east bank of the River Chindwin. From the jetty here river boats ran to Kalewa on the west bank and from there a track led to Assam and India. I did a recce and was so appalled at the state of the road to Shwegyin, I thought I would be very lucky to get any guns to Shwegyin. I imagined this would be the 'Dunkirk' of the Burma Army. Guns would have to be jettisoned at Shwegyin. On return from my recce, I told Brigadier Welshman at General Slim's HQ what I had seen. I was taken in to see General Slim. After listening to my description of the road, and my telling him that no guns of any kind could be got to Shwegyin, Slim summoned his CRE and G1 ops. I cannot but think that Slim took swift action, because the road was vastly improved during the next few days.

Despite the improvement, the last stretch of road was atrocious, along the edge of a chaung. I only managed to get four guns through. I was told to break all the rules for deploying AA guns and put them close together like field guns. This I did on a track leading to the jetty, about two hundred yards from the jetty.

Trooper Robert Morris
C Squadron, 7th Queen's Own Hussars
Before we got to the final stage we had to pass through Yenangyaung, the centre of the Burmese oil industry. I was carrying a load of high-octane petrol, and others with trucks full of ammo, with flames licking the sides of the vehicles as we drove through. It was keep going or remaining behind and being captured.

When we had ferried hundreds of troops back towards the Chindwin, we returned and reloaded our normal stores, and returned to the Chindwin at Shwegyin. It was hoped that ferry boats would carry the tanks across the river, but for lack of crews there weren't enough boats, so the tanks were destroyed. We took the drain plugs out of the engines and ran them until they seized. Breechblocks were taken from guns and thrown away, wirelesses blasted with tommy guns, and petrol poured on the tanks and set on fire. When Burma was recovered, the tanks were found where we had left them. We destroyed our trucks, as well as throwing ammunition into the river.

We were taken to a ferry spot, where there were only enough crew for one ferry, but it was big enough to lift large numbers of troops. By then we were all mixed up with soldiers from other units on the other side. The Gurkhas were holding the enemy off.

Private Neville Hogan
2nd Battalion, Burma Rifles Armoured Car Section
After driving north to cross the Chindwin, we destroyed our trucks and crossed. At Kalewa we were grabbed by an officer who put our party to work burning money notes, and throwing cash in the river. The walk to India was in pouring rain, carrying our possessions in a bundle on a bamboo pole. No one seemed to care. It was chaos, your boots got clogged with mud, the road was unsurfaced. If a truck came along, you had to press yourself against the side of the hill. You could not ride the truck. It carried wounded or rations, as far as I could tell.

At Imphal we had no means of identification, so we had problems proving who we were. After being sent to Ranchi, we were checked out in hospital, and given ten rupees each. The first thing I bought was a huge tin of cream cracker biscuits and a tin of Australian butter. I wasn't going to share them with anyone, and ate the lot. We were not in too bad a condition, we were still schoolboys, and treated the whole thing like boy scouts.

Trooper Robert Morris
C Squadron, 7th Queen's Own Hussars
On the other side we moved along smugglers' trails, used before the war. We slithered up and down the muddy tracks, sometimes so steep we slid on our backsides. We moved all night, we were dog tired, in little groups, sometimes single file.

Mrs Margaret ('Beth') Bootland
Wife of Captain, commissioned from RSM, 1st Battalion, King's Own Yorkshire Light Infantry
After our short stop in Calcutta, we were evacuated to a hill station. I had had no news of Alan. One night I went to bed really downhearted. I dreamt it was

my wedding day at Pontefract, except I was dressed in black, the flowers were withered, and Alan wasn't there. I told Lotte, 'This is a message to tell me he is gone.' That morning a telegraph boy came to the bungalow, and gave me a telegram. I asked Lotte to read it to me. It was from her husband, in Bareilly hospital. He said, 'Alan arrived in hospital this morning, badly bent but not broken, writing.'

I went to see him in hospital. He had been shot through the shoulder and the jaw. His jaw was fixed up by a man who had been the dental surgeon to the King. He made a silver splint for the broken jaw by melting down florins.

Trooper Robert Morris
C Squadron, 7th Queen's Own Hussars
At Tamu there was a reception organisation, and the sick were taken by truck, and we were sorted out into units. The worst part of the campaign was that march, by then we were exhausted, hungry, and under considerable strain.

Eventually we were moved through Imphal, to a camp we called 'dysentery hill'. Although we were there for only a few days, everybody seemed to get dysentery. To get to the cookhouse there we had to cross through a field of thick grass, and every time we ended up covered in leeches. I hated them.

Major Charles MacFetridge
Officer Commanding 3rd Indian Light Anti-Aircraft Battery
By the morning of 10 May three of my guns were deployed at Shwegyin. I realised that in the darkness that the Japs had started attacking the troops holding the hills overlooking the ferry boats evacuating the army. The surviving companies of the 1st Royal Jats were exchanging fire with the enemy. They were to be relieved by the 7th Gurkhas, an amalgamation of the 1st/7th and 3rd/7th Gurkha Rifles. I asked their CO if he had any mortars, and he did not know. The two COs agreed that the 7th Gurkhas should not relieve the Jats but reinforce them. I told the two COs that I had only three Bofors deployed that could support them, but I was a mountain gunner who had fought on the North-West Frontier, which they seemed to find reassuring. The CO of the Jats, Godley, placed his HQ by the guns and used them as match winners.

The Japs managed to get one of their mountain guns forward to shell the ferry site. My Bofors gunners picked up this gun arriving and as it was being brought into action it was destroyed by my Bofors firing over open sights. In the course of the battle the Gurkhas were committed to scale the hill overlooking the ferry site and reinforce the Jats. They wore yellow screens as they would have done on the frontier. This enabled my gunners to see where they were and to fire in their support without hitting them.

We were told to withdraw that night personally by General Cowan GOC 17 Division. As he drove off in his jeep after leaving us, his ADC was wounded by small-arms fire. When the time came to start the withdrawal, I was puzzled as to how Colonel Godley would pass his orders to his forward troops. He asked for two pairs of signallers, and he then gave both of them orders, which they were to give to the company commanders. The senior VCO told them to repeat the orders back. I doubted they would ever find the forward company commanders, but they did. The withdrawal was a model of its kind. I still had plenty of ammo, and devised a fire plan to bring down the heaviest fire possible to cover the withdrawal. At the end I ordered the detachments to withdraw. And merely said, 'Walk march to India.'

In reserve were the 1st/4th Gurkhas, under Lentaigne, he reckoned that in the chaung leading to the ferry there were at least three thousand troops awaiting evacuation, and they owed their survival to the actions of the Bofors manned by Punjabi Mussulmen gunners, and the two battalions; a fitting end to the longest withdrawal in the history of the British Army.

Major Michael Calvert
Officer Commanding Bush Warfare School, Maymyo

We arrived at Shwegyin having been chased by the Japanese and found ourselves on the enemy side of the battle. We lay in dry jungle, with tall trees interspersed with small shoots with large leaves, but no other cover. We lay in this hot, steamy jungle, on the receiving end of a British barrage, while the British and Indian soldiers fired off all their ammunition before destroying their guns and tanks.

We were going to wait till dark, but it was so hot and we were longing to have a drink. So we went to the riverside and drank and drank. We found a boat, but it was holed. We found another, and that had a hole in it. So I made a raft using empty water bottles and our packs. Private Medally could swim on his back, but my sergeant wasn't a good swimmer. I am a good swimmer, so I towed the packs and water bottles, which just floated. The Chindwin is about four hundred yards wide. There were Japs on both sides, but we cast off in a rainstorm. We got quite a long way across, when the sergeant said, 'I can't go any further.' So I said, 'Hang on to the packs,' and I let him use them while I swam free.

Medally was doing all right, but being on his back kept swimming in the wrong direction. Some Japs started to fire on us from the bank we had left, but not accurately. Finally we got to the west bank. Unfortunately the sergeant had let go of the packs and they drifted away. We had only what we stood up in. I had shorts, a revolver and a thousand rupees in coin. Medally and the sergeant had nothing other than shirts, socks and shorts.

We took a risk and followed a path: without boots we could not go through the jungle. We found some food dropped by refugees, including some sugar, which we licked up, despite the ants. We were emaciated. We huddled together at night.

We eventually came across about a hundred Indian refugees. They received us with open arms. They were from Orissa and had been employed in Burma as railway coolies. They had their complete families with them, and covered about six miles a day. They did not have cholera, thank goodness. They gave us some hot sweet tea, with marvellous jaggery sugar (Guhrr), and chapattis. We were emaciated, without weapons and bearded. They had seen the retreat of the British Army, their lords and masters, yet they behaved like that quotation in the bible: 'I was naked and you clothed me, I was hungry and you gave me food.' They gave us saris to cover up our beards. We walked along with the Indian women. We passed through a village, and there were Japanese soldiers leaning against the houses with cigarettes hanging out of their mouths, Medally saying, 'What a laugh, what a laugh. Wait until I tell my old dad.'

I told him to shut up. Our tactic would have been to scream and run off. We got through this village. When we felt stronger, I gave the Indians seven hundred of my thousand rupees, and we went ahead to find the British, still wearing Indian clothes. We eventually reached 17 Division commanded by Major General Cowan. The Divisional Intelligence Officer, whom I knew, rocked with laughter when he saw us. He made me go to see General Cowan, who said, 'I don't want to see any refugees.'

I stripped the sari off my face, and he said, 'My God, Michael, what are you doing?'

40

Second Lieutenant John Randle
Officer Commanding B Company, 7th/10th Baluch Regiment
The Japs fought with great ferocity and courage. We were arrogant about the Japs, we regarded them as coolies. We thought of them as third rate. My goodness me, we soon changed our tune. We had no idea about jungle fighting, no pamphlets, doctrine etc. Not only were we raw troops, we were doing something entirely new. In the early days we used to hack our way through the jungle, until we realised that this was useless, you made so much noise and it was so exhausting.

Striking Back

The Arakan Round One

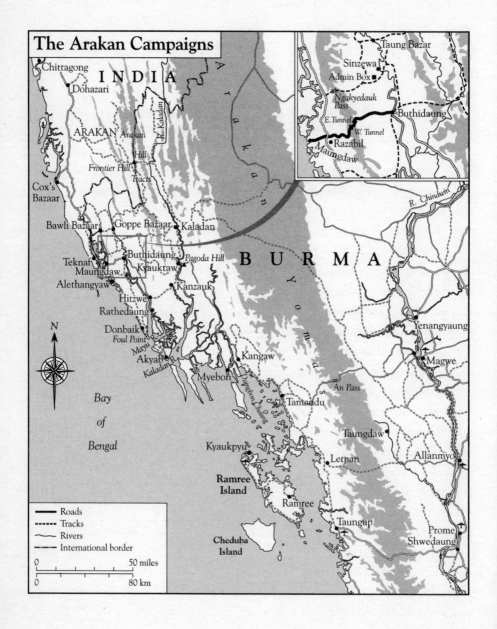

The Arakan Campaigns

INDIA

Chittagong

Dohazari

ARAKAN   *Arakan*   *R. Kaladan*

Hill

Frontier Hill

Tracts

Cox's
Bazaar

Bawli Bazaar   Goppe Bazaar   Kaladan

Teknaf

Maungdaw   Buthidaung   *Pagoda Hill*

Alethangyaw   Kyauktaw

Hitzwe   Kanzauk

Rathedaung

Donbaik
Foul Point

Akyab

Kaladan

Myebon

Kangaw

Bay

of

Bengal

N

BURMA

R. Chindwin

Y

O

M

A

Yenangyaung

Magwe

An Pass

Taungdaw

Dalet chaung

Tamandu

Letpan

Allanmyo

Kyaukpyu

**Ramree
Island**

Ramree

**Cheduba
Island**

Taungup

Prome
Shwedaung

	Roads
	Tracks
	Rivers
	International border

0 ———————— 50 miles
0 ———————— 80 km

(inset)

Taung Bazar

Sinzewa

Admin Box

*Ngakyedauk
Pass*

E. Tunnel

W. Tunnel   Buthidaung

Razabil

Maungdaw

A corporal said, 'Wait, wait, sergeant major,
these Brens and rifles won't fire.'
I didn't believe him and got down behind a Bren. One round fired and
then the gun jammed. I went through all the drills, but nothing would
work. I slung it aside in disgust.

Having followed the retreating British as far as the River Chindwin, the Japanese stopped. They had no plans for an immediate invasion of Assam or the conquest of India, although they did prepare plans for an advance to seize Imphal and Akyab, and exploit to the River Brahmaputra. This was aimed at preventing the Allies using the airfields in Assam and eastern India, thereby choking off supplies to China.

The British plan for a comeback involved a thrust from Imphal into northern Burma. But so much work on logistics and communications would be required to mount both of these attacks that neither the British nor the Japanese could undertake major operations in Assam until 1944.

In the interim, the British decided on a limited offensive in the Arakan, beginning in mid-December 1942, to clear the Japanese out of the Mayu Peninsula and take Akyab Island, which controlled the mouths of the two big rivers in the Arakan, the Kaladan and the Mayu. The British saw this as a means of raising morale in their own army following defeat in Burma, and preventing the Japanese from taking the initiative in this area. For although the capture of Akyab would not open the way for a British return to Rangoon, the Arakan was a possible Japanese invasion route to India.

The British advance on both sides of the Mayu River, as a precursor to capturing Akyab Island, stalled in the face of Japanese defences at Donbaik and Rathedaung. The British 6th Infantry Brigade, part of the British 2nd

Infantry Division, which had been practising amphibious assaults in India, and was earmarked for the assault on Akyab Island, was sent to Donbaik where stalemate had set in. Meanwhile the Japanese brought up their 55th Division to mount a counter-offensive in the Arakan.

As part of the British fightback the RAF mounted sorties at an increasing rate.

Flight Sergeant Deryck Groocock
99 Squadron, RAF

I was only nineteen with three hundred hours' flying experience and was sent to deliver a Wellington to Cairo from England via Gibraltar, down to West Africa and across to the Nile. We were very heavy taking off from Gib, with extra fuel tanks, and scraped over the sea wall at the end of the runway by inches. We had to fly a long dog-leg out into the Atlantic to avoid French Vichy fighters from Dakar who, according to rumour, were paid five hundred dollars by the Germans for each British aircraft they shot down. Quite a few aircrew got lost flying over Africa on one of the legs to the Nile at Khartoum.

We expected to join a squadron in the Middle East, where aircrew were sent back to UK on completion of a six-month tour. But we were stuck in a transit camp, and when I saw a notice asking for volunteers to ferry a Wellington to India, I and my crew volunteered for lack of anything better to do. We eventually arrived at 99 Squadron in Assam. I got out and said to the CO, 'Here's your aircraft, how do we get back to Cairo?'

'Cairo! What makes you think you're going back to Cairo? You're in India now. Are you single or married?'

'Single,' says I.

'Right, a tour in India for a single man is four years. Three years for a married man.'

At the age of nineteen, four years seems like a lifetime. The squadron was just settling down to bombing ops over Burma. I had been the captain of a Wellington all the way from UK, but because of my inexperience of ops, I was made co-pilot, with the same crew, but with a more experienced captain. We bombed airfields, ports and railway marshalling yards, mainly at night for about six months in late 1942, early 1943, dropping 500-pound bombs from around ten thousand feet. Finding the target was not easy. There was not a lot of opposition. We were attacked by a night fighter once. We went low-level and corkscrewed, and lost him. We had flak over some targets, but nothing like the flak over Germany. I had taken part in one of the thousand-bomber raids over Dusseldorf. Our main worry was ditching in the jungle. We were ill-prepared for survival. We had a silk scarf map of Burma, and a little compass. We had no money, just the Burmese version of the 'goolie chit'.

Flying Officer Cecil Braithwaite
60 Squadron, RAF
I carried out numerous sorties between August 1942 and January 1943, some in support of the first Arakan offensive. We were often attacked by Jap fighters, they buzzed around but were distracted by the Hurricanes and Mohawks. We respected the Jap pilots, but their aircraft could not take damage, they were not armoured. If attacked, one ploy was to fly low, as close to the ground as possible. Some Jap fighters had telescopic sights, which required the pilot to put his eye to it to aim, unlike the gunsight in most fighters which allowed the pilot to fly 'head up'. With his eye to the sight, the pilot could not fly low and fast without risking piling into the ground.

Although the Blenheim was slow, it was well armoured. Ours were well maintained by our peacetime-trained and skilled ground crew. All the same, not many of us expected to live all that long. We were issued with rudimentary will forms, which few of us bothered to complete. At twenty or twenty-two years old you don't have much to leave anyway.

Sergeant Sidney Savin
Section Commander, B Company, 2nd Battalion, Durham Light Infantry
The whole brigade, plus the 1st Battalion the Royal Scots, moved by rail to Chittagong. Each time the train stopped, someone would rush forward to the engine with a billycan to get hot water. The journey took about a week and shortly before our arrival we were told to prepare for a seaborne landing on Akyab. We arrived at Chittagong on Christmas Day 1942. The town was deserted and many of the shops were boarded up, but in a few places you could buy a cup of tea and a handful of Burma cheroots. We were now in a highly malarial area with a very high rainfall. Fortunately the monsoon was over and the ground underfoot was quite hard. We spent the next few weeks doing landing exercises with the navy, in assault craft, in preparation for the Akyab affair.

The idea was to land on Foul Point to use this as a jumping-off point for a landing across the mouth of the Mayu River on Akyab. But we were told that things had not gone well for the 14th Division in their advance down the Mayu peninsula, and so our seaborne assault on Foul Point was called off. We were told that we would try to crack the Jap positions at Donbaik, which 14th Division had tried without success, taking quite heavy casualties.

Corporal Ernest Galley
Section Commander A *Company, 2nd Battalion, Durham Light Infantry*
The battalion was going into action again for the first time for two years. We left Chittagong by boat, landed at Cox's Bazaar, and from there by foot.

Sergeant Sidney Savin
Section Commander, B Company, 2nd Battalion, Durham Light Infantry
We marched the fifty or so miles to the Donbaik positions over a period of three days, marching by night and stopping at rest camps by day. The road was very dusty, it was unpleasant and we wondered why there was no transport for part of the way. Donbaik was a village on the coast some six miles from Foul Point. The Japanese occupied strong positions in well-sited deep bunkers with good fields of fire. The two main strongpoints were known as Sugar 4 and 5. They were so strong that they could withstand fire from 25-pounders and 500-pound bombs dropped from the air. There were other strong points in the vicinity to support these two positions: the Shepherd's Crook in the bed of a deep chaung which ran down from the jungle to the sea; two positions called Twin Knobs; and the Elbow. In the distance there were two other positions that gave the Japs a commanding view of the whole area. When you moved around there you were in their sights.

In the beginning of March 1943 we relieved a Punjab Battalion of the 14th Division early in the morning. Our Company faced Sugar 4 and 5, I suppose we were three hundred or four hundred yards away. From our positions we could see them, and they looked like mounds of earth. There were many dead in no-man's-land, it was impossible to get them out. When the wind blew our way there was quite a stench. These were the dead from earlier attacks. The Japs had shut themselves in their bunkers, and at the right time opened the hatches in the firing slits and picked off the attackers. We didn't have flame-throwers then. You could get on top of the bunker, but you then came under fire from other bunkers that were supporting them.

Corporal Ernest Galley
Section Commander, A Company, 2nd Battalion, Durham Light Infantry

My platoon was right on the beach. Somewhere to our left there were some Punjabis. Sometimes, when the tide came in, the sea came into our slit trenches. We had tree trunks over our trenches with soil on top. We were always told in our training, never fire at night, unless you can really see the whites of their eyes. The Japs want you to fire and give away your position. The Japs would respond with mortars.

Evening came, dusk fell, I told off the sentries, and went to sleep, to be rudely awakened by the sentry. He told me there were tram cars coming. I thought 'here we go'. He said he was a Liverpool lad and had seen some Liverpool trams. I stood with him and convinced him it wasn't tram cars. Then half an hour later, he said he could see Japanese walking about. We had a good field of fire. I could see there were no Japs, and quietened him down. No sooner had I got him quietened down, when there was rifle fire on our left, heavy fire. I stood everyone to, hundreds of rounds were being fired by people on our left. Mortar bombs going down. There was nothing happening where we were. Next day we found out it was an Indian battalion blasting off. The Japs blasted back with mortars.

One day, the Japs started shelling, the shells fell behind our position. We could see the guns firing. We asked for artillery support but couldn't get any response over the field telephone or by the Number 18 wireless set. Our platoon sergeant joked, 'I can get Henry Hall and his dance orchestra on the BBC, but not company HQ.'

So we sent the lad who kept seeing trams back to company HQ who ran out a new line to us. Meanwhile the Japs went on shelling, rounds falling all round us. Eventually the battery of 25-pounders began to fire back. The platoon sergeant gave corrections to the guns. But the Japs were pretty good at moving their guns to avoid retaliation. For four hours it all went quiet, and then shells started falling again.

We eventually sent the lad who saw trams back. He wasn't frightened, but kept on seeing things. He never came back.

We were never attacked in that position. The Japs came up as far as the wire, sometimes you could hear them shouting, 'What regiment there?' 'I've been wounded, can you help me?' They might lob a grenade. Sometimes it was difficult to hear exactly what they were shouting. You couldn't see them.

They would try to put the wind up people. They were trying to pinpoint the position. The Indians on our left fired and got the 'crap' thrown back at them. We were a disciplined battalion.

Corporal Fred Cottier
Section Commander, 2nd Battalion, Durham Light Infantry
The day was spent in the slit trench, reading or sleeping. In the day we had one man on sentry in each. At night there were fatigue duties carrying water or rations up. Stand to was at dusk and first light, waiting for the Japs to attack – often nothing happened. At night there would be twenty-five per cent on duty. If an attack came in, you spent the next day collecting casualties, reinforcing positions, digging and so forth. After stand down, the Japs would attack at say midnight, knowing perfectly well what our routine was. An attack might go on until daylight.

We had rest periods at the Arakan, we would be relieved by another battalion, and go back, not far, still within range of the enemy artillery. We could wash our clothes in a stream, and have a hot bully beef stew or curry. We could relax and write a letter, have a haircut and shave off our beards.

The Arakan campaign was the best training we ever had for fighting in Burma.

Sergeant Sidney Savin
Section Commander, B Company, 2nd Battalion, Durham Light Infantry
We learned that the brigade was to capture Donbaik. It was decided we would do what the Japs did, get round the back; not attack head on, but bypass the Jap strongpoints, set up our own company strongpoints and hold them. Then the main assault on Donbaik village, by the 2nd DLI and 1st Royal Welch Fusiliers, would go ahead. The other battalions remained in reserve.

This attack was preceded by a heavy artillery and mortar barrage. The Royal Welch Fusiliers went in first and overran some strongpoints in the area of Shepherd's Crook, but they could not get inside them, and they sustained heavy casualties from Jap mortars.

Sergeant Clifford Jones
Commanding Anti-Aircraft Platoon [Brens] under Command Battalion
HQ, 1st Battalion, Royal Welch Fusiliers
At 0500 hours the attack began. All hell was let loose. Three-quarters of A
Company got into the bunker but they couldn't hold it. They got into some of
the trenches on the outside which were empty. I came in from the right and
lost half my men trying to attack similar bunkers. I was told over the radio to
move up to A Company, and take over. I wriggled forward and grabbed hold of
the first man I could see and asked what was going on. He pointed to an
officer doubled up down in a foxhole. The officer said, 'Are you taking over?'

'Yes,' I replied.

'Leave me here and get on with it.'

I then got the message to go back to the CO, who said, 'D Company are cut
off. The Royal Scots are going to reinforce us and attack to get D Company
out. I'm coming with you to A Company,' which he did.

The Japs were very astute, and shouted out in English things like, 'British
soldier why are you here? Your wives are waiting for you.'

The CO shouted in Welsh through a loudspeaker to D Company to hold
on. This flummoxed the Japs.

A Company and the Royal Scots' attempts to reach D Company went well
for the first fifteen minutes, but then came under Jap bombardment. After two
hours of fighting, we did get out about forty men of D Company. There were
no officers left alive.

Sergeant Sidney Savin
Section Commander, B Company, 2nd Battalion, Durham Light Infantry
The DLI then went in and my company managed to reach its objective
without any trouble. Other companies suffered casualties. We had a fairly easy
ride. We moved through the scrub jungle for cover.

Company Sergeant Major Martin McLane
C Company, 2nd Battalion, Durham Light Infantry
Before the battle my company, along with the battalion, had been issued with
ammunition manufactured at Kirkee in India, which proved to be defective.
My company formed up in a dry nullah bed. There were a series of them every
few yards. We were carrying an average of sixty pounds of kit. The artillery fire

An attack in the Arakan, Indian soldiers on the start line.

CSM Martin McLane

was going over, and everything was dusty in the early morning light. The company commander gave the order 'Bayonets on, smoke if you want to'. The men dragged on their cigarettes, and were hanging on to them for grim death, because, let's not be heroic, a man is only going to do a job if he's ordered to. He's going into an attack and the chances of him being killed is tremendous.

The order came, 'Right, get ready, over the top.'

I had the signallers and company clerk with me. We went over the top. I saw a Jap. I up with the tommy gun and the bloody thing wouldn't fire. I was disgusted, here was I a professional soldier, and I couldn't hit him. He had been throwing grenades, but scarpered.

I never heard our Brens firing, only desultory shots from rifles, which died away. I had been in attacks in France and knew what it sounded like. All there was was Japanese firing, nothing of ours at all. The CO spoke to me on the wireless set. He asked what was happening.

I said, 'This is the funniest attack I've been in. I can't hear a Bren, I can't hear a rifle. There's nothing moving, all I can see is bodies.'

He replied, 'Do something about it then.'

'What can I do?'

'Get the men in.'

Well I only had company HQ with me, the other two platoons were on their own, one was detached. I found the company commander wounded. He'd been wounded in France in the knee and his same leg had been hit again. He was bleeding badly. I dragged him back through the nullah, found A Company Commander and put my company commander on a stretcher.

I returned to my own company HQ, spoke to the CO on the wireless, and was ordered to get moving. I was leaning on the lip of a nullah when a shell burst nearby. A splinter hit the set. I could hear the CO, but could not transmit. I ordered company HQ to stay put while I went to find the two rifle platoons. I passed a stretcher on which was Lieutenant Greenwall, one of the platoon commanders. He was full of shrapnel from a Japanese plastic grenade, lying smoking a cigarette. He said, 'Well, sergeant major,' stroking his 'old man', 'they didn't hit that.' He was newly married.

I found seven of the platoon lying down. I shouted, 'Come on lads, bayonets.'

A corporal said, 'Wait, wait, sergeant major, these Brens and rifles won't fire.'

I didn't believe him and got down behind a Bren. One round fired and then the gun jammed. I went through all the drills, but nothing would work. I slung it aside in disgust.

'Give us your rifle.'

I fired it but the bolt stuck solid and I could not eject the round except by putting the butt on the ground and booting down the bolt with my foot.

I located the other platoon in a nullah bed, where they were being showered by Jap grenades. The casualties included the platoon commander. All the officers were out of action. By now my signaller had got the wireless working again, and I arranged with the CO for mortar and artillery smoke and HE to cover our withdrawal. I told the platoon to stand by to move when the fire came down, to take the wounded and leave the dead. Some were very badly wounded. They looked at me beseechingly. Although they call you what they like, the sergeant major is the kingpin of the company, and the men depend on him for so much. I went back and picked up some more wounded, but our artillery started dropping short among us. We were very lucky to have only two more casualties.

After reorganising, the defective ammunition was all dumped in a chaung and replaced by serviceable rounds.

Corporal Ernest Galley
Section Commander, A Company, 2nd Battalion, Durham Light Infantry
This was the one attack made by the battalion down there. It seemed fruitless. The enemy positions were well dug in. There had been numerous attacks on these positions, and no one had broken through.

Sergeant Sidney Savin
Section Commander, B Company, 2nd Battalion, Durham Light Infantry
As far as we were concerned things quietened down. Just the usual firecrackers at night. Then we came out of the line to rest. I got malaria, which took a toll higher than our battle casualties. I was evacuated along the beach by ambulance, and eventually put on board a hospital train at Dohazari which took me to hospital at Dacca.

With malaria you get a chilly feeling, your bones ache, you are generally lethargic and have a high temperature. You can't carry on soldiering. You don't eat and lose weight. The treatment is mepacrin and quinine. A bout would last two to three weeks. I remained in Dacca until the battalion was withdrawn from Arakan, by which time it had fought at Indin, and at Maungdaw.

Second Lieutenant Satoru Nazawa
Company Second in Command, 112th Regiment, Japanese 55th Division
The night attack on Indin was the first time that I was acting as deputy head of company. So I was nervous to the maximum point, and the soldiers, the men under my command, were mostly senior to me by age, and they had already experienced actual battles. On the other hand, I was a young lad, who just arrived from Japan. I was really nervous, but well I tried to remember all the fighting tactics that we were taught in school, on the night attacks by platoons and companies. And so I organized the system based on these fighting tactics, and went towards the enemy camp. And at first we went very slowly and quietly, and we went close to the enemy without them noticing, and I put one platoon on the north of the enemy, and two platoons from the back to the side, going around, and they went to the side, the side of the enemy. And so I wnet to guard the soldiers who were attacking the side, and from there we went into the village, and then the enemy were shooting back at us, and throwing hand grenades. They were throwing and throwing, and they exploded fiercely. I was thinking, oh this must be the end for me. then the head of the first platoon, sergeant Yamamoto, took a very bad injury to the stomach. Sergeant Abe of the second s a piece of shell in his eyes, and he can't see anymore, and I could hear many voices saying that they were being beaten, and I didn't know what was going to happen. In the end we won because it was very dark. The night wasn't the enemy's strongest point.

Corporal Ernest Galley
Section Commander, A Company, 2nd Battalion, Durham Light Infantry
Next we were told that we were surrounded. While we were watching the Japs at Donbaik, they had gone inland, and come round the back. We heard that brigade HQ had been attacked: the brigadier and staff and hospital wiped out.

If you built a defensive position they would go behind, cut the road, then attack. We were told we were going to pull out. Our CO, Lieutenant Colonel Theobalds, took over command of the brigade. This was my second evacuation, Dunkirk being the first. I had been fighting for over two years, and only taken part in evacuations.

The beach was like a parade ground, all the brigade's carriers were on the beach, the Japs were on the hill tops firing down. The carriers provided some protection. We pulled out marching in threes. We marched the full length of the beach (three or four miles), covered by the carriers. It must have taken the Japs by surprise because I don't think we had one casualty. Maybe they didn't see us. We then went inland to hill positions. We had just got in there when we heard that the Japs were on the move, to a place called Indin, a supply base for our attack on Donbaik. We stormed into Indin. The whole place was on fire. The Japs had left and destroyed it, leaving a sniper in a tree.

A lad called Bonnie killed the sniper with a Bren. He was cock-a-hoop. Confusion reigned, no one knew where the Japanese were. My good friend Jock McCleavy, a corporal in 2 Platoon, had to provide a patrol to find the Japanese. Jock went out with his section. Early in the morning, we heard they had been ambushed. Jock was badly hit. One was missing, dead or prisoner. Jock was whipped off to Cox's Bazaar. I saw him off. I was told to take out my section to find these Japs. I took with me a bloke called Ward, known as the 'Mad Mullah'. He had been in the army before, and his ambition was to win the VC. Another chap with us called Wilkinson was known as 'Brylcreem'. I was not excited by the prospect.

We set off through the forward positions. I had two scouts out front. I had a map and compass. To begin with we followed the route the other patrol was supposed to take. But I didn't like this, and took a bearing on where we thought they had been ambushed, and circled round to come in the other way. Near where we were heading we saw some Japs. They were lying around celebrating, that's what it looked like. Ward said, 'Let's get stuck in.' We had two grenades apiece. I said, 'Our instructions were to come out here, find the Japs, mark the position on a map, and go back, and not have any contact.' We had already lost half a patrol. Young Brylcreem said, 'He's in charge.' I reckoned there was nearly a company of Japs there.

I lost a friend that day. 'I can't get my medal,' Ward says. Anyway we came back. As we did so, we had to pass through C Company who had a forward listening position. They had changed its location, and hadn't told us. But we got back, and I gave the map reference to Company HQ, and the 25-pounders hit it.

Sergeant Frank Harrison.

Sergeant Frank Harrison
Section commander, Mortar Platoon, 2nd Battalion, Durham Light Infantry
We were in action with our mortars set up in the river bed. We could not move often enough and as soon as you opened fire, you got mortared back. I was hit by shrapnel: one in the chest and one in the top of my arm. I didn't feel it, no pain, said to my lance corporal, 'I've been hit.' I was given an injection of morphine by a stretcher-bearer. They carried me to the RAP, and then back to Maungdaw where I was in a straw basha hospital in a bamboo bed.

Corporal Ernest Galley
Section Commander, A Company, 2nd Battalion, Durham Light Infantry
We then withdrew to Chittagong. I got as far as there and started shivering and discovered that I had malaria. So I went to hospital at Dacca. Before we got back there, we were told that if anyone was wounded or sick and put in hospital, they must return to the 2nd Division because so much time had been spent on combined operations training; they must tell whoever was in charge that they were part of the 2nd Division and not to be sent anywhere else.
When some of us had recovered, a senior officer paraded us and detailed us to join some other regiment, and we refused; our hair was standing up on the backs of our necks. Someone told him that we were ordered to say that we were in the 2nd Division and would join no other. This officer walked off. So next time our names were posted on orders. We went to our huts and refused to move. We were threatened, but did not move. Some of us went to see this officer, and he damned and blasted us. We asked if he could send a signal to 2nd Division to ask.

Next morning all members of 2nd Division were ordered to parade and get on trucks and all taken to Ahmednuggur where the division was.

Sergeant Frank Harrison
Section Commander, Mortar Platoon, 2nd Battalion, Durham Light Infantry
From Maungdaw I was sent to a convalescent hospital at Comilla. I didn't like it. Some people there had no intention of leaving the place and get back to fighting. I really wanted to get back to my unit. Here there were more lads from the DLI. One night I went round to them and said, 'I am going, if you want to come with me you can. Just bring your shaving gear.'

'How are you going to get back there?'

'I will get a train at Comilla station.'

They said, 'We'll come with you but go out by road.'

Three gharry wallahs came along. Six of us got in, and we had no money so we jumped out about half a mile from the station. They were shouting, but that was that.

When we got on to the station there was red caps, and all different types of soldiers. When the train came in, they said, 'What now?'

'Bide our time,' I replied.

We got on, and got right to Chittagong where the battalion had gone out of the line. I went to our own company commander, and told him what I had done. He said you have done right. I couldn't raise my arm too far. But I was OK. I was always told to get back to your own unit.

Second Lieutenant Satoru Nazawa
Company Second in Command, 112th Regiment, Japanese 55th Division
And so we went to the line of Buthidaung. And here, we made the enemy retreat further away from this line to the north. And in Maungdaw, there was another field storage of the enemy. We saw that there were mountains of corn beef, bacon, cheese, cigarettes and rum lying around. I had never tried corn beef before that. they had water in a bottle, and we kicked it around, but when someone said it's an alocholic drink called gin, there were soldiers who were gulping down the gin, happier than ever. We had this kind of excitement, or more like comedy. We thought, my goodness, these people are fighting in such a luxurious condition. If they came and took our camp, well, they would just find a bit of dried fish and a bit of rice, nothing else.

Striking Back
The First Chindit Expedition

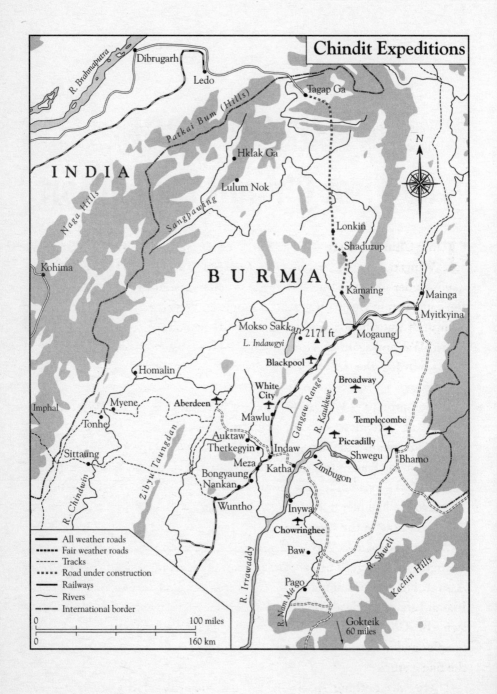

Wingate believed that you should take ordinary troops and turn them into a special force, and this would be an example to the rest of the army. 'If those people can do it so can we.'

The Chindits were the creation of a gunner officer, Major Orde Wingate. At the request of General Sir Archibald Wavell, then Commander-in-Chief India, Wingate was sent to India in early 1942, while the campaign in Burma was still in progress. Wavell had been impressed by Wingate's unorthodox soldiering methods in Palestine before the Second World War and again in Abyssinia in 1941. On each occasion Wingate had been awarded the DSO as the successful commander of guerrilla-type operations.

Wavell promoted Wingate to Colonel and sent him to the Bush Warfare School at Maymyo, in Burma, to organise long-range penetration operations against the Japanese. In the event the Japanese advanced too quickly for such an enterprise to be mounted from within Burma itself, and Wingate was posted to the staff at Wavell's HQ in Delhi. While at Maymyo, he had met that remarkable soldier, Michael Calvert, who was to play a key role in the Chindits.

Wingate persuaded Wavell to allow him to raise a special force of brigade strength to mount long-range penetration operations into Burma from Assam. He was promoted to Acting Brigadier, and told to raise the 77th Indian Infantry Brigade for this purpose. He chose as his brigade formation sign the Chinthe, the mythical beast, which stands guard outside the temples and monasteries of Burma. It was mispronounced as 'Chindit', and the name stuck.

There was nothing special about the majority of the soldiers in 77

Brigade. Most were either young and inexperienced, or overage and inexperienced. Few were well trained. The British 13th King's Regiment (Liverpool), raised for coastal defence in England, had been sent to India for internal security duties. The soldiers, whose average age was thirty-three, were mainly Scouse dockworkers, and liable to revert to their pre-war trade union habits when life got uncomfortable during training. Unable to strike, they demonstrated their disapproval of their new role by going sick in large numbers.

The 3rd/2nd Gurkha Rifles consisted in the main of under-eighteen-year-old recruits. The Gurkhas also provided leaders for the extra mules required by the brigade over and above those already with battalions.

The understrength 2nd Battalion Burma Rifles was composed of Karens, Kachins and Chins of the British Burmese Army who had been through the first campaign and fought their way to India. They were seasoned troops.

The 142nd Commando Company were far and away the best soldiers: volunteers from every regular battalion in India, augmented by men from the United Kingdom. They were the only picked men in the brigade.

Wingate broke up his brigade into columns, each of about four hundred men. His concept was that columns should march independently, be self-supporting for a week, and be supplied by air. He was aiming at mobility and security. Mobility would be achieved by not having wheeled transport, and therefore avoiding being tied to overland lines of communication; so columns could, in theory, go where they wished. Security would, again in theory, be achieved by the difficulty the enemy would experience in finding mobile columns in the jungles and teak forests of northern Burma, and on the ability of columns to disperse in smaller groups. Wingate planned to concentrate two or more columns for specific tasks. He would communicate with columns by wireless.

Wavell originally intended to use Wingate's Brigade ahead of an Allied offensive consisting of an attack across the Chindwin by IV Corps from Assam, a Chinese advance from Yunnan across the River Salween, and the American General Stilwell's Chinese–American forces pushing south from Ledo. For logistic reasons, the Allied offensive had to be postponed for many months, but Wingate was allowed to go ahead with his operation. This consisted of entering Burma in mid-February 1943, cutting the railway between Shwebo and Myitkyina, harassing the Japanese in the Shwebo area, and, if possible, crossing the Irrawaddy to cut enemy communications with the (Chinese) Salween front.

Wingate had many attributes that would have qualified him to rank as a great commander and man. Unfortunately he was also flawed. It is difficult to get a dispassionate judgement on him from anyone with whom he came in contact. He was either hated or worshipped. 'There was no middle ground with Wingate,' remarked John Masters, who took part in the Second Chindit expedition. This comes across from the voices both in this chapter and the one covering the Second Expedition.

Much of what he advocated strategically, operationally and tactically was flawed, and some of it was sheer nonsense. Yet he could inspire men to achieve things they had thought impossible. All who met him, including those who found him exasperating, such as General Slim, agree that you could not ignore him. That great fighting soldier Mike Calvert followed him unhesitatingly, whereas the young and inexperienced Dominic Neill of the Gurkhas, later to become one of the most accomplished jungle soldiers in the British Army and with vastly greater experience in that art than any Chindit, came to loathe Wingate, rightly regarded his tactics with contempt, and, given the choice, would not have followed him anywhere.

TRAINING

Major Michael Calvert
Officer Commanding Bush Warfare School, Maymyo and Chindits
When I got back from the Henzada raid, there was a man sitting at my desk. He got up and said, 'I'm Wingate.'

I replied, 'I'm Calvert, and that's my desk.'

'I'm sorry.'

I'd never heard of Wingate. He took me for walks, I found that when he talked about guerrilla warfare he was miles ahead of anybody I had met.

On arriving in India, Wingate sent for me, and George Dunlop who had also been fighting in the retreat from Burma. We were both suffering from malnutrition and disease. He said he was forming this brigade and would like us to help, and could I bring as many people from the Bush Warfare School as possible. Initially members of the staff of the School carried out the training of the brigade.

Major Walter 'Scottie' Scott
Officer Commanding 8 Column, 13th Battalion, King's Regiment (Liverpool)

I met Wingate for the first time in Central India. I was very impressed by him. He inspired us with his aims, and was completely dedicated to the end that we should be fit and trained before we crossed the Chindwin. During training up to twenty-five per cent were left out, and the numbers made up with fitter men. At the end of the training period, Wingate gave me command of Number 8 Column.

Private Charles Aves
7 Column, 13th Battalion, King's Regiment (Liverpool)

I was about twelve years younger than most of the men in my battalion. We heard about this man Wingate of Abyssinia. We thought he must be a freak who had done very well as a guerrilla in Ethiopia. He came to see us in Secunderabad and addressed us. He created a great effect on most of us. I felt I was in the presence of somebody really extraordinary, the type of person I had never come across before. He exuded an aura of power. And yet he didn't speak in that manner, he spoke quietly and convincingly, and we gradually came to the conclusion that he was talking about going to be trained to infiltrate the Japanese lines in Burma and in fact we were going to be the first troops to fight back since the debacle of the loss of Burma. He realigned our perception of what was possible for ordinary people like ourselves. He lifted us. We were left realising that our cushy life in India was coming to an end. He told us we were to be in for a very hard time training. We were going to show the Japanese we could do better. We were in awe of him. He convinced us that we could do it. He was a great man.

Lieutenant Denis Gudgeon
3 Column, 3rd/2nd Gurkha Rifles

From the time I joined the 3rd/2nd Gurkhas in March 1942, we trained to go to the Western Desert, learning the use of sun compasses, and our vehicles were painted yellow.

At end of June 1942, we were moved to Saugor to train on a secret operation, with 13th King's Regiment (Liverpool), the Burma Rifles and 142 Commando Company in 77th Indian Brigade under Brigadier Wingate. I was a bit annoyed, we had spent all this time training to go to the Western Desert and now we had to forget all that and start jungle training. We were a bit apprehensive. We had heard about Wingate and that he had been very successful in the campaign in Italy against the Italians.

We knew that he was ruthless and eccentric. I only met him when I was a young subaltern attending sand table exercises and TEWTs. Those I dreaded. Wingate would pick a hill several hundred feet high, and we would have to run up it and the last officer to get in would have to run down and up again. I was terrified of being asked some detailed military question as he would point his ruler at you, and fix you with his clear blue eyes. My mind would go a total blank.

He carried a Flit gun with him everywhere, which was a bit disconcerting when you were eating lunch and he puffed Flit about the place. He also carried an alarm clock about with him. We thought he was mad.

I did not like him. Not many of the Gurkha officers liked him. You couldn't have a rapport with him, he was aloof, never said very much. He issued reams of instructions, and we were terrified of him. We thought he was anti-Gurkha. We were split up into columns and the Gurkhas did not like being split up like that.

In the 3rd/2nd Gurkhas I was in C Company, my company commander was George Silcock. But when we became Chindits, I became administration officer of Number 3 Column. I was in charge of the RV where the mules were sent, coordinating supply drops, collecting parachutes, collecting supplies, and distributing supplies to the men.

Lieutenant Harold James
Number 3 Column, 3rd/2nd Gurkha Rifles
The Gurkhas expect very high standards from their officers: courage, to look after their interests, get to know their language, and have a good sense of humour. Out of the blue came the order that three of us were to go on a company commander's course at Jhansi. We arrived in January 1943. We were met by the adjutant, who asked, 'You know why you are here?'

'To go on a company commander's course.'

'No you are not, you are going into Burma. By the way, have you made your wills?'

We were pitchforked into Wingate's Chindits. We felt excited. I was nineteen.

I was in Number 3 Column. Originally there had been eight columns, but one had been disbanded so the force eventually consisted of seven, although we all kept our original number. The force had been training for months; it was a mistake on Wingate's part to bring in twelve hundred Gurkha troops and British officers at such short notice who had not a clue what it was all about, the various drills and so forth. As a result he went into Burma with a lot of untrained people, like me. He had suddenly decided that there should be more muleteers. Even the British column would have Gurkha muleteers, some of them recruits. Some hadn't fired a rifle, and certainly none of them had ever seen a mule. The other point was that we and other British officers were in columns with men we had never met before. Gurkhas like to know their officers. I was lucky, my column commander was Michael Calvert. An amazing man, a great leader, I have the highest regard for him. He could not speak Gurkhali, and had to rely on Captain George Silcock to translate for him. But the Gurkhas recognised in Calvert a man they could follow.

Lieutenant Denis Gudgeon
Number 3 Column, 3rd/2nd Gurkha Rifles
As we arrived at Saugor the monsoon started. It flooded and we had to climb trees. We lived up trees for several days, I tied my gramophone and records to a branch. About ten members of the force were drowned when the nearby river overflowed its banks and swept through camp very quickly. Gurkhas can't swim.

Private Charles Aves
7 Column, 13th Battalion, King's Regiment (Liverpool)
We went to Saugor, near Jhansi. The surrounding jungle was similar to the area of Burma in which we were to operate. We did long marches all through the night. We had bad and inadequate food. The monsoon started. We were never dry, night or day. There were mud holes four or five feet deep. It was an appalling month. We had our first casualties. A number of men returning in camp to their tents were drowned in what had been a small stream which had become a swollen torrent. I and plenty of soldiers went down with malaria, and lots of people went down with dysentery.

Those of us who had taken to the training and stuck it we called 'PKs', or 'pukka King's', those that opted out we called 'jossers'.

Many of the officers hated Wingate. I overheard an officer say to another officer, referring to Wingate, 'This man is mad.'

One day Wingate decided to hold a church service in the jungle. I was introduced by my column commander, Major Gilkes, to Wingate to discuss the hymns we would sing, which I would accompany on my accordion. I stood next to him as he conducted the first part of the service. I found him kind and considerate. Whenever we met on a one-to-one basis, which was not very often, he would ask how I was getting on. On one occasion he said, 'How are you finding the rations?'

I replied, 'There is not enough. We are hungry all the time.'

He just nodded his head and said, 'You will be pleased to know that we are going on general service rations. There will be more food and more variety.'

He went on his way. I felt proud to have spoken to Brigadier Wingate.

Major Michael Calvert
Commanding, 3 Column

We trained our men in the basing-up or bivouacking drills that would become a daily feature of life on Chindit operations. As the column approached the end of the day's march, the column commander would be near the front, and he would find a suitable place. You couldn't hesitate for long with four hundred or so men behind you. Some of the essentials were water and bamboo to feed the mules. Provided it was possible to combine it with water, we would try to find a place with fairly high ground so our signal sets would carry the two hundred miles back to India. We would set up a defensive position off the path, while the rearguard marched on as a deception before brushing away the footprints, and setting up an ambush to catch any Japanese following up.

Within five minutes of getting in, every unit would be lighting fires. We had been trained in this detail by Wingate who pointed out that often, just as we arrived at the bivouac area, the rain came at about four or five o'clock. He told us to collect dry sticks from the previous night's fire and put them in our packs. The wireless would be set up. The column commander would sit down and his batman would bring him a mug of hot sweet tea. Then the signals would start coming in. Our first signal out would give the position of the column to the base back in India.

The muleteers, one to each two mules, would go out and cut bamboo for their mules; you didn't need to carry fodder if there was enough bamboo nearby. The men would go to fill their water bottles. The upper piece of the stream was for water bottles, the next piece for mules, then for washing, and the lowest for defecating. We always tried to use running water for latrines, so it would be washed away and not give away our position.

We rarely stayed in a bivouac for more than one night, occasionally for two to three days. After the column commander had given orders, the column would settle down to eat and sleep. While the fires were still alight, we'd make a second quantity of tea, and put this in a spare water bottle, before burying the water bottle in leaves or earth just beside where one slept. In the mornings, before light, you drank warm tea and ate a Shakapura biscuit. The routines were carried out with few words being spoken, four hundred men and 120 animals going into their places with no fuss; the same in the morning. I would like to start the column moving just before dawn, and, if possible, get two hours' marching away from our previous bivouac before we settled down to breakfast.

Underlying all the training was Wingate's firm belief that his Long Range Penetration Force would outdo the Japanese. I don't want to be too hard on the British and Indian armies at the time, but they were to a large extent demoralised, they thought that the Jap was invincible. There were well-meaning posters up all over India showing cruel Japanese bayoneting children. Instead of making people want to fight the Japanese, it made them frightened. We had to build up the morale of the British to remember they were tough. I think this was why Wingate said that beards would be allowed. I personally would not allow mournful beards. I insisted that we should have aggressive beards, like conquistadores.

Lieutenant Dominic Neill
8 Column, 3rd/2nd Gurkha Rifles

Having been selected for a commission in the Indian Army from the 60th Rifles in the United Kingdom, I was sent as a cadet to Bangalore where the training was below standard, and all aimed at warfare on the North-West Frontier. We learned very little. Our weapon training was minimal, as was our map reading. When I joined our regimental centre our training was equally poor. My company commander was an ex-tea planter, and knew nothing about soldiering at that stage.

One day three other subalterns and I were called to the commandant's office and told that we were to join the 3rd Battalion under Brigadier Orde Wingate. Only one of the four of us was sent to command mules in a Gurkha column, the other three would go to the King's columns to command Gurkha muleteers. I had one Gurkha officer and fifty-two Gurkha Other Ranks, mostly from 10th Gurkhas and about half a dozen from other Gurkha regiments. When I joined 77 Indian Infantry Brigade I hoped I would get more training. I did not.

The 77th Infantry Brigade consisted of three rifle battalions and 142 Commando Company, which was a commando/demolition outfit. The brigade was organised into an HQ, and Numbers 1 and 2 groups. In Number 1 group were the four Gurkha columns, and in Number 2 group the three British columns, seven columns in all; around three hundred men in each column, and about ninety mules and three chargers. Each column had a headquarters; three rifle platoons; a support platoon with two Vickers medium machine guns and two 3-inch mortars; a reconnaissance platoon of Burma Riflemen and a section of 142 Commando Company. The training that the brigade had received had virtually finished by the time we joined at Saugor: mainly river crossing and tactics. On contact with the enemy a bugle would be blown, signalling dispersal. Troops would then disperse, under sub-unit commanders, and return to the former halting place. I could not believe my ears. Neither I, nor my Gurkha soldiers, received any tactical training whatsoever until we came face to face with the Japanese.

Lieutenant Denis Gudgeon
3 Column, 3rd/2nd Gurkha Rifles
We left Jhansi by train in mid-January 1943, crossed the River Brahmaputra by steamer, and by train to Dimapur railway station. We were met on the platform by Major Calvert, who was to be our column commander. We marched by night along the road through the lovely hill station of Kohima, which was to be flattened a year later, and eventually arrived at Imphal.

I was immensely impressed by Calvert, a dynamic character, he had been an army boxer, and had a flat nose and cauliflower ears. General Wavell came up and had a long conference with Wingate and finally gave his approval for us to go into Burma. He actually saluted us, and not the other way around.

71

Lieutenant Dominic Neill
8 Column, 3rd/2nd Gurkha Rifles

I was to join Number 8 Column, commanded by Major Walter Scott. Wingate came to visit us a day or so after the brigade farrier had branded each mule's number on their hooves. This was the first time I had met Wingate. He wandered down the mule lines with me and asked me one of the mule's number. I said that I did not know, they had only recently been branded, and haven't memorised their numbers yet. He said, 'Boy, you should know the numbers by now,' and passed on.

He looked very closely at the mules, but totally ignored the newly arrived young Gurkha soldiers, very peculiar.

After he had departed, I met Lieutenant 'Tag' Sprague, who I thought was very impressive. He was about four years my senior, had fought with 1 Commando in Norway, and was an experienced soldier. Originally the Gurkha columns were commanded by their respective company commanders, all of whom spoke flawless Gurkhali. On the eve of leaving India, two of the columns were given new commanders, neither of whom could speak a word of their language.

We had a lecture on how to handle mules, feed and water them and so forth, but had no practical training; we learned as we went along. I had never seen a mule in my life before. The Gurkhas had seen mule trains in the hills of Nepal, but never led them.

I was introduced to Major Scott, known as 'Scottie', but not to his face. He was an excellent chap. He gave my men and me a very warm welcome indeed, which was much appreciated. I was given a British sergeant, William Ormandy, an ex-17th/21st Lancer, very knowledgeable about horses, but he did not know much about mules. I also had twenty British Other Ranks (BORs) to lead the first-line mules in Number 8 Column. The mules were divided into two parties, first and second line. First-line mules carried support weapons, the heavy wireless set, ammunition, and some spare light machine guns. Second-line mules carried bedding, spare rations, and other stores. First-line mules were led by BORs, second line by Gurkhas.

The final exercise was a long hike across country of about a hundred miles. What the scheme was supposed to be about I have no idea at all, because from the start to finish in my time in Number 8 Column I was never called to one of Scottie's O Groups, even when we were in Burma. I was so inexperienced that it never occurred to me to suggest that I should attend. My orders were given to me via the sergeant major.

Lieutenant Harold James
3 Column, 3rd/2nd Gurkha Rifles
At Imphal Wingate had his HQ in the golf club, the floor was covered in maps. We went in every day in our stocking feet while Wingate held forth. He always carried a Flit gun and every now and then he would spray the room, it was dreadful. At one point Wingate asked if there were any questions and one of the doctors, a Canadian, said, 'Tell me, why do you have to use that Flit pump?'

'What do you mean?'

'It's bloody unsanitary.'

'Get him out,' said Wingate.

We were suddenly told that if anyone was wounded and could not keep up, he would be left in a village; if seriously wounded he would be helped on his way with a lethal dose of morphine. Officers were given a supply of morphine in things like miniature toothpaste tubes with a hypodermic needle on the end.

ACROSS THE CHINDWIN

Lieutenant Dominic Neill
8 Column, 3rd/2nd Gurkha Rifles
At the end of January we left Imphal for Tamu and the Chindwin. We marched through Palel and over the Shenam pass. As we approached the Burma border we marched by night. On 14 February 1943, we reached the Chindwin just north of the village of Tonhe, where there was a wide sandy beach on our side of the river, which at that point was about two hundred and fifty yards wide. Just before we started to cross, Bill Williams, the second-in-command, came and told me that a signal from Wingate had been received giving quotations from the Old Testament, which had to be interpreted by the column commander digging out his Bible. I suppose Wingate did it to try to fox the Japanese.

Wingate (centre) with two staff officers planning on the map on the floor of the golf club at Imphal before taking his brigade across the Chindwin.

General Sir Archibald Wavell, C-in-C India, inspects the Chindits before the first expedition. Nearest camera, Major Bernard Fergusson, commanding Number 5 Column, the badge on his hat has been obscured by the censor. Wingate is on the far right in the picture.

Lieutenant Harold James
3 Column, 3rd/2nd Gurkha Rifles

We had to cross the river Chindwin without the Japs finding out. The first objective was the Rangoon–Myitkyina railway, so Wingate divided the force into two groups. One group, the northern group, went with Wingate and his HQ, consisting of two Gurkha columns, including mine, Number 3, and three British columns, 5, 7 and 8; Fergusson's, Gilkes's, and Scott's.

The other group consisted of just two Gurkha columns, Numbers 1 and 2, commanded by Lieutenant Colonel Alexander, the CO of the 3rd/2nd Gurkhas. The southern group were the decoy. They crossed the Chindwin openly, and, combined with other tactical deception moves by other units not involved in the expedition, tried to attract the attention of the Japs while we went further north and crossed at Tonhe.

It worked because the Japs at that time were not all that well established on the Chindwin anyway. We were in the northern group aimed at blowing up the railway. We spent two nights marching on tracks through the jungle to the Chindwin. The river was about four hundred yards wide. None of the Gurkhas could swim. Wingate had made no attempt to teach them to swim, and indeed some British troops could not swim. Yet we were marching across the grain of the country and having to cross rivers. The British officers and commandos had to get the mules and horses across the river. It took a long time and much effort.

Lieutenant Dominic Neill
8 Column, 3rd/2nd Gurkha Rifles

When our Burma Riflemen were collecting boats from the villagers, we had another signal from Wingate in code, telling us that once we crossed the Chindwin any man wounded and unable to move would be left in a friendly village to his fate. I thought that to give an order like that on the eve of battle would cause the men's morale to dip. I know the British soldiers were not best pleased. I did not pass on the order to my Gurkhas. In those days none of them spoke English. Having received that boost to our morale we started to cross the river. We tethered the mules to the stern of the boats and swam them across; we were successful, other columns had problems. We were over by about 1700 hours or so. I remember going to sleep feeling very excited at the prospect of the operation ahead.

Swimming mules across a river.

Lieutenant Denis Gudgeon
3 Column, 3rd/2nd Gurkha Rifles
We crossed by boat, and the mules were swum across. This was very disheartening as some mules, having got almost to the other side, would panic and turn back again. Several times I got a free ride across the Chindwin by hanging on to the tail of a mule. It was broad daylight and luckily there was no sign of the Jap air force.

Lieutenant Dominic Neill
8 Column, 3rd/2nd Gurkha Rifles
That night was uneventful, as was the following day and many days thereafter. We moved north-east and received our first air drop. The dropping zone (DZ) was on an area of rice paddy. The mules were based in a bamboo forest to wait in safety during the drop.

This was the first parachute drop most of us had ever seen. While loads on parachutes were being dropped, the aircraft flew over the DZ fairly high. But the sacks of rice were free-dropped and planes came in quite low. We could see the dispatchers at the doors chucking out the sacks of rice, each weighed about 160 pounds. These came tumbling out turning over and over quite slowly, but hit the ground with a tremendous whack, and would have killed any mule or soldier had they hit.

My muleteers and I took the food back to our bivouac area. The rations were Shakapura biscuits, like square dog biscuits, rice, small tins of cheese, tinned meat and vegetables, powdered milk, tea and sugar. From this the BORs made a sort of porridge: crushed biscuits in a mess tin, with sugar and raisins sprinkled over, and either hot or cold powdered milk poured over it. It was very good indeed, but sadly my Gurkhas did not like it very much. They preferred to eat the rations straight.

Lieutenant Harold James
3 Column, 3rd/2nd Gurkha Rifles
I had a good view of our first air drop: I took a platoon to guard Bobby Thompson, our column RAF officer who was organising the drop. He later became Sir Robert Thompson of Malaya fame. The Brigade Rear HQ, a squadron of Dakotas, and supplies were located back in Agartala near Dacca. When a column wanted supplies it would radio requests and give a map

reference for the DZ (at night we would light fires to guide the aircraft in over the DZ). This was all new to us, none of us had done it before, and we thought that you needed a nice open area like a paddy field for a DZ.

Squadron Leader Robert 'Bobby' Thompson
3 Column, RAF Liaison Officer

I would be sent ahead to select a place where supplies could be dropped and signal the location back to base. Sometimes we came across Japanese patrols, but usually we got plenty of warning of their approach from the local inhabitants, and we hardly ever ran into them unaware.

We got quite a lot of food in the villages. Once we paid for a meal of rice and curried fish and vegetables that was being cooked for the enemy. The main supplies were dropped to us by DC3s. We lit fires to show the dropping area. Grain was dropped in sacks, food by parachute. The ration packs consisted of paratroop rations, each pack was intended to last for two days and contained: six packets of biscuits, three packets of dates, one packet of raisins and nuts, four ounces of cheese, four ounces of chocolate, four ounces of sugar, two packets of dried milk, tea and salt, forty cigarettes, and two boxes of matches. Later on the chocolate was left out because it melted in the hot weather, but one column that wanted it particularly sent back a request for four hundred pounds of it. One of the restaurants in Calcutta took the job in hand and worked all night making the chocolate and the following day it was sent straight out to them by the officer in charge of base, whose name was Lord. One day one of the columns sent back a message 'Oh Lord send us bread'. And got the answer 'the Lord has heard thy prayer', and a full supply of bread followed. Anything you might specially need later was left behind with the supply officer and could be sent out to you. One officer had a replacement monocle sent out after he broke his. He got through several monocles during the course of the campaign.

Sergeant Douglas Williams
Wireless Operator/Gunner, 194 Squadron, RAF

Flying conditions in Burma were atrocious, there was always tremendous turbulence because of the heat. The bouncing up and down made it difficult moving supplies to the door to despatch them. We often flew through lightning. On a Hudson operation over the Chin Hills at sixteen thousand feet, we flew through a storm, the lightning flashed along the wing tips, lighting up the inside of the Hudson and the pilot's face white and tense with the strain of controlling the aircraft which bucked and dropped, thrown about like a ship in a boiling sea.. The pilot was very strong and held it while we plummeted from sixteen thousand to twelve thousand feet. But we got through, dropped our supplies, and returned to base pretty shaken.

Flight Sergeant Deryck Groocock
194 Squadron, RAF
In the monsoon you had fantastic thunder storms, towering cu-nims, air currents, low cloud bases and violent rain. We knew just about every valley in our area of Burma, so we knew which valleys we could fly up without coming to a dead end. Often there were clouds on the mountain tops, and you had to fly up a valley underneath. When trying to find a DZ, you hoped to find a hole in the cloud, find a valley leading in the right direction, drop and climb back up through the hole.

Lieutenant Harold James
3 Column, 3rd/2nd Gurkha Rifles
The rations were pitiful. Eventually, because of difficulties of getting air drops when you needed them, one day's rations had to last four days or even longer. You might get rice from villages, if you were lucky, but getting enough rice for three hundred and fifty people from a small village was not easy. When you are marching an average of ten miles a day, fighting and so forth, you got very hungry; it affected morale.

I was very fit, and coped very well with the rigours of the expedition. At first I noted in my diary what I was going to eat, and kept some reserve. Most difficult was the lack of water. When we got into the dry zone there was very little water, you had to dig for it.

Because I was so fit, Calvert made me permanent rearguard platoon commander. The worst place to march was in a long snake behind all those people and mules. There was a concertina effect with people at the back sometimes stopping for five minutes followed by running fast to catch up. Although platoons were changed over every few days, I was always rearguard commander.

We reached the railway line on 6 March without seeing the Japs. They were looking for our lines of communication, which did not exist. We marched on tracks and paths. Mike Calvert was trusted by Wingate implicitly, the only column commander who was. He allowed Calvert's column to go off on its own which is why we did better than the others.

We approached the railway at Nankan near Wuntho, between Mandalay and Myitkyina. We set off to blow up bridges. Wingate sent off one party to blow bridges north of Nankan under George Silcock and Lieutenant Geoffrey Lockett, a British commando. While Calvert and I went south to blow another bridge, an ambush was laid in the village of Nankan under the senior Gurkha officer, Kumarsing Gurung. The mules were sent to a safe RV.

My party with Calvert set off. On the way we heard firing at the station at Nankan, but continued on our way. As soon as our bridge was blown Calvert decided to go and help our party at Nankan. On our way back a Gurkha Rifleman came running up to say that the Japs had arrived in the village in lorries and that Kumarsing Gurung had ambushed them, killed a few, and was holding up the rest of the Japs. We were walking along the railway line, and had reached the path which joined the railway, when I looked up and saw a bearded face looking at me, and then a whole lot of more bearded faces; huge surprise, it was a Dane called Eric Petersen from 7 Column and his chaps. Mike Calvert, never one to lose an opportunity, said, 'How would you chaps like to join us in a little battle?'

So we all set off again along the railway. Meanwhile Kumarsing Gurung, realising they were being overwhelmed, moved away from the village towards the RV. At which point we arrived, caught the Japs napping, had quite a fight in the village, and blew up a lorry and an armoured car. The Japs withdrew, and as it was getting dark by now, Calvert decided to pull out to the RV about six miles from the station. We couldn't get to RV in time, so we based-up for the night. Calvert remarked, 'It's my birthday today, I'm thirty.'

I replied, 'If I'd known I would have bought you a present.'

Calvert laughed, 'I could not have asked for a better present than blowing up a couple of bridges and killing a lot of Japs.'

Calvert believed that boldness paid off and did not care a damn about the Japs. He lit a fire and made tea. We had just had a battle with Japs, were several hundred miles behind enemy lines, and here we were like a lot of happy campers. All the Gurkhas were asleep and contented, and not worried because they had such faith in Calvert, and had seen off the Japanese. This was our first action, and we didn't have a single casualty.

It worked well mainly because of Calvert and his 2i/c, George Silcock, a very good Gurkhali speaker, who supported him well. We reckoned we despatched fifty or sixty Japs. Mind you, you always think you have killed more people than you actually have.

To our north Fergusson had blown up the Bongyaung Bridge, but had suffered casualties and the southern group had also blown some bridges.

Lieutenant Denis Gudgeon
3 Column, 3rd/2nd Gurkha Rifles

I wasn't involved in the Nankan battle, I was in the RV with mules. The column blew up three box girder railway bridges, put charges on seventeen different places on the railway lines, ambushed a Jap lorry, and inflicted quite a lot of casualties. I could hear the bridges being blown and the lorry being ambushed.

The mules were a curse in battle. They had no 'discipline' as far as water was concerned, as soon as they smelt water they would bolt. They were very cunning and when being loaded, would blow out their stomachs so that the girth was not very tight. They loathed anything that rattled, or made a noise, and would get rid of it as soon as possible.

Lieutenant Dominic Neill
8 Column, 3rd/2nd Gurkha Rifles

After our first supply drop we marched about thirty miles due east to the Zibyu Taungdan, which we called the escarpment, and took a narrow footpath. Our mules started getting bad galls on their withers and bellies. The stench of their galls was dreadful as you marched alongside them, like a rotting corpse. If there were any heroes of the Wingate expedition it was our mules. After crossing the escarpment, 8 Column turned south-east towards the Irrawaddy. At that time I had neither map nor compass.

Up to now there had been no aggressive role for 8 Column, and I was getting bored. We marched towards the Irrawaddy, crossed in the same area as brigade HQ and 7 Column. Looking across the river I could hardly believe it was so wide, in some places up to two miles across. The villagers produced country boats paddled by villagers. We crossed satisfactorily. Some mules got loose but still got over.

Lieutenant Harold James
3 Column, 3rd/2nd Gurkha Rifles

As we approached the Irrawaddy, Wingate ordered everybody over. It was important to get across the Irrawaddy without the Japs knowing, so we marched most of that day, and all that night, traversing the Meza a couple of times to throw people off the scent. Eventually, in the early hours, we reached a jungle-covered hill where we stopped to rest. The order was that nobody was to move out of the perimeter. At daybreak there was a fusillade of fire, and the whole column got ready to move out. We discovered that a Gurkha and a Karen had very stupidly gone down to the river for water, we were very short at the time. They had been seen by a Jap patrol. We moved out very quickly leaving booby traps. We hadn't gone very far when we heard mortar fire, and shouts of Japs charging into the position, and then a couple of blasts of booby traps going off, which pleased us no end. Calvert now had to get to the Irrawaddy and throw the Japs off our track. So we had a very nasty twenty-four hours while he went one way and then the other, like a fox. Eventually in the early hours of the morning we stopped for a long time. As rearguard commander I was out of the picture. I heard mortar bombs about a mile off, so went on to the head of the column, and found the men collapsed, absolutely exhausted, in a flat area. I located Calvert, woke him up, and told him that the Japs were mortaring us. He said, 'I know,' which took the wind out of my sails. 'They don't know we're here,' he continued.

I believed him. It was probably true. He told me to stay by the chaung with my platoon and form a rearguard, and went back to sleep. The chaung was about two hundred yards wide, with thick elephant grass on both sides, and a few hundred yards away there was an open space with the whole column absolutely flat out exhausted. About two hours later I was catnapping and my havildar woke me up, saying, 'Come along sahib, come quietly.' We were in the elephant grass, which completely hid us. Peeping out I could see this Jap soldier, he was looking right across to where the column was, he couldn't see us. The havildar asked, 'Shall I kill him?'

I thought if I shoot him the Japs will open fire on the column, and also on me as my position will be compromised. So I said, 'No.' I sent a runner with a note to Calvert to tell him what was happening. The runner couldn't find Calvert. He and Lockett had gone off on horses to the other side of the island to see if they could find some boats. Luckily the runner chanced on George

Silcock, who immediately shook out the column into defensive positions. They were almost all deployed when the Japanese opened fire. With the first burst of machine-gun fire we took only five casualties. The Japs still didn't know where I was, and my Bren gunner opened up on them, putting some of them out of action. The Japs came down opposite us in the elephant grass and fired on us, badly wounding the number two on the Bren. Eventually we seemed to silence them; it went dead quiet. Just as I had got up to cross the chaung with my havildar to check if any enemy still there, Calvert appeared, and said, 'What are you doing standing in the open?'

He was always standing in the open. I didn't want to tell him I was going to cross the chaung, and said, 'I was going to get the men in the right positions.'

'Oh,' he said. 'Oh well, get in position here and keep the Japs at bay, while we cross the river.'

I had a wounded Gurkha, shot to bits in great pain, and dying. After agonising for a bit, I gave him a lethal dose of morphia. He went out very quietly, the Gurkhas were amazing, they just accepted it. We covered him with a blanket. We stayed there for some time, until a message came for me to join the main column with George Silcock. On arrival, I found only George, a section of Gurkhas and some Karens, the rest had gone off.

To my horror I found another very seriously wounded Gurkha there. I said, 'I've just had to do it.' George looked at me as if to say 'you do it again'.

I protested, 'There is no way I'm going to do it twice.'

He gave the chap a lethal dose. We were lucky: out of three hundred and fifty we had only three killed and four wounded. We moved off towards the main column where Calvert had started to organise the Irrawaddy crossing in some boats. Most of the Gurkhas were already over, and Calvert decided to put across only sufficient mules to carry essential equipment like wireless sets, MMGs and 3-inch mortars, the rest would be abandoned.

Eventually we set off into the interior, with my platoon at the rear. We passed a bullock cart loaded with straw, and on it were the four wounded Gurkhas who were going to be left in a village. The Gurkhas gazed at it; I think that this was the first time they really realised what would happen to them if they were wounded, and it went through them like being hit by a bullet. They had accepted giving a lethal dose: the chap was dying, and the officer sahib was doing the best for him. But this was quite different. This was when the seed of lowered morale was sown. It didn't appear then, but later.

We moved off. I can still see that bullock cart to this day with those four people lying there.

Major Michael Calvert
Officer Commanding 3 Column

The MO and I went the nearest village, asked them to look after the wounded we had crossing the Irrawaddy, and hand them over to the Japanese if they came along. I wrote a note to the Japanese, saying that I left the men who had been wounded, fighting for their king and country, just as they were. They have fought courageously, and I am sure that with your *bushido* you will look after them. I signed it. The Burma Rifles translated the note into Burmese. I felt that the Japanese would look after them, and they did. After they arrived in the prison camp, some of the other prisoners of war believed that they had given away secrets to earn good treatment. They had no secrets to give away.

Lieutenant Harold James
3 Column, 3rd/2nd Gurkha Rifles

Once we had crossed the Irrawaddy, we were in dead trouble for two reasons. First, which Wingate didn't realise at the time, we were in the dry zone, and at that time of year there was very little water.

Second, until then we had been spread out in jungle, so the Japs had trouble locating us. We were now in an area where columns were all within fifteen miles of each other. We were in a trap. To our east and north, the Shweli River flowed in a big curve into the Irrawaddy. A network of roads (the exact location of which we were unaware) ran to the Irrawaddy throughout the area. To our west lay the Irrawaddy, which was the lid of the trap, because the Japs took all the boats from the east bank of the river over to the west bank. So getting back over was going to be very difficult. The Japs knew where we were, realised we were supplied by air, and had gathered together a large force to smash us.

Wingate told Calvert that he would be joined by Number 5 Column, commanded by Bernard Fergusson, and that the two columns, under Calvert, were to march to the Gokteik viaduct, and destroy it. This pleased Calvert.

We set off in the direction of the viaduct, and had to cross the Nam Mit Chaung, a tributary of the Shweli River, to get there. Calvert organised a supply drop near a chaung on our route where we could dig for water, and gave everyone a good rest for three days. Up to that time officers slept with their own groups, but on this occasion, Calvert decided that all officers were to come to HQ. We started to sing popular songs, but stopped because we were not supposed to make unnecessary noise. He told us to sing on. It was a remarkable sight: eight British officers mostly bearded, very scruffy, singing songs three hundred miles inside Japanese lines. This was because Calvert was allowed to operate alone, and didn't believe in being dictated to by the enemy.

Calvert planned to cross the Nam Mit Chaung, RV with Fergusson, and go for the Gokteik viaduct. We reached the chaung at night, and first thing next morning we heard shots from where Calvert had sent a small patrol of Burma Rifles to do a recce. They had bumped some Japs, who had fired without hitting anything. So Calvert decided to set an ambush on the road near Pago, where there was known to be a Jap garrison. He selected me to set the ambush. I had a platoon of Gurkhas, a section of British commandos, and CSM Bob Blaine, a very tough character. We set up the ambush on the track, and waited. Soon a Burmese villager came along, and we grabbed him. I had a Karen with me who asked him where he was going. He said he was travelling from one village to another. We searched him and found a letter written in Japanese, which he said he had been told to take from the garrison in his village to the garrison commander in the next village.

I sent a note to Calvert on which I had rather cheekily written, 'May I suggest you come and join us for an attack on Pago?'

A little later, a Jap patrol walked into my ambush, and some of my Gurkhas, not being fully trained, fired too early and we did not kill them all; one or two escaped, and fired at us. I and my havildar decided to get rid of them. He fired a rifle grenade at the enemy while I worked my way round with a tommy gun, found one Jap there, who I put out of action, and rejoined the havildar.

At that point all hell broke loose as lots of Japs came on the scene. They struck the ambush behind us, and came round the flanks. In addition, thirty or so Japanese came rushing around to the front of my position. I had a section of Gurkhas with me. The Japs stopped for a moment, in a bunch, gazing at the enemy we had already killed; they were sitting targets. We let them have it with everything we had. Some were lying moaning, but there was no way we were going to look at them, they were treacherous even when wounded. But half a dozen or so may have escaped to my left. Then I heard a lot of firing

Chindits crossing a minor river.

from my other two sections, under the jemadar to my left, and Blaine to my right, so I told the havildar to move out. But before we could do so, we were attacked by about six Japs coming out of the jungle behind us. My Bren gunner stood firing from the hip. There was a bit of a melee, three Gurkhas were killed, one was wounded, and my havildar was killed by a bayonet. I had the satisfaction of despatching the chap who had killed him. We killed all the Japs.

Now there were just four Gurkhas, the Karen and I left unwounded. We started to move out. The place was full of Japs, and I wondered how we were going to get clear. It was thick scrub country. Suddenly our 3-inch mortar bombs started landing in among the Japs. Calvert, as soon as he realised that I had landed in something big, ordered the mortars to fire, which caused a gap in the ring of enemy through which we ran to join the main body. Sergeant Major Blaine turned up with his men saying he had had a great time, a whole lot of Japs had appeared in front of his position and he had wiped them out.

The main column remained in the position for about an hour and the Japanese never counter-attacked. But it was sad too, we lost nine people.

We moved out to go to the Gokteik, but that night received a wireless message to return to India independently. Now you could begin to tell that despite the troops fighting well at Pago, it was coming to the point where they had given practically everything they had to give. We were in tatters, stinking, hungry, thirsty. Everyone began to realise that if anything happened to them now they would be in a bad way.

DISPERSE AND RETURN TO INDIA

Major Walter 'Scottie' Scott
Officer Commanding 8 Column, 13th Battalion, King's Regiment (Liverpool)
When Wingate ordered the columns to split and return to India, I decided to cross the Shweli and hook round and cross the Irrawaddy. We had taken a supply drop at Baw but Japs closed in on us in a ring; not in great strength, but in patrols that could bring in more enemy as required.

I asked the RAF to drop me a floating rope and some rescue dinghies. I planned to cross the Shweli, using the rope and RAF dinghies. The chaps pulled themselves across with a looped rope over the grass rope, which was knotted at intervals. After getting about forty men across, one of the sergeants got his loop rope jammed on one of the knots on the grass rope. He panicked and pulled out his dah to cut the loop; instead he cut the main rope. He went sailing down the Shweli in his dinghy, on into the Irrawaddy, and was captured. I was left on one side of the Shweli, and my second-in-command with some men on the other.

The RAF dropped another rope and more boats the next night enabling me to get most of my chaps across. By then my second-in-command and forty men had been given authority to head for India. But he was killed and most of his chaps captured. I picked up four of them later.

Lieutenant Dominic Neill
8 Column, 3rd/2nd Gurkha Rifles
Just before we crossed, Scottie told us that we would shortly be returning to India. He told me to kill a mule to provide meat. I shot the mule with the worst galls with my pistol, between the eyes. Unfortunately the meat was very unpleasant and very tough. We were now only about seventy miles from the Chinese border. Return to India was very much on our minds, and when it would be. I wondered why on earth we had come to Burma, we in 8 Column had done nothing except a minor contact in Baw.

From the Shweli we marched north for two days. Tag's platoon was sent off on recce, while a platoon was left in a deep dried chaung bed, and the rest of us moved off to a forest rest house. We were marching in single file, all the men bunched as usual. No one in Wingate's brigade seemed to worry if troops bunched. If you bunch, you present a target, and if hit you take casualties. The vegetation was jungle, but not very thick. Suddenly there was rifle fire in front. It sounded like Jap fire, I saw the BORs in the leading platoon running back shouting, 'Japs!' I stood in the middle of the track, thinking would I see my first Jap? Suddenly I saw one, range twenty yards. I put my rifle up to my shoulder, had taken the first pressure, and was about to fire, when a BOR's head popped up and blotted out the target. The Jap fired, the bullet hit the sand between my feet. There was confusion in extreme up front. The remainder of the leading platoon came back with terror in their eyes, and my men in sympathy turned and ran. I shouted at them in Gurkhali, 'Don't run,' and, bless them, they slowed to a walk. As the animal transport officer I now found myself as rearguard. I thought, 'At last, I shall kill a Jap.' But not a bit of it, they didn't follow up.

We got back to the chaung bed where we had a firm base. I asked the leading platoon commander what had happened. He told me they had bumped two Japs, only two, and the leading platoon had carried out Wingate's dispersal drill to the letter. The only thing missing was a bugle call. Wingate had really opened up a Pandora's box when he told them to carry out dispersal drill on meeting the enemy. It was a shambles. There were a lot of young men in 8 Column that evening who hung their heads in shame. If a field commander teaches bad tricks in training, the chaps will react badly when they meet the enemy. It was a lesson I hoisted in then. After that incident Scottie ordered us to march to the Irrawaddy, which we reached at the beginning of April. We were, as far as I could gather, not far from Inywa; about seven hundred men were there from HQ and other columns as well as us. Some men had been sent across by Wingate to form a bridgehead. Not long after I reached the area of the river there was heavy firing from the other side, Jap 4-inch mortar and medium machine-gun fire; theirs had a much slower rate of fire than ours. It sounded just like a woodpecker.

I could not see any of the bridgehead platoon. Next I saw a group coming towards me led by Wingate like a figure in the Bible, with a huge beard and sola topi [pith helmet], his pack was bumping up and down on his back, his eyes were wide and staring, and as he passed me and my group, he shouted, 'Disperse, disperse, get back to India'. I can remember the words to this day. I thought the man had gone stark staring mad. Here we were, with a force seven-hundred strong, one platoon already across the river, and he was not prepared to carry on with the crossing. I realised we would have suffered casualties if we had persisted with the crossing, but far fewer than we eventually did by splitting up into small groups and getting back piecemeal to India.

Private Charles Aves
7 Column, 13th Battalion, King's Regiment (Liverpool)
Wingate decided to recross the Irrawaddy at the same place as he had crossed on the outward journey, counting on the Japanese not thinking that we would do this. In the early morning we approached the river, Number 7 Column was sent ahead. Some boats were found from somewhere, and some Burmese to paddle them across. I was on the third boat. As we approached the other side the Japs opened up with machine guns and mortars. My boat wasn't hit. One

behind was hit, and everybody in it killed or drowned. When our boatload got ashore, we crawled up the bank. I found one of the officers standing eating a piece of cheese from a tin, unconcerned. The firing was about four hundred yards north of where we landed.

The officer pointed to a paddy field, told me to go out there and launch some grenades towards the enemy. He produced a grenade launcher and two grenades. I had never used one before. It is difficult to cross a paddy field; it consists of mud, water, and banks called bunds. I could not walk along the bund for fear of being shot by the enemy. I crawled my way to where the officer had told me to go. I found I was the only person who had crossed who was doing anything. I could not see where the enemy were. I didn't know what to do and decided to return, which took some time. I told the officer that I hadn't fired, he told me not to worry, and that we were moving off anyway.

Here I learned that Captain Hastings, an officer I admired and respected so much, had been killed on the boat that had been hit and sunk. Sixty-five of the column landed, a captain, a lieutenant, a second lieutenant, four sergeants, a couple of corporals, and about fifty private soldiers. We went inland to a place already designated as an RV after crossing the river. We waited twenty-four hours to see if anyone else turned up. Although the opposition where we crossed was not big, I learned later that Wingate had decided to stop crossing there.

Lieutenant Dominic Neill
8 Column, 3rd/2nd Gurkha Rifles

Number 8 Column marched east away from the Irrawaddy; talk about the grand old Duke of York. That night I got a warning order from Scottie that mules and chargers were to be driven away because they might be a hindrance to us in our return to India.

I hated the idea. My charger, whom we called Rathi, the Gurkhali name for red deer, started nuzzling my face. I was glad it was dark, and no one could see me, the tears were running down my face. The following morning off we marched, leaving our mules and chargers where they had spent the night. We took one mule to carry the wireless. Many of our animals followed and we tried to shoo them off. But my beloved horse followed for hours, eventually leaving us in a big field of sugar cane. I saw his red rump disappear. I looked round at my syce, Dalbir, and he was weeping too. That night there was much talk of what orders we would receive. I asked Tag if he and his commandos would accompany me and my Gurkhas if we split up, and to my intense relief he agreed. We had a final air drop of ten days' rations and I was called to my first O group. It was a big day, all columns would split up into small groups. Wingate had played us his last ace card. He had taken us so far but he wasn't going to take us back, and for that I have never forgiven him. He took us one river too far.

The single wireless set would go with Scottie, and he told us to tell him our chosen route, so that before we split up he could issue us with maps. Tag and I said we would go north to the Irrawaddy, cross between two villages of Bhamo and Khaso, and head west to the Chindwin. We collected our set of maps and compasses.

We knew the Japs would make every effort to catch us. Tag was our salvation. Sergeant Ormandy volunteered to come with us. I was given four hundred rupees in silver coins from Scottie's treasure chest. All my equipment weighed what seemed like a ton. Never again in all my combat soldiering was I ever faced by such a test as getting my men back to India. Each group was given a section of Burma Rifles, and I had an exceptional young soldier called Tun Tin, a Karen, mission-school educated, who spoke excellent English. We took three days to reach the Irrawaddy.

Lieutenant Harold James
3 Column, 3rd/2nd Gurkha Rifles
After Calvert had been told to return to India independently, he decided to return to our earlier camp to collect the three days' worth of rations we had cached there. We then set off to cross the Shweli river and go up into the Kachin Hills where the tribes were loyal, and work our way out through China. The Shweli, although not as wide as the Irrawaddy or Chindwin, was still quite an obstacle as well as being fast flowing. There were no villages nearby for boats. So Calvert decided to make 'sapper sampans' out of groundsheets and bamboo. While we started to build these he left me to guard the rear. He sent Blaine across to the other side. Not long afterwards a Jap patrol walked into Blaine's position. Blaine exterminated the lot of them but Calvert, having decided there was no way he could linger and cross the river as the Japs would soon be upon us, ordered a quick move away at once.

When I came forward to rejoin the column, and reached the riverbank, to my horror I saw two Gurkhas on the other side. The 'sapper sampan' had been brought back ready to take another load across, when Calvert ordered the move. Calvert had left the Gurkhas, he could not wait. We marched away from the river, and had a long discussion with the other senior officers, who had suggested breaking up into small dispersal groups and making our way back to India in these groups. Calvert was against this. He felt the column had worked so well up to now that it would be wrong to break it up. In the end he agreed to what was a right opinion. He decided to break up in an ordered manner. We took an air drop, he decided on the groups and who was to command them. He ordered a good supply of maps, rations and machine guns to be dropped. Some rum was also dropped. The officers gathered and drank a toast to the king, and to Number 3 Column. Calvert said, 'Well, here we go. We will all meet again in India.' We broke up into our groups, and off we set.

Lieutenant Dominic Neill
8 Column, 3rd/2nd Gurkha Rifles

Eventually we reached the village of Zimbugon. I sent Tun Tin and some of his riflemen in, dressed in civilian clothes; they all carried civilian clothes in their packs. I told him to ask the headman if the village was friendly, and if they would hire us boats. He came back and reported that the villagers were indeed friendly, there was Jap presence in Shwegu about twelve miles upriver from Zimbugon, and the headman promised to give us early warning should the Japs approach his village. As a counter to that, we were told that it would take a day or so for the headman to collect sufficient boats for us. We spent a very tense day in a reed-covered sandbank.

We waited and waited, and early on the night of 11 April 1943, four or five large boats appeared. It took us half an hour or so to get across. I noticed that the sandbanks were not in the same position as marked on our maps. But as our maps were made in 1910 it was understandable. We disembarked on the other side at about 2100 hours. Having paid and thanked the boatmen, we moved off to some high ground about five miles off, which we picked off the map as it was shown as being jungle covered. We based up and posted sentries, and slept for the rest of the night. I felt elated at crossing that first huge barrier.

Lieutenant Denis Gudgeon
3 Column, 3rd/2nd Gurkha Rifles

I was rearguard in Calvert's party. When we got back to the Irrawaddy we discovered that the Japs had moved all the boats to the western bank. Calvert decided that we would build 'sapper sampans'. Unfortunately our groundsheets were rotten and our boat would not float. As I had a party of twelve in which the only people who could swim was the Burma Rifleman and me, I decided to march along the Irrawaddy. After several days we got to a village and hid in some thick undergrowth nearby. The Burma Rifleman went into the village, found a boatman, and after a lot of hard bargaining I arranged to pay the boatman some of my precious silver rupees with which we had been issued. He got us safely across to the other side that night. I had no maps of the area, but had a prismatic compass and if I marched on a bearing of 330 degrees it would take us more or less to where we started. I got progressively weaker as we marched, and eventually I ordered my men to go on and leave me. I was then on my own, and knew I must be near the Chindwin, and two days later on a small path I waylaid a Burmese fisherman who was selling dried fish. He said he would take me in a boat across the river, and get me to the British lines. Actually he took me to a village and handed me over to the local Burmese militia. They took me to the nearest Jap garrison and this fisherman got a reward of fifty rupees.

Lieutenant Harold James
3 Column, 3rd/2nd Gurkha Rifles

My group consisted of my platoon and Captain Taffy Griffiths, Burma Rifles: cool, brave and older than me. Half of the groups decided to head for the Irrawaddy much further south than where we had crossed. Others decided to go the way we had come.

We were now going across the dry zone, there was no water, and we were very thirsty. We had to avoid a huge forest fire. As we were going through burnt-out black scrub, suddenly a little line of green appeared in front: it was a cool clear chaung. We had a good drink, and filled our water bottles. Taffy sent a couple of Karens forward to recce the river. We knew that the Japs had removed boats. As we approached the Irrawaddy, in broad daylight, the Karens came back to say they had a boat. It was a big sampan, the home of a Burmese family. They had come to our bank to fix something in the boat. It was sheer luck. There it was at our feet, and could take about twenty people. We sent a small party across in a small boat, which the bigger boat carried, to check that there was no enemy there. We then crossed in two parties, and who should turn up but Bobby Thompson, and he used our boat too. After Bobby, Calvert turned up and used the same boat. We had sheer luck in broad daylight, but we had come a long way further south from the other crossings, and crossed the danger zone quickly before the Japs could get into position.

Private Charles Aves
7 Column, 13th Battalion, King's Regiment (Liverpool)
We needed to get some food, as we had had no air drops. Some of the men were ill and worn out. A friend of mine, Freddy, said, 'I can't go on.' I knew his mother, whom we had visited when on leave. So I said, 'It's all right for you to give up, but what about your mother? She's waiting for you to come home. She's all on her own.'

We took his rifle and his pack. You become very close in these circumstances. Even if you would have nothing in common in civilian life, a bond forms between you. Freddy did get out of Burma. We had to go to a village to get food. The officers had maps and money, so could buy food, a ball of cooked rice wrapped in a banana leaf.

The next day the officers decided to rest, and set up camp in a nullah, a dried river bed. We were spread over sixty yards, with two sentries out. I was with Corporal Hickman, near the sentries. We brewed up. We were tired. Suddenly the two sentries ran past us, saying that they had heard firing. Corporal Hickman said, 'Don't run.' We stayed for a few seconds. We didn't know if they were Japs or Burma traitors. My friend Stan Allnut said, 'Let's go.' We left our packs, and ran. On our way we picked up two packs, I didn't know whose they were at the time.

We clambered up some rocks nearby. We emptied our rifles towards the area where the Japs had been, but there was no reply. The firing stopped. There were eleven of us: one officer, one sergeant, Corporal Hickman and eight privates. The rest had disappeared. I would have been lost if it hadn't been for Stan. The lieutenant, I don't remember his name, asked how many water bottles we had. There were two. The pack I picked up had in it all the maps, all the way to the Chindwin. It was Captain Oakes's, he had left it behind. Corporal Hickman's pack belonged to the other officer Lieutenant W, my platoon officer, and in it were three hundred rupees. Both packs were left behind by people who shouldn't have left them behind.

The lieutenant said two water bottles were not enough, that we must find some more, and that we would have to go back. So bravely we went back to the area of the attack. We could hear the Japs talking. The lieutenant changed his mind saying it was too dangerous, and we would march west as soon as possible. All of the eleven of us were pretty fit. We made off into a bamboo forest, and rested.

Major Walter 'Scottie' Scott
Officer Commanding 8 Column, 13th Battalion, King's Regiment (Liverpool)
I had my CO, Lieutenant Colonel Cook, with me, who was very sick. I headed for an area of the Irrawaddy we hadn't used before, twenty miles below Bhamo where the river races through a narrow defile. The villagers said that all the boats had been taken by the Japanese. But I noted that the Burmese boats poling up the Irrawaddy were moving very slowly up through the gorge. After a while one came quite close to our side of the river, and grounded in shallow water about fifteen yards offshore. So I, and several others, waded out, and captured it. By that night, I and my party had got across the Irrawaddy. We only had one mule, the wireless mule. I gave the boatmen five hundred silver rupees, more money than they would have made in a year.

We went off into thick jungle. We still had the wireless, but the mule soon died. I sent a signal to say where we would be in four days' time, and asked the RAF to drop me fourteen days' rations. The signal went on to say that a week later I would be at such and such map reference, and take another drop. I planned these so we would have these drops all the way out of Burma.

A few nights later I walked out into the clearing we had given the RAF as a DZ, it was about fifteen hundred yards long and about four hundred yards wide. I thought right away how we might set up a rescue. If they come to supply us they could fly out the sick and wounded: fourteen men and my CO, who certainly would not have made the Chindwin.

The RAF came across as arranged and dropped our rations, but our wireless was dead. Using the first lot of parachutes we laid out a signal: PLANE LAND HERE NOW. WOUNDED.

The next aircraft circled twice, tried to land, couldn't make it, but he dropped a message on a streamer. It said, 'Hold on here.'

Lieutenant Dominic Neill
8 Column, 3rd/2nd Gurkha Rifles

After the Irrawaddy, we had one more major river to cross, the Chindwin, and many smaller rivers in between. I reckoned that as the crow flies we had about two hundred miles to reach the Chindwin. The monsoon was due to break in late May or early June, and even the minor rivers between us and the Chindwin would be tremendous barriers if flooded.

It took two days, marching to cover the twenty-five miles or so to the Kaukkwe Chaung. Where we crossed, the Chaung was about twenty-five yards wide, with steep twelve-foot-high banks, and waist-deep water. On the west bank I sent Tun Tin to recce a village about two miles to our south. We followed them closely in case they got into trouble. A short while later Tun Tin sent scouts back to say that the village was clear and we would get a warm welcome. We moved into the village and begged the headman for some rations, which he gladly said he would supply. It was now early morning on 14 April.

We got a sock full of rice per man and a few chickens. I had had a very sore toe for some time. I sat on my pack and took my boot off for the first time for days, and saw a huge abscess on my big toe. I didn't know what to do. I put on my boot and hoped for the best. I was very worried; we had no drugs or medicines to deal with such a problem.

After collecting our rations, and as we were about to leave, I saw a villager get on a bicycle and leave the village on the track we were about to take. I paid no attention, and we moved off. We were now marching north along a narrow track. I had some Gurkhas ahead of me, and Tag, plus Tun Tin and some others to my rear.

We had not gone far when an ambush exploded to my left. I shouted, 'Take cover right,' and dived into cover myself. I wasn't actually frightened but certainly shocked. Never in my training had I been taught the appropriate contact drills. I did not know what to do. A Jap machine-gunner was firing across the track from me so close I could see the smoke from his muzzle, the bullets hit the trees above my head, cutting leaves and bark, which fell on my pack and down my shirt collar. Rifle fire came in as well. Altogether I am sure that the ambush was not all that long in length along the track. I don't know how long I lay there, perhaps a minute and a half. I heard the Jap gunner change the magazine, and decided that the next time he did so we would

Major Scott's signal to a Dakota 'Plane land here'.

move. My heavy pack kept me pressed to the ground with my head bent down, and I could not fire my rifle easily.

I heard him change magazines again, and roared above the noise of rifle fire, 'Everybody up, follow me,' calling to my men to follow me away from the ambush into the jungle. Some of my men ran, but there was no sign of Tag or Tun Tin. I saw one of my men hit.

My men on my flanks began to close on me. I saw one of Tag's men drop his pack and thought him a fool to do so. Then I saw Tag and some more of his men. I called out again to close on my position. I suggested we lay an ambush to catch any Japs coming for us, and hope that the majority of my men still dispersed could catch up. Tag, an experienced soldier, said no, if we waited here in ambush we could get cut off. We did not know where the missing men were, we had no means of communicating with them. Our aim was to get back to India without further delay. He was right.

We took stock. We had two British officers, eleven Gurkhas, six BORs of Tag's platoon, one Burma Rifleman, a total of twenty; all the others were missing. I felt very guilty at not doing better, I had failed completely. Our first contact with the Japs after leaving 8 Column had ended in disaster. The villager must have warned the Japs so we must put the maximum distance between ourselves and the village. We must leave the others and hope that some of them joined up with other escape parties. We must head north.

That night I told Tag about my frustration at not having a tommy gun in the ambush, and Tag told his Corporal White to swap his tommy gun for my rifle. White was delighted at getting a lighter weapon. I thought now if we get hit again, I will have a better weapon.

I found that my sore toe was not hurting. I took off my sock and it was full of blood and pus. My mind was in a turmoil with utter guilt and shame. I vowed that night if I survived I would teach myself and my soldiers proper contact drills and counter-ambush drills.

Lieutenant Harold James
3 Column, 3rd/2nd Gurkha Rifles
The next danger spot on the way to the Chindwin was the railway line, but we got across that all right, followed by crossing the escarpment, a high ridge of mountains. By this time we were very short of food. We resolved not to look for trouble and attack the Japanese. We had to go into a village to get

some rice before we crossed the escarpment, as there was no food there. Then along comes Bobby Thompson and his group. We decided to join up and be double strength, which made it safer to go into a village, which we did, and got some rice. After this we went off into foothills, camped, and had a good meal. Just as we were moving off we heard machine-gun fire. I thought of the wounded Gurkhas, as did others. I saw two Gurkha sections coming along, totally ignoring the battle behind us, and taking no notice of any orders we gave them. I don't know what the firing was about.

We went up onto the escarpment. We lost touch with half a platoon, although they did get back safely. It was a most unpleasant feeling. I realised that everyone, except Calvert, would do things that they would not normally do. Hunger, tension, thirst and fear built up. Getting back became the overriding urge. This operation was quite different from the normal battle.

It was a terrible march. But Bobby was one of the world's best map readers.

Private Charles Aves
7 Column, 13th Battalion, King's Regiment (Liverpool)
We came to the railway line in the evening. The lieutenant said we would hole up and see if we could spot any Japs. He wisely decided to cross at night, having waited one night and the next day before doing so. We got across and just as we arrived on other side we heard a shout, we froze, and whoever it was didn't spot us. It was pitch black without a moon. After that we moved off and marched west day after day. We had a man with us who read us a verse from the Bible every day. We all fitted in very well with each other.

When we got to villages, the phrases I had learned back in India came in very useful. I was the only one who had any knowledge of the language at all. I went in with the lieutenant, speak to the head man, and ask if any Japs were about. We could pay for our food. We went to about six or seven villages and always looked about to see if anyone disappeared. Only one village caused any problem. Immediately we got in we knew there was something wrong. The lieutenant said, 'Let's go,' and we left immediately. We were right, because when we got out of Burma, we learned that a party ahead of us had been attacked after entering this village.

Lieutenant Dominic Neill
8 Column, 3rd/2nd Gurkha Rifles

The next two or three days were hard, over ridges rising four thousand feet. Tag's men were becoming despondent. The BORs wanted to take the British rations from the DZ where supplies had been dropped before, and then head for China. Scottie had been told and had given us the grid references of where supplies had been dropped so we could collect rations from them. Tag and I reckoned this would be suicide, the Japs had seen the supplies being dropped, would ambush the DZs. Tag explained this and strongly advised against heading off on their own. In the end his sergeant said they could not exist on rations from villages, and must have British rations. Tag eventually agreed to their plea, they already had a compass, and he gave them maps. We wished them well. They were never seen nor heard of again.

I was quite glad when Tag's men left. Their morale had gone down very much since the ambush. I think Tag made the correct decision. He still regrets it.

Apart from our physical weakness through hunger, we were only fourteen men and this was a concern. We were the quarry and the Japs were the hunters. There was little thrill in being hunted, just terror. We had about sixteen miles to go as the crow flies to reach the Myitkyina–Rangoon railway. About five miles from the railway line we came across some paddy and a small hut. The man and woman inside told us how far we were from the line. They had no uncooked rice they could sell us but gave us some cooked rice folded in banana leaves, which we ate then and there. They also gave us some tiny lumps of unrefined sugar, or ghurr.

We had to get on to beat the Japs and coming rains. I had cut my trousers to shorts and my legs got scratched and developed jungle sores. My heavy pouches caused further sores on my hips. At midday when we stopped to brew tea, we took off our shirts and had a lice hunt, killing about a hundred on each occasion. The next landmark was the Mawhan–Mawlu Road which we crossed very quickly in extended line, and brushed away our tracks in the dust with branches of leaves. Having crossed the railway and into the Mawhan Forest, we hid near a village and sent in the Burma Rifleman to buy food, while we hid nearby. He returned with some rice in a sock and a chicken. We crossed the Meza river, and it was almost dry and easy to cross. From here was the escarpment, the Zibyu Taungdan.

Major Walter 'Scottie' Scott
Officer Commanding 8 Column, 13th Battalion, King's Regiment (Liverpool)
Two days later we got another supply drop, and one plane dropped another streamer telling me to lay out a landing strip. I laid out parachutes across the area to mark the strip. He landed at the second attempt, brought in another wireless set, and took out my CO and fourteen wounded. Two hours later they were in hospital in Imphal. I got a signal saying hold there, they might try to rescue more of us. But Dakotas were in short supply and in any case the Jap garrison at Indaw close by would be bound to react soon, so I decided that we had better get out. I set out to walk to India.

Soon after leaving the strip, we came to the Kaukkwe Chaung; it was about sixteen to thirty yards wide and was lined by small parties of Japanese. We were crossing on bamboo rafts and had got practically everybody across, except for about ten men, when the Japanese opened up on us. I blew the dispersal signal, and we dispersed. I lost about twelve men there. My best colour sergeant was hit in the leg; the bullet went right through. I tried to lift him up, and he said, 'Your duty is to get the rest of these men out. You won't make it with me. Leave me.'

We had to leave him, and he was never heard of again. We linked up at an RV between the Kaukkwe Chaung and the railway.

Lieutenant Dominic Neill
8 Column, 3rd/2nd Gurkha Rifles
The men's knowledge of what we could eat in the jungle was our salvation, one of the favourite being the tips of a fern, tasty if boiled with rice. We used only game trails, for fear of bumping a Jap patrol on the wider tracks. At night we would leave the trail and bed down for the night. I had long since stopped posting sentries; the men needed all the sleep they could get.

Major Walter 'Scottie' Scott
Officer Commanding 8 Column, 13th Battalion, King's Regiment (Liverpool)
We crossed the railway, didn't meet any enemy and had a trouble-free march to the Chindwin. I chose the densest area I could to move through. We got boats from a village, and crossed in one night about thirty miles north of where we had entered Burma.

Lieutenant Dominic Neill
8 Column, 3rd/2nd Gurkha Rifles

One day we met three or four buffaloes in a deep-sided chaung. I told Tag to take one of the Gurkha soldier's rifle, knowing him to be a good shot. He fired, killing one, the rest scattered. I got the men to drag the dead buffalo out of the chaung, we knew we had to butcher and cook the buffalo as quickly as possible before a villager came to look for his missing buffalo. We cut stakes of wood and skewered buffalo meat to cook and smoke. The men knew exactly what to do. It was butchered and cooked in a very short time. As the long strips were cooked, we ate them before they were properly done. The blood ran down our chins, until our shrunken stomachs were bursting. We could hardly believe our luck. We hung strips of meat on our packs. We would occasionally chew them on the march, and cook them at halts. Unfortunately some of us kept these strips too long, they became fly-blown and stank horribly. I continued to eat mine. How I did not get stomach problems I don't know, I must have had the constitution of an ox.

We now avoided villages because of Jap garrisons, which we knew were in them. It was now mid-May, about another month before we would reach the Chindwin. Marching became slower and slower, we could manage only forty minutes' marching, followed by twenty minutes' rest, in the hour.

We thought that to use our outward route across the escarpment would be fatal, as the Japs would ambush it, and we were proved right when they ambushed other escape parties. We eventually picked a route off the map following a chaung. It was very hard going, either full of water or damp sand. Tag caught fever and was near to collapse, but he kept going; a less resolute man would not have made it. Eventually it burnt itself out. We reduced our pace to marching for half an hour and resting for half an hour.

We were so desperate that we decided to risk visiting another village, a Kachin village, it was not on our map, just a few houses. We got enough rice for one sock full per man, and some ghurr, and some cheroots in lieu of our cigarettes, which had long run out. While paying the headman, Tag and I noticed the headman's pretty daughter standing there, and I was glad that I had trimmed my beard. But she had no eyes for me, just for the silver rupees. The stinking, sore-covered scarecrows were of no interest to her at all. When we had packed the food in our packs, we thanked them and went off.

We were fearful of encountering the Burma Traitor Army. They wouldn't take on a large party of Chindits, just report it to the Japs.

Private Charles Aves
7 Column, 13th Battalion, King's Regiment (Liverpool)

The rest of the journey to the Chindwin went without incident. Suddenly we came across a patrol of Seaforth Highlanders. They were looking out for Chindits. We were in tatters. This patrol had been attacked by Japs the previous day, and were looking for the Japs to deal with them. Our lieutenant volunteered us to help. To our great relief, the officer of the Seaforths declined, saying that they were here to help us to safety not to get us killed. They took us to boats and we crossed to the other side, north of where we met the Seaforths.

We were taken to Imphal. It felt wonderful. Except that I went down with malaria. To my great pleasure, we were visited by Wingate, who smiled and said, 'I'm glad to see you here.'

I told him my story about the packs we picked up. I was disgusted at the way they were abandoned. He said, 'We won't wash our dirty linen in public, will we?'

I have not talked about it since.

I was lucky to survive.

Lieutenant Dominic Neill
8 Column, 3rd/2nd Gurkha Rifles

We hit a track leading to the Chindwin. Could we take the risk? We had to, in order to get ahead of the monsoon. We were marching along; about forty yards away there was a left-hand bend in the track. Suddenly, a Gurkha said in a low voice that an elephant was coming. Sure enough there was one approaching down the track. A mahout was sitting on the elephant's neck and standing in the howdah was a man with a white helmet and tunic. Just as I was thinking he must be a district officer, he bent down, picked up a rifle, pointed it at me or Tag, just beside me, and started to shoot. The elephant was towing a fifteen-hundredweight truck loaded with some fifteen Japs. They leapt out, took up fire positions and opened up at us. We were within a few miles of the Chindwin, we could not take on the Japs. So within half a second I roared out follow me, and we dashed off into the forest. We were all in good order. I waited for the sound of a thwack and a bullet hitting my pack. But I wasn't hit. We ran and ran, despite the fact we were exhausted, we ran and kept together. I realised the Japs had ceased fire. We ran on and didn't seem to be following up. We eventually halted in a hollow. We were all there except my orderly. A chill swept through me. There was nothing we could do for him. I told Tag.

We walked on, goodness knows how far, based up, and had something to eat. Huddled up under my damp blanket that night, I regretted the serious error of judgement in using the track, and the lack of correct reaction on my part. I was ashamed.

Next morning we set off to the Chindwin, now only thirteen strong. It took us ten more days. My havildar went down with malaria, his skin was like yellow parchment and we thought he would die. We took his rifle and pack. We wouldn't leave him. He staggered along following us, using a stick. About this time I found that the sole of my left boot had a hole in it, and I marched on my sock. The right sole was tied on by parachute cord.

Major Michael Calvert
Officer Commanding 3 Column

The Gurkha columns commanded by Gurkha officers failed. Whereas mine and George Dunlop's columns succeeded. Dunlop's column got back after most of the others, and did not get the publicity the others did. He did not disperse and carried out some excellent operations on the way back. By the time he got back the press had lost interest.

I sometimes wondered if I should have carried out the dispersal. We were told that IV Corps has patrols across the Chindwin who would meet us. Unfortunately the Corps commander withdrew his troops back across the Chindwin before we arrived near the river. When we reached the Chindwin we relaxed. I went further south than my dispersed groups, and blew the railway in order to attract the Japanese on to me so as to make it easier for the other dispersal groups to get back to the Chindwin. When we got to the Chindwin, I got on to a boat with some Burma Riflemen and drifted down the river, standing up shouting that we had arrived. I wore shorts, the Japanese didn't wear shorts.

When we eventually arrived we all marched in to the Indian Army base, to show we weren't a defeated army.

Lieutenant Harold James
3 Column, 3rd/2nd Gurkha Rifles

Our party eventually reached the Chindwin where we were met by the Sikhs who looked after us very well, with a huge curry. We should have been told not to eat too much, but even our Doctor who was with us wasn't going to hold back. At Imphal we were put into hospital, and our lice-ridden clothes were burnt.

Lieutenant Dominic Neill
8 Column, 3rd/2nd Gurkha Rifles

Early one morning we heard the noises of a village, it was Myene. Tag and I went to the headman's house. He said there had been no recent enemy movement in the area. We said our goodbyes and left. We marched to the Chindwin, about five miles from Tonhe, where we had crossed on the outward journey. We found a game trail and met a villager. The Burma Rifleman spoke to him. He said he would take us to the tiny village nearby. We asked if we could hire boats. He said that all boats had been collected by the Japs and taken to Homalin, about twenty miles away. There was nothing on our side of the Chindwin. Our spirits fell. We moved to the Chindwin, and scanned the river of our dreams. It was about two hundred and fifty yards wide and fast flowing. Tag and I could have swum across without our weapons. But this was academic. We could not leave our men. We decided to build rafts as we had done to cross the Shweli. But I tried to think of something else. I stood in an open clearing looking across, and heard a call from the other side in Nepali, 'Who is it?'

I replied, 'We are the 3rd/2nd Gurkhas. Have you got a boat that side? We have none.'

He said he had one and would get it.

The men of course had heard my conversation with what I assumed to be a V Force Levie, I knew they recruited Gurkhas, and were delighted. The Gurkha brought a dugout across, it took four men only. I put in the havildar and three men. After a while, the boat came back after what seemed like hours. We sent four more men across. It came back; there were now five of us, including Tag and me. We sent off the three and Tag and I stayed until last. We hid behind the bank, and waited. I put my safety catch to automatic. We looked towards the jungle and wondered if the Japs would get us at the eleventh hour, or would we get away with it. There was the boat coming back. We clambered in, and we crossed. I pulled out my last cheroot and lit it, as happy as a sandboy.

We came to a V Force post. There was a young captain commanding the V Force post, I can't remember his name. I asked him what date it was, he said 6 June; we had long since lost any idea of what day it was. That is one date that I will always remember.

Major Michael Calvert
Officer Commanding 3 Column

When we got back General Scoones made me write down all the points I could remember on patrolling. It was eventually published as *Notes on Patrolling* by General Scoones.

Lieutenant Dominic Neill
8 Column, 3rd/2nd Gurkha Rifles

After leaving the V Force post, we reported to the 3rd/10th Gurkhas' camp. We had a shower and were given clean clothes to wear. We were given whisky and sodas, and slept like the dead that night.

Next morning we were told that a signal had arrived from the V Force post, which, after sending a recce across the river, reported that a Jap fighting patrol of platoon strength had been tracking us for about a week. It had arrived on the eastern bank of the Chindwin about half an hour after we had crossed. It was just luck that we escaped. Had we stopped to construct rafts we would have been caught. Had I not been standing in the clearing and the Gurkha levy not seen me, likewise.

We were taken by transport to a Field Supply Depot. As we were eating a meal we saw the rain coming down like stair rods, the monsoon: we had beaten it by two days. The rain delayed our return to Imphal, but while at the Field Supply Depot, two things stick out in my memory. I calculated from the maps that the distance we had marched from Dimapur to the Shweli and back must have been about a thousand miles, give or take a hundred miles. Second, finding and stealing a four-pound tin of plum jam, which Tag and I ate in about five minutes, without any biscuits.

We went off in trucks to Imphal to IV Corps HQ and hospital. When we got off our trucks, three staff officers appeared from out of a tent, smelling of roses. One of them said, 'They must be from Longcloth,' in the same tone of voice that he might have said, 'There is the sweeper.' They must have seen the expression of fury in my eyes, as they turned and left.

We went to hospital to be checked over, and were told to shave off our beards. Wingate appeared. He looked at me and said, 'I see you are out.' Fortunately I did not reply as I thought, 'No thanks to you sir.' That was the last time I saw him.

Lieutenant Denis Gudgeon
3 Column, 3rd/2nd Gurkha Rifles
I was rather rude to the first Jap I met. I was reading a Penguin book, and went on reading. He got very angry, and when he interrogated me, although he could speak perfect English, he spoke through an interpreter and kept the point of his sword pointed at my throat. I didn't disclose that I was in the Chindits, I told him I was in a foot patrol across the Chindwin from troops guarding the other side, and he seemed to believe this.

I was questioned again and this time he tried a different tactic, giving me sake and sweets, but I wasn't taken in by that. I was put on a train, and during the journey we were strafed by a Beaufighter. I did think of trying to escape, but was rather weak and didn't. At the Ava Bridge I had to detrain because it had been blown. I ended up at Rangoon station where I was interrogated again, taken to Rangoon Jail, and spent the next two years as a POW.

Major Walter 'Scottie' Scott
Officer Commanding 8 Column, 13th Battalion, King's Regiment (Liverpool)
I didn't lose weight on the expedition. What did we achieve? We realised that the Japanese were not the supermen that we had been brought up to believe. They were very brave soldiers, and even if they were outnumbered, they would attack.

Lieutenant Dominic Neill
8 Column, 3rd/2nd Gurkha Rifles
The newspapers back in India had banner headlines about Wingate's expedition. We couldn't believe our eyes. We had achieved absolutely nothing; we had been kicked out by the Japs again. The publicity was the work of the authorities in GHQ Delhi grasping at any straws after the defeat

in 1942, closely followed by the disastrous Arakan Campaign of 1942/43. Only Number 3 Column, under Mike Calvert, had achieved anything of any significance.

Ours was the very last party to escape from Burma. I had been posted missing, but fortunately no one had sent a telegram to my mother. I spent all the remaining silver rupees drinking the king's health on leave in Kashmir. The 3rd/2nd Gurkhas took heavy casualties, we lost the CO and adjutant, plus two officers, and some two hundred and ninety GORs killed in action, or died of starvation, or as prisoners.

In my opinion Wingate's concept was sound and daring, but the training was inferior. Arrangements for casevac were inadequate, as were communications. Splitting up groups was a bad decision. Columns could have called for air resupply, and posed such a potent fighting force that in the time available the Japs would not have been able to concentrate against them. In small groups we were fair game for platoon-size hunting parties. Wingate's failure to train his troops in contact drills caused frequent and unnecessary casualties. He also went too far. By crossing the Irrawaddy he overstretched himself dangerously. His achievements beyond that river were negligible, and a great number of casualties were caused by having too long a retreat. We did not have enough maps or compasses. Wingate ruled by fear. Officers feared to query his orders.

The Struggle for the Arakan
Round Two

I watched this attack by the Gurkhas, shouting 'Ayo Gurkhali', their
battle cry. They had kukris in their hands, rifles slung across their
shoulders and advanced throwing grenades.
They threw the Japanese out. It was a beautiful
sight and etched in my memory.

The monsoon of 1943 shut down all but minor operations on all fronts in Burma. With the onset of the dry season in November 1943, the British and the Japanese began to stir.

The British aimed at driving the Japanese out of Burma. To this end, Admiral Lord Louis Mountbatten, now Supreme Allied Commander South East Asia (SEAC), ordered a four-pronged offensive.

As related in the next chapter, in northern Burma a Chinese force led by the American General Stilwell would head south from Ledo, take Myitkyina, and thereby connect Ledo with the Burma Road. This would enable the Americans to supply China by road for the first time since the Japanese invasion of Burma, instead of the hair-raising air route over the 'Hump', the nickname for the eastern end of the Himalayas that lay between the air bases in Assam and China.

On the Chindwin front, IV Corps was to undertake a limited push. In support of these two operations Wingate was to lead a hugely increased force of Chindits on a second expedition aimed at disrupting the Japanese lines of communications to their troops facing Stilwell and IV Corps. Meanwhile, XV Corps was ordered to secure the Maungdaw–Buthidaung Road as a precursor to further operations to eject the Japanese from the Arakan.

The battle-experienced 70th British and 5th Indian divisions were now being shipped in from the Middle East. They were joined by the recently raised 7th Indian Division, new to battle, but commanded by the charismatic Major General F. W. Messervy, fresh from fighting in the Western Desert.

Lieutenant General A. F. P. Christison's XV Corps began the Arakan offensive by pushing down the Mayu Range with the 7th Division to the east and the 5th Division to the west. As the two divisions probed south they hit the Maungdaw–Buthidaung Road, the only lateral road fit for wheeled traffic until the Taungup–Prome Road two hundred miles further south. Along the sixteen miles of road, the Japanese had a continuous sequence of defences in steep, jungle-covered hills. They had also built three heavily fortified positions: in the two tunnels carrying the road under the Mayu hills; at Letwedet east of the tunnels; and at Razabil to the west. These were constructed in the hills with thirty-foot-deep dugouts, supported by machine-gun nests, all linked with tunnels.

The 5th Division was ordered to take Razabil, while the 7th took Buthidaung followed by hooking in to take Letwedet from the south. Thirty miles to the east, the third division in XV Corps, the 81st West African, was told to advance down the Kaladan valley, capture Kyauktaw, and cut the Kanzauk–Hitzwe Road. In so doing the division would cut the main Japanese supply route between the Kaladan and Mayu Rivers.

To support operations west of the Mayu hills, Christison ordered another road, capable of taking tanks, guns and supply trucks, to be constructed about five miles to the north of the Maungdaw–Buthidaung Road. The road, driven over the Ngakyedauk Pass, nicknamed the 'Okeydoke', was fully serviceable by the end of January 1944.

The enemy, as is their inconvenient custom, had their own ideas. In this case the Japanese, whose strategy was to remain on the defensive in Burma, decided that the best way to spoil any British offensives would be to mount limited offensives themselves. Lieutenant General Renya Mutaguchi, commanding the Japanese Fifteenth Army, planned to take Imphal and Kohima in his area of responsibility. Before this, the Japanese Twenty-Eighth Army under Lieutenant General Shozo Sakurai was to attack in the Arakan. The intention: to keep Lieutenant General 'Bill' Slim, commanding the British Fourteenth Army, looking towards the Arakan, while the main attack went in at Imphal. But, if the Arakan offensive went

Lieutenant General Sir William Slim, Commander Fourteenth Army.

well, the Japanese might exploit further and even invade India.

For the Arakan offensive, timed for 4 February 1944, and codenamed *Ha-Go,* Sakurai had the elements of three Japanese divisions, the 54th, 55th, and 2nd, and an Indian National Army (INA) force. The attack would be in a pincer movement so favoured by the Japanese. The northern pincer, a force commanded by Major General Tokutaro Sakurai (not to be confused with the commander of Twenty-Eighth Army), would seize Taung Bazaar on the Kalapanzin River (as the upper reaches of the Mayu were called), block the Ngakyedauk Pass, and hook down to attack the 7th Division. Concurrently, the 1/213 Regiment would attack the Arakan Road to cut Christison's lifeline back to India. Meanwhile the southern pincer, consisting of most of 143rd Regiment was to hit 7th Division from the south.

Although there were signs of an impending Japanese attack, Christison had no idea how big it might be, and his troops continued with their own attacks. By now the troops were starting to benefit from their training, although there was still much to learn.

Captain Alexander Wilson
Argyll & Sutherland Highlanders, attached British 2nd Division
I had fought the Japanese in Malaya. Just before the surrender of Singapore I, and my commanding officer, were ordered out, so we could pass on our experiences to the army in India. I joined the British 2nd Division and took over all jungle training.

Most British people, brought up in towns, are never in the dark. So few of our soldiers had ever been alone at night. We have lost much of our sense of hearing and smell. These are basic animal-like characteristics. The Japs smelt different to us, and you had to learn how you could smell them in a defensive position, or if they had passed down a track.

At night you are on your own. You are susceptible to noise made by the enemy, and shooting at noises and shadows, which you mustn't do. The antidote is endless training: practising movement by night, the use of pole charges to attack bunkers, and bringing down supporting fire from mortars and guns very close to us. There was a very great deal to learn.

There were problems with wirelesses in jungle and hills caused by blank areas for communicating, especially at night. You had to find the right spot for good communications, by moving around. The 6th Brigade had been detached from 2 Div in Arakan, and we learned a great deal from their experience.

We learnt about their siting of defensives and use of local materials (logs, parts of buildings etc) to build bunkers, which were shellproof, even against anti-tank guns, and marvellously well concealed. You seldom saw a Japanese move by day. They took pains to conceal their tracks because by 1944 we had superiority in the air and in artillery. They realised this and they trained to operate at night. Their positions were well sited to support each other. They tunnelled and connected firing positions with covered ways. They could call down their own gun and mortar fire on their own positions. They cleared fields of fire, but not in such a way that it gave away the location of the bunker. What you could do was try to draw their fire at night; by shooting at them, moving about etc. They did it to us. Bill Slim's adage was 'the answer to noise is silence'. It was almost a crime to shoot without having a corpse to show for it the next morning. We used the PIAT for bunker-busting, and sometimes wheeled up a 6-pounder anti-tank gun, which was very risky.

Captain Kristen Tewari
Divisional Signals 25th Indian Division, attached 51 Brigade
I didn't belong to what the British called a martial class. I joined the army because a friend of my father's, Colonel Kilroy the recruiting officer at Jullundur Cantonment, said I should because war was imminent. Some members of my family asked why join the British Army and fight for Britain, Indian independence was more important. No doubt there was conflict in my mind too. But better sense prevailed. I learned a lot during the war. I joined in a spirit of adventure. I saw Indian soldiers at drill at Jullundur and wanted to be like them. I joined the Officer Training School at Bangalore in 1942. We had British instructors for drill and PT. I admired them.

As far as the Indian National Army, the INA, was concerned, we called them JIFs. Although we knew that people had joined them, we would not break our oath. Personally I had no sympathy for those who joined the INA.

After joining the 25th Division I went on jungle training. It was very useful, I came from the plains of Punjab and had never been into a jungle. We had to build our own shelters, we learned to live in the jungle and be comfortable in it. We saw wild elephants, tiger, and snakes galore, which we learned to cope with. It was all very useful, especially as there were lots of snakes in Burma. We learned to respect and make use of the forest. We lost one or two people on that training to snake bites.

EASTERN ARAKAN

Pilot Officer Roger Cobley
20 Squadron, RAF

I flew the Hurricane Mk II C which was fitted with two 40-mm cannons for anti-tank work. They made the aircraft a bit unwieldy and you couldn't do aerobatics safely. We carried high explosive or armour-piercing shells. Each gun was loaded with only sixteen rounds, which you had to fire singly, not in bursts like 20-mm cannons or machine guns. You had to line up very accurately on the target, and attack one at a time.

We were supposed to have Spitfires as top cover, but didn't get it to start with. But operating very low as we did, with jungle trees below, it was difficult for Jap aircraft to see us, and in any case there weren't many about. I commanded a section, a pair of aircraft.

In the Arakan in late 1943, we started by operating from a jungle strip called 'Brighton', near the coast just behind our front line, after which we moved even nearer the front and flew from a strip on the beach, called 'Hove'. This was an agreeable place, living in bamboo huts. We swam, but had to look out for stingrays. We had a ration of drink dropped to us by parachute: four bottles of beer per month for the airmen, and one bottle of gin or whisky for the officers. We had a good mix of over half Commonwealth chaps.

Our targets were bunkers, river boats, and occasionally trucks. We lost quite a few people, shot down by flak.

Lieutenant Michael Marshall
Officer Commanding B Company, 4th/5th Royal Gurkha Rifles

The battalion's task was active patrolling. Each company took turns to send out fighting or standing patrols for three or four days at a time. As I was totally inexperienced, I went out and soon learnt what I ought to be doing. This was not easy as I had a limited knowledge of Urdu and my knowledge of Gurkhali was not much better. On one patrol I had ten men, plus Subedar Indrabir Thapa, a very experienced Gurkha officer; he always spoke to me in Gurkhali and, if I didn't understand, in Urdu. It was only when I got back to the battalion and heard him talking on the inter-company telephone system to the CO in perfectly good English that I realised that he had no intention of making my life easy, and knew I would only learn Gurkhali by speaking nothing else.

In late October 1943, I went out at night with a standing patrol, with a jemadar from my own company and about six men. Two things occurred. At about two o'clock in morning we were shot at while crossing open paddy. We all got down into the water, and stayed for about half an hour. It was probably a small Jap patrol who had moved on after hearing us. Every one of us had forty to fifty leeches hanging off us, and we spent a good half-hour removing them. Some leeches can go through lace holes in boots. The most fearsome were elephant leeches, some six to nine inches long, in flooded chaungs and rivers. We took them off with a lighted cigarette.

Having reached the patrol position, on the second morning, the jemadar pointed out to me that he had seen through his binos a small sampan containing a Jap officer, a soldier and two villagers, coming down the Ngakyedauk Chaung, about twelve hundred yards away. They were on their way from Jap positions on the ridge in front and coming to Awlinbyn Village. My instructions on leaving the battalion location were to take evading action only, unless absolutely necessary; my main task was observation. As the sampan got closer to us, I felt that we ought to do something about it. When it was seven hundred yards away, the jemadar agreed he would open fire with the LMG. The occupants of the sampan disappeared. Later we were told that a senior Jap officer and his orderly had been killed. Although not due to leave the patrol position for a further four or five hours, I decided it prudent to do so, and we left for the company base at Taung Bazaar. This took us about twelve to fifteen hours. After we left we heard mortar fire approximately on the position we had left, and a great deal of noise from the Jap positions.

When I reported to the CO his views were mixed. However, the following night a patrol from another company occupied approximately the same position I had been in; not very clever of them. During the night the Japs sent in a patrol, killing one and wounding another of our patrol. Despite my having disobeyed instructions, I think that our action established the positions of the Japs and this proved valuable for what happened thereafter.

Major Harry Smith
Officer Commanding HQ Company, 4th Battalion, Queen's Own Royal West Kent Regiment
On being moved to India from fighting in the Western Desert, we carried out jungle training near Ranchi, and at the end of December we embarked in a troop ship, the *Ethiopia*, which deposited us at Chittagong. From Chittagong we entrained and went fifty miles south to Dohazari, and then marched. In order to avoid the heat, and being spotted by enemy aircraft, we marched at night; two hundred miles at twenty miles a day for ten days. It was nice swinging along on an earthen track in the warm darkness, through clouds of fireflies. After being ferried across a chaung, we reached the forward area.

The countryside in the Arakan along the coast consisted of a lot of jungle-clad hills interspersed with paddy fields. Our brigade took over the sector from the coast inland to a range of much bigger hills, called the Mayu Range.

Private Leslie Crouch
Pioneer Platoon, 4th Battalion, Queen's Own Royal West Kent Regiment
In November 1943 we took up positions facing the Japs. We were advancing and pushing them back at Maungdaw; it was really just a village of mud huts and straw roofs. We dug in and the Japanese attacked, we came off best. They were attacking frontally. We were in trenches. We hadn't heard a lot about them, except that they were fanatical.

Captain John Anderson
HQ, 33rd Brigade, 7th Indian Division
Brigades in the Indian Army were in the main formed of three different races or castes, usually one British battalion, one Gurkha, and one Indian. It worked really well. There was a bit of rivalry and leg-pulling; but a lot of friendships.

I moved by sea to Chittagong with the brigade transport. Our division was moving to the eastern side of the Mayu range. There were no roads in this area, only a track, like a footpath. The division crossed from Bawli Bazaar by the Goppe Pass and on southwards. There was no question of getting transport by that route, so we were left behind. Eventually the call came, the division had found a better track which the engineers worked on; the

Private Leslie Crouch.

Ngakyedauk pass. It ran parallel with the Goppe pass but several miles further south. At first the engineers made a track driveable by jeeps, and I took the brigade transport and crossed the range at night, through thick jungle with steep banks on one side of the track. After a while you came out into a clearing at Sinzweya where the rear echelons of the division were located in an administrative box.

Ultimately the track was made bigger and shortly before the balloon went up, the 25th Dragoons with Lee-Grant tanks got across. Having got to Sinzweya, both sides started prodding each other to find out where weak spots were, by patrolling, artillery fire and so on.

Lieutenant Michael Marshall
Officer Commanding B Company, 4th/5th Royal Gurkha Rifles
In January 1944 the whole brigade began a general advance through the foothills of the Arakan Yomas, the intention being to cut the Japanese supply lines to the south of the Mayu river and capture Buthidaung. During all this period I was acting company commander of B Company and was joined by 2 Lieutenant Tom Briscoe who had been at school at Christ's Hospital, was captain of rugger and head boy. We became immediate friends. Two months later he was killed.

As we advanced through the foothills, among dense trees, not jungle, we had a series of brisk actions against the Japs. One I well remember was rather macabre: after an afternoon battle, where D Company and my own B Company were involved, we had killed about twenty Japs. It was very close fighting. It was the first time I had heard Gurkhas actually shouting 'Ayo Gurkhali', a fearsome noise, and it undoubtedly scared the Japs. It was the first time I had seen them using their kukris at close quarters. They mostly went for the throat, often putting down their rifles to do so. The Japs ran. We suffered considerable casualties. The Japs were not properly dug in otherwise they would not have run. They only had small one-man foxholes.

The next morning I was told to take two platoons back to this position to bury the dead. I instructed the jemadar to bury the bodies, and went off. Instead of digging graves, the Gurkhas used the foxholes dug by Japs. Because the Jap dead had rigor mortis, and would not fit, the Gurkhas cut up the bodies and stuffed them into the holes. I stopped this, but they thought I was being pernickety. The Gurkha has all the nicest characteristics of the British:

he likes games, drinking, women, gambling. However, he has little feelings for the dead, either the enemy or his comrades. Once gone, they'd gone. They had no feelings of sadness nor remorse. At the time of killing the enemy they'd get elated, and it is an interesting fact that Gurkhas going into action at close quarters get bloodshot eyes and look fearsome. They still take orders from officers. But in close-quarter fighting no one is giving orders to anyone.

The Jap was a very courageous opponent and suffered enormously. But the Gurkhas were better. I was glad I was with them, not against them. My battalion took no prisoners until well into 1945; none of our men were taken prisoner. At this time in the war the Japs were thought to be invincible by some people, including many British troops. This was not the attitude of my Gurkhas. The Gurkhas didn't like the smell of Japs, it was a very strong smell, something to do with the bad fish and bad eggs they ate.

Private Ivan Daunt
Pioneer Platoon, 4th Battalion, Queen's Own Royal West Kent Regiment

Never known a nation that wanted to die, except the Japs. We retreated, they don't. You picked up skinny Jap bodies, with their eyes popping out of their head. You would advance on a Jap lying there with a grenade waiting to blow himself up. What can you do? Shoot him?

I saw a British plane came in to pick up a wounded Jap. It landed on the road, we put him on the plane, and the pilot said, 'I'm not for this. I don't know what he is going to do.' We told him we had checked the Jap over. He was badly wounded. He was needed for interrogation.

You knew they were there at night, they gave the game away, you could hear them moving. We let them come close and opened up on them, and found them in the morning. If you were armed only with a rifle, it was not a lot of good at night-time, so you relied on grenades. But you were limited to the number you had. We used Brens as well.

The Japs dug one-man round pits. When we captured them, we would expand each to a two-man slit. Once Freddie Clinch and 'Tosh' Hill shared a slit next to mine. Both had bayonets fixed on their rifles. The time came for 'Tosh' to go to sleep; one should stay awake, while the other sleeps. But both fell asleep. A Jap crept up to them, and went to throw something into the trench, a grenade maybe. But in leaning down, he rammed his face down on

Freddie's bayonet, and let out a squeal. They jumped up and shouted, 'Somebody here.' The Jap was in a state; they took him prisoner.

Lieutenant Michael Marshall
Officer Commanding B Company, 4th/5th Royal Gurkha Rifles

On 4 February 1944 we were instructed to attack a Jap position together with C Company. The two companies set off at 0630 in the typical early morning mist that hangs over the paddy in the Arakan. We climbed up through jungle to within some four or five hundred yards of what we thought was a Jap position. C Company Commander told me to attack with my company at about 0900 hours. The attack went in. There was considerable Jap fire coming back. We used our 2-inch mortars and grenade dischargers. Eventually the position was taken by us.

We suffered one killed and thirteen wounded, one being me. I was wounded together with my orderly by a Jap grenade falling behind me, and hit in the backside, back, and left arm. We all carried morphine syringes in our kit, and my orderly, who was badly wounded in the legs, managed to extract the syringes and we both injected. Luckily my haversack contained my binoculars, compass and two grenades, which were badly dented, but took most of the blast. Without them I would probably have been killed.

I was taken back to C Company, unaware of what was happening. The Jap position was mopped up by my company. I was then taken by stretcher-bearers to battalion HQ. While I was there, my CO was informed by brigade HQ that the whole advance had been stopped, and an immediate withdrawal ordered. So the whole action and the previous month's work had to be aborted. This was because the Japs, during the night of 4 February, had sent in a task force of nine thousand men to cut the supply lines to 7 Div. This force, complete with artillery but relying on captured supplies, came through the mist in the paddy in the early hours of the morning.

Life did not become pleasant for me. I was carried on a stretcher for two days to the 114 Brigade Box at Oktaung near Kwazon. I was put in a temporary hospital with many other wounded, and after two or three days found I had gas gangrene in my left arm. Others were also suffering from gangrene. As there were no anaesthetics, limbs were being amputated without. Two large British orderlies knocked out the patient with a punch to the jaw after he had been given a large tot of whisky. This happened to my

Lieutenant Michael Marshall, taken after the war.

orderly, both his legs were amputated. He didn't survive. At this stage there was only one surgeon who had hung on to his kit. He told me I would have to have my arm off. One of my fellow officers came to see me, and said he had some of the latest sulphonamide tablets, which no one else had. He gave them to me, and I did not have to go through the unpleasant experience of amputation. On 17 February a landing strip was built at Kwazon to which the whole brigade had moved. I was lucky enough to be first to be evacuated by L-5 light aircraft.

Captain John Anderson
HQ 33rd Brigade, 7th Indian Division
Early in February 1944 Japs attacked us. The Japs were trying to open up a route northwards to Chittagong and to Calcutta.

Gunner Bert Wilkins
284 Anti-Tank Battery, 24th Light Anti-Aircraft/Anti-Tank Regiment, Royal Artillery
We acted as infantry, we were sent up the road to form a roadblock and a staff officer came up, all excited: 'No one goes back from here. You stand here.'

We had to turn all the stragglers back and put them up on the hills, but as fast as we put them up on the hill, they came down and ran off again. There were a lot of Indian non-combatants, and in the end we took their automatic weapons off them and used them ourselves. I had a tommy gun, and then a Bren. In the end we dug about three different positions, I don't think anyone knew what was happening.

In one position they told us to collect hot stew, which had been brought up to a nullah behind the position. It was raining, so by the time you go back to your trench, your mess tin was overflowing with water and stew.

Captain Peter Gadsdon
Officer Commanding A Company, 4th/14th Punjab Regiment
I had standing patrols out in the paddy fields. They heard troops coming and said, 'Halt who goes there?' Some Indian replied, 'Tikka bai, it's all right, don't bother, no problem.' and they walked straight past. The sentries came and reported this to us. There was very thick mist and we could see absolutely nothing. This column appeared to have gone through our position. We took it

Peter Gadsdon, taken after the war.

to be some of our own ration parties. In fact it was the Japs with INA pushing the sentries on one side.

Our carrier platoon commander, Jemadar Pir Gul, a Pathan, sent a carrier out into the fog to investigate, and came back with a dead Japanese on the carrier.

I am sometimes asked about the attitude of our soldiers to the INA. They would kill them, and regarded them as traitors. The INA surrendered very quickly in battle. To the Indian Army they were traitors. To the Congress they were heroes. Now in India they are heroes, and people think they were responsible for getting the British out.

Captain John Anderson
HQ 33rd Brigade, 7th Indian Division
The Japs succeeded in cutting us off completely. We were entirely surrounded, they got to the Ngakyedauk Pass, and held that. But there were two things that saved our bacon. One was air supply, the RAF were even dropping to individual companies. The other was the 25th Dragoons and their tanks. Without doubt the Japs were fine soldiers. They had gone through Malaya like a dose of salts, and as soon as they came up against opposition they split and outflanked it, which is demoralising.

I was at brigade HQ some miles south of the divisional HQ, and suddenly there was a complete collapse of communications, brigades were trying to get in touch with division and couldn't. It had been overrun and all radio sets captured. The brigade commander, Loftus Tottenham, told me to borrow a Bren gun carrier from 4/1 Gurkha Rifles and try to find out what had happened. I set off with two Gurkhas, a driver and a Bren gunner. Halfway up the track we were shot up by Jap machine guns from a small hill some way off, and the driver was shot through the mouth, and I got some grazing hits in my arm from bullet fragments or bits chipped off the carrier. I took over the driving and pushed on, having taken note of where the Japs were. My chief concern was for the driver, the Bren gunner was not touched.

Gunner Bert Wilkins
284 Anti-Tank Battery, 24th Light Anti-Aircraft/Anti-Tank Regiment,
Royal Artillery
Div HQ had been overrun and our regimental HQ had been overrun.

Eventually we dug in on this hill, to begin with just thirty of us. Then two companies of Gurkhas moved in. We were there for about three days. I was young and foolish and volunteered to be a runner. This officer, a major from our unit, told me to run from trench to trench, and told everyone to watch for the flashes of Jap snipers shooting at me, and to open up on them. I thought it was quite exciting.

We were attacked by Zeros. I didn't really know what was happening. The ordinary soldier doesn't. We were shelled heavily, and the Japs dragged up 75-mm guns and fired them point-blank. We were knocked off this hill, and we had to go back in again. As we were going forward, I got hit. I rolled down the hill and a couple of blokes dragged me behind a tree. This officer crawled up to me, and said, 'I'll take your Bren gun and give you my revolver and a grenade. You'll know what to do with it if they come out for you.' The Japs used to come out and finish off the wounded if they could. So you didn't shout or make a noise. If they heard someone crying out in pain they would come out and finish you off. I was wounded by a bullet just behind the hip bone.

Lieutenant Colonel Gerald Cree
Commanding Officer, 2nd Battalion, West Yorkshire Regiment
Brigadier Evans told me to bring my whole battalion, less one company, into the 7th Division Admin Box. One company had to remain behind with the 3rd/14th Punjab Regiment still up in the hills next to our own division, the 5th. He said I must keep two companies in mobile reserve for counter-attacking, and only one company for static defence. I got in touch right away with Lieutenant Colonel Cole, the commanding officer of the 7th Division Light Ack-Ack Regiment, who had been in charge of the defence of the Admin Box up to that time, and discovered what he had done. As a result I put C Company into a static defence role, occupying a hill just above the eastern entrance to the Ngakyedauk Pass.

Colonel Cole had mustered every man he could find to defend the place, all the Indian followers, contractor wallahs, admin people and so on. They were holding their positions and acting like soldiers. We found by lending out our troops, putting one British soldier in a platoon of bakers and butchers etc, it provided moral support. My battalion headquarters was in adjoining trenches to brigade and divisional HQs.

Captain John Anderson
HQ 33rd Brigade, 7th Indian Division

Approaching Sinzweya, where the box was, the steering went, and I couldn't turn right. Then much to my delight I saw a 25th Dragoons tank, and asked him if he could give me a tow. So he passed me a bloody great chain, big enough to hold the *Queen Mary*. I hooked it on to my carrier, and he pulled me along the steep roads. We came to a right-hand bend, I couldn't turn right, and the carrier, with three of us in it, slipped off the road down a khud on the end of the chain. Suddenly to my surprise I found myself being towed up the slope. The tank commander had no idea what was going on behind him, and had just kept on going. We were pulled up on to the track, and eventually got to what became divisional HQ, because Messervy, the GOC, had escaped with several of his staff. This was when the defensive box was formed with scores of troops from different units, Gurkhas, Indians, British, engineers, signals, administrative folk.

Gunner Bert Wilkins
284 Anti-Tank Battery, 24th Light Anti-Aircraft/Anti-Tank Regiment, Royal Artillery

My leg was dead. I tunnelled into a bush and lay up all night. Next morning, to my surprise someone grabbed my ankles and yanked me out. It was a Gurkha officer and a Gurkha. They piggybacked me down the hill, to where all the wounded and the dead were being assembled in this nullah. The road was cut so they had to take us into the box on the backs of tanks and Bren carriers. I was in a Bren carrier beside a dead man. We got to a bend in the road and the officer in command of the column said, 'The road is cut on this corner. All those who can walk beside the tanks, walk. The rest of you, duck your heads down and hope for the best.'

So all the tanks opened up on the hill overlooking the road with machine guns to keep the Japs' heads down. The tanks and carriers cut across off the road; we got through.

Captain John Anderson
HQ 33rd Brigade, 7th Indian Division

I took my driver to the Main Dressing Station (MDS). It was just getting dark, and I asked the chaps there, two or three of whom I knew, one a major, and

A Lee-Grant tank of the 25th Dragoons blasting a way through the Ngakydauk ('Okedoke') Pass.

asked him to attend to him. I had my arm dressed and was then told by a doctor to hand in my pistol. I didn't have an army issue revolver, I had a German 9-mm Parabellum, which fired Sten gun ammunition. I was given it by my father, who had taken it from a German artillery officer in the First World War. I said that no way was I going to hand it in. So the doctor said, 'You can't stay.'

I said, 'Fair enough.' I had my arm in a sling and walked out with my pistol. For a time I stood chatting to a Gurkha officer I knew. After I left him, I found a job in one of the defensive positions being constructed at the time.

Gunner Bert Wilkins
284 Anti-Tank Battery, 24th Light Anti-Aircraft/Anti-Tank Regiment, Royal Artillery
We had casualty labels on, and when we got to the box an MP stopped us and checked that we were casualties, not stragglers. He said, 'Dead bodies to the right, casualties to the left.' They had graves dug in rows and the dead were put down there. The seriously wounded were seen to first, naturally. An orderly said to me, 'You've got a field dressing on, we'll see to you later.'

He took me over to a ward for walking wounded: a tarpaulin on bamboo poles. We were just across the track from the ward with the seriously wounded. That night the Japanese broke in. We heard all the screaming from the ward across the track and bullets came through our tarpaulin. We all jumped up. Four of us grabbed a chap on a stretcher, he had his leg in plaster. We ran out into the river that ran at the back of the tarpaulin, and stood there, but there was still stuff flying about, whizzing into the water. So we crossed the river and hid in the bush, about two hundred yards away. We could see the Japanese bayoneting and killing, and running about. Then it all died down. Out of six doctors there was only one left alive and most of the sixty wounded were killed. They smashed the operating theatre.

Private Henry Foster
Carrier Platoon, 2nd Battalion, West Yorkshire Regiment
We were sent in the middle of the night, two or three o'clock in the morning, with a carrier to try to get to the hospital, which was at the top of a very steep rise from where the stream ran in a valley, to see what was happening. There was gunfire and screaming. We only got halfway up, got grenaded and turned

130

back. We had never been up there before, and the track was bordered by trees and jungle.

Lieutenant Colonel Gerald Cree
Commanding Officer, 2nd Battalion, West Yorkshire Regiment
My A Company, supported by B Squadron 25th Dragoons, cleared the Japanese out of the MDS. They found that the enemy had camouflaged their machine-gun posts with stretchers in the wards and theatres. The bodies of thirty-one patients and four doctors were found, as well as seventy Japanese.

That night the Japanese pulled out after our counter-attack and started trickling down a chaung that ran up into the main dressing station. Both sides of the chaung were held by our Brigade B Echelon personnel: muleteers, orderly room staff, sanitary men, quartermasters' stores, chaps like that, nearly all old soldiers, including the Regimental Sergeant Major. They twigged what was happening and let the Japs have it. They killed an enormous number of them in the chaung, which became known as Blood Nullah. These were the chaps who had raided the dressing station, so we felt we'd avenged that one. They continued to come down this chaung, although it was a stupid thing to do. Perhaps they'd been ordered to some rendezvous.

Captain John Anderson
HQ 33rd Brigade, 7th Indian Division
Next morning there was a hell of a muddle. People were trying to get themselves into useful jobs. I can remember seeing a 5.5-inch gun firing over open sights at the Japs on the surrounding hillsides. It was all a bit hectic for a few days.

Gunner Bert Wilkins
284 Anti-Tank Battery, 24th Light Anti-Aircraft/Anti-Tank Regiment
Royal Artillery
After this I was properly dressed, a Scottish doctor looked at my leg, and said, 'No exit wound, eh laddie. Never mind, you'll cough it up one of these days.' He filled up my wound with powder using an ordinary spoon; all the equipment had been destroyed. I was there for eight days. I was glad to get out of the dressing station, because I was unarmed, and I didn't like it.

Walking wounded used to parade every day and company commanders from the various units would come along and say, 'Can I have this man?'

Gunner Bert Wilkins, in Belgium at the end of the war.

The medical officer would say, 'He's got a big hole in his back. He can't carry a pack.'

The officer would ask, 'Can he fire a rifle, that's all I'm interested in?'

Being a wireless operator, and our regimental HQ having been destroyed, I went to the Gurkhas, and they carried on dressing my wound. I could limp around.

Private Henry Foster
Carrier Platoon, 2nd Battalion, West Yorkshire Regiment
There was a clear patch of paddy which made a good dropping zone. The first time they tried they were driven off by Japanese fighter planes, but after that they had a big escort, and came in daily.

Sergeant Douglas Williams
Wireless Operator/Air Gunner, 194 Squadron, RAF
We located the DZ, but as our aircraft flew over Jap positions near it, it came under fire and was hit in the port engine. The pilot closed it down to avoid a fire, meanwhile the navigator and second wireless operator were busily despatching loads.

I noticed black smoke streaming past the door, and rushed up to tell the pilot. He told me to alert the crew to take up positions for a crash landing. By now we were down to about three hundred feet above the ground, and had lots of supplies still on board. The pilot was having a problem maintaining even that height, we threw out the supplies as fast as we could. Slowly the pilot gained height, and the navigator gave him the course for home. We managed to get over the Chin Hills, and eventually made a good landing back at base.

Private Henry Foster
Carrier Platoon, 2nd Battalion, West Yorkshire Regiment
We used to go and pick up supplies in our carriers. There were shells for the artillery and the tanks and there were big notices on the boxes, 'Dangerous Do Not Drop'. We didn't do too badly. We had plenty of water, we could go down to the stream and wash our clothes. We didn't have too bad a time. By the time we got to the Arakan, those of us who had fought in the Western Desert had got used to the way of life in action.

We lived quite well in the carrier platoon, because we had been out on a patrol and come across a ration dump left by our people in no-man's-land. We got a lot of crates of tinned milk and tinned fruit. We lived on porridge and with the tinned milk we could make really good porridge. We got bags of sugar but they'd poured paraffin or petrol over it.

We got attacked by air two or three times, they came in low over the hills and there was no warning, there was no radar. A troop of ack-ack guns were quite near where we were dug in, about forty yards away. They got attacked one day by Japanese fighter-bombers and they actually got a couple of bombs right on the target. They made a right mess. I could see the pilot, he came that low. I could see the bomb falling and it fell at the side of my carrier. Luckily only a small one. I was only two or three yards away but in a trench. It just blew the track off my carrier.

We supported the rifle companies when they were attacking the hills held by the Japanese. They used to dig themselves in these wooded hills, and dig right through so that when artillery was being fired at them, they would go through tunnels to the back of the feature. We didn't have guns that could fire in a high trajectory and get to them on the back of a hill. So a plan was devised that as the infantry attacked they were given supporting fire just over their heads. We used to do this with our Bren guns.

Captain John Anderson
HQ 33rd Brigade, 7th Indian Division
Eventually we managed to break out of the box, and I was taken back to brigade HQ in a tank. The 'Okeydoke' Pass was re-opened and we went on the offensive. We pushed further south to the road from Maungdaw to Buthidaung, which ran through the tunnels.

Second Lieutenant Satoru Nazawa
Company Second in Command, 112th Regiment, Japanese 55thDivision
But here, the men of the Tanahashi regiment, the 112th Regiment, were all like half dead, even the ones who were alive, because we were just so hungry. We didn't eat anything. We didn't have water, and our mouths were dired up. And so sometimes, a bit of chaff would be distributed, but even if they distribute chaff, we were the ones who had to polish it. So we would put it in our iron helmets, and we would use a stone to pound it. And then we would

Private Henry Foster.

blow on it, and then we would take one grain out at a time, and then put that in our mess kit, and would cook it and call it a rice gruel, but even if we cook that, we would only have a line of rice in our bowls. We would have rice gruel in the morning, rice gruel for lunch. And at night, we would finally have rice porridge.

Major Harry Smith
Officer Commanding HQ Company, 4th Battalion, Queen's Own Royal West Kent Regiment
Our first encounter with the Japs consisted of the battalion infiltrating round one of the Jap positions, while the 4th/7th Rajputs put in an attack at night, with the idea of cutting off the Japs while they withdrew. This was quite successful: we got into position behind the Jap outposts, and without being spotted. The Rajputs had quite a tough fight of it, coming up against Jap bunkers, which were very difficult to deal with. Eventually some of the Japs came back through us and were duly accounted for.

But soon after that we had a bit of a tragedy. The Japs must have spotted one of our Bren gun carriers bringing forward supplies and they fired at our positions with 105-mm guns. The Company Sergeant Major, Provost Sergeant, and the RSM all went down to unload the carrier, a shell landed beside them. The Company Sergeant Major was killed, as was the Provost Sergeant. The RSM was so badly wounded that we didn't think he would live, but in fact he did. These were our first casualties in this campaign, and very serious too. After that the war in the Arakan consisted of us eliminating the Japanese positions on these jungle-clad hill tops which rose up like pimples out of the plain; until we came up against the main Jap position at Razabil.

CSM Herbert Harwood
C Company, 4th Battalion, Queen's Own Royal West Kent Regiment
After the RSM, CSM of HQ Company and a couple of others got killed or wounded, I was promoted in the field from sergeant to CSM.

The Arakan was covered in hills running down to the sea. The Japs had been there for nearly a year and were well established. In one place we captured they had dug right through a hill from one side to the other. It was bombed by Mitchell bombers, and it made no difference. We went by night and cut them off from behind. We used cart tracks and dried-up chaungs.

These little hills delayed us. You had to send a patrol of about section strength up each to find out if they were held. Some would be held by only three or four Japs. But that was enough to hold you up. You harboured up, hit them with mortars, and the Japs might disappear during the night. But you could not be sure until you had sent a patrol to investigate. As soon as you put a patrol on top, it would be under observation, and they would mortar or shell the patrol. So as soon as you realised the hill was unoccupied, you kept going down the other side to avoid the pre-registered mortar or artillery fire. It was time-consuming to check a feature. It could take a day to travel two miles in the hilly jungle.

Major Harry Smith
Officer Commanding HQ Company, 4th Battalion, Queen's Own Royal West Kent Regiment
When we came up against Razabil, the Japs were entrenched in almost impregnable bunkers, and we were held up. So the brigade embarked on an ambitious outflanking movement round Razabil. By first light we were behind the Japanese position and encircling it. A heavy barrage from another brigade in front of Razabil heralded our actual attack from the rear. This was successful and the Japanese were ejected from the position, but many were caught in their bunkers as we fought an odd battle in which the dry jungle grass caught fire, and we made our way through blazing undergrowth to eliminate the last Japanese defenders in their bunkers.

CSM Herbert Harwood
C Company, 4th Battalion, Queen's Own Royal West Kent Regiment
On one of the round-the-back hooks, we were at the back of the column, and due to get in position in the enemy rear by dawn. We were still out in the open when light came, but we took cover in a chaung. I examined Razabil fortress after its capture; it was like an enormous underground hospital. You could exist there for months, provided you got supplied. It was all dug by hand.

Eventually we got down to within the sight of the entrance to the two tunnels. We clambered to the top of the ridge with the tunnels underneath. The Japs had used them as a supply base. B Company was in front of us. They called for artillery support from our own guns and you heard the shells coming over and exploding in front of us. I heard somebody shouting, 'Stop them bloody

The West Tunnel on the Maungdaw-Buthidaung Road, looking towards Maungdaw. In the distance the Razabil Ridge.

guns, they are shelling B Company.' We had the job of taking the place of B Company. Moving through them I have never seen anything like it, bodies, arms hanging in the trees; they lost about twenty killed and forty wounded, sixty people out of a company of about one hundred and fifty strong. It is a wonder the Japs didn't attack us. We were very confused and disorganised.

Major Harry Smith
Officer Commanding HQ Company, 4th Battalion, Queen's Own Royal West Kent Regiment

This was a tragedy, but it does happen in war. I took members of the pioneer platoon to the foot of the hill to dig a communal grave, and under very unpleasant Japanese mortar fire we buried the shell-torn victims.

When we captured positions we sometimes found Jap bodies with their right hands cut off. If they had time, the Japs cremated a dead soldier's right hand, and sent the ashes back to his relatives. We also found flags and bugles. They blew bugles and waved flags in the attack.

Private Bert Wheeler
Stretcher-Bearer, 4th Battalion, Queen's Own Royal West Kent Regiment

At the tunnels I had to bring back what I thought would be just one wounded man, but in the end it was ten. You had to pick the ones who would live to take back first, and help the walking wounded last. Being an inexperienced medical orderly, not a doctor, it was difficult to pick the worst wounded, but everybody stood by what you decided.

Most wounds were caused by shrapnel from mortars and artillery. If a man had shrapnel in his chest with maybe the heart or lungs exposed he wouldn't have much hope. Broken limbs and less serious wounded had priority. Walking wounded walked with you as you carried the stretchers, but you had to keep an eye on them. On one occasion I had shrapnel in the arm, and a broken rib, but was walking wounded.

You took the wounded to the Regimental Aid Post (RAP) where the MO worked. Conditions were primitive: he would operate on a stretcher, not a table. There was blood everywhere. He did not carry out amputations.

As a stretcher-bearer the only time you were stationed in the RAP was when you were not attached to a company. We also had to dress wounds. With fractures you put on splints, which you carried in your bag, the small

ICSM Herbert Harwood as a corporal before going to Burma.

ones only, bigger splints you did not carry. On bringing the wounded in, you reported to an NCO first who prioritised everybody.

Men with flesh wounds were treated in the RAP unless there was a risk of infection, in which case the wounded man was evacuated. There was a big problem with infection. I have seen quite a lot of gangrene; this usually required an amputation.

We used acraflavine, for cleaning wounds, one of the main treatments at the time, dressed them with a cream, bandaged them up, and hoped for the best. When you picked them up you stopped the bleeding, dressed the wound; nothing more. The distance from the front line to the RAP could vary from a few hundred yards to three miles.

Ambulances came from the ambulance company in the Casualty Clearing Station. An ambulance would take two stretchers, and you piled in as many walking wounded as you could.

In addition there was malaria and dysentery. As a precaution against malaria we took mepacrin tablets daily, usually after the evening meal; it was a parade, a medical orderly put the pill in your mouth, supervised by an officer. It was an offence not to take mepacrin.

If you caught diarrhoea it caused a problem because you were excused mepacrine, and given quinine, which was not as effective against malaria. Bad attacks of dysentery, such as passing blood, were evacuated. Men with ordinary 'trots' were treated by the MO, and stayed with the battalion.

Major Harry Smith
Officer Commanding HQ Company, 4th Battalion, Queen's Own Royal West Kent Regiment
Before another attack could be mounted, the battalion was withdrawn to fight elsewhere as the whole division was moved to Assam.

Captain Kristen Tewari
Divisional Signals 25th Indian Division, attached 51 Brigade
Our Division relieved 5 Division in the area of the tunnels. The Japanese knew they had fresh troops opposing them, and the first night the Japs sent a 'jitter party' with crackers. One of the battalions opened up on their fixed lines, followed by the next company, and the next battalion, and so on. Our defence platoon guarding the brigade HQ fired away. I was sitting on the

exchange, and the brigadier spoke to the general, and immediately the divisional artillery fire was called for. After about two hours the fire died away. The next morning the general came to our HQ to check up on the ammunition state; everyone had fired all their first line.

The area between the two tunnels was dominated by Hill 551, which the previous division had failed to capture after several attempts. The hill dominated the road and the Japanese brought down shellfire on the road when they saw movement. We lost a lot of men killed by Japanese shelling the road, including two of my men.

Our division attacked the hill, using Gurkhas from another brigade. I watched this attack by the Gurkhas, shouting 'Ayo Gurkhali', their battle cry. They had kukris in their hands, rifles slung across their shoulders and advanced throwing grenades. They threw the Japanese out. It was a beautiful sight and etched in my memory. The hill was almost bare of vegetation, just a few bushes were left.

Before advancing south we stayed in defensive positions in the tunnels area until the end of the monsoon.

THE WEST AFRICANS IN THE KALADAN VALLEY

Lieutenant John Hamilton
Platoon commander, 1st Battalion, Gambia Regiment
Some Africans may have seen jungle at home but the conditions in Africa are different from those encountered in Burma. Many Africans did not live near jungle as most of it near the coast had been cleared, especially in the Gambia. But Africans could perform well in jungle, they were used to living hard, they didn't expect sprung mattresses on their beds. They liked food but did not have fancy ideas. They could see and hear better than most Europeans. They could live as sparingly as the Japanese. They could dig trenches and cut through trees quickly. We cut a jeep track seventy miles long through the jungle using just machetes or pangas.

Patrolling along a path in the Arakanese bamboo was like taking a tank along a dyke in Holland: you couldn't get off the path easily, it is like giant grass. The bamboo grew in single stems so close together you had to turn sideways to get through it. If wearing a pack on your back, this is almost

Climbing a hill before a daylight attack in the Arakan.

impossible. Then you are faced by another, and have to zigzag to get through: exhausting. If you try this at night, even with a moon, you can't see the man in front of you.

When on top of hills, you can't see down to the bottom. The hills consist of razor ridge, the streams run in knife-slice thin chaungs. The beds of the streams are slabs of sandstone, all higgledy-piggledy – it is very difficult to walk along in a narrow stream bed.

In some places in Burma the jungle is different and you can follow the ridges, but in the Kaladan you couldn't. Because of the bamboo, any trees on the ridges don't grow branches until about twenty feet up, so climbing a tree to get a view was difficult, but not impossible for the Africans.

Sergeant Nana Kofi Genfi
Company Clerk, 7th Battalion, Gold Coast Regiment
The Burma jungle is not like the Ghana jungle. In Ghana the bamboo grows in groups, but in Burma it was like a plantation stretching for miles and very hard to pass through. There was segregation in the regiment; the white NCOs had a separate mess from black NCOs, but the whites painted their faces black in the jungle so they wouldn't stand out from their troops.

Lieutenant John Hamilton
Platoon commander, 1st Battalion, Gambia Regiment
On the march to the Kaladan in January 1944 it was very hot indeed. The nice thing about jungle paths is that you march in the shade, but on the jeep track the sun beat down full blast at midday. We had one advantage over other British troops: we Europeans did not carry our large packs, only our haversack. We had 'boys' who were 'enlisted followers'. They wore the same uniform, but weren't armed, and their job was to be a batman. They were paid the same as the soldiers: a shilling a day.

We marched in what British troops called battle order. Wingate would have 'gone spare' at officers not carrying huge packs. We lived on air supply for far longer than the Chindits did, and covered far more ground. We didn't carry as much as them, but survived better. When we arrived at a defensive position, the officers didn't dig the trenches, but went to the company O Group, supervised the administration and so forth. That is why the British Army provides an officer with a batman, so that the officer can take care of

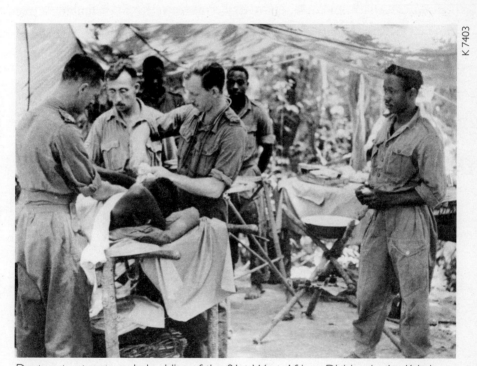

Doctors treat a wounded soldier of the 81st West African Division in the Kaladan Valley.

everybody else, and isn't bogged down looking after himself, cooking a meal etc. Chindit columns lost lots of officers through sickness and fatigue. We had nothing like those casualties. We were the first people to be on air supply at divisional strength. Our air drops were to battalions and even to brigades. The Chindits were trying to organise air drops for half battalions, spread out all over the place; very wasteful of aircraft.

The whole division marched along the jeep track over Frontier Hill; on the other side the hills went up to two thousand feet. Then we pushed down the Kaladan. The initial opposition was light, just outposts. In the first Arakan performance the British had sent a small force into the Kaladan, not by our route, but by Taung Bazaar, a more tortuous route, more or less due east. It emerged in Kaladan village, and was called the SoutCol route after Lieutenant Colonel Souter who was commanding a Baluchi battalion.

The Jap counter-attack began in the Kaladan when two battalions of the 213 Regiment disposed of the Baluchis at Kyauktaw, while the third battalion made its way across country, attacked Kaladan village and pushed out the Indian troops defending it.

Private Ali Haji Abdul Aziz Brimah
Signaller, 5th Battalion, Gold Coast Regiment
The Japanese had been told that we were cannibals and devils with tails as a propaganda trick. We started by not taking Jap prisoners, because they were not to be trusted and we had heard stories of what *they* did to prisoners. After a while we were told to try to take prisoners. We found it was no use. We didn't let our officers see, and killed the prisoners. They would kill themselves anyway. War is not child's play.

Lieutenant John Hamilton
Platoon commander, 1st Battalion, Gambia Regiment
The Jap 55th Division was facing XV Corps in northern Arakan, initially leaving the 1/213 Japanese Battalion in the Kaladan. Eventually this battalion was ordered to join the remainder of the 55th Division for the push that resulted in the Battle of the Admin Box. They were replaced in the Kaladan valley by the cavalry, or reconnaissance regiment of the 55th Division. The first people we bumped into were outposts of 1/213 stiffened by some locally recruited people. We called them the Arakan Defence Force, or Burma Traitor Army

(BTA). They didn't put up much of a show. 4 Nigeria Regiment drove in the outposts on the Kaladan. My company drove in another, and the remainder of the battalion a day later, on a different line, drove in yet another outpost.

The Japs assumed we would have to use the river as a line of communication. Of course we didn't have to use anything as a line of communication as we were being supplied by air. There was no Jap air threat at all, as they were in the process of losing command of the air.

We advanced to Kyauktaw, but this overstretched us and at Pagoda Hill we were forced back and operations in the Kaladan valley were closed down for a time.

I and my platoon sergeant were the last to leave Pagoda Hill. The Japs were boneheaded; they had been told to capture Pagoda Hill, they did, but didn't know what to do next.

Operation Thursday
The Second Chindit Expedition

Northern
Burma

Roads
Tracks
Railways
Rivers
International border

R. Brahmaputra
Dinjan
Ledo
Tezpur
Jorhat
Fort
Hertz
Sumprabum
Hukaung Valley
I N D I A
Dimapur
Kohima
Shaduzup
Kamaing
Myitkyina
CHINA
Mogaung
Tengchung
R. Chindwin
B U R M A
Silchar
Imphal
Shuganu
Indaw
Bhamo
Wanting
Mombi
Tamu
Sittaung
Katha
Kachin
Hills
Kyaukchaw
Loiwing
Tuitum
The Chocolate
Staircase
Tonzang
Tiddim
Kennedy Peak
Fort White
Kalewa
Shwegyin
Chin
Hills
Yeu
Lashio
Shwebo
Gokteik
Gorge
Gangaw
Monywa
Maymyo
Mandalay
Ava
Kabaw Valley
Yu R.

0   100 miles
0   160 km

We did have our bad times; so much rain that we remained wet for
weeks. Sometimes we were without water for two days at a time. We
carried enormous loads, varying from seventy-two pounds just after a
supply drop to fifty-seven pounds just before one.

Of some three thousand Chindits who had marched into Burma on the first expedition, 2,182 returned four months later. About 450 were battle casualties, 210 were taken prisoner, of whom forty-two survived; the remainder were missing. So little was achieved by the expedition that for a while after his return Wingate thought he would be court-martialled.

Instead, he was sent for by Winston Churchill, whom he accompanied to the Anglo/American Conference at Quebec in August 1943. Here Churchill paraded Wingate before the American President and Chiefs of Staff, as an example of how the British meant business in Burma. Meanwhile the press in India and in Britain was encouraged to trumpet the fact that the expedition had penetrated far behind the Japanese lines, which was true; other details were not passed to the press. What we would now call the 'spin doctors' busily milked the Chindit story for all it was worth. It worked. Slim remarked, 'Whatever the actual facts, to the troops in Burma it seemed the first ripple showing the turning of the tide.' Wingate's eloquence at Quebec convinced the American President, Roosevelt, and the Combined Chiefs of Staff that long-range penetration (LRP) could play a decisive part in the war in Burma. He was authorised to expand his force massively. To his original 77th Indian Infantry Brigade was added Brigadier W. D. A. 'Joe' Lentaigne's 111th Indian Infantry Brigade, which was already training for the LRP role. In addition he was given the experienced 70th British Division, fresh from the desert, which he broke up to form columns and LRP brigades. He also took under command the 3rd Brigade of the 81st West African Division.

Eventually, after many changes of plan, Wingate was tasked with supporting the American Lieutenant General Stilwell in his mission of advancing south from Ledo, to take Myitkyina, and connect Ledo with the old Burma Road into China. Wingate planned to achieve this by cutting the line of communication of the Japanese opposing Stilwell. It was not the intention that the Chindits should seize objectives in pitched battles with Japanese main force units.

Wingate returned from Quebec with a private air force assigned to him for ninety-nine days: the American Colonel Cochrane's Number 1 Air Commando USAAF, consisting of thirteen C-47 Dakotas, twelve C-46 Commando transports, twelve Mitchell B-25 medium bombers, thirty P-51 Mustang fighter-bombers, 225 Waco gliders, 100 L-1 and L-5 light aircraft and six helicopters. For major troop moves, resupply, and close air support tasks, the RAF and USAAF Troop Carrier Command would be needed to augment Number 1 Air Commando. Morale soared among the Chindits when they realised that no longer would sick and wounded have to be abandoned; the light aircraft would come and get them.

Originally Wingate's command included a three-thousand-strong US Army infantry regiment, Merrill's Marauders, named after its commander Brigadier General Frank D. Merrill. Well before the Chindits moved into Burma, Stilwell demanded Merrill's men back. Wingate's response was to tell the American officer bearing the order, 'You can tell General Stilwell he can stick his Americans up his arse.'

Wingate originally intended that his force would march into Burma. On arrival each brigade was to choose a stronghold as a base of operations, including an airstrip and a dropping zone (DZ) for supply by parachute. The enemy was to be induced to attack the stronghold, and while doing so, would be attacked in his turn by 'floater columns' operating outside.

In mid-January 1944, Wingate was told that the Japanese had closed up to the Chindwin in strength, and were keeping close watch on all crossing places south of Homalin. Although Wingate did not know it, this was in preparation for the Japanese attack into Assam (covered in the next two chapters), and was nothing to do with Japanese suspicions that Wingate planned to repeat his 1943 performance. But it caused Wingate to change his plans and fly in all his force, except for Fergusson's 16th Brigade, which would be trucked to the road head on the Ledo Road at Tagap Ga, and march to cross the Chindwin just upstream from Singaling Hkamti, well over a hundred miles north of Homalin.

Wingate chose three main objectives: Indaw, the railway from Mandalay to Myitkyina, and the road from Bhamo to Myitkyina. The fly-in brigades would be taken by glider and Dakota into four landing zones (LZs) named Piccadilly, Chowringhee, Broadway, and Templecombe. Early glider loads would carry light bulldozers and engineers to construct airstrips for Dakotas. The LZs were some distance from the objectives, and he relied on the brigades approaching their objectives under cover of the thickly wooded and rough terrain. His plan was as follows:

- Fergusson's 16th Brigade march from the Ledo Road, starting in February, and secure the two existing Japanese airfields at Indaw.
- Calvert's 77th Brigade land by glider and Dakota at Broadway and Piccadilly, and set up a block on the Mandalay–Myitkyina railway.
- Lentaigne's 111th Brigade land by glider and Dakota at Piccadilly, and head for the area south of Indaw, to protect the southern approaches of 16th Brigade's operations there. The Blaine Detachment of commando engineers (Bladet) was to operate in the same area, and demolish key railway bridges.
- Morris's 4/9th Gurkha Rifles (Morrisforce) land by glider at Chowringhee, march to the mountains east of the Bhamo–Myitkyina Road, and raid the road.
- Dahforce, consisting of Burma Rifles commanded by Lieutenant Colonel 'Fish' Herring, to land by glider at Templecombe, raise guerrilla bands from the Kachins and support Morrisforce.

The remaining brigades, 14th, 23rd and 3rd West African, were kept for a second wave, planned as a relief for the first wave in about two to three months. It was thought that ninety days was the maximum that Chindits could spend behind enemy lines. In the event the back-up brigades were flown in much earlier.

16 BRIGADE TO INDAW

Colour Sergeant Harold Atkins
21 Column, 2nd Battalion, Queen's Royal Regiment
After the Tobruk battle the battalion was due to be sent to Syria, but because of the Japanese entry into the war, we were sent to Colombo to defend Ceylon. Suddenly, out of the blue, we were told by the CO that the whole of 16 Infantry Brigade, which we had been part of for the whole war, was to join the Chindits and move to Jhansi for jungle training. We were there for three months living in jungle, as we would in Burma, and trained hard.

Wingate gave us a pep talk at the conclusion of the last major exercise at Saugor. I can't remember exactly what he said, except that we would have air support and casualty evacuation by air, so no man need worry if he was wounded; he would not be left behind. We would have supplies dropped to us. We were well trained and would show the Japs that we were better than them. I certainly wasn't inspired by Wingate. Nor were some of the other lads. Our concern was how much the press had built up the Japs as being invincible and merciless. We nursed the thought, 'What happens if you get captured?'

Private Arthur Baker
71 Column, 13 Platoon, 2nd Battalion, Leicestershire Regiment
The 2nd Leicesters were a marvellous battalion, the nucleus was all regulars. They had been all through Tobruk, fought in Syria, and were experienced. Corporal Brown commanded our section. He was a regular soldier, and had served in Crete, Syria and Tobruk.

The training was rigorous, if you weren't fit you would not survive it. Wingate visited us and spoke to us. We thought he was mad to begin with but he proved his point, he never expected anyone to do anything he couldn't do himself. But not many of the 2nd Leicesters liked him.

Lieutenant Peter Taylor
45 Column, 45th Reconnaissance Regiment
I was in the 45th Recce Regiment, part of 70 Division. We had to retrain from being a mechanised recce regiment for the desert. We were split into 45 and 54 Columns. I was in Number 45 Column commanded by the CO, 54 Column was commanded by the 2i/c. We did too much marching in training,

MH 7873

At Hailakandi airfield in Assam before the fly-in of the Chindits on the second expedition. L-R: American liaison officer, Colonel Allison USAAF, Brigadier Calvert, Captain Borrow (Wingate's ADC), Wingate, Lieutenant Colonel Scott, Chindit officer.

and exhausted ourselves before we even started operating.

Lieutenant Arthur Binnie
Blaine Detachment (Bladet)

I joined the Chindits because it had an aura of being special. We trained very hard, and the troops were proud of being trained this way, it was enormously satisfying. Wingate was about during our training, and we were impressed by his personality, with almost a manic attitude to jungle training. Although a small man, his personality came over as someone one would like to follow.

My first operation was to carry out a recce for Fergusson from the Ledo Road to the Chindwin, in February 1944. Our small party of British and West African soldiers were dressed as Americans because there were no British troops there until Fergusson's Brigade arrived. We wouldn't have fooled anybody. West Africans speak differently to American Africans, and our accents were different too. I had a packet of opium with which we bribed the village headmen.

Private Alexander Preston
22 Column, 8 Platoon, B Company, 2nd Battalion, Queen's Royal Regiment

Wingate visited us by the Ledo Road, waiting to go into Burma. We had to wait for a fortnight for extra kit to arrive. He said, 'You are going into Burma, imagine yourself climbing up one side of a house and down the other in mud, and you think it's impossible. It is not, because that is just what you are going to do.' He was right. It rained all the time while we waited. We got covered in leeches.

Colour Sergeant Harold Atkins
21 Column, 2nd Battalion, Queen's Royal Regiment

I was the Column Company Quartermaster Sergeant, equivalent to the Regimental Quartermaster Sergeant in a battalion. After our final training we moved to Assam/Burma border near the Ledo Road. We moved into a jungle clearing assembling for the march ahead. To get there we had to travel quite a distance along the Ledo Road in US trucks driven by Chinese drivers. It was an atrocious road, and was still under construction by hand by thousands of coolies – Indians, Chinese, all sorts of people, and some US giant equipment. The road, being carved out of a mountainside, consisted of masses of S bends.

The Ledo Road.

It climbed above the cloud level, and then down into ravines, crossing rivers on wooden bridges constructed out of material from the jungle. I wouldn't have trusted even a Dinky toy to cross some of them, let alone a truck. Coupled with the dangerous road, and the hair-raising way the Chinese drove their lorries, we were glad to get off the trucks after each day of a frightening journey; but at least it was a ride. The mules and muleteers walked. All the time it rained and rained and rained.

After some days we arrived in the jungle clearing. Here we got some more equipment, including some infantry flame-throwers.

Brigadier Bernard Fergusson
Commander, 16th Brigade
The brigade I commanded walked in and very tedious it was too. There were four thousand men and seven hundred animals strung out sixty-five miles from end to end, one abreast, because the paths and tracks were not wide enough to have two men walking abreast. If the leading man was in Richmond Park, the last man would be in the New Forest. Or if the leading man was on Glasgow Green, the tail-end Charlie would have been in Fort William, or Roxburgh or Carnoustie. The hills are half as high again as in the West Highlands and covered with jungle.

Colour Sergeant Harold Atkins
21 Column, 2nd Battalion, Queen's Royal Regiment
The 2nd Queens were given the lead of 16 Infantry Brigade. A battalion of six hundred men, seventy mules, twenty ponies, strung out in single file covers a huge distance. There were two columns of the Queens, two columns of the Leicesters, plus another six columns, so many people had to wait for days before setting out. Before we started the march a team of sappers went ahead to cut steps in the steep Naga hills that rise up to six thousand feet. Because we were heavily laden, as were the mules, and with all the rain, we could not have got up the hills without properly revetted steps. But within half a day, the steps were washed away by the rain.

Brigadier Bernard Fergusson
Commander, 16th Brigade
The mule leaders had the worst job of all, looking after the mule's load as well

as their own, and ensuring that the mule's back did not get sore. The most important loads on the mules were wireless sets, charging engines, mortars, machine guns and ammunition. Going off the air was the thing we dreaded most.

Colour Sergeant Harold Atkins
21 Column, 2nd Battalion, Queen's Royal Regiment

The worst part of the march was from Tagap to Hklak, it took us the best part of seven days to cover thirty-five miles; it beggars description, the physical exhaustion that was inflicted on men and mules. Sometimes the mules fell over the side, down two or three hundred feet. Men had to dump their packs, climb down, unload the mule, and help it up. Strangely very few were badly injured. They loaded them up, only to have it happen again with another mule. It was as hard to go down the hills as climb up. At times you were running and felt your knee joints under strain, it was as exhausting as climbing. In some places we had to offload the mules and send them off sliding down on their haunches, and put the loads on bamboo slides to manhandle the loads down. You arrived at the bottom to see another ruddy great climb up, it seemed never ending and went on like that till we reached the Chindwin. We never met the enemy. We went through several villages. We did not have anything to do with them.

Brigadier Bernard Fergusson
Commander, 16th Brigade

The signallers and the cipher operators had to work while we brewed up and rested, sending off the signals for supplies, and receiving orders. They were all the real 'heroes'. They had to put up aerials by throwing a stone tied to the end of the aerial over a tree branch.

We did have our bad times; so much rain that we remained wet for weeks. Sometimes we were without water for two days at a time. We carried enormous loads, varying from seventy-two pounds just after a supply drop to fifty-seven pounds just before one. We saw very little of the sky. Sometimes you would come out into a clearing, perhaps around a village, and we would halt for a few minutes extra.

Lieutenant Peter Taylor
45 Column, 45th Reconnaissance Regiment
Wingate said you couldn't punish a man, for sleeping on sentry or sleeping with a local woman, by giving him twenty-eight days' detention or court-martialling him, so he would be flogged. This was accepted by the men.

Two of my men were caught stealing rations, and my CO was so bloody wet, he attempted to punish them by distributing all their chocolate around. But all their friends instantly gave them the chocolate back. Typically British.

Colour Sergeant Harold Atkins
21 Column, 2nd Battalion, Queen's Royal Regiment
When we arrived at the Chindwin the training paid dividends. Dakotas came over and dropped rubber boats, but not enough to take everyone over in one lift. If you had well-trained mules, you could swim them across in a bunch with their muleteers, although there was always the chance that one would turn round and go back. Some hung on to mules with their gear rolled up in a groundsheet like a sausage. I did this, I wasn't a good swimmer. This river crossing was part of our training.

When we reached the far bank of the Chindwin we were sitting on the bank of the river brewing up, waiting for the rest of the column to cross and two characters were walking along the banks of the river. One had a towel wrapped round him and a monocle and an enormous beard. That was our brigadier, Bernard Fergusson. The other was General Wingate looking fearsome and scruffy. I remember wondering what the top brass would think about these two senior officers.

From the other side of the Chindwin it was a matter of getting on to our objective, Indaw North. We were told that the Japs were in the vicinity of the bridgehead, but didn't see them. Eventually we arrived at the stronghold of Aberdeen. Morale was quite good. But physically we were becoming very tired.

Aberdeen was well behind Japanese lines in an area near the River Meza near a village, we constructed an airstrip big enough to take Dakotas. It nestled in a valley surrounded by hills, and if one had not been behind Jap lines it would have been a very pleasant interlude. It was subjected to Jap air raids to try to knock out the airstrip.

We were told we were getting to the meat of what we were here to do: to

Peter Taylor, taken after the war.

harass the Japs, and cut their communications and to cause chaos in the area of Indaw North. We were originally told it was planned that we should capture the Jap airfields at Indaw North and the Jap supplies for their attack on Imphal and Kohima.

Private Arthur Baker
71 Column, 13 Platoon, 2nd Battalion, Leicestershire Regiment
We built a strip at Aberdeen. The West Africans came in to provide the garrison at Aberdeen. We built it with machetes and shovels. First we flattened the banks in the paddy and then the gliders flew in carrying light bulldozers.

Lieutenant Peter Taylor
45 Column, 45th Reconnaissance Regiment
When we got to Aberdeen the other two brigades were flown in. They looked as fit as fiddles, while we were exhausted. To add to that, we had hardly got to Aberdeen when we were ordered off to carry out an attack on Indaw.

Colour Sergeant Harold Atkins
21 Column, 2nd Battalion, Queen's Royal Regiment
From now on it becomes a tale of indecision and poor results, bearing in mind the effort we put in to get there. We set off from Aberdeen, but because the columns were so stretched out behind us it was going to take three or four days before the brigade could concentrate to start the operation to take Indaw North. It was originally intended that us and the Leicesters should attack Indaw and the airfields. The other columns were to play minor roles. But because the concentration of the brigade took so long, the plan was changed. My column was sent in a long hook to attack Indaw from the south, with the Leicesters coming in from the north. But things went wrong. We tried to move south without being seen, but villagers probably reported our progress to the Japs. We arrived at the Meza Chaung, and had had a supply drop the evening before. After this we set off in a hurry, and made towards the start line for the attack on Indaw. We arrived on the day after the supply drop, towards dusk.

Lieutenant Peter Taylor
45 Column, 45th Reconnaissance Regiment

During the Indaw operation, we came to Thetkegyin. I was recce platoon commander, with two sections of British, and one section of Burmese, unfortunately in my case Burmans, that is townsmen, not hill men like Karens or Kachins. Instead of carrying out reconnaissance, my proper job, I was guarding the CO's party. We were attacked while still wearing our large packs by a bunch of lightly equipped Japs in what amounted to PT kit. The CO ordered dispersal, but at the RV there were more Japs.

The CO was over thirty-six, too old, and a great gent, he wouldn't have his pack carried on a mule or pony. As a result he was played out. He changed the RV. So he sent me with a sergeant and one Burman to find the column and tell them where the new RV was. So off I went; it was nearing dusk. I luckily found the mules of the mortar platoon and told them where to go. Then I found the rifle company under an excellent fellow called Ron Adams, and he had collected together one or two others, and I told him where to go. Then I came on what I thought were some more of our chaps, and I shouted the codeword which was Namkin. They all stopped dead. I said it again, as my mouth was rather dry, and suddenly I realised they were all Japanese. Fortunately my sergeant, a marvellous chap, shouted, 'This way sir,' and he fired away and I was able to run straight into a thicket and joined the rest of my party.

We were not in jungle, but in teak country, where there is not a lot of cover from view. I found the track of the company and followed it. We were terribly short of water; for some reason water discipline had broken down since leaving Aberdeen, mainly because we had not had any contacts with the enemy and were getting slack.

Having found the company we went to a village where the Burmans said we would get water. It was held by the Japs. The company rushed in and a lot of chaps were sprayed by Jap fire. Ron Adams was wounded, and had to be left behind; God knows what happened to him.

I found myself with about half a dozen chaps, mainly my recce platoon, and we hid up in lantana, very useful stuff, it gave us cover in this rather open area. Travelling by night we got back to Aberdeen, where remnants of the column had collected. The CO was flown out, got rid of, a Burma Rifles chap took over.

Private Arthur Baker
71 Column, 13 Platoon, 2nd Battalion, Leicestershire Regiment

At Auktaw we had a brush with the Japanese, and we charged with fixed bayonets across a river held by Japanese and Burmese. Corporal Flowers dropped dead by my side, the first man I saw killed in action, by a sniper tied to a tree. Corporal Brown shot the sniper, and he hung from the tree suspended by his ropes.

Around the perimeter of the village was a bamboo fence, and each time a man went through the gaps in it, the Japs fired at them, so I dived through it and got stuck in the fence by the pack on my back and had to be pushed out from behind. But all our platoon got through. The Japs would feign death and shoot you from behind if you did not kill them as you went by. We didn't bury the enemy dead, or our own. The CO was wounded in the arm, but stayed with us for the attack on Indaw.

Colour Sergeant Harold Atkins
21 Column, 2nd Battalion, Queen's Royal Regiment

The CO decided that we could go no further that night. Although he and some of his group had noticed tyre marks on a track they had crossed, whether they gave it sufficient importance I cannot say. But we were ordered to bivouac in that area. We were still moving in and had not completed getting the column in to all-round defence when it became completely dark, and all of a sudden we could hear the roar of engines. To start with we thought it was aircraft, but it was half a dozen lorryloads of Japs who drove slap-bang into the middle of our bivouac.

Chaos reigned. It was dark. The Japs jumped out of their lorries, there were grenades going off, there was screaming and shouting. The CO was wounded. People were milling around, people had taken off their packs, leaned their weapon against a tree, and started to brew up. Some people were close to their weapons, others weren't.

My group had not had time to get packs off. We took cover on the banks of a small wadi. The issue of orders was difficult. The night progressed. My name was called out a number of times, 'C/Sgt Atkins.' It might have been an officer trying to contact me, against all the rules of training in the jungle, under fire, that was wrong: he should not have shouted my name, indeed not shouted at all. That gave the Japs the clue where he was. I was always convinced that it was this officer, but it could have been the Japs hearing my name and continuing to shout it.

I was engaged in trying to locate my administrative officer who was with the CO to find out what to do with the mules. Nobody knew where anybody was. One chap was shooting, and crawled across and asked him what he was shooting at. He said he didn't know, but that everybody else was shooting so he thought he had better join in. I told him to stop: he might be shooting at our own people.

There was close-quarter fighting. One young soldier held a Jap while his chum bayoneted him.

The second-in-command took command and gave orders to evacuate the bivouac and move across the chaung. In a huge state of pandemonium we crossed the chaung, and several men drowned, as it was quite deep.

We went on for a mile or so leaving the Japs in possession of our bivouac area. In daylight we discovered that about seventy men were missing, nearly every mule was gone, and nearly all the wireless sets and medical stores. The mules had panicked and went in all directions; we found a few eventually. The main concern was the loss of our wirelesses. We could not communicate, coordinate the attack, take supply drops etc.

There was a system to cater for what had just happened. You were given a short RV, which would be in force for 24 hours, or a long RV three days' hence. And you made for one or the other, depending on how long had elapsed since the dispersal of the column. A lot of the blokes did turn up at the RVs. Many men lost their packs with all their rations. All the remaining rations had to be gathered in and redistributed. The CO sent for me and asked me if I had a pistol as his had been blown out of his hand by a grenade. I had just given out all the spare pistols. I took one off a soldier and gave it to the CO.

My column for the next few hours was disorientated and unnerved. Our CO addressed us later and gave us a terrific harangue and said we were a rabble and it was to stop.

Private Arthur Baker
71 Column, 13 Platoon, 2nd Battalion, Leicestershire Regiment
We captured the airfield but there were no reinforcements so we had to abandon it in the end. The Japs put in some ferocious attacks but we saw them

off. The Japs had suicide squads, one would carry a white flag, with a machine gun strapped on his back, so the man behind could fire it when the lead man threw himself down. They ended up twenty yards off crossing a dried-up chaung. We rolled grenades into it and caught them in the bottom. We had American carbines, which had been dropped to us after Auktaw.

We were in jungle green, they wore khaki. Some of the first of our chaps into Auktaw found some South African khaki uniforms that the Japs had captured in Rangoon, and put them on because their kit was so ragged. Later they were found at Thetkegyin, killed by the Japs, mutilated. A man wearing a South African bush hat had been beheaded, men with South African shirts had their arms cut off, and those with South African trousers had their legs cut off.

Colour Sergeant Harold Atkins
21 Column, 2nd Battalion, Queen's Royal Regiment

We got into contact with brigade HQ using a short-range wireless set that we still had. We were told to go to the road, find the Japs and be 'bloody', give them hell. That we started to do, but they had vanished and we did not contact them. Then we were told to get ready for the attack and to go in on a given signal and attack Indaw.

We waited at the forming-up position. All the muleteers stood by their mules so they would not make a noise. We lay up all night on the southern fringe of Indaw. Some of the men had only a machete, having lost their weapons the night before.

We waited and waited and the signal did not come. We learned that some of the other columns had come under attack. The Recce Platoon was ambushed trying to find water. The Leicesters were discovered somewhere near their forming-up position north of Indaw and were attacked. All this put paid to a coordinated attack on Indaw. The brigadier gave orders to withdraw to Aberdeen.

The journey back to Aberdeen was full of hair-raising episodes. We had halted and started searching for water. Most of us got back, but two chaps disappeared, and they were never heard of or seen again. When we were about to cross the single-track railway line from Katha to Indaw in the dark, we heard a train chugging up the line. I don't think I've seen so many men disappear into jungle so quickly. We were still very disorganised and with low morale and not about to get involved with the Japs again if we could avoid it.

One of the men sitting on a pony with a fractured thigh was yanked off the pony. He did not utter a word. He took it very well.

We lay there looking at the train loaded with Japs going off to Indaw. One Jap shouted a sort of challenge, but we did not answer it. We remained quiet and continued to Aberdeen after the train had gone.

THE OTHER BRIGADES FLY IN

Lieutenant Colonel Walter 'Scottie' Scott
Commanding Officer, 81 and 82 Columns, 1st Battalion, King's Regiment (Liverpool)
The plan was that my 81 Column would land at Piccadilly, and 82 some thirty miles to the north in another clearing known as Broadway. The role of these columns was to clear the area and hold it so that bulldozers could be flown in to construct airstrips. In the late afternoon of 5 March 1944, Colonel Cochrane had sent a photo recce flight to both strips. General Wingate, Calvert and myself were standing at the head of the glider train when a photograph of Piccadilly was shown to us. There was a silence. The clearing I had known so well from 1943 was covered in logs.

Wingate took the photograph to General Slim and after several minutes came back and handed the photograph to me and turned away with his head bent and hands clasped behind his back. He looked a forlorn and lonely figure as he walked towards the setting sun. He returned and after a brief conference returned to General Slim.

He came back and gave me fresh orders, so clear and concise that it was as if Piccadilly had never existed, I was to go to Broadway. Someone had made a bold decision. Who it was I do not know.

After I had given orders to my column commanders, he took me off and told me something that was for my ears alone and always will be. All his planning and hopes were on the line but as we shook hands not the slightest tremor betrayed what was conflicting within.

As my glider rose into the purple dusk on the hills to the east, my thoughts were not on what lay beyond, but rather of General Wingate's unforgettable display of cool, determined and inspired leadership. I believe that if ever I saw greatness in a human being I saw it in General Wingate that night.

Private John Mattinson
20 Column, Commando Platoon, 1st Battalion, Lancashire Fusiliers
Initially the Lancashire Fusiliers were the floating battalion, to patrol outside the stronghold and attack the Japanese before they could reach the block. I was in the Commando Platoon, fifty-two strong, commanded by Captain Butler of the Guides Cavalry. We were taught how to drive in case we captured Japanese vehicles. We were taught the basics of explosives. Each man was issued with condoms for underwater demolitions. You inflated it, put explosive in, with safety fuse and match inside, and tied it up. It would float and you could swim out with it to the bridge pier. Then you untied the condom, struck the match on the fuse, it burned underwater. You could use the cloth ammunition bandoliers as cutting charges by packing in explosives in every pocket, and wrapping the belt round a girder. We were told that our job was to blow a bridge near Tonlon village.

The night before the fly in, we were watching a film, and Colonel Cochrane took the mike and said, 'Now lads, the time has come; tomorrow night we shall hit the Japs in the guts. Good hunting. I know that some of you will not be coming back.' A big cheer went up.

I wasn't supposed to be going that night, but someone came up and said, 'You are going tonight, in number five glider, into Broadway.' So I flew in with Lieutenant de Witt, some American engineers and some of ours. We were to help clear the strip ready to take the C-47s the next night. I looked out of the little window in the glider and I could see the Irrawaddy and it looked like a road in the moonlight. The pilot said, 'It looks like a hell of a mess down there. But I'll see what I can do.' I thought what the hell is he doing, going straight for trees. He flew in between two trees, the wings came off, and just the body went on a bit further. But everyone got out all right.

Private William Merchant
20 Column, Commando Platoon, 1st Battalion, Lancashire Fusiliers
As we landed a Bren hit me on the side of the head, I wasn't too badly hurt. One chap had a broken ankle. But the first glider down crashed because of ruts in the paddy where teak logs had been laid out to dry, so the ground was corrugated. We got down about 10.30pm; we wondered if we would ever live to see India again.

Private John Mattinson
20 Column, Commando Platoon, 1st Battalion, Lancashire Fusiliers
There were gliders scattered all over, with quite a lot of injured; two of the American engineer officers were killed. Lieutenant de Witt went up to Colonel Allison who was sitting in a jeep, and he told him to start helping clear the strip, cutting the lantana and other trees, digging and laying out portable lights with a small generator to bring in the C-47s carrying more men and equipment the next night.

Captain Donald McCutcheon
40 Column, 3rd/4th Gurkha Rifles
We were having a party to drink the mess profits before we went into action. Brigadier Lentaigne and Jack Masters were there, both 4th Gurkhas. An officer came in with a signal saying 'Move your men now. Get to Tulihal tonight and fly tomorrow morning'. We spent the whole night packing up.

Surprise, surprise, the next morning a lot of large trucks arrived and took us to Tulihal. Then, typical army, we sat around for a couple of days.

Although we had had a certain amount of glider training, we had never actually been up in gliders. We were then told, 'You are not going by glider. You will follow in the 4/9th Gurkhas by Dakota to an airstrip called Chowringhee.' This was not the one we were originally going to, because that had been covered in logs. The snag was that Chowringhee was on the wrong side of the Irrawaddy, but all right for the 4th/9th, who were going to join up with the North Kachin Levies.

Lieutenant Richard Rhodes-James
Cipher Officer, HQ, 111 Brigade
It was extraordinary to be landing at night in a Dakota on a strip with a lit flare path in enemy territory. We had total air superiority. After landing we got into defensive positions and waited for the morning before moving to the Irrawaddy. We were to have landed at Piccadilly, north-west of the Irrawaddy, but when the plan was changed we landed east of the river at Chowringhee, so had to cross to reach our area of operations.

Warrant Officer Deryck Groocock
194 Squadron, RAF

The Dakota was a marvellous aircraft, light on the controls, with very reliable engines, and you could land it on a five-hundred-yard-long strip at night. I flew into all the Chindit strips by night and day: White City, Broadway, Blackpool and Chowringhee. Aberdeen was the worst, especially at night, it was short with hills on three sides. You had to circle at seven thousand to eight thousand feet, waiting until you were called down by the controller. You circled down, and landed one way on the five hundred- to six hundred-yard-long strip. You took off in the opposite direction. One night I came in too high, and knew I wasn't going to make it. So I opened up full throttle, found a little valley, and staggered along this at about seventy-five knots, managing to get away with it and come in for another approach.

One of our flight commanders, 'Dinger Bell', was attacked by a Jap night fighter while circling overhead Broadway. Both engines were knocked out, and four or five of the twenty or so soldiers in the back were killed. He managed to do a dead-stick landing and get away with it – fantastic.

Major Alexander Harper
94 Column, 4th/9th Gurkha Rifles

I was originally in the Deccan Horse. I was posted to the Governor of Bengal's Bodyguard, volunteered for the Chindits, and went to the 4th/9th Gurkhas. I joined them in February 1944 at Jhansi, and went into Burma a month later. The 4/9th were in two columns, 49 and 94. I was in 94, commanded by Peter Cane, of 4th/9th Gurkhas, a regular. As a cavalry officer I was supposed to be able to handle animals and so was in charge of the mules for the fly-in.

We had a ramp for loading the mules into the Dakota door which was about four feet above the ground; they couldn't jump in, but could jump out if need be. We loaded fifty planes with mules, and then got them out again, because we were told that the LZ was no good. So we loaded again the next night for a different LZ.

We flew in to an LZ on the east bank of Irrawaddy, called Chowringhee. Glider-landed troops had improved the LZ and Dakotas flew in the heavier stuff, including mules. The flight was OK. We had no trouble, although on one Dakota a mule misbehaved, and was shot. The Dakota flew back to India with a dead mule on board.

Pilot Officer James Thirlwell
194 Squadron, RAF

Even in monsoon storms when you had very little say in what happened to you, plunging down three thousand feet and up again two thousand in torrential rain and lightning, the Dakota was a wonderful aircraft. It had one snag: the cockpit leaked badly in heavy rain, and we used to put oilskins over our knees to keep the water off our laps.

Broadway was a difficult place to land at night because of mountains on either side. You approached downwind at eight thousand feet to clear the high ground, turned on to finals at eight thousand feet, and tried to pick up the light of the goose-neck flares marking the strip. There was no glide-path indicator, you went right in from eight thousand feet to touch down. My first landing there, the chap ahead of me with twenty-four soldiers on board made a nonsense, and tried to go round again; all I could see were his landing lights as he went straight into a hillside beyond the runway. I was at about six hundred feet at that stage, and just held on, all I could see was a flaming aircraft ahead. I made it OK.

Private John Mattinson
20 Column, Commando Platoon, 1st Battalion, Lancashire Fusiliers

The next night at Broadway, Captain Butler came in with the column and the rest of the platoon, and I was the guide to show them where they were to go. We worked for four days, before getting our marching orders and setting off for the Central Valley.

Major Percival Leathart
Officer Commanding D Company, 3rd/9th Gurkha Rifles

The CO and Intelligence Officer were to have gone in first. Their glider crashed soon after take off. They were all right, but the small bulldozer and horse in the glider were damaged. That was a bad start for the CO who came in with us the next day. We flew in Dakotas, each towing two gliders on long nylon ropes. They had to climb to over six thousand feet to get over the hills into Burma.

It got colder and colder as we climbed. Then we started to come down. It was a remarkable sight seeing the open space all lit up in the middle of the Burmese jungle. As we marched in the night, past the paraffin-burning lights

James Thirlwell, taken after the war.

that marked the edge of the strip there was a smell of death that accompanied us for the rest of the campaign. It came from crashed gliders; nobody had had time to remove the corpses. It was a chilling experience.

Lieutenant Arthur Binnie
Blaine Detachment (Bladet)

On the main operation, I went in as a special decoy group under Major Blaine, fifty men and five officers. Blaine had been much admired by Wingate on the first expedition. He was given an immediate DCM and promoted to officer in the field from being a CSM. Blaine was a tough Scot trained as an engineer. He was given the task of collecting a group of engineers and muleteers who would carry out whatever Wingate wanted, called Bladet, standing for Blaine Detachment.

When the main body went in our job was to disrupt the Myitkyina railway, to make the Japs aware that troops were operating further south of the main operation, which might make the Japs wonder how many troops were operating in the area.

We flew in five gliders from Imphal and landed in paddy fields near the Irrawaddy, in an LZ prepared by Gurkhas who had gone in before us. We landed in moonlight and ploughed straight into the jungle. The wings fell off, the body of the glider fell apart, and we walked out of the wreckage. My group was intact. The glider carrying the mules seemed to loop-the-loop, but landed all right. The mules walked out and started to graze.

After landing it was revealed to me that I was to take command as Blaine had been injured in the landing. This was my first time on active service, but as the senior of five lieutenants I took command. Blaine gave me my objectives before being flown out in a light plane. It was a little bit nerve-shattering.

We were told to conceal ourselves as best we could. It was likely that Burma traitors would spot us, but we were not to get seriously engaged. Our main task was to blow up the railway line. With only fifty men you were limited in the amount of damage you could cause.

Private John Mattinson
20 Column, Commando Platoon, 1st Battalion, Lancashire Fusiliers

After marching for five days we had an air drop of explosives for our task at the bridge near Tonlon, and a top-up of rations. The drop was into elephant grass, it was sharp and cut like a razor. One chap fell into a mud wallow made by elephants, and broke his leg. He was flown out the next morning by light aircraft.

For the supply drop we lit a line of fires. We saw the aircraft coming round, and Captain Butler flashed a green light twice. Six chutes came out, and a free drop of mule fodder as well. We had one chap killed with a broken neck; a bundle of fodder bounced and hit him. But morale was high, and everyone was raring to go.

The bridge was a five-pier bridge with H girders. I was in the chaung by the bridge, putting explosives in a bag, and the others were hauling it up to the bridge. We had started to lay the charge, and a shout went up, 'Jap truck coming down the road.' Captain Butler gave orders not to fire.

The truck was coming fast. It got to a level crossing and pulled up and stalled. The troops in the back sat there, they were wounded. We didn't fire, but sat looking at them. We were hidden so close, that one chap got spat at in the eye by a Jap.

Eventually the Jap truck drove on. We put a lead pencil delay fuse on the charge to give us a chance to get away. Lieutenant de Witt said to me, 'I'll give you the honour of pulling the pin out.'

Captain Donald McCutcheon
40 Column, 3rd/4th Gurkha Rifles

We, with brigade HQ, now had to cross the Irrawaddy before we could go to our objective in a north-west direction. Things started to go wrong from the beginning; it was an IMFU, or Imperial Military Fuck Up. The outboard engines we had dropped to us kept breaking down. Also, we did not cross on a wide-enough front. Came the dawn when we should have been across, we were not. Brigade HQ had got across, and half the battalion was over. We, the other half, were left on the other side.

Orders were given to 40 Column to join the 4th/9th Gurkhas as an extra column. The journey north was frustrating as the 4th/9th had been ordered to move as fast as they could to join the Levies. We were about thirty-six hours behind, and it was difficult with the Japanese stirred up. Almost level with Bhamo we ran into the Japanese and had minor engagements with them from time to time. We ambushed and destroyed the Bhamo–Myitkyina Road as we went along.

Chindits preparing a bridge on the Mandalay-Myitkyina railway for demoltion.

SE 7922

Private John Mattinson
20 Column, Commando Platoon, 1st Battalion, Lancashire Fusiliers
The next day the bridge blew successfully and we set off again to harass the Japs. The point men came back and told Lieutenant de Witt that there were some Japs by the road having a rest in a clearing. We approached, took up fire positions. Captain Butler said, 'When I throw grenades, you are to open fire.' He threw five grenades, shouting, 'Here, you yellow bastards, share these between you.' They screamed and fired at us, we didn't fire a round. We killed five. The rest ran off.

The man by me said, 'I've sprained my ankle.' A bullet had gone through his boot. We carried him back on a stretcher. When we got out his pack to do a brew, we found a hole where a bullet had gone through his mess tin, and through his rations. We cut an airstrip for a light plane and he was flown out.

Next day we got a message to head for White City.

Private William Merchant
20 Column, Commando Platoon, 1st Battalion, Lancashire Fusiliers
So we made our way into the White City block. Brigadier Calvert came out on a horse to meet us and rode in with us. It was the size of a city park, surrounded by wire. The Bengal Sappers and Miners had blown the bridge north of Mawlu. They had taken sleepers from the railway line to make overhead protection for slit trenches, making them into bunkers. They built a light airstrip inside the block, and a Dakota strip just outside on the far side of the railway.

Pilot Officer Joe Simpson
194 Squadron, RAF
On one occasion I flew a load of water, including a small water trailer, in to Broadway. The Chindits didn't want the trailer, they just wanted me off quickly. So I just opened the taps to drain it, before lashing it well forward in the aircraft for take-off. I must have been a bit flustered and disorientated, because I saw two lights on the runway and was opening up power, when a chap with a torch rushed out and waved and screamed, 'Those are the last two lights on the runway, you are facing the wrong way.' I turned round and took off, and in the confusion forgot to make the fifteen-degree right turn immediately after take-off. I heard trees bashing the bottom of the aircraft, did a stall turn to the right and the Dakota responded. On my return the fitter said, 'Where have you been? The engine cowling is full of twigs and leaves.'

Lieutenant Arthur Binnie
Officer Commanding Blaine Detachment (Bladet)

We had a long journey to get to the Mandalay–Myitkyina railway line, including going through the dry belt which was not a pleasant experience, surviving with very little water for two or three days when the jungle is burning with the heat and no water in sight. It was one of the few occasions in my life when I thought I would kill one of my friends, I could hear the water in his bottle sloshing around, as we were marching towards where we hoped we would find water. I thought I might kill him and drink his water; it was a passing thought.

We tried to avoid villages, as we believed that the villagers were spotting us and might give information to the Japs. At one stage one of the chaps in the rear section of the column came forward and told me that two men with rifles had been following us for half a mile or so. I said that we would have to get them, and told an officer to take some men, ambush and kill them. They killed one and the other was brought to me slightly wounded in the foot. The problem: what to do with him? I decided that he knew where we were, and our strength. I had no option but to execute him. This was my duty. The attitude of the troops under my command made this clear. So I did it. I have lived with it, but don't feel guilty. It was more important to do that than risk the lives of my men.

We did not run into the Japanese at this stage. We blew up the railway line. Then we withdrew aiming to join the main force. We had done our job. It was a long trek. We were covering about twenty miles a day. The engineers laid booby traps on our tracks and by the railway, which would blow the Japs' feet off. Food was at a minimum. My batman, Private Whiting, came to me and said he had a fever. So I told him that I would have to leave him behind. Whiting immediately got surprisingly better, and was considerably better the next morning.

Major Alexander Harper
94 Column, 4th/9th Gurkha Rifles

My column was going to operate near the Chinese border, and ambush convoys on the Bhamo–Myitkyina Road. After this it was to link up further north with a Kachin local force raised by 'Fish' Herring.

We began by ambushing a Japanese truck on the road: two Japs were killed.

One hid, was captured, and shot. We were supposed to take care of any Jap prisoner, as they were rare, and send them back as quickly as possible. We could not do that.

The next ambush, the truck had ten Japs in it. Although it went over a mine, the Japs dashed into the jungle and fought back. They moved to some paddy fields and lay down behind the bunds and returned our fire. We killed them all but it took about forty minutes. They would not surrender. We did not suffer a scratch. The Gurkhas were most impressed by the Japanese persistence and courage.

Major Percival Leathart
D Company, 3rd/9th Gurkha Rifles
The next morning at Broadway we started digging foxholes and laying wire that had been dropped to us, and after about a week we had a really strong position. The RAF based some Hurricanes there. One of our companies acted as floaters to provide warning of any approaching Japanese.

One day about twelve Japanese bombers came over and bombed us, but caused remarkably few casualties because our foxholes were quite deep. A day or two later, the floating company was attacked by Japs but they did not press their attacks.

Wingate paid us a visit early on in an American B-25. When he left, I went with him and his ADC to the plane. Two American war correspondents tried to hitch a lift, and Wingate hauled them in, although the pilot said the plane was overloaded.

We then heard that the plane was missing. His death knocked the stuffing out of the Chindit campaign.

Lieutenant Colonel Walter 'Scottie' Scott
Commanding, 81 and 82 Columns, 1st Battalion, King's Regiment (Liverpool)
The last I saw of Wingate was when I said goodbye to him at Broadway, and a cloud came over all of us in Special Force. We didn't know what was to happen to us, whether we would be disbanded or someone else would take over command. Though it was very difficult for General Lentaigne to take over after Wingate, he did a damn good job, he was a good soldier.

But to most of us there could only be one Wingate. He had a lot of things that one could get annoyed with, but overall he was one of the greatest men I have ever met. Even those who disliked him had to admit that he was an outstanding leader. He was never afraid, even in a tight corner. His leadership and his drive I shall remember always. During that second campaign we were all inspired by what we did on the first campaign.

Lieutenant Richard Rhodes-James
Cipher Officer, HQ, 111 Brigade

We wondered if the operation would come to an end when Wingate was killed. Our brigade commander, Lentaigne, was made head of Special Force, so we had to get him out by air. The Brigade Major, Jack Masters, was made commander of the brigade.

The brigade blew up roads and supplies of ammunition on the Japanese route to their operations in the north of Burma. The problem with the column organisation was that it was not suitable for conventional attacks on a strong objective, because there was no reserve, and hence no flexibility. Some COs reverted to a proper battalion organisation.

Major Desmond Whyte RAMC
Medical Officer, HQ, 111 Brigade

A doctor in the Chindits was his own surgeon, own dermatologist, own orthopaedic specialist with just your medical orderlies to help. You had one pannier carried on one side of a mule for medical supplies. It was never large enough. Of all the medicines, mepacrin to suppress malaria was the most important.

In the jungle you carried a carbine. At night the enemy could be only a few feet from you. We had no antibiotics, but sulphamine drugs had just been issued, and on my first air drop after arriving in Burma I had my first sulpha drugs dropped to me; the first time I had seen them. We did not have tents, and therefore no cover from the elements. We had no mosquito nets.

Wounded who were immobilised were dragged behind mules on a bamboo stretcher, with the front on the mule's saddle, and the back of the stretcher on the ground. Four men with ropes walked alongside to help the stretcher up over the bumps on the ground and steer the mule.

Most wounded did very well, but in the great heat it became difficult to

Giving a wounded Gurkha soldier a drink.

keep them alive. Shortage of water was a problem. We carried chaguls, canvas bags to hold water; it evaporates through the canvas to keep the water cool, but loses water in the process. The casualty would sometimes have a tube down into his mouth and into his stomach through which we poured water. Sometimes I added brandy, and occasionally hot sweet tea.

With our training we always felt we were the masters of the jungle. Our number one enemy was malaria: everybody got it. Every morning if the enemy situation would allow, everybody was lined up and the NCOs checked that everybody took his mepacrin. Your eyes went yellow. After a bit you didn't care. Word spread through the Gurkhas that this made them impotent; as the Gurkha is a very virile man, we had to scotch the rumour.

Our ration was the American K Ration. It was excellent for a short time. It was all pre-cooked. If the enemy allowed, you could heat it up. You could eat it cold. The difficulty was that although it gave you three meals a day, you soon knew what was coming up next. More serious, a day's ration gave you only four thousand calories, whereas we were burning up six thousand calories, and from the start burned up our own flesh. We had the occasional 'paradise' drop of luxuries. We didn't always get our regular drop, for example, if the enemy was near, they would mortar the DZ. If there was a ground mist the RAF and USAAF were told if you don't get the correct signal, don't drop. The signal was changed every five days.

We were running down in condition. Men died of malaria, sepsis, pneumonia, and meningitis. I always took the seriously ill or wounded from the other columns, this meant that the brigade HQ moved very slowly with a long trail of casualties. The brigadier didn't like this, but we talked him into it; an excellent person, John Masters.

We arranged for a fly-out from time to time. Several light planes would come in. The doctor with Gurkha escorts took the casualties to a place where the Gurkhas could cut a strip and hope the planes would come before the enemy came. One of the rescue planes crashed on take off, and the pilot survived, scrambled out, and said, 'Aw shit, I ought to be shot.' I said, 'You soon will be, the Japs are coming.' We got the two dead out of the plane and buried them in the jungle. I always carried a little prayer wrapped in cellophane in my pocket. I said a prayer and moved on, knowing that the shallow grave would not keep the jackals out.

We didn't have too much trouble with teeth, more with glasses. Men who

Loading a casualty on to an L-5 light aircraft.

wore glasses took in a spare pair, but if they broke the second pair they had to have another pair flown in.

Psychological cases occurred towards the end. Every man has his breaking point, and we were reaching this. You could see people going downhill. Some even died in their sleep.

The Gurkhas were the most resilient in our brigade. The Gurkha has a very tough upbringing in Nepal, and is used to hardship and disaster.

Lieutenant Arthur Binnie
Officer Commanding Blaine Detachment (Bladet)

I had one muleteer, a bit of a rapscallion, who my CSM said needed discipline. So I told the muleteer that he was impeding the progress of the operation, and that I would deduct three days' rations from him and give them to other soldiers. I added that if he did not accept my punishment or made further difficulties I would shoot him. He accepted this, and worked very well.

We were heading for the main force, very tired and hungry. All we wanted to do was find our own troops and see what happened next. We were sitting in light jungle near paddy, and I was talking to CSM Chivers who had been on the first expedition, a very good man. We had taken a supply drop but were running short. Chivers believed that because we were lost and our wireless had gone unserviceable, we should march back to Imphal across the Chindwin. He had done it before, but now the Japanese were attacking in the area. I thought it was a hopeless idea. But I said, 'If you want to take the men that will go with you, you can. But I will take the others and find our own troops'. We had got almost to the stage of doing this when we saw two Gurkhas walk out on to the open paddy a few yards away. They were part of a column that we had not seen in the jungle, despite being only about two hundred yards away. It was Colonel Brennan's Cameronians. They took us in and fed us on rations they had just taken on a supply drop. Brennan sent a wireless message to General Lentaigne who had taken over from Wingate. He told him that we were totally exhausted and useless as fighting troops, and must be evacuated. I was told to head for Aberdeen and be flown out.

Major Charles Carfrae
Officer Commanding 29 Column, 10th Battalion, Nigeria Regiment

We were split into two columns, Number 29, which I commanded, and

Number 35, commanded by Peter Vaughan, a Welsh Guardsman, who also commanded the battalion. We told the West Africans that they would find the Japanese a very different kettle of fish from the Italians, whom some of my more experienced NCOs and men had fought in Eritrea. They had little respect for the Italians. Until they met the Japs they didn't believe how formidable they were.

I flew in on 5 April with the advance party of the battalion in a Dakota, which took off just before dark and landed in a big defended position, White City, commanded by the most famous Chindit of all after Wingate, Brigadier Michael Calvert. He was a very fine commander, the finest I ever came across. He was determined, enterprising, brave and a strong magnetic personality, he has been described as flamboyant, but he wasn't, he wasn't a show-off. He talked quietly, always gave his orders in a conversational rather than a peremptory tone. He was often quite vague in his conversation. But his soldiers would do anything for him. He wasn't mad at all or impetuous, despite his nickname.

Our battalion's job was to form part of the garrison of White City. We had a platoon of Africans who were flown in to help unload artillery flown in by glider.

There was firing quite close by and in the gloom it was impossible to tell where attacks were coming from and indeed if any of the figures passing us in the dark were friendly or enemy. Eventually we bedded down under the wing of a glider on the airstrip just outside the main fortress. Next morning Calvert's RAF officer led us into the fortress itself. We were given a position to dig near a platoon of the South Staffordshire Regiment.

Major Alexander Harper
94 Column, 4th/9th Gurkha Rifles

We moved on, blew a hole in the road and ambushed it to catch the Japanese coming to mend it. In the middle of the night the Japanese arrived in a column marching down the road. We held our fire and caught them perfectly. It was pitch dark and we couldn't see what we were firing at. Some must have escaped by jumping into the ditch by the road, and crawling away. Some Japanese began to mortar us from another direction, so we pulled back. We exchanged some shots with the Japanese while we waited for the party that had been in an ambush further south. They had been surrounded but managed to break out. We then pulled back to the main body of the column overlooking the road, a bridge and a village the Japs were using. We were about two thousand feet up.

Major Charles Carfrae
Officer Commanding 29 Column, 10th Battalion, Nigeria Regiment
Our second night at White City, the first within the fortress, the Japs attacked in force and we all stood to. In daylight, before the attack started we were mortared by a huge Jap mortar known as the 'coal scuttle', firing a tremendous projectile about five feet long which went off with a huge noise – it was a 5.9-inch mortar obtained from the Germans after the First World War. At this time the British officers had not dug slit trenches, so we leapt into a hole about twelve feet by six feet, full of unsavoury tins and rubbish. The Africans had half dug their holes but with no overhead cover. Every time an orange flare went up from our mortars we looked around to see if we could spot a Jap. Our bit of the fortress was not attacked, the nearest was about two hundred yards away. But it was very noisy and went on for several hours. Next morning we were attacked by about half a dozen Zero fighters who bombed the air strip and then machine-gunned us but they were nothing like as frightening as the mortars. It was a very abrupt introduction to war, in twenty-four hours or less, from peace without a shot being fired or enemy within hundreds of miles, suddenly we were in the thick of it.

I went to Calvert's brigade major, an old friend of mine, to try to find out what had happened to the battalion, but he did not know. On the eighth day I saw our brigadier and brigade major getting out of a light plane landing on the strip within the defences. I rushed up to ask what was happening to us. He said that as well as the Jap attacks on White City, bad weather in Assam had prevented any aircraft taking off. But the battalion had flown off the day before and landed at a stronghold called Aberdeen, were marching to White City and would arrive the next day.

Private William Merchant
20 Column, Commando Platoon, 1st Battalion, Lancashire Fusiliers
The Japs used to shell the block by day and attack at night. There were hundreds of dead Japs hanging on the wire outside the block. We planted landmines and booby traps within the wire perimeter. We dug pits and put in

sharpened stakes for them to land on when they fell in. The Japanese were very brave but stupid, always attacking in the same place. I was hit in the leg by shrapnel, but the MO dug it out with a pocket knife. It was from a Jap plastic grenade.

Private John Mattinson
20 Column, Commando Platoon, 1st Battalion, Lancashire Fusiliers
Patrolling to find the place from which the big mortar was firing at us, we went out through a zigzag in the wire, which was closed up behind us. We found some weapon pits dug for the Japanese to wait in while forming up to attack. We booby-trapped them. We found tins of fish, Japanese cigarettes and photos of their wives and children. We took the fish and cigarettes, but didn't take the photos because if the Japs had taken us they would have killed us.

Private William Merchant
20 Column, Commando Platoon, 1st Battalion, Lancashire Fusiliers
Coming back into the block we saw some people, thought they were enemy and opened fire. It went on for some time until we realised they were our own people. We killed one of them, a corporal.

Private John Mattinson
20 Column, Commando Platoon, 1st Battalion, Lancashire Fusiliers
In attacks the Japs would sometimes throw themselves on the wire so others could run over them. On one occasion they got in and overran positions on OP hill. In the morning we went up and turfed them out, killed the lot of them. In the dark the jackals would come and eat the bodies on the wire. The crows would come by day.

Major Alexander Harper
94 Column, 4th/9th Gurkha Rifles
We sent one party with machine guns to attack the village the Japs were using. But they came after us with superior force. We would have had to have a pitched battle, and this was something we tried to avoid unless one held an airstrip from which to evacuate casualties. So we withdrew that night without many casualties and joined up with 49 Column.

At this stage I was told to leave and fly to Broadway, the main stronghold, and take command of the 3rd Battalion there, the stronghold garrison, because the CO had gone sick.

We had made a little airstrip just across the Chinese border on some flat fields. We flew out in American L-1s and L-5s. I went in the last one and we landed at Broadway without any problems.

Private William Merchant
20 Column, Commando Platoon, 1st Battalion, Lancashire Fusiliers
On one occasion the Japanese got in to an OP behind us. In the morning we turfed them out. We threw grenades in the weapon pits and bunkers they occupied.

Our latrine trench was about eighty feet long with just a pole over it. It was full of maggots. One of our chaps was equipped with a flame-thrower; he emptied the fuel into the latrine to get rid of the maggots, sat on the pole, and chucked a match in after lighting a cigarette. He was so badly burned he had to be flown out. We thought it a huge joke at the time.

Private John Mattinson
20 Column, Commando Platoon, 1st Battalion, Lancashire Fusiliers
The Japanese attacks on White City were massive. We had three rings of wire round the place, and machine guns. I had a 2-inch mortar and a rifle. I used to fire one illuminating then one HE, one illuminating, one HE.

We used mortar bombs or shells that had been damaged in air drops and were unfit for firing, and attached explosives to them; made them into booby traps.

The Japs would shout during their attacks. Things like 'Thik Hai Johnny', which is Urdu for 'It's all right'. We used to shout back at them.

One night I was filling a gap where two of my friends had got killed. I was sat in the slit with my Bren, and shouting, 'Come on you yellow bastards,' and a voice behind me was shouting the same. I thought it was some of the blokes in other bunkers, but it was someone standing behind me. I said, 'Get down, you stupid bastard! Are you tired of living?'

He said, 'All right, it is only me'; it was Calvert.

Private William Merchant
20 Column, Commando Platoon, 1st Battalion, Lancashire Fusiliers
The Japs would shout at us, trying to draw our fire. They attacked using Bangalore torpedoes. My job was to fire grenades from an EY rifle at the Japanese from a small slit trench at night. I used to spend all day priming grenades. One night I fired over a hundred grenades. The Japs came across the paddy banging and shouting. I was wounded in the back with shrapnel. My mate had been wounded earlier, so I was the odd one out. The sergeant used to say, 'Wait until someone is killed, and you can muck in with his mate.' The trouble was that most seemed to get killed or wounded in pairs because they shared the same slit trench.

Lieutenant Peter Taylor
45 Column, 45th Reconnaissance Regiment
Rumours were flying around that we were going to be flown out. But not a bit of it, we were loaned to 77 Brigade, Mike Calvert's block at White City. Bernard Fergusson thought we would be flown in to the White City, but Mike Calvert was under the impression to the contrary. So ourselves, the Gurkhas and the Lancashire Fusiliers were told to attack the Japs who were attacking the White City.

Major Charles Carfrae
Officer Commanding 29 Column, 10th Battalion, Nigeria Regiment
Still the battalion did not arrive. Eventually a chap called Jerry Bladen, the recce platoon commander of our sister column, came in to the block, and told us that our two columns were lying up in the jungle a couple of miles away. All the wireless sets had broken down, and although the CO had heard the noise from the White City he could not find out what was going on. As he didn't know who was in possession, he sent Jerry Bladen to find out.

Our next step was to rejoin our battalion, led by Jerry Bladen. We learned that we were no longer to be garrison battalion, but to join in attacking the Japs investing White City from the south. With the rest of the striking force we occupied a deserted village within range of the Japanese attacking White City. The Lancashire Fusiliers and Gurkhas attacked the Japanese, and Peter Vaughan with his column went off to attack Mawlu, a village occupied by the Japs south of White City. We did very little, occupied a nearby village, of no particular significance as a foot on the ground. A lot of wounded Gurkhas came in and we sent them by bullock cart to where a light plane strip had been made.

Lieutenant Peter Taylor
45 Column, 45th Reconnaissance Regiment

We were still following jungle warfare tactics, moving in single file although we weren't in jungle. I was behind the leading scouts. Suddenly we were fired on. We managed get across a chaung and then we were held up. No one else got over, so we were told to withdraw. I was told to go back to where we had dropped our packs in the charge of some Nigerians.

On the way back, with about half a dozen men, I came across a corporal giving water to a sergeant who had been shot in the head, he was blinded. This corporal had not deserted him, some people just buggered off. I was able to take him on with me.

Major Charles Carfrae
Officer Commanding 29 Column, 10th Battalion, Nigeria Regiment

At nightfall we received orders from a galloper to move. We assembled everybody and were ready to move when we received orders from another galloper to go back to our positions. We were all going back when there was a burst of automatic fire and two grenades went off very close. I was alarmed. But nothing more happened. We sat it out.

At dawn we heard a single shot, and soon a platoon commander came in and said there were two dead Japs near, and his best corporal had been killed. This corporal and a Bren gunner had blundered into the two Japs in the night. The Bren gunner had despatched them. The platoon commander took us to the spot. The single shot had been the platoon commander finishing off one of the Japs who was wounded and had tried to throw a grenade at him.

I collected a party of Africans to view the corpses so they could see what the Japs looked like. This went down well because two Japs had been killed and for the loss of only one African. The only person who was unnerved was the African sergeant major, he roared like a bull on the parade ground, but was virtually useless for the rest of the campaign.

The next day Calvert was to make another attack on the Japanese attacking the White City. Our column was to set an ambush on the road leading to White City. At four o'clock in the afternoon a truck came along. I intended to fire my Very pistol to set off the ambush when the truck was opposite me, but someone fired a PIAT before it got there. The bomb exploded on the ground, and the troops jumped off the truck and ran off into the jungle. I was furious.

The next day at dusk we heard several lorries grinding slowly towards us from the north, very slowly, with Japs walking ahead, probing the road for mines. When they were directly opposite us, within feet, this time the Very light went off at exactly the right moment. The leading vehicle was in flames, and after I had blown my whistle to stop the firing, you could hear the Japs groaning.

I sent out a couple of platoons to mop up. We lost about four or five dead, but the Japs lost forty-two. We had hit six trucks. I got my soldiers to pull the bodies out of the trucks and we laid them all beside the road. We had three prisoners – I told the Africans not to kill them. The Africans were very puzzled at this. But as I was telling them this, there were loud shouts behind me. A Jap NCO had shaken off the hands dragging him from the lorry thinking he was dead, and was brandishing a bayonet trying to shove it into the nearest African. His tunic was stiff with caked blood. One of my British sergeants shot him dead with a pistol.

Lieutenant Peter Taylor
45 Column, 45th Reconnaissance Regiment
We had one more action. We were ordered to Broadway, about two or three days' march away. We bumped into some Japanese, and everybody was very jumpy, and fled. I and three others found some Nigerians and put them on the right track to find our column.

After the first show after Thetkegyin everybody thought I was a goner, but I turned up, and then after this action, I turned up again. We arrived at Broadway and were flown out. We were emaciated, after living on K-rations. You didn't know you were exhausted until you saw someone else. Marching in was a waste of time. The chaps who flew in did lots before we even arrived. We could have flown in.

Colour Sergeant Harold Atkins
21 Column, 2nd Battalion, Queen's Royal Regiment
The brigadier and higher HQ decided that 16 Brigade had shot their bolt. We had spent February to May on operations. We were told to make our way to Broadway and be flown out to India. This took five or six days over quite mountainous terrain. We passed quite close to the Mawlu block, the White City.

Eventually we arrived at Broadway, and were given permission to use food stocks there. The column was flown out in Dakotas over the next two or three days. We were in not too good shape. We were tired, it was nerve-wracking, one very rarely spoke above a whisper. There was always uncertainty: was one going to be ambushed or not?

Lieutenant Arthur Binnie
Officer Commanding Blaine Detachment (Bladet)
We cleaned ourselves up and left for Aberdeen. We were climbing up a slope in light jungle when we were fired on. This shook us up a bit. We could see very little. John Urquhart was hit on his compass that was over his kidney, and a bullet grazed him just over his left nipple. We eventually managed to break contact. The muleteer I had punished was hit in the knee; we carried him to Aberdeen, where a plane arrived to take us out. We got in, and after about half an hour sitting on the ground the American pilot came and said, 'Say you boys, I guess we have trouble with the engine here. If you'd like to wait we can fix it in an hour or two. In the meantime there is another plane over there, would you rather go in that one?' You have never seen people scamper so quickly from one plane to another. Having survived so far the idea of flying in a plane with a doubtful engine didn't appeal at all. We very valiantly rushed to the other plane, and got taken to Shillong, a lovely hill station in Assam.

We drank a lot of booze, and had a riotous party. I went to bed and woke up thinking my God this a hangover of all hangovers. I tried to get up, but had to get back, my head was thumping as if it was being hit by hammers. I told my batman I was ill. He got me to hospital. I was unconscious for three days with cerebral malaria. One does not normally survive that, in the condition I was in. I was given intravenous quinine.

When I came to I asked about my troops. Every single one of them was in hospital with some malady or other.

MARCH NORTH TO HELP STILWELL

Private William Merchant
20 Column, Commando Platoon, 1st Battalion, Lancashire Fusiliers
By now I was ill with malaria. They gave me twenty mepacrine tablets. I was delirious. They thought I might have cerebral malaria. The brigade was going to take Mogaung, but I wasn't fit to march. They took me to a slit trench by the strip to fly me out to Aberdeen, and on from there to India. Every time the pilot tried to take off, the Japs shelled the strip. So they carried me, a sergeant who had lost both legs, and a West African without an arm, back to the slit trench. Eventually they left us in the plane, and when there was a lull the American pilot who returned to the trench dashed out and took off. When we landed at Aberdeen it was attacked by Japanese bombers. They left me because I couldn't run for cover. The next day I was flown out to Sylhet. I was there for almost a week and given liquid quinine. I weighed just under eight stone.

Lieutenant Richard Rhodes-James
Cipher Officer, HQ, 111 Brigade
After carrying out demolition operations we were sent further north to attempt to replicate what 77 Brigade had done in the south of the area: set up a block to sever the Japanese communications with their forces fighting Stilwell's Chinese. We chose the wrong position. It was only able at a distance to block the railway. It was too near the enemy front line, whereas we were meant to be operating in rear areas. It was itself surrounded by country which could easily be occupied by the enemy and dominate our position.

Jack Masters recced the position. It may be he was hustled into holding there by higher command, and possibly there was nothing better. The position was on a range of hills overlooking the railway valley.

Major Desmond Whyte, RAMC
Medical Officer, HQ, 111 Brigade
We had air drops of barbed wire and began to prepare a landing strip outside the wire. The enemy attacked on the second night. When day broke the wire was littered with Japanese corpses. In the heat of the day the corpses swelled and stank, limbs putrefied, and millions of flies came in from the jungle. The

Richard Rhodes-James.

next night the Japs attacked in the same place again, broke through in one or two places, but were thrown out. They came the next night, same again. We got no sleep. Enemy planes attacked us. My dressing station began to fill up.

Then we had three days without attacks. The Dakotas came in, the strip having been levelled with a small bulldozer landed by glider. The Dakotas brought four 25-pounder guns. The enemy let us alone. We got in two AA guns. Then we heard the Jap 100-mm and 105-mm guns ranging on our position. The USAAF couldn't find the enemy gun positions. The Japs plastered our positions. We couldn't spare anyone to sortie and destroy the guns. The dressing station was hit. The monsoon broke with heavy rain. When a thunderstorm hit us, the mules stampeded. There was death and misery everywhere.

Pilot Officer Joe Simpson
194 Squadron, RAF

The technique for dealing with Japanese fighters in daylight was to stay in cloud if you were flying at height. When below cloud, fly low, right at tree-top level. If the fighter gets close, close one engine and do a steep turn. But most of the time we had RAF fighters to keep the Japs busy. Our biggest problem was the weather, particularly cu-nims stuffed into grey cloud so you couldn't see them, as well as poor maps and no navigational aids. We developed good techniques for overcoming these. You took the maximum possible fuel, and if the DZ was covered by cloud, you stooged around, until a hole appeared, and went in to drop. There were few aborted drops.

I crashed at Blackpool one night. As I was in the circuit, I could see a lot of people going round again. I thought, I won't do that. So I dragged it in at sixty-eight knots, got to the end of the runway over a huge tree and plonked the aircraft down. The undercarriage on the port side cracked and caught fire, while I belted down the runway holding it up on one wheel. At the end I swung it off to the left, clear of the runway. As we came to a stop the aircraft was getting hot. We all got out of the hatch in the roof, because the load had shifted, blocking the way to the door. I remembered we had the mail on board, right by the door, so I got a chap to give me a leg up so I could snatch the mail bags from outside.

They didn't clear the very end of the runway because the bulldozer broke down. I hit a mound of earth, which they had left unflattened.

Lieutenant Neville Hogan
Burma Rifles, attached 111 Brigade

I was flown into Blackpool. At about ten o'clock at night I was at the airstrip and a sergeant came along, called out our names and we emplaned in a Dakota. I prayed the plane wouldn't take off because of the weather. But we did take off. Watching the faces of my platoon, every one was scared of the unknown. Down we came; there were guides on the airstrip to lead us to our defensive positions round the airstrip.

The next morning a sergeant from the Cameronians gave our NCOs the fields of fire, and pointed out the water points, and where the enemy were on the other side of the airstrip.

We had one young officer straight out from England who had volunteered for the Burma Rifles, dead keen to go into action. That night the Japs attacked and he got shot through the penis, the right testicle and the bullet lodged in his right thigh; his first night of action. He was flown out.

Our job was to defend the airstrip. Not long after this the Japanese started attacking across the airfield with bayonets fixed, and the Bofors guns were firing over open sights.

Lieutenant Richard Rhodes-James
Cipher Officer, HQ, 111 Brigade

Every bombardment we had about twenty people killed. We were slowly pounded to bits. When our aircraft were overhead their artillery didn't fire in order not to reveal their positions. They then mounted infantry attacks. A fresh battalion, the 3rd/9th Gurkhas, arrived to help, under a very good CO.

Lieutenant Colonel Alexander Harper
Commanding Officer, 3rd/9th Gurkha Rifles

At Broadway I took command of 3rd/9th Gurkhas. They were not a Chindit battalion but had been commandeered by Wingate to act as garrison, and had not undergone the training. However, we were now told that Broadway was to be abandoned.

Stilwell had been complaining that we were not doing enough to help him. He had two Chinese divisions coming down the Ledo Road. So we were told to stop what we were doing and move into closer contact with his lot. We were to move further north to a new position called Blackpool, which the bulk of 111

Brigade were holding to block the railway and road north to Myitkyina.

After giving the battalion a few days' training in moving about the jungle, which they did perfectly well, we moved off to join 111 Brigade and arrived after an uneventful march. Originally we were told to split into two columns like the rest of the Chindits, but this was changed and we were told to operate as a complete battalion.

Major Percival Leathart
Officer Commanding D Company, 3rd/9th Gurkha Rifles, ex-77 Brigade, now 111 Brigade

We got to Blackpool after several days' march. We heard and saw Japanese mortars and artillery crumping down on the block. The CO decided that we would spread out and march straight in across the open paddy and hope for the best. It worked: we got in without any difficulty.

The commander was Jack Masters. The first time I saw him he was wearing nothing but a pair of shorts made from an old parachute.

We were there for several very unpleasant days. The Japanese attacks were vigorous despite heavy casualties. The block was a mess of Jap corpses outside, and inside the stench of death and latrines. I took over positions in the stronghold from a British battalion, can't remember which. When I jumped into a slit trench to check the field of fire before I put anyone in it, there was a soldier in the trench looking out. He didn't take any notice of me. I tapped him on the shoulder, and he toppled over. He had rigor mortis. I don't know how long he had been dead. Nobody seemed to know he was there.

Lieutenant Neville Hogan
Burma Rifles, attached 111 Brigade

After a day or two, I was summoned by Jack Masters. I was told to take a patrol of the King's Own across the Namkwin Chaung up the hills to meet the Nigerian Regiment of 3rd West African Brigade who were cutting steps up the steep hillside. We ran into an ambush so I didn't make contact with the Nigerians, and we were ordered back to the block. On my way I was joined by Captain Kershaw with a platoon of the King's. He took command of the two platoons. He sent my platoon back to the Namkwin Chaung to look for a crossing. I crawled through elephant grass and lantana to the Chaung, and the other side, about thirty yards away, the enemy was rustling about. We all took cover. I said, 'Don't fire until the order.' All of a sudden there was movement, followed by fire, and we fired back. A cultured English voice could be heard asking what the ammunition state was. It was a chap called Tony Gowan, a Burma Rifle officer, who we were firing at. 'Cease fire, cease fire,' I shouted, ran across the river, and embraced Tony. We sat down and counted what casualties we had. I had one chap shot in the heel of his boot. Not good, considering how much ammunition we fired.

We returned to Kershaw, and found that we were evacuating Blackpool.

Lieutenant Colonel Walter 'Scottie' Scott
Commanding Officer, 81 and 82 Columns, 1st Battalion, King's Regiment (Liverpool)

It was a poor site and eventually Jack Masters was ordered to evacuate it. My battalion formed the rearguard. It was no fault of Jack Masters, or those that served under him, that we had to hand it to the Japanese.

In the closing minutes we were fighting hand-to-hand with the Japs in the block. Colonel Thompson of the King's Own and myself had two small parties of three or four men each. Right in the middle of the block there was a tree. Although it had lots of branches blown off, it was a solid tree. Behind it stood two lieutenant colonels throwing grenades up towards where the Japanese were trying to come down the slope. But the grenades rolled back without hurting the Japanese. Colonel Thompson was firing round the left side of the tree, and I was firing round the right-hand side. All of a sudden there was a 'whumph', and Colonel Thompson went down with a wound in his left shoulder. I bent down to pull him in and I was hit. Something was gushing down my leg. I put my hand down, it wasn't blood; my water bottle had been hit.

Major Desmond Whyte RAMC
Medical Officer, 111 Brigade

We managed to cut the wire in the north, and as the barrage lifted we began to move out through the wire, with a rearguard holding the enemy off, in a series of fallback positions, we fought them back. Before we left we gave a lethal dose of morphia to those so desperately badly wounded that we could not take them with us so they would not fall into Jap hands alive. The others, some of them blinded, we walked and carried out. We had to climb a mound of at least one thousand feet in full view of the enemy. They did not follow us up. There was only one possible explanation; they had had such a mauling. Four days of nightmare followed.

Lieutenant Neville Hogan
Burma Rifles, attached 111 Brigade

We helped carry the wounded. There was a British sergeant with his boots on his hands, dragging both wounded legs behind him, but still giving orders to his men.

My Karens were marvellous, very cheerful. They knew what roots and leaves could be eaten. They brought me a mess tin of something that tasted like Bovril. I asked what it was and they told me it was boiled up roots. We took some of it to the sick and wounded.

We marched to Mokso Sakan, and set up an all-round defence perimeter.

Major Percival Leathart
Officer Commanding D Company, 3rd/9th Gurkha Rifles, ex-77 Brigade, now 111 Brigade

Halfway over the mountains we came across the West Africans, who were walking about with nothing on, a good way to keep your clothes clean in the mud. They were very helpful, but the Gurkhas were rather shocked, as they are very prudish about being naked.

We arrived at Indawgyi Lake, and had to re-equip with air drops. The casualties were all lying there under temporary shelters. But someone came up with the idea of landing Sunderland flying boats on the lake, and over a number of days the casualties were taken out by the Sunderlands.

One day I saw a herd of wild elephants when I went to the top of a hill to look at some birds. When I told my friends that I had just seen a most wonderful sight, referring to the elephants, one of them said, 'We have heard something even better, we have just heard over the radio about the D-Day landings in Normandy.'

Lieutenant Colonel Alexander Harper
Commanding Officer, 3rd/9th Gurkha Rifles

The British battalions were completely exhausted by now, and had both sick and wounded. Wingate had believed that we could not stay in for more than three months and we eventually were in for five and the rations were inadequate. This sort of operation was not intended for pitched battles because without an airstrip you could not evacuate sick or wounded. If you went sick on the march, you were left behind, so you kept going.

We marched further north of Indawgyi Lake in order to attack the road nearer Mogaung. That took some days. The ground was in a terrible state. We took twelve hours to cover a track seven miles long. Another battalion later took three days to complete the journey on that same track.

Major Percival Leathart
Officer Commanding D Company, 3rd/9th Gurkha Rifles, ex-77 Brigade, now 111 Brigade
A few days later, we were told to march north towards Mogaung. The Japs were using a stream flowing into the Indawgyi Lake as an approach route, and we were ordered to go to a village on this little stream where the Japs were supposed to have a position and we marched off and I decided to attack at dawn. We set up a base and had an evening meal, before creeping up to this village in darkness. We spent a most uncomfortable night being bitten by mosquitoes. In the morning we sent one platoon in one direction, and one in another, as stops. I, with the central platoon, went into the village. The platoon on the right came into contact with some Japs apparently coming into the village and had a bit of a battle. A section commander was hit, and I went to see if I could do anything for him. But he died. I went back into the centre of the village, with my Gurkha officer, to see what was going on. Suddenly there was a loud bang, and I was almost knocked off my feet by something hitting my left arm. I looked down and saw my forearm hanging down, with a lot of blood. My Gurkha officer said, 'I have also been hit.'

In fact he hadn't, a bit of my ulna had flown off and hit him in the chest, damaging him slightly. He then recovered and put a tourniquet on me. My orderly, who had seen where the Jap had fired from rushed into the jungle and killed the fellow with a kukri. After that I had moments of unconsciousness.

I was very weak. The Gurkhas carried me. From time to time they were engaged in skirmishes with the Japs. They could have left me but of course they didn't. Eventually we got back to the doctor. He treated me with sulpha powder. The battalion then moved on, leaving me with my orderly and a small escort. My orderly looked after me, built a hut and a bamboo bed. He gave me morphine injections, and actually made a bed pan out of a kerosene can. His service to me was exceptional and wonderful. The men with us went out into the rice paddy and constructed an airstrip. The battalion had sent a wireless message to have me picked up. One day an L-5 came in and flew me to an American base near Mogaung, where I was flown in a Dakota to Assam.

Lieutenant Colonel Alexander Harper
Commanding Officer, 3rd/9th Gurkha Rifles

We moved again and attacked a position on hill 2171 on 9 July 1944. This task was given to my battalion, which was the fittest. As CO I followed up B Company who carried out the frontal attack while C Company came in from a flank. We captured it and held it against further Japanese attacks. The commander of C Company, Major Frank Blaker, a gallant, aggressive and dashing officer, charged a machine gun and it got him and he was killed, but his example kept the momentum of the attack going. The attack was so successful we had few other casualties: twenty or thirty.

If you took up a position that threatened the Japanese, they seemed to think they had to attack it or they were 'dishonoured'. And they would throw in attacks from a tactically unsound direction, sometimes again and again. We let them do this for about a week. Although we took casualties from their mortars and artillery, we held them. We had improved their positions, we had wire dropped to us and made a very strong position.

We then marched off to Mogaung.

Lieutenant Arthur Binnie
Blaine Detachment (Bladet)

I was sent back to base and Blaine was there to receive us. I had lost three stone. When I was fit I was told to train twelve others to lead flame-thrower operators, and flown to Myitkyina, and on by light plane to Mogaung to play a part in the battle of Mogaung, where Calvert was about to take the town. We were quickly involved with what was left of a company of King's commanded by Fred Reeman, who I knew quite well. We were to go by night into a village that was holding up Calvert's advance to Mogaung. We were to spread fire here and there. The troops behind us thought it was great. We went in under our own mortar barrage to keep the Japs down, they were all in bunkers in this village. We never saw sight of them. We were told to advance in front of the company of King's, and to 'turn the f . . . . ing lights on'. They were very happy to have the flame-throwers in front of them. It was a fantastic sight, the whole village in flames. We went through the village with twenty or thirty yards of flame shooting out in front.

The Japs were in bunkers and fired along the line of the flame, so the troops behind shouted, 'Put out the f . . . . ing lights.' It seemed to have a good effect on the Japs anyway, and many of them ran off. I was blown up by a Jap grenade, and had little bits of grenade through my trousers in my legs. It did not hurt much, and I got up and carried on.

The poor CSM of the King's was shot in the head and killed, a wonderful guy who had been through the whole operation. I then realised that my right eye wasn't seeing properly. I went to the doctor, and he seemed to take my eye problem seriously. I was in a queue with Field Marshall Wavell's son, who had had a hand blown off.

Brigadier Michael Calvert
Commanding 77 Brigade
When we captured Mogaung, we heard on the BBC that the Americans and Chinese had captured Mogaung. So I sent a message saying, 'The Americans and Chinese have captured Mogaung. 77th Brigade is proceeding to take umbrage.'

When I was ordered to move to Myitkyina, still in Japanese hands, I closed down my wirelesses for fourteen days and marched out. I was summoned to Stilwell's HQ at Shaduzup to explain my insubordination. He said, 'You send very strong signals, Calvert.'

I said, 'You should see the ones my brigade major won't let me send.'

I hit the right note, because he roared with laughter. From then on we got on very well. He didn't realise we had done the glider-borne invasion, didn't realise we'd blocked the railway at White City for almost five weeks, four of them against repeated Japanese attacks. He didn't realise my brigade had not only been decimated but had had other bits taken off to help other brigades. We had no artillery; he didn't realise these things.

He kept on saying, 'Why wasn't I told? Is this true?'

His staff admitted it was.

Captain Donald McCutcheon
40 Column, 3rd/4th Gurkha Rifles
American command under Stilwell was very badly coordinated. We got the

Brigadier Calvert, talking to Lieutenant Colonel Shaw at Mogaung. Major Lumley in singlet looks on.

MH 7287

impression that American senior officers had no idea of how lightly we were equipped and therefore we were ordered to attack strongly dug-in Japanese positions with no support and not enough ammunition; the attacks failed.

On one occasion we had air support, we were told that the bombers were flown by Chinese. Instead of flying in the way we asked for, across our front, they came over us, and dropped the bombs far too close to us. It is very unnerving to see the bomb doors open and the bombs apparently coming straight for one. Luckily they missed.

Eventually we were all pretty exhausted by these fruitless attacks. A lot of chaps were flown out, and I found myself commanding about forty men that were left.

My CO was killed. We were forming up to attack a village and had moved up in four groups, the intention was that on arrival the assaulting troops would go in, all groups together. As 2i/c I was moving in the rear. We were not expecting any opposition on the move, but I heard on the radio that the CO had been shot, and I was called to take over. He had been called up to the lead when the column hit opposition. Unfortunately he was jumped by a small patrol of Japanese who shot him dead. As I suspected something like this might have happened, myself and my orderly went forward, you always moved in pairs in the jungle. My orderly had a grenade in his hand, suddenly I saw a couple of Japanese who started blazing off at us. I threw myself into a bush and started firing back. Then I heard an enormous crump close by, the orderly had thrown a grenade into the bush, fortunately it missed me but shook up the Japs. We went on forward and there was the colonel lying dead.

Then the fun started, like a cavalry charge, a horde of Japs all shouting 'Banzai', a big party of Japs who had come out from Myitkyina swept towards us. But by this time we had formed into little defensive squares so we didn't suffer much.

Towards the end we were not scared of the Japs. They never followed us into the jungle. They were not all that splendid jungle fighters, they were good fighters, but not jungle experts. They were very brave. At Myitkyina, against two Chinese divisions, they held out when most people would have given up or gone away.

My last contact with the Japanese was on a wooded hillock with an open glade leading down to a village called Maingna near Myitkyina on an island in the Irrawaddy which the Japanese used as a washing place. I was told to observe the area. We saw quite a lot of Japanese coming up, outnumbering my patrol. So I ordered a withdrawal, and I stood up, and felt a thump at the back of my head. I thought it was someone throwing stones. It was a bullet going through my hat which blew it off. Apart from a stiff neck I suffered no injury.

Lieutenant Richard Rhodes-James
Cipher Officer, HQ, 111 Brigade

We had a medical inspection at the insistence of Masters, and out of two thousand men in the brigade only one hundred and twenty-five were fit to carry on operations. Most of our casualties were sick, not battle casualties. Eventually Stilwell got the message and gave orders for us to be evacuated. We were flown out from Myitkyina, which had been captured by the Chinese under Stilwell.

Some people were never properly fit again. After being assembled after leave we were told there would be another operation, a glider-borne attack in the Rangoon area, but the powers that be saw sense, and we were disbanded. We weren't sorry.

Crisis Point
Kohima

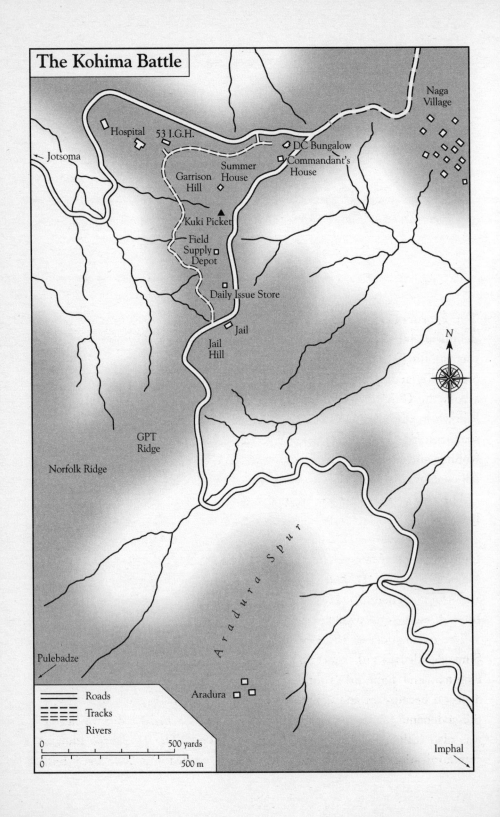

The Kohima Battle

Naga Village

Hospital

53 I.G.H.

← Jotsoma

DC Bungalow

Commandant's House

Summer House

Garrison Hill

Kuki Picket

Field Supply Depot

Daily Issue Store

Jail

Jail Hill

N

GPT Ridge

Norfolk Ridge

A r a d u r a   S p u r

Pulebadze ↙

Aradura

Roads

Tracks

Rivers

0   500 yards
0   500 m

Imphal ↘

I couldn't imagine that I would ever see England again, or even get out of
this battle. A feeling that set in with me was I couldn't care less if I get
killed. I accepted it. It wasn't fear.

In February 1944, reports from patrols and OPs on the Chindwin indicated that Lieutenant General Mutaguchi's Japanese Fifteenth Army was building up for an offensive aimed at the British bases in Assam; principally at Imphal, but also at Kohima. Mutaguchi's plan was to attack across the Chindwin on nine routes between Tamanathi in the north to Kalewa in the south. In a series of pincer movements, he would cut the road from the railhead at Dimapur to Imphal in several places, and capture Kohima and Imphal, his aim, as outlined in Chapter 2, being to prevent the Allies using the airfields in Assam to supply the Chinese.

The area was the responsibility of Lieutenant General G. A. P. Scoones's British IV Corps, the bulk of which was deployed well forward of Kohima and Imphal covering the main routes west from the Chindwin. The 17th Light Division (Major General D. T. Cowan) was in the south at Tiddim; Major General D. D. Gracey's 20th Division was at Tamu and Sittaung; and Major General O. L. Roberts's 23rd Division deployed north-east of Imphal, but also responsible for Kohima.

The commander of the Fourteenth Army, Lieutenant General William Slim, decided to pull back Scoones's IV Corps to the Imphal Plain and Kohima, and fight on ground of his own choosing. He arrived at this decision because in addition to patrol reports, he had access to ULTRA, the codename for the reading of Japanese (and German) radio traffic. He was also influenced by logistical considerations. The IV Corps lines of communication on this front ran through rugged jungle-covered hills, whereas east of the Chindwin the Japanese had comparatively good supply lines. By withdrawing, IV Corps would be falling back on well-stocked bases, shortening its lines of communications, while the Japanese would be stretching theirs to near breaking point through the difficult country west of the Chindwin that the British had abandoned. If Slim could hold the Japanese for two months the onset of the monsoon would make the Japanese supply lines almost impassable.

With the Japanese held up on the Imphal Plain, Slim, reinforced with formations from the Arakan and India, could destroy the Fifteenth Army. A potentially winning card in Slim's hand was air power. By now air supremacy had been wrested away from the Japanese. By using the two good airfields at Imphal and several smaller strips in the locality, as well as air-dropping supplies, Slim could ensure that even troops cut off by the enemy could fight on. Both Imphal and Kohima were already well stocked with supplies.

Mutaguchi took a chance on capturing the British stocks within three weeks to feed his troops, and tailored his logistic plans accordingly. Until he was able to seize the British supplies, his men would have to exist and fight with whatever they could carry on their backs, or on a small number of horses and mules, supplemented by meat on the hoof in the form of cattle that accompanied their columns.

To this day there is disagreement on whether or not Mutaguchi intended to stop at Imphal. He favoured pressing on into India, and with help from uprisings by Indian nationalists in India, throwing the British out. He thought this might induce the British to abandon the war against Japan, and that the Americans might do likewise; all highly speculative, and very much in line with Mutaguchi's improvisational approach to war.

A possible indicator of Mutaguchi's aspirations for exploiting into India was the inclusion of the 1st Indian National Army (INA) Division in his plans. The INA was ineffective in battle so Mutaguchi's motive for saddling himself with seven thousand useless mouths could only have been to use them for propaganda on arrival in India.

Although the fighting at Kohima and Imphal took place concurrently, I have dealt with events at Kohima first; not least, this was the key to Slim's plan. Indeed the Japanese nearly beat him to the draw here. While the 17th Division was still fighting its way north (covered in the next chapter), it became clear that instead of just one regimental group heading for Kohima and Dimapur, the whole of the Japanese 31st Division was coming this way. Kohima had a small garrison, but Dimapur none. If the Japanese besieged Kohima, the road to Imphal would be cut: dangerous, but not disastrous. Whereas Dimapur in enemy hands would end any hope of relieving Imphal, as well as threatening the whole of the Brahmaputra Valley, its airfields and the line of communication to India.

Accordingly, Slim changed the plan for the reinforcement of Imphal by the 5th Division, ordering its 161st Indian Infantry Brigade to be flown direct from the Arakan to Dimapur. He also asked for Lieutenant General M. G. N. Stopford's XXXIII Corps Headquarters and the British 2nd Division, both training in India, to be sent in. Stopford was to take over responsibility for clearing the road from Dimapur to Imphal, while Scoones concentrated on the battle around Imphal. Slim ordered that Kohima and Dimapur were not to fall.

Kohima was both the civil administrative centre of Nagaland, and a military supply depot, hospital and staging post, about a third of the way between Dimapur and Imphal. The names of features around Kohima reflect their military or civil use at the time. The road from Dimapur climbed in a curve round the 53rd Indian General Hospital (IGH) spur, and after passing the Deputy Commissioner's (DC's) Bungalow, it turned in a sharp hairpin to the south-west whence another road ran east to the village of Kohima. From the DC's Bungalow the road ran south along the Kohima ridge past Garrison Hill, the Kuki Picket, Field Supply Depot (FSD) Hill, Daily Issue Store (DIS) Hill, Jail Hill (for civil prisoners) and General Purpose Transport (GPT) Ridge. Most of the personnel at Kohima were administrative.

THE JAPANESE ATTACK

Ursula Graham-Bower
Naga Watch and Ward Scheme and Women's Auxiliary Corps (India) (WACI)
I was educated at Roedean before the war. My parents could not afford to send me to Oxford, so instead I went to live among the Naga tribes and carried out

ethnographic work. When war broke out I joined the Women's Auxiliary Corps (India) and in August 1942 helped start a Watch and Ward scheme in Nagaland. My job was to collect information on the Japanese and send it back by runner.

But it had its problems. There was no hope I could conceal myself in the Naga village. First of all I am too tall, and light skinned, my hair was sun-bleached: I was blonde. In Burma when British officers were occasionally hidden, the Japs tortured the villagers until the officer gave himself up.

I fixed up with Namkia, the headman, that I wasn't going to be taken alive. So I would shoot myself, and he would take my head in, if the pressure on the villagers became unendurable.

Lieutenant Colonel Gerald Cree
Commanding Officer, 2nd Battalion, West Yorkshire Regiment

My battalion, having been flown to Assam from Arakan with the remainder of the 5th Division, was diverted to Dimapur instead of being sent to Imphal. I motored to Kohima, and had just completed putting together a defence plan agreed with Colonel Richards, the garrison commander, when Major General Ranking, commanding 202 Lines of Communication Area came in and ordered me back towards Dimapur to hold the road in a series of company detachments.

This was a most foolish thing to do. The road was jam-packed with refugees trying to get out of Kohima and others trying to get in. If I split the battalion into four detachments over forty miles of road, I'd have no control over them, couldn't have affected the battle at all, and would have been mopped up in detail. I disobeyed and we went back to Milestone 10 and settled there for the night.

Suddenly the general appeared. I thought, now I'm for it. However, he didn't mind at all. I explained what I felt, and he agreed, and said, 'Tomorrow go back to Kohima and help defend it.' So back we went, took up positions around the place and prepared for a long siege.

I occupied the matron's quarters in the former hospital. We found a harmonium there, which greatly pleased our padre, so we lifted it, and it accompanied us for the rest of the war. After a couple of days, orders came that the West Yorks were to move to Imphal, and transport was sent for us. Colonel Richards was rather dismayed, being left naked again without anybody to defend him, except the odds and sods of the convalescent depot. I couldn't have been more pleased.

The vehicles arrived. We piled on to them, and went off down the road to Imphal like scalded cats. We were the last people to get through. We passed some military policemen on the way, and I asked them what they were doing. They replied, 'Directing traffic.'

Major Harry Smith
Officer Commanding HQ Company, 4th Battalion, Queen's Own Royal West Kent Regiment
The whole division was moved to Assam. Two brigades of 5 Div were flown in to Imphal, and our brigade, 161, flown to Dimapur to defend Kohima. No one imagined at the time that Kohima was in any danger. We were told that only scattered Japanese forces were in the area. We thought that Kohima was unapproachable from Burma because of the huge jungles intervening. We embarked in our aeroplanes at Dohazari, in a light-hearted manner. Quite a lot of us had never flown in an aeroplane before. We loaded our Dakota with ammo and stores to the extent that he couldn't get the tail of the plane off the ground. He was an American pilot and he said, 'Sorry fellows, shift some of that junk further forward and I'll try again.' We did and he took off. After a short flight, we landed at Dimapur on a flooded airfield, and wound our way by truck up the road to Kohima. We were totally ignorant of what we were to do, but glad to get up to five thousand feet, out of the heat of the plains. We were expecting only very light Japanese forces.

CSM Herbert Harwood
C Company, 4th Battalion, Queen's Own Royal West Kent Regiment
We got to Kohima and were allocated our positions. We had no sooner got organised than we were trucked back to Dimapur.

THE SIEGE BEGINS

Ursula Graham-Bower
Naga Watch and Ward Scheme and Women's Auxiliary Corps (India) (WACI)
We were suddenly in the middle of no-man's-land, utterly bewildered, hardly armed, sharing no-man's-land with an unknown number of Japanese. We had

a very dodgy three weeks, not knowing what was going on, but trying to find out and pass back intelligence.

Major Harry Smith
Officer Commanding HQ Company, 4th Battalion, Queen's Own Royal West Kent Regiment

We left the meagre garrison at Kohima and various odd bodies from the convalescent depot. No sooner were we back at Dimapur, than orders came through for the brigade to move up once more, but by this time the leading Japanese spearheads were on the outskirts of Kohima. As we wound up the road again, we met crowds of frightened non-combatants. The battalion was leading the brigade column and as it approached Kohima it came under heavy fire from machine guns and artillery. Getting out of the trucks as quickly as possible the battalion sprinted up the hlll overlooking the roads at the bottom and established itself in positions already allotted to it. The other two battalions and Brigade HQ stayed on the road because there was no room for it on Garrison Hill.

Major John Winstanley
Officer Commanding B Company, 4th Battalion, Queen's Own Royal West Kent Regiment

Garrison Hill was a pleasant pine-covered hill round which there was a 'ladies' walk'. On a spur, which ran towards the main road, cut into the side of the hill was the District Commissioner's Bungalow. The District Commissioner, the DC, was an Indian Civil servant. Behind the bungalow was a clay tennis court. On our side of the court was a small clubhouse.

Private Leslie Crouch
Pioneer Platoon, 4th Battalion, Queen's Own Royal West Kent Regiment

Some of the lorries were set on fire by shellfire. All we had was our small packs and rifles, Brens etc. We went up the hill through the District Commissioner's Bungalow, past the tennis court. It was a lovely place when we first arrived. We got to our positions and dug trenches. We were above the tennis court, about a hundred yards away, on a steep bank.

Private Ivan Daunt
Pioneer Platoon, 4th Battalion, Queen's Own Royal West Kent Regiment
We started getting out of the trucks and getting our kit out. Mortar bombs and shells began falling around us. The drivers were screaming and hollering, and didn't know what to do. We got off the road and lay down in a ditch. We crawled up the hill and stuck it out until night time. We were told to go back and get our kit out of the trucks. Some were on fire.

We then moved up above the tennis court, and started digging in. We didn't know what was going on.

Major John Winstanley
Officer Commanding B Company, 4th Battalion, Queen's Own Royal West Kent Regiment
At first B Company were only observers on Kuki Picket. After five days, we were ordered to relieve A Company on the tennis court. My second-in-command, Tom Coath, was taken to command C Company, whose commander had been wounded, so I had myself, two officer platoon commanders, Victor King and Tom Hogg, and Sergeant Williams commanding the other platoon.

Our position was on the fringe of the tennis court and included a mound above the court occupied by my right-hand platoon, my middle platoon was in the clubhouse, with my left-hand platoon holding a bank that fell away from the tennis court. The tennis court was no-man's-land. On the other side the ground fell away; that's where the Japs were, only fifty yards away.

CSM Herbert Harwood
C Company, 4th Battalion, Queen's Own Royal West Kent Regiment
We went to DIS Ridge. We dug trenches and only just got them dug in time. The road went in front of DIS Ridge, and off to Imphal. Near us was Jail Hill, a bit higher than us. Next thing I knew was one of my blokes pointing out two Japs on Jail Hill. I opened fire on them, didn't hit. But it warned people the enemy was about. Nothing happened that night. Eventually the Japs got on to Jail Hill in strength.

The Japs made a frontal attack on our company, and we let them have it with grenades and Brens. They got into the many huts in the place and some of these caught fire. In the light of the fires, lots of Japs were killed by

213

Sergeant Tatum with a Bren, as they ran and jumped down to the road. By the time he had finished there was a big mound of bodies on the road.

Private Bert Wheeler
Stretcher-Bearer attached C Company, 4th Battalion, Queen's Own Royal West Kent Regiment
There was a lot of rock in the soil on the hill. You dug as deep as you could, unfortunately not deep enough, so you were half exposed when standing. I shared a slit with another stretcher-bearer.

There was nowhere to evacuate the casualties to. You just had to dress and treat them as best you could. If it was a superficial wound, you dressed it and the chap carried on. If it was serious you took him to the dressing station in HQ Company. The MO decided if he should go back to his company or stay lying around the dressing station.

You had to run the gauntlet between shells arriving. It wasn't healthy but you had to do it. If a salvo came over, you knew you had a couple of minutes before the next one. But it wasn't always easy to judge. As we were in such a confined space you only had to go about one hundred and fifty yards at most to collect a casualty. Someone would shout 'stretcher-bearers', and if you didn't hear it at once, it would be shouted along the line. You crawled out, and sometimes you had to crawl back with the stretcher, dragging it with you.

Sometimes you went out with a patrol. If a man was wounded seriously you had to bring him back using a fireman's lift. If the wound was too serious you had to use your revolver.

CSM Herbert Harwood
C Company, 4th Battalion, Queen's Own Royal West Kent Regiment
We were attacked two or three nights running. They didn't manage to shift us. Sometimes during the night you would hear them shout, 'Indian National Army, come over, you are surrounded.' The Japs were across the road on Jail Hill. After a heavy shelling, one solitary Jap came out in bandages. I imagine that they were trying to entice our medical people to go in and help him. At night it was possible to shoot your own side. Our colour sergeant, while bringing up rations, was shot by our own people.

The company commander was wounded and the second-in-command. Eventually the remnants of the company was made into a platoon, I was the platoon commander, and we were attached to D Company. In the end it got so tight, we had to withdraw and leave DIS Hill as part of drawing in the perimeter.

Major John Winstanley
Officer Commanding B Company, 4th Battalion, Queen's Own Royal West Kent Regiment
The perimeter shrank and shrank until it only included the tennis court and Garrison Hill where the final stand took place. The battle took place on the tennis court – we shot them on the tennis court, we grenaded them on the tennis court. We held the tennis court against desperate attacks for five days. We held because I had constant contact by radio with the guns and the Japs never seemed to learn how to surprise us. They used to shout in English as they formed up, 'Give up.' So we knew when an attack was coming in. One would judge just the right moment to call down gun and mortar fire to catch them as they were launching the attack, and by the time they were approaching us they were decimated. They were not acting intelligently and did the same old stupid thing again and again.

We had experienced fighting the Japs in the Arakan, bayoneting the wounded and prisoners. So whereas we respected the Afrika Korps, not so the Japanese. They had renounced any right to be regarded as human, and we thought of them as vermin to be exterminated. That was important – we are pacific in our nature, but when aroused we fight quite well. Our backs were to the wall, and we were going to sell our lives as expensively as we could. Although we wondered how long we could hang on, we had no other option. We had not thought of surrender at any level; we were too-seasoned soldiers for that. We couldn't taunt the Japanese back as we couldn't speak Japanese, but there were some JIFs on the other side and we taunted them in English.

Anonymous INA corporal
I joined the INA after hearing *Netaji*. The Japanese were not cruel to anyone. They said the Asians should fight for their independence, and all Asians should be independent. We were fully confident that the Japanese would hand independence to India, as they had done to the Burmese, the Malays, the Thais; all the Asians. The Japanese remained in Burma because Nehru said on the radio that he didn't need any help from outside.

Private Bert Wheeler
Stretcher-Bearer attached C Company, 4th Battalion, Queen's Own Royal West Kent Regiment

As the days passed the casualties built up and you had to step over them in the dressing station. They had no cover: luckily it was not monsoon time. It was under shellfire. Some wounded were killed, others were wounded a second time. The MO was operating under very primitive conditions. He sometimes ran out of dressings. You couldn't clean the wounds. Gangrene developed.

The terrain changed from being covered with trees to an open space and stumps, with no cover at all. Casualties were heavy. There were some dead you couldn't reach, close to the DC's Bungalow and tennis court.

Halfway through, we were out attending casualties, we saw a flash from a gun, and dived towards a slit trench. The chap I was with, another stretcher-bearer, was hit by shrapnel in the neck and killed instantly. I was lucky and caught shrapnel in the arm which damaged the muscles. I had no grip with that hand. I walked to the dressing station, putting a dressing on myself, and saw the MO. He said, 'I'm sorry there is nothing more I can do.' He inserted ointment in the wound, and covered it with a dressing; this saved my arm.

The dressing station was under fire. I changed my dressings as and when I could when dressings were available. You just sat around, and assisted the other stretcher-bearers using one arm: feeding the wounded, giving them a drink, wetting their lips, anything you could do. We were supplied by air, on a daily basis. Dressings were dropped as well as drugs and medicines. There was enough water for cooking and drinking, but not for washing or shaving. There was rum amongst the air drops which was very acceptable. Water was dropped in metal jerrycans by parachute.

As soon as you were killed and certified dead, your comrades dug a hole, wrapped you in a blanket if one was available, and the padre buried you.

Major Harry Smith
Officer Commanding HQ Company, 4th Battalion, Queen's Own Royal West Kent Regiment

Incessant shelling was the pattern of the place. It became extremely dangerous to walk about in daylight. On one occasion a Japanese infantry gun bombarded my positions at close range, so close that the shell arrived before you heard the report of the gun, very disconcerting. The Japanese took enormous casualties from the Brens, rifles and grenades of the battalion. Their attacks went on night after night, all night. The sheer weight of the attacks threatened to overwhelm the battalion. The outer part of the defences became piled up with Japanese corpses.

Major John Winstanley
Officer Commanding B Company, 4th Battalion, Queen's Own Royal West Kent Regiment

Besides Brens, the other weapon that was so effective were grenades used by Victor King's platoon who showered them with grenades as they formed up. As Kohima was a depot, we didn't lack grenades, but we were very short of 3-inch mortar bombs. We were supplied from the air, but much of the loads went to the Japs. They had captured British 3-inch mortars, and most of the mortar bombs dropped for our use fell into enemy hands.

We had a steady toll of casualties mainly from snipers. Showing yourself in daylight resulted in being shot by a sniper. They also used their battalion guns in the direct fire role, in morning and evening 'hates'. This caused mayhem among the wounded lying in open slit trenches on Garrison Hill. We heard that 2 Div were being flown in to relieve us, and could hear the sound of firing to our north, as the division fought its way down to us.

After five days I was relieved on the tennis court by the Assam Regiment and moved to Hospital Spur. The tennis court held; the Kuki Picket changed hands several times.

Major Harry Smith
Officer Commanding HQ Company, 4th Battalion, Queen's Own Royal West Kent Regiment

We very soon ran out of water when the Japanese cut the only piped supply. Luckily a spring was discovered near my company area, and hazardous trips had to be organised every night, most of which was taken up to the casualty centre which was under continual mortar fire.

The area became festooned with parachutes as medical supplies, ammunition and water were parachuted down.

The smell of death increased as the days passed and bodies decomposed. Day after day our hopes were dashed when expected relief did not arrive. We began to walk about like zombies because we had little chance of sleep. The

The tennis court and terraces of the District Commissioner's Bungalow at Kohima.

IND 3483

rifle companies on the perimeter were steadily pushed back as they were forced to give ground by overwhelming numbers of enemy.

The Japs had Urdu speakers with loudhailers who would shout mainly to the Indian gunners and sappers we had with us to surrender. None of them deserted.

2nd British Div was arriving at Dimapur and clearing the road to reach us, but it seemed to take a long time. The situation got graver and graver as our numbers diminished.

Lieutenant Trevor Highett
Officer Commanding Carrier Platoon, 2nd Battalion, Dorsetshire Regiment
When we arrived at Dimapur, the Japs were only forty miles away. There were huge supplies of stores, which nobody seemed too bothered about. There are few things more unpleasant than a base in a flap. It was full of people who never expected to fight, and who couldn't wait to get out. 'Take what you like,' they said, 'just give us a signature if you've got the time.' We were pretty arrogant in 2 Div and not impressed. I acquired two armoured cars, which proved very useful. We picked up masses of stores, ammo, food, drink etc. We could carry it in the carriers. The Dorsets and 2 Div weren't short of anything.

Private Tom Cattle
17 Platoon, D Company, 2nd Battalion, Dorsetshire Regiment
Taking just a few carriers, jeeps and water bowsers, we went on to join the battalion at Zubza on the road to Kohima, where all the divisional artillery was dug in and shelling the Japs. I rejoined D Company. We were reserve battalion and guarding the Div Artillery.

We were told that the Japanese had got as far as Kohima, and the troops defending Garrison Hill were the Royal West Kents and a few Burma Rifles and were cut off as the Japs had cut the road behind them, and they were being supplied by air.

Our division was trying to push up the road from Dimapur to Kohima cut out of the hillside, with a deep ravine one side and steep hill covered in thick jungle on the other. It was difficult to advance along this narrow road.

Major Harry Smith
Officer Commanding HQ Company, 4th Battalion, Queen's Own Royal West Kent Regiment
On the night of 19 April, it was arranged that the leading troops of 2 Div with tanks would relieve the West Kents. As I was about to make my way to battalion HQ to receive orders for the relief, a mortar bomb burst on the front of my trench and a fragment entered my head just above the cheek bone. It knocked me out cold. I was treated at the RAP, given a shot of morphia and ceased to know any more until early the next morning. I came to in time to see the leading troops of the Berkshires in their nice clean uniforms making their way up to the top of the hill, covered by a very heavy barrage of 2 Div's artillery down the road. Soon I was being helped down the hill to the waiting ambulances, together with the remnants of the battalion, who were filing down ragged, bearded, looking like scarecrows. Tanks were engaging enemy positions on the road.

I never thought we would be overwhelmed as the Japs were taking enormous casualties. I was taken to the hospital at Dimapur and had a restless night listening to the cries of the wounded.

Major John Winstanley
Commanding, B Company, 4th Battalion, Queen's Own Royal West Kent Regiment
The 4th Royal West Kents, the Assam Rifles and odds and sods defended Kohima against an entire Jap division in a fourteen-day siege.

THE RELIEVING FORCE BREAKS THROUGH TO KOHIMA

Major Francis 'Frankie' Boshell
Officer Commanding B Company, 1st Battalion, Royal Berkshire Regiment
My battalion was the first into Kohima, and my company was the leading company of the battalion. We took over from the 4th Royal West Kents who had had a terrible time. To begin with, I took over the area overlooking the tennis court, although only my left forward platoon could see the court. The Dorsets were responsible for the positions closest to the court itself. The lie of

the land made it impossible to move by day because of Japanese snipers. We were in Kohima for three weeks. We were attacked every single night. On the worst night they started at 1900 hours and the last attack came in at 0400 hours the next morning. They came in waves, like a pigeon shoot. Most nights they overran part of the battalion position, so we had to mount counter-attacks. When part of my right-hand platoon was overrun, we winkled them out with the bayonet. I lost two platoon commanders, but good sergeants took over, and did better. Water was short and restricted to about one pint per man per day, so we stopped shaving. Air supply was the key, but the steep terrain and narrow ridges meant that some of the drops went to the enemy. My company went into Kohima over one hundred strong and came out at about sixty.

Warrant Officer Deryck Groocock
194 Squadron, RAF

My worst incident took place on a supply drop north of Kohima. We were flying at 8,500 feet, the mountain tops went up to seven thousand feet, but there was a layer of thick cloud between us and them. Getting near where the DZ should have been, we couldn't see anything. I thought with a bit of luck we'll find a hole and go down, so I told the two wireless operators to get the load ready to drop; it was bags of rice by free-fall that day. They started to pile the bags of rice by the door. All of a sudden, the air speed started to drop off. The natural reaction is to put on more power, but this makes the problems worse because it puts the centre of gravity back and pulls the nose up. I put on more power, and the speed dropped. Suddenly she flipped into a spin. I knew we had fifteen hundred feet to go before hitting the mountains. We dropped straight into the cloud, descending at fifteen hundred feet per minute. The altimeter unwound past seven thousand feet, and I thought any moment now. I took the correct recovery action, opposite rudder and nose down, and we came out of the spin below cloud at 4,600 feet, with two bloody great peaks on either side of us reaching up into the cloud. We collected our wits.

The aircraft had been badly loaded to start with, and by stacking the rice by the door the aircraft's centre of gravity had been put out of limits. In the spin, it all fell forward putting the centre of gravity right, so the aircraft would fly OK. Fortunately no one had bailed out, because they couldn't get their parachutes on in time. We staggered along the valley, saw a column of smoke, it was the DZ – an absolute miracle. We dropped our load, the only aircraft out of twelve who made it that day. The others all turned back.

Private William Cornell
A Company, 2nd Battalion, Durham Light Infantry

After we took over from the West Kents, we were told we were to attack the Japanese. I thought, 'I've been OK up to now, now what?', because Lieutenant Connelly said it was going to be a nasty one. We were told that at 'five o'clock in the morning we are going to move out up this track here', and he drew a little sketch, and he said, 'We expect to meet the Japs somewhere near here, in a defensive position, and we are going to clear them out.' It was the Kuki Picket.

It was just getting light, and we started to move off up this hill, it was a very narrow track. We hadn't gone very far, Corporal Breedon was leading the section, behind him a lance/corporal. I was number one rifleman. There was a tremendous racket as a Japanese machine gun opened up. There was a terrible scream, it cut Corporal Breedon right in half. We couldn't get to him where he fell down the hill.

I couldn't imagine that I would ever see England again, or even get out of this battle. A feeling that set in with me was I couldn't care less if I get killed. I accepted it. It wasn't fear. The only thought was 'will I get wounded or will I get killed'. Right round me it was chaos, shouting and screaming; stretcher-bearers running about.

The word was passed that we were going to carry on to attack the Jap position. The jungle thinned out and I saw flashes of the Japanese firing at us. I thought it's now or never, the pace quickened, and I thought, 'In we go.' We started to run forward, I was all keyed up, rifle ready, grenades ready, and the next thing I knew was a tremendous bang, which seemed right underneath me. I was blown into the air, right up the bank, and landed on the ground, it was a mortar bomb, don't know why it didn't kill me. I found myself on my own, and thought, 'What do I do?' I crawled into a little bit of cover, I wasn't in pain. Then I felt something pouring down my leg, and thought, 'Is my leg off?' I moved my toes, and no they worked all right. I started investigating and it was water from my water bottle, punctured by a piece of shrapnel. If it hadn't been for my water bottle, it would have gone through me. There was just a gash in my body. I wasn't in pain. I took out my FFD and put it on. The battle was still going on. I thought would the Japanese come, would our troops come and pick me up?

I said to myself, keep yourself under cover, and don't move until you are sure that it was your own people. I had no water, and lay there for about two hours. On one occasion, 'ping', someone shot at me, I don't know who. I had no idea what was going on. Then a faint voice shouting, 'Corny, Corny, where are you?' It was a lad from my own home town, Tommy Hunter.

'I'm glad I found you Corny.'

'So am I'.

He had a look at me, and said. 'You will be all right.'

The next feeling was immense relief, you are wounded, not serious, but it will get you out of this for a bit.

Lance Corporal Henry Bell
Signaller, 2nd Battalion, Durham Light Infantry

The night I was with D Company on Garrison Hill, they came in shouting, 'Tojo Tojo,' throwing phosphorus grenades. I was in with the signallers and dying for a smoke, so I crawled under a blanket and lit a cigarette. The company commander, 'Tanky' Waterhouse shouted, 'Who's smoking?'

'Me, sir.'

'For God's sake light me one,' he replied.

C Company ahead of us were overrun, with heavy losses.

Company Sergeant Major Martin McLane
C Company, 2nd Battalion, Durham Light Infantry

I was woken by shouts from my company commander, Major Stock. Green phosphorus was pouring into one end of the trench. I was covered with it, which causes deep penetrating burns. I was rubbing the stuff off me with earth, then the Japs came in yelling and shouting. They were in among us and just ten yards away there was a fearsome-looking man waving a sword.

The ammunition stacked on Garrison Hill exploded and parachutes from supply drops hanging in the trees caught fire. We stuck out like sore thumbs. After fierce fighting we cleared the position. My company commander, the runners and the signallers were all dead. A shell had landed right in the hole where they were located.

Henry Bell as a sergeant.

Private Tom Cattle
17 Platoon, D Company, 2nd Battalion, Dorsetshire Regiment
We were now taking heavy casualties on Garrison Hill, and the Dorsets took over the 2 DLI positions. The only way up was on the road in carriers to a place called Mortuary Corner. Anything approaching this point came under Jap mortar and artillery fire. So carriers, in relays, each took about six men up to a point out of sight of the Japs spotting for their artillery and mortars, the carrier stopped, everyone out, and back to pick up some more. From the road Garrison Hill was almost perpendicular, the monsoon had started early and every step you tried to pull yourself up, you slid back, with all your kit. At the same time being sniped at, machine-gunned and mortared and shelled. We got to the top and were given our positions, the original positions dug by the Royal West Kents. There were bodies lying around. We scrambled into a slit, three of us, me, Lance Corporal Des Walford and someone else. There was only enough room for three of us, about eight feet long, two feet wide with a roof on it. Without the roof you couldn't have stayed long.

Our position looked down on to the continuation of the road to Imphal. It was very steep. To the right of us was Kuki Picket, which the Royal Welch Fusiliers were still trying to take. The Japanese to our left were dug in on the tennis court and the DC's Bungalow beyond. We were on the top of a ridge that ran out from Pulebadze, which was about seven thousand feet high. The ridge extended down from Kuki Picket to Garrison Hill, down on to the DC's Bungalow and the tennis court, to the road leading to Kohima village.

You couldn't get out of your trench in daylight, or the Japanese snipers would have you. So many shells and mortar bombs had hit the hill that all the trees were shattered and the stumps were draped with parachutes that had come down with supplies. It was a desolate and desperate situation.

Water was dropped in two-gallon cans. We were connected trench to trench by ropes, so we could pull supplies, water cans and ammunition across from one trench to another. On one occasion we were pulling a water can to our trench and it got caught on the stump of a tree, and we couldn't move it. And Des the Lance Corporal said, 'I'll have a look and see.' He stood up, and fell back, shot dead, straight through the forehead. He had to stay in the trench with us until dark. He was such a nice chap, and we'd been together for such a long time.

Our Sergeant, 'Yorky' Seal, from Yorkshire, a regular soldier, had been with

Garrison Hill, at Kohima.

CRISIS POINT - KOHIMA

the battalion for a long time, in France and Dunkirk, a very brave man. He was one of those people who would volunteer for everything, including fighting patrols. So we had to go with him. You did not want to but had to. Patrols were sent to find out where the strongest and weakest Jap positions were. The only way we were going to progress was by winkling the Japs out, and the infantry were the people who were going to have to do it. To find out where they were you had to probe and poke and get them to fire so you could see exactly where the positions were.

I went on one patrol to find out where the enemy were in relation to the DC's Bungalow. We had to go down the side of a hill from our positions and try to work round the hill at the bottom towards the road because they seemed to be dug in to the ridges with their machine guns. The only way in was from the front. This night, and it is difficult moving at night, people were jittery as you moved through your own positions going out and coming back in. We got to the bottom and started to move forward and we could hear the Japs talking. It is difficult to move at night without making a noise. Suddenly all hell broke loose as they opened up with machine guns, mortars, grenades, and we had to pull back and take what cover we could as showers of grenades came over. The sergeant told us to pull out.

Major Alexander Wilson
Brigade Major, 6th Infantry Brigade, 2nd British Division, Argyll & Sutherland Highlanders

The fighting on Garrison Hill was worse than the battles at the Somme remembered by the Divisional Commander, General Grover, who had fought there in the First World War. 2 DLI had more casualties on Garrison Hill than anyone else. In A, C and D Companies there was total of four officers left. Of the original 136 men in A Company, only sixty were left. The pioneer and carrier platoons also lost many killed and wounded. The fighting was hand-to-hand. Men were kept going by training, regimental pride, and the will to survive. If you let the Japanese in you'd had it.

At night the Japs sent in fighting patrols to beat up brigade HQ, but were seen off by our defence platoon. The first morning we counted twenty dead Japs, including a young officer.

Lieutenant Gordon Graham
Platoon Commander, C Company, 1st Battalion, Queen's Own Cameron Highlanders

I was on a combined operations course when the Japanese attacked Kohima. I had met the girl of my dreams in Bombay and had just got married. I was flown in a bomber from Calcutta, which stopped at Imphal, and then on to Jorhat near Dimapur. I got there in two days, straight into the battle. I rejoined the battalion in Kohima, sad that some of my closest friends had been killed. Two sergeants of whom I was very fond had been killed by our own guns. All by accident of course.

I walked up the steep jungle-covered hillside above Kohima village, which my battalion had partly captured, but part was still held by Japs. I went over to my platoon and greeted the Jocks. The men in my platoon were a mixture of Yorkshiremen from the mining towns of south Yorkshire, and Highlanders, the original Camerons from northern Scotland, round Inverness and Skye, so you had a mixture of crofters and miners; they got on wonderfully. They were people of sterling qualities, used to the hard life, took their hardships stoically. The camaraderie between officers and men that already existed in the battalion was essential for survival in the jungle. Most of the senior NCOs were regular soldiers.

There, fifty yards away, were the Japs, also dug in. There was a curious sense of almost intimacy with the enemy in jungle warfare. In the patrols which I made in the next few days you constantly found Japanese. You were constantly intermingling with the enemy. I found it exciting.

The patrols were mainly quite long range, you went out with one NCO and five or six privates, your duty was to locate the Japanese and report back, because the command in jungle warfare is actually blind, you can't see what the hell is going on and life is full of surprises. That is one of the democratising elements of jungle warfare. The brigade command is just as vulnerable as the humblest private soldier. They were just as much exposed as anyone else, so they were always anxious for information.

The first patrol I went out on the day after I arrived, we spotted some Japanese and took a note of where they were. They didn't see us. On the way back we found the corpses of a previous British patrol that had been wiped out and I said to one of the Jocks we'd better cut off their identity discs so we can report who they are. While he was doing this a Japanese patrol opened up on

Gordon Graham, as a Lieutenant Colonel at the end of the war.

us, but we got back with only one wounded. But again that was a piece of vital information. We could say exactly where that patrol was, and also indicate where there was clear country where it might be possible to advance. In the next three or four weeks I must have led about a dozen patrols.

PRISING LOOSE THE JAPANESE HOLD

Lieutenant Sam Horner
Signals Officer, 2nd Battalion, Royal Norfolk Regiment
The CO, Robert Scott, called an O Group. He said, 'Now the 4th Brigade – less the Lancashire Fusiliers, who are detached to 5th Brigade, so we're only a two-battalion brigade – with Brigade Tac Headquarters, we're going to do a right hook and try and come in behind the Japs, get on to the road that led from Kohima to Imphal, cut the road, shoot them up the arse.' It was as simple as that.

Sergeant Fred Hazell
D Company, 2nd Battalion, Royal Norfolk Regiment
We were issued with one hundred rounds of ammunition in addition to what we already had. This dangled round our necks in two bandoliers. Blankets were cut in half, rolled up and put on the back of our pack. Every third man was given a shovel, every third man was given a pick and the other third were given two carriers of mortar bombs.

Sergeant Albert 'Winkie' Fitt
Officer Commanding 9 Platoon, B Company, 2nd Battalion, Royal Norfolk Regiment
Around my web belt I had grenades all the way. I had five or six bandoliers, about fifty rounds in each. On top of that we had our ammunition pouches full. We didn't expect the climb and the march to be quite as fierce as it was.

Lieutenant Sam Horner
Signals Officer, 2nd Battalion, Royal Norfolk Regiment
There was a map showing where we were going. It was absolutely white

because it had never been surveyed, nobody had ever been there, the Nagas said they didn't go there, because there was a lot of superstition about it – there were witches and that sort of thing. All there was, drawn from aeroplanes, was a few little nalas, watercourses, and the rest of it was white – so it was a fat lot of use having a map.

Sergeant Fred Hazell
D Company, 2nd Battalion, Royal Norfolk Regiment
God, what a night that was. What a climb. Very steep, wooded, a lot of undergrowth. There were a lot of paths, but occasionally we had to cut our way through. I stepped on a moist tree root, lost my footing and fell flat on my back. My legs went in the air, and I unfortunately caught the chap in front on both his legs, just above the knees and he was the biggest chap in the battalion. He came down on my stomach and, God, he knocked every ounce of wind out of me. You couldn't hang about because it was pitch blooming dark, and if you lost the chap in front you could end up anywhere.

We finally arrived at this village at about two o'clock in the morning. Somebody from headquarters came up and said, 'Put your platoon in there.' I woke up, the sun was shining through the chinks in the walls of the hut, and I thought God's strewth, I never posted a sentry. I opened the door and there was a big Naga standing outside, on guard with his spear. Then somebody appeared and said, 'Have breakfast, we're moving off at ten.' Breakfast was three biscuits and a brew up.

Lieutenant Sam Horner
Signals Officer, 2nd Battalion, Royal Norfolk Regiment
We were moving across country. We had to climb up one after another of these ridges, and slide down the other side, it was very, very exhausting. We even used ropes sometimes to get up the very steep hills, which were so slippery that you went forward one pace and back half a pace. But with the Nagas' help we made it. But it was slow. Secrecy was important, we didn't want the Japs to know we were coming in behind the Jap lines – but there weren't any lines. We were well away from the actual battle going on in Kohima.

Private Dick Fiddament
2nd Battalion, Royal Norfolk Regiment
That part has the heaviest rainfall in the world. It comes down in a solid sheet. You think to yourself, if it doesn't stop soon beating against my poor skull, I'll go insane. The whole area becomes a quagmire. Combined with the rain you've got the humidity, and you're sweating – the straps of your pack, your rifle sling, and anything else you are carrying tends to chafe and rub. Your skin becomes all tender and raw. Your feet, however tough and hardened, are saturated and become sore with constant rubbing, however well your boots are fitted.

Bugler Bert May
HQ Company, 2nd Battalion, Royal Norfolk Regiment
Leeches used to get through on any part of your body that was open. We tried to keep the bottom of our trousers and sleeves closed as much as we could. If we got leeches on us we never pulled them off because the head stayed in the flesh and that made a very nasty ulcer. So you used to get a lighted cigarette, stick it on his tail, and he used to pop off.

Lieutenant Sam Horner
Signals Officer, 2nd Battalion, Royal Norfolk Regiment
The CO called his O Group for the attack on GPT Ridge. The light was failing fast so he said, 'Get your pencils out, I'm going to give you the fire plan first, it's important, you should have it written down while you can see to write.' I wrote down the fire plan in my notebook. By then it was dark. He said, 'Orders, memorise the lot, they're going to be simple.'

The doctor had dug a hole for the Regimental Aid Post. Robert Scott had strict orders from brigade that there were to be no fires lit whatsoever. He disobeyed the order, told the doctor, 'Look here, get a fire going at the bottom of that ruddy hole of yours and I want every man to have some hot sweet tea, I think it's very important for morale.' There was little or no smoke, any that filtered up, there was somebody to swish it away. Brigadier Goschen discovered this was going on and practically placed Robert Scott under arrest – but not quite. Robert talked his way out of it.

Bugler Bert May
HQ Company, 2nd Battalion, Royal Norfolk Regiment
I received some tea in my mess tin – hot tea. You don't know what a cup of tea means to you after you've been three or four days marching without having one.

Private Dick Fiddament
2nd Battalion, Royal Norfolk Regiment
Everybody's frightened. If he says he's not, then he's either a liar, or a bloody madman. Because nobody wants to die, but nobody. I certainly didn't. But you're all pals together, there's a job to do and you get on with it the best way you can.

Sergeant Albert 'Winkie' Fitt
Officer Commanding 9 Platoon, B Company, 2nd Battalion, Royal Norfolk Regiment
I was happy as a platoon commander. I was prepared for a good scrap, if there was one coming along, and I didn't fear anything or anybody. I was keen to learn and I was also keen to try and protect the men under my command. I wanted to go into battle with thirty men and come out with thirty men. That was my idea and as far as leadership was concerned, I never asked troops under me to do what I couldn't bear or wouldn't do myself. I wasn't frightened. About a couple of minutes before the attack, you'd get a sick feeling in the stomach. But immediately you moved, that sick feeling goes away altogether as far as I was concerned. Everybody, I don't care who he is, is nervous to a certain extent before a battle. But when it starts then you've got one thing in your mind, it's either you or the enemy, but somebody's going to get killed. At the back of your mind it's the enemy, not you, or your men.

Sergeant Fred Hazell
D Company, 2nd Battalion, Royal Norfolk Regiment
When we got to the top of the ridge it was almost like World War One. There were four, five or six Japs, they suddenly leapt out of their holes and raced at us with their bayonets. They didn't get very far because the lads' machine guns just went 'BZZZTTT' like that. They threw their rifles at us but it was fairly simple to side-step them. They were about twelve yards away when they hurled them at us, as they dropped.

233

Sergeant Albert 'Winkie' Fitt
Officer Commanding 9 Platoon, B Company, 2nd Battalion, Royal Norfolk Regiment

We went from the forming-up place, got on the start line. Poor old Captain Fulton, he had been hit through the top of his head and the scalp was laying open. You could see his brain actually moving and he had a pleading look in his eye, more or less asking you to put a bullet through him and finish him off. Well you couldn't do that. But it was obvious he hadn't got long to go.

We should have had artillery support. That was all laid on to blast GPT Ridge before we attacked it. But things got rather desperate as we lay on the start line. We were getting shot up and hadn't got a chance.

I lost my Bren gunner, a chap called Grogan. I grabbed the Bren and I had a rifle slung on my shoulder. I called out to Davis commanding the left-hand platoon. I told him I had had enough laying here and not fighting. I was going forward. Lieutenant Reeve in the centre, he had to come with us.

Lieutenant Sam Horner
Signals Officer, 2nd Battalion, Royal Norfolk Regiment

Robert Scott decided, absolutely rightly, that the momentum was being lost and he kept it going. The battery commander said, 'What about the guns?'

'No, no. Forget it, we'll just get straight on through.'

He went on as far as it was possible to get. He ran off with A Company who were then spearhead and practically led the assault.

Sergeant William Robinson
A Company, 2nd Battalion, Royal Norfolk Regiment

The CO lined us up with Bren guns. Bob Scott at that time was ill with malaria. All he had was his pistol and his khud stick. His famous words were, 'Right ho, boys let's go.' That was it. The instructions were to fire at everything, spraying some down, some up and forward because there was a bunker there. Up to that time I hadn't seen any Japanese at all. But in this semi-clearing several got up and started running away. They didn't get far because the fire power was terrific, about twelve Bren guns. The bunker was taken.

Sergeant Albert 'Winkie' Fitt
Officer Commanding 9 Platoon, B Company, 2nd Battalion, Royal Norfolk Regiment
We took the position with the bayonet. I used the Bren for the remainder of the attack, using it from the hip. The Jap positions were facing outwards, so they had to come into the open if they wanted to fight us, and that suited us. We wanted them out in the open so we could see what was going on. We tore down GPT Ridge as fast as we could. About halfway down, I saw what looked to me like a flat piece of ground, and I thought it was a bunker facing the other way. I jumped on to this, and I was looking down the muzzle of a mountain field gun. I threw a grenade in. Three Japs got out, and my runner, Swinscoe, shot the first one that was running away from us. He twizzled him like a rabbit – a marvellous shot. We'd then got two prisoners.

I left them with one man, a soldier you could trust. Colonel Scott came up and when I told him about the prisoners, he said, 'Where are they?' I told him they were being brought up by one of the chaps.

'Good,' he said.

Well, up came this fellow, no prisoners, so I asked him where they were.

'Back up the track.'

'What do you mean? They'll be gone.'

'Never,' he replied. 'Never, they won't go anywhere. Remember my brother got bayoneted in hospital. I searched them. I took these badges off them. These are Royal Norfolk's badges. Well, I bayoneted both of them.'

When I told the CO we hadn't got the prisoners, he flew at me and said, 'Bring the person who let them escape to me.'

I said, 'They didn't escape, sir. He took these badges off them.'

'So what?'

'Well, his brother was bayoneted in hospital – he bayoneted them.'

Colonel Scott said, 'That's saved me cutting their bloody throats.'

Lieutenant Sam Horner
Signals Officer, 2nd Battalion, Royal Norfolk Regiment
Robert Scott got on the wireless and said, 'Objective captured.' Divisional headquarters started coming through to the brigadier saying, 'You haven't had the fire plan yet'. Then Robert sent a message to the divisional commander, 'If you don't believe me, come and bloody well look.'

235

Sergeant Fred Hazell
D Company, 2nd Battalion, Royal Norfolk Regiment

Someone shouted, 'We've arrived – dig in – prepare yourselves for a counter-attack.' We didn't appreciate when we stopped there was this confounded bunker about seventy yards in front of us with umpteen machine guns inside. At that moment Major Hatch appeared and said, 'Come with me, I want to sort out the company positions for the night.' We were standing in the open with this bunker on our left, all the time there were bullets whistling past our heads.

He said, 'Let's make ourselves less conspicuous,' and dropped on his hands and knees. I dropped with him. A shot rang out, I shouted, 'They've got my bloody nose.' I put my hand up, my nose was still there. It passed right under it. The Major said, 'It missed you, but I think it's hit me.' I looked and it had got him in the leg, in an artery. I tried to put a tourniquet on him, but had nothing ready to do the job properly. I dragged him back under cover, over the ridge and handed him over to the medics. I was very upset in the morning when they told me he had died in the night.

Private Dick Fiddament
2nd Battalion, Royal Norfolk Regiment

Suddenly Robert Scott comes along. There we are crouched down in our holes. Scott says to us, 'Come on you chaps, there's no need to be afraid, you are better than those little yellow bastards.'

Sergeant Albert 'Winkie' Fitt
Officer Commanding 9 Platoon, B Company, 2nd Battalion, Royal Norfolk Regiment

When Scott got scalped by a grazing bullet, he shook his fist at the Japanese, saying, 'The biggest bloke on the damn position and you couldn't get him. If you were in my bloody battalion, I'd take away your proficiency pay.'

The plan was to attack the Norfolk Bunker from the front. It consisted of about seven or eight bunkers. My platoon was spearhead in attacking the centre, and 12 platoon on the right. Number 10 platoon was in reserve with a support platoon consisting of machine gunners and so forth under the Carrier Platoon commanded by Captain Dickie Davies.

We moved and got about halfway to the base of the hill. Captain Randle, now company commander, staggered twice before we got to the bottom, that told me that he had been hit fairly heavily in the upper part of his body. I shouted to him to go down and leave it to me, you could see that he had already lost blood. He said, 'No, you take the left-hand bunker, I'm going to take this one.'

I got mine by coming up underneath and before they could spin the gun on me I had a grenade in the bunker. After four seconds, it went up. I knew that everyone in the bunker was either dead or knocked out.

I saw Captain Randle at the bunker entrance. He had a grenade he was going to throw in. I just stood there, I couldn't do a thing. If he had held on for three minutes, I'd have got on top of the bunker, and knocked it out. But he had been hit again at point-blank range. As he was going down, he threw his grenade into the bunker and sealed the entrance with his body. So nobody could shoot from it. But he killed all the occupants. I thought, 'That's the end of Captain Randle.'

A Japanese rushed out of the back door of the next bunker, which was behind me, and fired at me. I didn't see him. He got me through the side of my face, underneath my jaw, taking my top teeth out, fracturing my maxilla, the bullet burning alongside my nose. It felt like being hit by a clenched fist. It didn't hurt as much as a good punch in a fight in the past. I just spat out a handful of teeth, spun round, and he was a few paces away, facing me. He had a rifle and bayonet. I pressed the trigger, I'd got no ammunition. As he came towards me, I felt it was either him or me. I was an instructor in unarmed combat. I let him come and threw the light machine gun in his face. Before he hit the ground I had my hand round his windpipe and I tried to tear it out. It wouldn't come – if I could have got his windpipe out, I would have twisted it round his neck. I managed to get his bayonet off his rifle and finish him with that.

I stood up and had a call from 12 Platoon telling me they were pinned down from another bunker I couldn't see. I asked them where it was. They told me. I threw a grenade. It went over the top. A chap who could see shouted a correction. I threw a second grenade. It hit the ground short, and bounced in killing the occupants. There were still more bunkers. One of my corporals spotted another bunker slightly over the crest. He started going for it. I yelled at him to stop. He continued for four or five paces and was shot down.

Captain Dickie Davies
Officer Commanding Carrier Platoon, 2nd Battalion, Royal Norfolk Regiment
There were other bunkers further down the ridge towards the road. We couldn't throw grenades at them, so you got your bayonet out and made a hole in the top and dropped a grenade in through the hole. Four Japanese ran out of one of the bunkers. I pressed the trigger, and nothing bloody well happened – my Sten gun jammed. They always jammed, a useless weapon. I threw it at them I was so annoyed.

Sergeant Albert 'Winkie' Fitt
Officer Commanding 9 Platoon, B Company, 2nd Battalion, Royal Norfolk Regiment
At the RAP I met Colonel Scott, the first words he said to me was, 'They got you then, Fitt?'
  'That's right, sir.'
  'Let's have a look.'
  The MO removed the field dressing. Colonel Scott stood in front of me and he went, 'Ho, ho, ho! You never were any bloody oil painting.'

Captain Dickie Davies
Officer Commanding Carrier Platoon, 2nd Battalion, Royal Norfolk Regiment
I took shelter in the main bunker. It was full of dead Japs. They sent us down some bully beef and my batman said, 'Let's have it.' I said 'OK.' He got his hankie out of his pocket – it was filthy. He put it over the bare tummy of a dead Japanese. He pulled this warm bully beef out with his fingers, put it on a biscuit and said, 'Here you are, sir.' I couldn't eat it, I was sick.

Private Tom Cattle
17 Platoon, D Company, 2nd Battalion, Dorsetshire Regiment
We needed to get the Japs out of the DC's Bungalow and the tennis court. They tried to bring up a tank to provide direct fire to help take out the bunkers. The first tank found it too steep. So an armoured bulldozer was used to tow the tank, but in the end the big Lee-Grant tank pulled the bulldozer back. The next time the bulldozer cut a track and we got a tank up into the D Company position.

The next day we were to attack the tennis court positions. The difficult part was taking the tank over the perpendicular drop down on to the tennis court. We lined up, a terrific barrage from our artillery fell on the Japs, and an airstrike. We knew that the Japs were so deeply dug in that it wouldn't make any difference. But we moved forward and the tank slithered down over the ridge, a Lee-Grant with a 75-mm gun, it fired its 75-mm and machine guns into the Jap bunkers as we advanced.

Lieutenant Trevor Highett
Officer Commanding Carrier Platoon, 2nd Battalion, Dorsetshire Regiment
I rode in one of the tanks because I had a good idea of the layout of the land, having used the armoured cars I acquired at Dimapur to take ammunition to the forward companies. I was not the commander of the tank. One of the unsung heroes of Kohima was Sergeant Waterhouse, the driver. He had to go down a vertical drop of six feet on to the tennis court. If the tank had been out of action on the tennis court it would have been a disaster. We were firing point-blank at the Jap positions from about twenty to thirty yards. I was firing one of the machine guns. The longest part of the operation for me personally, which took about two hours, was waiting on the edge of the drop down to the tennis court, while the driver made up his mind if he could do it. It was probably only a few seconds. But we were aware that there were anti-tank guns around, and we were stopped.

Mopping up took time. D Company used pole charges. Richard Sharp of the BBC covered it live. Afterwards it was rather like a celebration, lots of people milling about, then the Jap artillery opened up, and the scrum of spectators dispersed rather quickly.

Sergeant William Cook
Platoon Sergeant, 18 Platoon, D Company, 2nd Battalion, Dorsetshire Regiment
My objective was a black water tank. I took one section with me, when I came under fire. I dropped off a Bren to cover the enemy, came under fire again, and dropped off another Bren. This left me with one Bren, another man and myself to take the black water tank. The tank had fired a few rounds into the black water tank, it was shot to pieces and there was no water in it. The Japs had dug trenches all round the tank, which was about twelve feet square, and

underneath it I had a pole charge, an eight-foot length of bamboo with gun-cotton tied on the end with a fuse attached. When I jumped down into the enemy trench, and looked round the corner, there were three or four Japs. There shouldn't have been any left alive – the tank was supposed to have killed the lot. So I had no option but to put the pole charge in. We had been told that if you pushed the charge in before pulling the fuse, it would be pushed out by the Japs on to you, so I pulled the fuse, counted five, and put the charge in, and it must have blown the Japs to bits. Unfortunately I forgot to close my eyes, and I was temporarily blinded by debris being blown out from the fifteen-inch gap between the bottom of the tank and the trench underneath. The explosion blew out a Japanese sword, and I could feel this thing, and said, 'There's something here.' A corporal said. 'You've got a Japanese sword there.'

The other two sections had gone round the other way and did their work winkling out the Japs. I'd done my bit, but couldn't see, so missed the mopping up. I was in the MO tent for four days, before they washed the dirt out, and I fully regained my sight after about a week.

People behave differently in action from their normal behaviour. One chap, Corporal Day, normally a mild-mannered man who wouldn't hurt a fly, had the Bren when we reached the black water tank. He stood on the top of a little trench shouting and cursing the Japanese, he was in another world.

Private Tom Cattle
17 Platoon, D Company, 2nd Battalion, Dorsetshire Regiment
Suddenly some of the Japs started running. And we knew we had done it. We mowed them down as they ran. There were bodies that had been there weeks, covered in flies and maggots, the stench was terrific.

We still had to winkle some of them out of their trenches. We pushed pole charges into the firing holes in the bunkers. Some of the Japs didn't seem to know what they were, and pulled in the bamboo pole, which was exactly what we wanted. Some were pushing them back out, so we cut the fuse to two seconds. We got on to our objective, as did other companies, and we had won the day. We still had a problem where the Japs were on Kuki Picket and Jail Hill. But we could get tanks forward now and help the rest of the division. This had all taken from mid-April to the capture of Kohima on 13 May.

Lieutenant Trevor Highett
Officer Commanding Carrier Platoon, 2nd Battalion, Dorsetshire Regiment
The Japanese were magnificent in defence. Every army in the world talks about holding positions to the last man. Virtually no other army, including the Germans, ever did, but the Japs did. Their positions were well sited and they had a good eye for the ground. They relied on rushing and shouting in the attack. We thought they were formidable fighting insects and savages. We took few prisoners, about one or two in the whole war. We wanted prisoners for information, but wounded men would have a primed grenade under them, so stretcher-bearers were very careful.

Private Tom Cattle
17 Platoon, D Company, 2nd Battalion, Dorsetshire Regiment
We could now walk about without being fired on by snipers. But we were still being shelled by Jap guns being controlled by Japs on the high hills overlooking Kohima. I was filthy, unshaven, covered in impetigo, covered in lice, with boils on my arms. My feet were in a terrible condition. We were thin, hungry, thirsty and tired.

We went back to Zubza and we were stripped. They had cut large oil drums and filled them with hot water to make baths. My face was covered in sores, it was difficult to have a shave, but it had to come off. We were covered in purple gentian violet in our armpits and crotch, put there by the medical staff.

We were taken to Dimapur and had a rest. We were visited by an ENSA party including Vera Lynn. I got so thin, I was clapping so hard, off went my wedding ring and I thought I would never find it. But afterwards, with some other chaps, among all the mud, I found it. We had new clothes and boots, and were soon on the move again.

BEGINNING THE BREAK OUT TO IMPHAL

Lieutenant Sam Horner
Signals Officer, 2nd Battalion, Royal Norfolk Regiment
We were shown the ground for the attack on the Aradura Spur. I thought this is a straightforward nonsense from start to finish. There was a very steep hill, we knew the Japs were on top, we knew they'd be in a reverse slope position,

The 1st Battalion Queen's Own Cameron Highlanders bath in half oil drums at Kohima. L-R back to camera: Captain David Murray, Captain Neil White, and Major Alan Roy.

and we were going to assault straight up the front – not a hope in hell.

CSM Walter Gilding
B Company, 2nd Battalion, Royal Norfolk Regiment

The company were lined up on the base of the hill, it was all jungle covered, no tracks leading up to it, and must have been about one in four. You couldn't walk up it, it had to be scrambled up. The Royal Scots had a company on our left flank. Solid shot was to be fired from 25-pounders to break up the Japanese bunkers on the crest of the hill. The idea was to have two platoons forward, with one platoon back and company HQ, including me and my party. With us was Colonel Scott. We were all within touching distance, there was no space to spread out. The artillery fired and this allowed us to start scrambling up the hill, bypassing a clump of bamboo, or round a tree, you couldn't go straight up. We could hear the thudding of the shot on the top of the hill. We got almost halfway up when the artillery stopped and then the fun began. Small-arms fire, machine-gun fire and grenades – we got the lot.

Second Lieutenant Maurice Franses
B Company, 2nd Battalion, Royal Norfolk Regiment

Then some Japanese grenades started coming down, so we threw our grenades up to the top. The ground was so steep, there was a great danger of our grenades rolling back on us. So I tried to land my grenades on the very top, or a little further, so they wouldn't roll back.

CSM Walter Gilding
B Company, 2nd Battalion, Royal Norfolk Regiment

The leading lads got within twenty feet of the crest. Robert Scott came up and he was with the leading troops throwing grenades, shouting, 'Get on, get on, get at 'em.' By this time I was about ten yards from him. I had a Sten gun and was firing, scrambling up, grabbing hold of a tree, firing the Sten, going a little further, encouraging the lads. You couldn't see the bunkers or slits, they were so well camouflaged. I heard the stretcher-bearers being called as people were getting hit.

Second Lieutenant Maurice Franses
B Company, 2nd Battalion, Royal Norfolk Regiment

Robert Scott had always been a keen cricketer, and when he threw his

CSM Walter Gilding.

grenades he reminded me of a medium bowler lobbing. He was being seen, it was a big help to us all, it certainly was a big help to me. After a few minutes of this, a Japanese grenade came down towards Robert Scott and I think he decided to kick it away. He misjudged it slightly and it went off and brought him down.

CSM Walter Gilding
B Company, 2nd Battalion, Royal Norfolk Regiment

I saw him go down and the stretcher-bearers come to try to pick him up. They cut his trousers open to put a field dressing on his wounds. This uncovered his bottom and through all the noise that was going on, Robert shouted out, 'COVER MY BLOODY ARSE UP.'

Private William Cron
Carrier Platoon, 2nd Battalion, Royal Norfolk Regiment

I had a go at the Japs with my Bren, kept their heads down while the stretcher-bearers got him out. If somebody hadn't fired at the bunkers they'd have popped him and the stretcher-bearers off. So I gave them two magazines of thirty rounds each. I got one through the arm – it didn't do much harm, it didn't stop me firing. By that time they'd got the old man on the stretcher and were getting him down to cover.

Private Tom Cattle
17 Platoon, D Company, 2nd Battalion, Dorsetshire Regiment

We were taken back up to Kohima again, the division had cleared the roads for a way. But soon we were the leading troops, and the Dorsets were to make a left flanking move instead of following the road. We started off and something went wrong and we had to come back again. By now a Field Dressing Station had been moved up into Kohima. We set off again, it was a long drag down to the paddy fields in the valley bottom. After marching all day in single file, we got to the bottom of Big Tree Hill and had to climb up to the Kohima–Imphal Road again and cut the road behind the Japs. We got to Big Tree Hill, it was getting on in the day. We were now at the bottom of Aradura Spur, it was hard climb in thick jungle. A patrol had reported that there were no Japs on Big Tree Hill.

We got so far and came under fire. It was decided that as it was getting dark we would go no further so we had to stay and dig in. Started digging, it was so hot, and we took off our equipment, we were in helmets, our battalion was not allowed to wear bush hats in the front line. I thought it was so hot and all we had to dig with was an entrenching tool. I got about a foot down. I took off my helmet, and the Japs attacked again. I felt a slap on the back of the head and I was knocked out. I fell down, and when I came round I was lying on the ground with blood pouring out of the back of my head. I shouted for a stretcher-bearer and someone bandaged me and put me on a stretcher. I was carried all the way back we had marched that day. We got back to Kohima, where the dressing station was. It was full of casualties. I wasn't all that bad. I had a bit of shrapnel in the back of my head. Others had lost legs, lost arms. People were shouting and screaming; such a lot of noise.

I was put into a bed and operated on, removing a bit of shrapnel. Three days later there was a terrific pain in the back of my head and down my neck. I told the sister and she had a look. She said it's gone bad. We hadn't got penicillin, gunshot wounds were getting gangrenous. I was a bit naive, I was only twenty. I thought that's it. I had another operation and it gradually got better.

Bugler Bert May
HQ Company, 2nd Battalion, Royal Norfolk Regiment
When it was all over you just felt 'Thank God'.

Lieutenant Gordon Graham
Platoon Commander, C Company, 1st Battalion, Queen's Own Cameron Highlanders
After the battle of Kohima, the division had to open the road from Kohima to Imphal.

Ursula Graham-Bower
Naga Watch and Ward Scheme and Women's Auxiliary Corps (India) (WACI)
There was one village that was friendly to the Japs. They took one hundred rupees to bring the Japanese my head. After the 'shouting' was more or less over, Bill Tibbetts of the Assam Rifles and I were touring the area. We came to the village, which clearly had a very bad conscience. We had our Assam Rifles with us. I think they were afraid we were going to take reprisals. There

was no point in doing that. The headman refused to appear. A very nervous young man appeared with a bottle of beer and a chicken, and sat looking at us with terror. I was tempted to point out that I was in possession of my head, and the Japanese weren't, and could I please have the hundred rupees that I felt was due to me.

The Turning Point Imphal

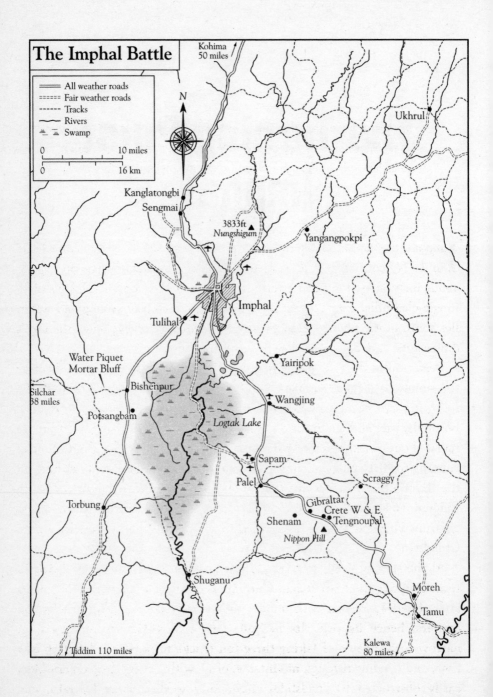

The Imphal Battle

═══	All weather roads
═══	Fair weather roads
- - -	Tracks
───	Rivers
⛰	Swamp

0 ————— 10 miles
0 ————— 16 km

N

Kohima
50 miles

Ukhrul

Kanglatongbi

Sengmai

3833ft
Nungshigum

Yangangpokpi

Imphal

Tulihal

Water Piquet
Mortar Bluff

Silchar
88 miles

Bishenpur

Yairipok

Potsangbam

Wangjing

Logtak Lake

Torbung

Sapam

Palel

Scraggy

Gibraltar
Crete W & E

Shenam

Tengnoupal

Nippon Hill

Shuganu

Moreh

Tamu

Tiddim 110 miles

Kalewa
80 miles

To my horror I saw that the barbed wire was firmly held in the ground by
big wooden stakes, it was insuperable. It seemed that every medium
machine gun in the world was opening fire on converging lines.

Imphal, the capital of Manipur State, the most eastern province of India in 1944, consisted of a small town and a group of villages on a plain about forty miles long and twenty wide, overlooked on all sides by high, jungle-clad hills. The Logtak Lake, a marshy stretch of swamp and water, lies south of the town. About twenty miles long by twelve wide, the lake's dimensions varied according to the season, wet or dry.

Beginning at the time of the retreat from Burma in 1942, Imphal became the supply base for Lieutenant General Scoones's IV Corps, and over the following two years the administrative units had mushroomed to include hospitals, fuel and ammunition dumps, workshops and airfields. Six roads radiated out from Imphal of which the three most important were: the road running for fifty miles north to Kohima; the one to Tamu and Sittaung on the River Chindwin, seventy-five miles to the south-east; and the road to Tiddim, 164 miles south of Imphal, known as the Tiddim Road, which continued beyond Tiddim for another fifty tortuous miles to Kalewa on the Chindwin.

At the start of the battle, on 15 March 1944, the most exposed British formation was the 17th Indian Light Division, which had been reorganised after the 1942 retreat with mules, ponies and jeeps replacing trucks and carriers, hence its title. Its headquarters was at Tiddim, reached by a narrow road capable of taking three-ton trucks in only one direction at a time, and winding through mountains, often with a sheer drop on one side; easily obstructed by landslides, frequently washed away by rain, and perfect for roadblocks. The 17th Division's two brigades were deployed well forward and in contact with the Japanese, as were other British formations further north along the Chindwin. The soldiers in these divisions, in fighting described at the beginning of this chapter, believed they had achieved an ascendancy over the Japanese in late 1943 and early 1944. They were, therefore, somewhat disgruntled when they learned that the plan was to withdraw to the Imphal Plain and fight the Japanese there. Slim, aware of the possible adverse effect on morale, told Scoones to withdraw only when he was satisfied beyond all reasonable doubt that a Japanese offensive was imminent.

Slim's proviso led to the withdrawal of the 17th Division being left too late. The Japanese were able to cut in behind the 17th Division and indulge in their favourite tactic of establishing roadblocks on the withdrawal route. But, whereas during the retreat in 1942, such tactics had disheartened the British and Indian soldiers, this time they fought back ferociously. They had some scores to settle with their opponents who had dealt them such a devastating blow at the Sittang Bridge two years earlier. In a series of brilliant battles the 17th Division utterly defeated the Japanese attempts to cut them off, and withdrew safely to the Imphal Plain.

The subsequent fighting at Imphal was mainly for control of the roads and tracks radiating out from the centre. Savage engagements, sometimes concurrently, sometimes following each other in succession, took place on a ninety-mile arc all round the plain; from Kanglatongbi ten miles north of Imphal Town, through the 5,833-foot twin peaks of Nungshigum, to Yainganpokpi on the Ukhrul Road, Wangjing and Tengnoupal on the Tamu–Palel Road, Shuganu south of Logtak Lake and Torbung on the Tiddim Road.

ALL QUIET ON THE CHINDWIN

Yuwaichi Fujiwara
Japanese Soldier
Wingate's Chindit first expedition changed Japanese thinking. We thought that the north Burma jungles were a defence against British advance into Burma. We now realised that they could be traversed by both sides.

The Tiddim Road, possibly Milestone 109, where the Japanese attempted to cut off the 17th Indian Division during the retreat to Imphal in March 1944.

We had no intention of advancing into India, just occupy Imphal and Kohima to further the defence of Burma. But Chandra Bose and Mutaguchi wanted to invade India after occupying Imphal. There was a serious anti-British movement in India, so it was hoped that the INA would operate in Bengal to assist the rising.

We had been successful because the British always fought on roads and in motor cars. The Japanese crossed jungle and attacked the British rear. The British were not tough. The Japanese were tough.

Lieutenant Harbans Singh
Indian National Army

We were told that it was our duty to fight for India, even take our weapons from the British. We were told to say to other Indians not to fight, to come to our side. We didn't care that *Netaji* was on the side of Hitler and Mussolini. *Netaji* said, 'I have travelled the world and seen the standard of the German Army, they will win.'

Second Lieutenant Shiv Singh
Indian National Army

After being captured in Hong Kong, General Mohan Singh and Bose said you must come and fight for your own country. You are fighting for a very small sum of money indeed, now come and fight for your own country.

We volunteered without any force being used. When I heard *Netaji* in 1939, I was very impressed, and thought he was number one leader, above Gandhi.

The Japanese were cruel, but were the most nationalistic people in the world. The Japanese were not cruel to us, because Bose was our leader. There were other prominent Indians in Thailand and Japan and they influenced the Japanese to treat us well.

Lieutenant Mahesh Sharma
70th Independent Field Company, Bengal Sappers and Miners

My father was a judge in the Indian Civil Service, the ICS. My uncle had retired from ICS, and was Prime Minister of one of the independent princely states. I joined the army because all vacancies in the civil service were reserved for Indians serving in the armed services. I was a sergeant in the

University Cadet Corps, I was a science graduate, and wanted to join the Bengal Sappers and Miners.

It was not the done thing to get involved in politics, hence I was not interested in the INA. After six months of training, after two and a half years of commissioned service, two of us selected to join 70 Field Company in 1943. I was the first Indian officer in the Field Company and the only Indian officer in 48 Brigade. It was quite a shock to be holding the standard for India. I could not make a mistake. I was initially in the Sikh platoon, then in the Mussulman platoon, and finally the Hindu platoon.

One of my first experiences under fire was at the latter end of 1943; the Japanese were advancing up into the Chin Hills. One company of the 2nd/5th Royal Gurkha Rifles under Captain Crossfield was supposed to attack a feature called Basha East. I was in support, I had to blow up the bunkers after the attack so the Japanese could not use them again. So, loaded with explosives, we marched.

Unfortunately Captain Crossfield was killed instantaneously by fixed lines fire, with six of his Gurkhas. The Jemadar, the company 2i/c, was very badly wounded. So it was rather worrying. I got a 'rocket' from an officer accompanying us from brigade HQ, because brigade had ordered that a green Very light would be used to signal success in capturing the bunkers. But the Japanese must have chosen this signal for their own artillery DF.

I was also given a rocket for taking so long to blow up the bunkers. But we had not captured them. There was Captain Crossfield lying dead at my feet.

I could see the bunkers, and started towards them. The Jap mortaring started, my batman was cut in two standing beside me. Ten minutes later and the officer from Brigade HQ came running, shouting, 'Get back, get back.' So I started withdrawing. One of my sappers got hit in the tummy and died the next morning.

You can imagine what went through the mind of a young officer not experienced in war.

Anonymous INA Captain

In Singapore I was given special training by the INA in intelligence gathering, swimming and how to sketch terrain. In 1943 we were on the Chindwin River, on one side of the river were the Japanese and the INA, and on the other the British Indian Army. From January to March I was going from village to village, on the other side of the river, collecting information on the deployment of the British and Indian soldiers.

I was in a small party of about thirty people who crossed into India and we made contact with a whole company of the enemy and we had to get past this company and we decided we had the spirit to do this. We had divided into four groups, and attacked in such a way that the enemy would think that we were a large party. We attacked with bayonets and they fled leaving behind their half-cooked food. We discovered later that they were a party of engineers.

We captured thirteen prisoners and sent them back. We failed to reach the bridge, which we had been told to demolish because there were so many enemy tanks and troops. We then decided that we must discover where our troops were on the road in to India. We went to a bridge right on the border. There we were fired on. I was wounded in the head, and another behind me wounded and another killed. There was a heavy bombardment and all the bamboos caught on fire and we had to run for it.

Captain A. M. Vohra
14th/13th Frontier Force Rifles

I chose to join the army because before independence there were really few professions open to educated Indians. The ICS was top, next the army, then railways, police and so on. Most of us in university wanted to go into one of these professions. I was in the University Officer Training Corps. This did not in any way stand in the way of our desire for independence.

We came into contact with the INA. In one night harbour, I heard our telephone operator talking. He was talking to a JIF. They had got jitter parties and were putting them at the extent of the harbour defence. I talked to some JIFS who were normal soldiers who had been told by the Japs that they would be able to free India. For example I spoke to a JIF who had been a havildar clerk, and highly trained.

Lieutenant Mahesh Sharma
70th Independent Field Company, Bengal Sappers and Miners

The INA were called JIFS, I had nothing but contempt for them. The Japanese did not arm them properly, or they might have been a problem. They surrendered very quickly. The JIFs did not get involved in any fighting to speak of. Quite a lot of INA gave themselves up. They weren't popular. The Gurkhas captured one and he was sent back to brigade HQ about quarter of a mile away, and somehow he never got there. The escort said he tried to escape.

Lieutenant Peter Noakes
1st Battalion, Northamptonshire Regiment

I was put in command of the carrier platoons of Gurkha and Punjabi battalions in our brigade as brigade carrier officer based at brigade HQ. My knowledge of Urdu was primitive and of Gurkhali non-existent. But as most commands in the Indian Army, like 'Halt', or 'Fire', were in English, you could get by. The VCOs could communicate in English. In my Punjabi platoon I had three sections, one each of Sikhs, Punjabi Mussulmans and Dogras. The Gurkha platoon was all Gurkhas. Each section was commanded by a VCO.

We arrived at Dimapur in time for Christmas 1943. My battalion had gone ahead to the Kabaw Valley, with instructions to reach the Chindwin.

Shortly after Christmas Day 1943 we loaded our carriers on to trucks and we drove along the road from Dimapur to Kohima, Imphal and on to the Kabaw Valley. Eventually we got to Kabaw valley at Moreh, and were given orders, 'Put the carriers in harbour and leave a skeleton crew behind for maintenance, you and your crews will return to your units.' The Gurkhas and Punjabis returned to their battalions and I took my platoon of Northamptons on foot to the battalion near the Chindwin.

Captain George Aitchison
Officer Commanding B Company, 1st/4th Gurkha Rifles

We were in patrol contact with the Japs on the Chindwin. The 33rd Japanese Divisional HQ was at Kalewa, a really good division. But, although we shot up the Japs on tip and run raids, they were surprisingly passive. They gradually pushed out troops about thirty miles west of the Chindwin. They patrolled often dressed as Burmese. We rather stupidly thought they had no aggressive intentions.

Just twenty-two miles south of Tiddim, a small town 162 miles south of Imphal, there was a very good defensive position. Called Point 8198, because it was marked as such on the map, it was a knife-edge ridge that marked the highest point between India and Burma in this area. It was a position that everybody coveted. It broadened out sufficiently to take at least a battalion; the 1st/16th Punjabis held it.

In October 1943, I was commanding B Company at Kennedy Peak six miles from this key position. I had outlying platoons, and visiting them involved climbing up and down a total of eighteen thousand feet. One day I visited the 1st/16th Punjabis, Sikhs and Punjabi Mussulmans. They were not alert; their sentries stood about plainly in sight. Nor did they have any proper perimeter defence. An orderly called up the colonel, and he wore beautifully polished brown chaplis and a starched uniform; chaplis were totally unsuitable, he must have thought he was still on the North-West Frontier. He demanded to see my identity card. I didn't feel welcome. There was a touch of luxury about them. I was pretty scruffy, and unshaven. We had to go down thousands of feet from my position to get water. They could get it at Fort White. I looked a shaggy and undesirable chap, and trudged six miles back to Kennedy Peak.

Lieutenant Peter Noakes
1st Battalion, Northamptonshire Regiment

Orders came for an attack on a strong Japanese position at Kyaukchaw, which dominated the river Yu and its confluence with the River Chindwin. I rejoined my old rifle company, Number 4 Company, which used to be D Company; renamed on the CO's orders. The company had one too many officers. My old platoon had been taken over by Stanley Hinks. One of us had to stay behind for the attack; every company had to keep back an officer, a couple of NCOs and a few men Left Out of Battle, LOB, to provide replacements for casualties. We tossed for who should go. I won and so I was LOB in reserve with rear battalion HQ.

The attack failed. Stanley was wounded in his right shoulder, I took back command of my platoon. One day I was out patrolling the Jap position at Kyaukchaw, and came to the conclusion that the Japs had gone in the night. So I struggled ahead, and cut the wire with my wire cutters, told my men to follow me in and we found the bunkers were empty. On our left was a platoon from another company commanded by John Hopkins. There were two big bunkers and the CO called one 'Hoppy', and the other 'Noakie'. Those names stuck. We occupied the Jap position without opposition.

Captain George Aitchison
Officer Commanding B Company, 1st/4th Gurkha Rifles
Eventually the whole of my battalion joined me on Kennedy Peak and made a good defensive position.

About three am on 13 November we were woken by terrific machine-gun and mortar fire. The Japanese made a furious attack on the 1st/16th Punjabis. Next morning a bedraggled lot came through our lines, shirts hanging out of trousers, wearing what they had on when surprised in their beds: plimsolls, chaplis, some unarmed. Many of the Sikhs had lost their pugrees and their hair was all over the place. It was a dejected, defeated battalion with a deep resentment and bewilderment evident in every man. There were a lot of casualties, including the CO and four other officers killed. The entire battalion had been scattered.

Lieutenant Peter Noakes
1st Battalion, Northamptonshire Regiment
In due course we were told to withdraw from Kyaukchaw and retire to the Kabaw Valley where the 32nd Brigade was concentrating at Tamu. When we got back I was told to mobilise the carriers. I got together the Punjabis and Gurkhas and my chaps and the carriers were ready to go having been maintained, and we were detailed to go back to brigade HQ as security and guard the perimeter.

We did our patrolling in the Kabaw Valley, which has a terrible reputation for disease: typhus, malaria, dysentery, you name it. Typhus was the chief killer. We were inoculated against it. The Japs died of it in droves.

One day the brigadier said, 'I want you to go to 100 Brigade HQ commanding the 2nd Borders, the 4th/10th Gurkhas and the 4th/13th Frontier Force Rifles, you are to report to Brigadier James who feels a bit exposed on his left flank and wants protection.' So I went down there, down the one and only dirt track, and was introduced to the brigadier, sitting in his command post with maps on the wall, with a very nice bar that he had the Gurkhas build. A real old Indian Army character, he said, 'Noakes, now look here. Before we start will you pour me out a gin and French, and pour one for yourself, a decent-sized one,' which I did.

He continued, 'The Japs are advancing up the valley, I've got the Frontier Force Rifles here, the Borders are blocking the Kabaw Valley, they've had a

few casualties and seem to be withdrawing. I want you to patrol down the left
– east – flank here into the jungle and make sure they're not going to encircle
us.'

Captain George Aitchison
Officer Commanding B Company, 1st/4th Gurkha Rifles
No counter-attack on Point 8198 took place for thirty days. It was decided
that on 12 December 1943 two battalions, 1st/3rd and 1st/4th Gurkhas, would
leave Kennedy Peak at 0001 hours and march the six miles to the Jap
positions, the artillery would lay down a creeping barrage. Things went
wrong. The barrage expended itself on nothing at all, because the Japs had
contracted into a small, superbly built defensive position, which, compared
with the 1st/16th Punjab treatment of the same piece of ground, was like a
Fabergé egg compared with a run-of-the-mill piece of work. There was no
point in a creeping barrage. The Japs were all inside this beautifully
constructed position in bunkers.

The two battalions advanced side by side, the 3rd Gurkhas on the left, and
the 4th on the right. The leading company of the 3rd Gurkhas found that the
final fifty yards before reaching the Jap position had been cleared of jungle
and ahead of them was a formidable barbed-wire obstacle five foot high and
four feet across. The foliage the Japs had cleared was woven in all over it so
you couldn't see the other side. The leading 3rd Gurkha company began to
scramble over the wire: the company commander was killed and every man
with him hit.

Our colonel said, 'We'll go right, where there's no jungle.' He shouted to
me that I was to take over C Company if the company commander, Major
Keeble, was hit. To my horror I saw that the barbed wire was firmly held in the
ground by big wooden stakes, it was insuperable. It seemed that every medium
machine gun in the world was opening fire on converging lines. Keeble was
hit, but moved forward to the wire, and he was hit twice more. A couple of
riflemen dragged him back, but he died of wounds.

The colonel, already wounded in the shoulder on a recce, was hit again but
his binos took most of the effect. But then he too was too badly wounded to
carry on. So there we were with the 3rd Gurkhas colonel dead, our colonel
wounded, and up against some extremely well-sited Jap bunkers behind very
strong barbed wire. Even to look at what we were attacking we had to be head

and shoulders over a slight crest. That meant they could fire at us without us being able to bring a rifle to bear, let alone anything more lethal. We had wasted all our 25-pounder shells dragged nearly two hundred miles from Imphal. There seemed absolutely no answer to the Japanese bunker. Only twenty yards away ahead of me was the little hollow where the 16th Punjabis had not made me feel welcome, and now containing the strongest bunker I had ever seen, and nicknamed Gibraltar. I realised the situation was absolutely hopeless; all there was in command was me and my Jemadar. He looked at me and I looked at him. We dropped down below the crest, and from a range of not much less than twenty yards the bullets from three bunkers with interlocking machine guns cut the crest just above our heads. We lay there wondering what the hell to do next. After a while the Japs stopped firing. Two Gurkha battalions lay there and no one had any contingency plans for what to do. We lay there all day.

We waited for someone at brigade HQ to give an order. But the brigadier was miles away, standing on Kennedy Peak six miles away, unable to see quite what was going on, although there was a suggestion that came forward somehow, that the next battalion should attack at dusk. But I thought no one has been able to patrol close enough to the Jap position to see that they have got this superb position.

After about two or three hours, a Jap officer or someone started shouting. The 3rd Gurkhas thought it was instructions to mount a counter-attack. Eventually it was decided that another attack would not succeed. So we all quietly trudged back, arriving twenty-four hours later, having achieved nothing. We thought how the hell are we going to retake Burma if this is what we will face. Between the two battalions we lost about two hundred men that day.

Corporal Les Griffiths
9th Battalion, Border Regiment

Imphal was a big flat plain; from there you drove along the Tiddim Road. You could see the odd lorry down at the bottom of the ravines. The mad drivers drove with one leg under them some of the time. On the way to Tiddim you passed the Chocolate Staircase, built by bulldozers, in a series of hairpin bends. The mud was the colour of chocolate and very sticky.

I rejoined the battalion on Kennedy Peak. It was a long walk from the road.

I was shown where I was to sleep, in a hole in the ground. It was covered with tree branches covered by earth. I could see thousands of feet down and miles and miles of treetops, and in the distance the silvery sheen of the Manipur River.

Lieutenant Arthur 'Mac' McCrystal
Officer Commanding 14 Platoon, C Company, 9th Battalion, Border Regiment

When I joined the battalion it was dark. I was taken to battalion HQ and my kit was put on a jeep, and taken to C Company HQ. Officers and soldiers didn't look any different from each other. Everyone wore greatcoats because it was cold up there. The jeep stopped by the side of the road. You could see the remnants of a small fire with people sitting round. I was accosted, what was I doing here? Who was I? I recognised immediately the twang of a Prestonian. I said that I expected a better welcome from someone from Fishgate, one of the main streets of Preston. This went down quite well. I was given food and introduced to my company commander.

Many of them had been together in England and India since 1940 training and so on. Everybody knew everybody. Suddenly you arrive in the dark, in the middle of Burma. You meet a sergeant who is your platoon sergeant and you find it difficult to get to know people quickly. The best way to get to know people is to take time. There was so little time. My sergeant was Bill Stoker from Newcastle. The average age of my platoon was twenty-nine, thirty, and Sergeant Stoker was thirty-one; remarkable people, very reliable. I was only a babe of twenty. My twenty-first birthday was on Kennedy Peak; quite a gap in age.

Corporal Les Griffiths
9th Battalion, Border Regiment

We carried tins of bully beef on patrol. In that heat the fat was liquid. So you punctured the tin with your bayonet, and poured out the fat into a small hole in the ground: you didn't want to leave any signs. Having opened the top of the tin, you ate the bully beef with your spoon.

PULL BACK TO IMPHAL

Lieutenant Peter Noakes
1st Battalion, Northamptonshire Regiment
The Japs had overrun quite a number of positions of the 2nd Border, who were astride the track. We went out into the jungle and it was very close country and very difficult to manoeuvre the carriers, so I dismounted the men, left a guard on the carriers, and we patrolled on foot in various directions to see if we could find the Japs. We didn't find any, so we stayed the night out, and the next morning I said, 'Right, we are going back to brigade HQ, there are no Japs here'. We had no wireless or any other communication. I had no communication between my carrier and the others, very primitive.

When I got to brigade HQ they'd gone. They had disappeared in the night. I think the brigadier realised he was in a very vulnerable position and had withdrawn his remaining troops and the remnants of the Borders through 32 Brigade. I said, 'We're here on our own, better go home.' So we drove back to our own brigade HQ.

A patrol from the Punjabis came in. They had ambushed a party of Japs and inflicted quite a few casualties, and the Indian officer in charge of this platoon-sized patrol reported that the Japs were advancing in strength with armour, which we hadn't come across in Burma before.

One night we stood to and heard the rattle of tracks down the track. By this time the brigade box had been reinforced by a section of 6-pounder anti-tank guns, and a troop of Bofors AA Guns, ready to fire over open sights at any advancing force. The Japs advanced up a dusty track, tanks with infantry support.

The Japanese tanks arrived. The commander of the box was the CO of the 9th/14th Punjabis, Lieutenant Colonel Booth. He gave orders that when he fired a Very pistol we could open fire. When they came right up to us, we opened up with everything we had. The anti-tank guns knocked out two tanks, the Bofors did the same. The Japanese infantry were engaged by my men with Bren guns, the attack failed. At daybreak we counted the bodies and tanks, and thought we had done well.

Captain John Randle
Adjutant, 7th/10th Baluch Regiment

We had no warning of the Jap offensive. The battalion HQ was at Saizang. When we were ordered to pull out of the Chin Hills we thought why the hell have we gone to all this trouble to build these good defensive positions, the Chocolate Staircase, and the road? We were rather annoyed. We were given a couple of days' warning to withdraw to Imphal. We pulled out of Saizang and harboured up in Tiddim. The battalion was sent to Tonzang where the CO commanded an ad hoc force called Tonforce. Our task was to provide a lay-back position through which the division could retire.

Lieutenant Arthur 'Mac' McCrystal
Officer Commanding 14 Platoon, C Company, 9th Battalion, Border Regiment

When the Japs attacked they cut across the main route into Imphal. For one hundred or so miles there were attacks coming in from the crack Japanese 33 Division. There were a number of positions along the route where there were supplies. We had supply drops as we withdrew. A battalion of Japs would attack and block the road. To break it troops would probe forward; there might be only twenty Japs, there might be a whole battalion. Having got rid of the block, fresh troops would go through you to the next block. At certain points where the terrain allowed you would create a box. Into the box would come the wounded, the animals. Sometimes you might be providing a perimeter guard on the box, or with your own company form part of an operation dislodging the next roadblock.

Captain George Aitchison
Officer Commanding B Company, 1st/4th Gurkha Rifles

Starting 8 March 1944, the Japs got in behind us and dug in on high ground. We were up against the 33rd White Tiger Division who advanced up the Tiddim Road. We had retreated in the face of 33 Division, and had formed a defensive position. We had our barbed wire about ten yards out in front. My CO didn't like this and wanted a greater field of fire. I said there was no advantage in doing so because the Japs will get up close and use good field craft to get through the wire at night, and you won't see them. He was not happy.

At last light I was told to get out, take the whole company, and move up on to Tuitum Ridge about two thousand feet higher than where we were and behind us. So in pitch darkness we managed to get up and at about midnight we met the 2i/c of the 10th Gurkhas.

Lieutenant Peter Noakes
1st Battalion, Northamptonshire Regiment

Things were not going all that well elsewhere in the Chin Hills. 32 Brigade HQ was rather exposed in the Kabaw Valley. The Brigade Commander, David McKenzie, told me to take a scouting party to the east of the valley and see if there was any Jap penetration there. We came across some open, very dry paddy fields. The bunds had been knocked down and made into a landing strip. And lo and behold a flight of Hurricanes landed. I drove over in my carrier, and the flight commander jumped out and said, 'Hello old chap. Everything all right?'

'What are you doing here?' I asked.

'I'm on a recce, where are the enemy?'

'About half a mile down the road,' I replied.

'Oh my God,' he said, 'this is no good.'

'I suggest you do a bunk. We'll protect you as you go off,' I answered.

We went back to brigade HQ and had orders to withdraw to Wangjing, outside Imphal. 32 Brigade used my carriers as rearguard, and the move went without incident, except losing a Punjabi carrier that conked out under Japanese shellfire. We abandoned it, pushed it over the hillside. There was no close contact with the enemy. We halted for a few days at Palel, and the battalion sent out patrols into the Naga Hills to see if the Japs were coming that way, and we finished up at Wangjing.

Lieutenant Junichi Misana
33rd Mountain Artillery Regiment, 33rd Japanese Division

Luckily, we were able to take the territory right in front of the enemy base. So we positioned a cannon one hundred metres away in front of the enemy. We would lie low, and dug a hole all night, and put the cannon in the hole. Then at dawn, we started attacking, and we were shooting at each other.

Captain George Aitchison
Officer Commanding B Company, 1st/4th Gurkha Rifles
Major Fairgrieve, 2i/c of the 10th Gurkhas, said, 'The Japanese have taken retaken Tuitum Ridge, a beautifully-sited position: from there they can dominate the whole of the valley for five or six miles as the road snakes down and crosses the Kaphi Lui River.' He continued, 'If they can augment their men with artillery we are going to be in a very difficult position. We will attack at dawn, you will do a left hook with B Company, and reach the crest to the left of the Jap position, and I will take both the other companies frontally. The Japs are using grenade dischargers.'

He added, 'The road is only one hundred yards to your left. On it there are piles of corrugated iron sheets. Get your men to take the sheets, get them to cut some sticks with their kukris, rest the iron sheets on the sticks, and that will give you cover from the Japanese grenades.'

The Jap grenade was a poor weapon, when it exploded it hit people with tiny fragments and did little damage. We did this and nobody was hit at all; although the Japs were lobbing grenades in showers.

Next morning, when we reached the crest, we were hit by Jap artillery fire. My orderly's cousin got a shell all to himself, he looked as though he had been run over by a large lorry. The ridge was very thinly held, which astounded me because it controlled miles of road. We had no difficulty winkling out the Japs. They had some small two-man bunkers that were easily taken out with grenades. We captured and held the whole ridge with three rifle companies.

We planted some anti-tank mines. The next morning the six light Jap tanks appeared. The first one hit a mine and blew up, the rest were hit by PIATs. The whole of the brigade managed to move over the Kaphi Lui Bridge without any casualties.

Lieutenant Junichi Misana
33rd Mountain Artillery Regiment, 33rd Japanese Division
We went after them and pursued them, but I got injured. You could hear the sound 'pyoo pyoo pyoo pyoo'. So I ducked down on the ground, and then the cannonball dropped somewhere in the back, and it got my leg. My right leg was injured, and my thighs too. And my toes, and my right first toe was wounded deeply and my toes were cut off. And there was a small one in my hip too.

Captain John Randle
Adjutant, 7th/10th Baluch Regiment
The Japs attacked at Tonzang at dawn, and overran one company, the company commander was wounded and we lost two good VCOs and a lot of soldiers. Another company was attacked in a half-hearted way by the INA. Our chaps jeered at them, 'We've come here to fight proper soldiers, not a lot of yellow deserters like you.'

Major Ian Lyall-Grant
Officer Commanding 70 Independent Field Company, Bengal Sappers and Miners
The Japanese thought by blocking the road back to Imphal, we would abandon our vehicles and guns and stream back to Imphal where they would defeat us, as we would have no weapons or equipment.

At the first big block at Sakawng there was a dramatic atmosphere at brigade HQ, where I was for a time, as the brigadier liked to have a sapper officer close by. We had never so far fought our way out of a Japanese block that had been there for some time. The brigadier was cool and cheerful as a cricket, and he asked one of the officers to sing a song, which he did. And we sat round the fire as plans were made for the next day.

Lieutenant M. Martin
Officer Commanding D Company, 2nd/5th Royal Gurkha Rifles
I set off at 0230, ahead of me was the reconnaissance platoon. C Company and battalion HQ followed. The terrain was abominable. There was no track, we heaved ourselves up steep slopes tree by tree.

Eventually we hit the unmetalled road to Imphal, on the other side was an earth cliff about fifteen feet high, and above that the Japanese. We and the recce platoon dumped packs and shovels and made ready to attack. The only way up this cliff was to make a ladder with bayonets and kukris. To our astonishment we took the Japanese by surprise. Our attack roared in and the Japanese fled, leaving five dead and lots of equipment.

Major Ian Lyall-Grant
Officer Commanding 70 Independent Field Company, Bengal Sappers and Miners

At six o'clock the mountain guns in support opened up. Then the Gurkhas attacked up the hill; they discovered that there was a gap between two Jap positions. One battalion went each side, followed by the brigadier. Our job was to dig a path up the hill so the mules could get up with ammunition. This took a couple of hours. The Gurkhas attacked, it was only about two hundred and fifty yards away. There was a tremendous rattle of automatic fire.

Lieutenant M. Martin
Officer Commanding D Company, 2nd/5th Royal Gurkha Rifles

The moment we started trying to exploit our success, we were subjected to sustained and accurate fire from medium and light machine guns, and mortars. I told the men to dig in. We had left our packs and shovels and scratched and scraped with kukris and entrenching tools. Our casualties that had been light to start with, seven killed and wounded, rose in a short space of time to thirty.

C Company passed through but their attacks failed on each occasion. The company commander and two VCOs were killed, and the adjutant sent up to take command was badly wounded.

Major Ian Lyall-Grant
Officer Commanding 70 Independent Field Company, Bengal Sappers and Miners

Then Colonel Hedley came back, a rather serious officer, known as 'Deadly Hedley', commanding the 5th Gurkhas, a very fine soldier. For once he looked a little bit excited, and I thought there is a trace of emotion showing. He said, 'Can I have all the guns and all the mortars for another five minutes?' He then sent a platoon round the back of the Japanese, followed by more firing, shouting and dead silence.

I went to see what had happened. There were two circles of Japanese, about twenty-five in each circle, about thirty yards apart, every one was dead. Two of the Japanese seemed to have blown themselves open with grenades, but everyone was dead. This was a change, our infantry had outfought the Japanese for the first time in a set-piece battle.

Lieutenant M. Martin
Officer Commanding D Company, 2nd/5th Royal Gurkha Rifles
We had no food until a patrol found a lorry on the road containing tins of pilchards in tomato sauce – not my favourite food. The wounded suffered greatly, we had to keep them overnight in a collecting post. If hit in the stomach, their chances of surviving were nil. The battalion lost thirty-seven killed and sixty-seven wounded.

Captain George Aitchison
Officer Commanding B Company, 1st/4th Gurkha Rifles
We leapfrogged our brigade over the other brigade, winkling out Japs astride or dominating the road, and it took us from 8 March to 10 April to get to Imphal. We dug in at Bishenpur. Behind us was an enormous supply depot, with three dry-season airstrips and one all-weather strip. It was crucial that the Japs should not take these strips or supply dumps.

THE SIEGE

Trooper Malcolm Connolly
7 Troop, C Squadron, 3rd Carabiniers
Imphal was beautiful, lush and green and surrounded by mountains. The regiment dispersed and squadrons were deployed round Imphal. In Burma we often fought in half squadrons of eight tanks, sometimes in a troop of four, and even as individual tanks. My squadron remained north of Imphal. Each squadron formed a box with infantry. We were in Lion Box and Oyster Box. Each night you went back into the box.

My squadron had the job of patrolling the Imphal–Dimapur Road. We knew the Japs were coming, but we didn't know when. Our job was to keep this road open up to the control post operated by the military police between Dimapur and Kohima. All of a sudden there was no traffic. We realised the Japs had arrived and we returned to Imphal. As we turned round, an MP came out of the jungle, still with his red cap on. We opened the door in the side of the tank and dragged him in. We took him back to Kanglatongbi, a huge ordnance supply base, manned by Indian non-combatants and various service arms. The MP never told us what had happened. When we got back to the squadron there was big flap on. We knew the Jap was somewhere in the vicinity, but where and in what numbers we hadn't a clue.

Flight Lieutenant Owen Parry
11 Squadron, RAF

My first operations were flying a Hurricane Mk IIC at Imphal. The weather was always a major hazard, monsoon or no.

The Imphal Plain was 2,500 feet high surrounded by mountains rising to around seven thousand feet. Clouds developed every afternoon, and cumulus especially fast. When returning from a sortie we sometimes found it difficult to out-climb the cloud, as we did not have enough fuel left to keep climbing at full power for long enough. There was a tendency to try to find a way through the mountains below the cloud.

On one occasion we were on a squadron 'effort' south of Imphal, in two flights, not in the monsoon. The CO was leading the first flight of five aircraft, and I the second of six, spaced five minutes apart. We were returning from the strike along a narrow valley leading to Imphal. The clouds were across the top of the valley and over Imphal itself, like a lid on a basin. We were below cloud height, which was well down the slopes of the mountains on each side. Suddenly we ran into a severe rain shower, like a curtain ahead. The CO carried out the correct action, put his aircraft into line astern and climbed up through the cloud heading for the top of the cloud over Imphal, hoping to find a hole through which to descend. He gave me fair warning what he was doing over the radio. When I came to the rain barrier, I decided I wouldn't climb up through it, instead I gathered my aircraft into close formation and went through the rain below the cloud. I reckoned that it was only an isolated shower, and not very deep, and if I held my course between the two mountain walls, I would come out into a clear spot. I did after a couple of minutes. Unfortunately three of the aircraft in the CO's flight were lost, either because of excessive turbulence in the cloud, or the inexperience of the pilots. Only the CO and the most experienced pilot got through. Yet he had done the right thing, I hadn't.

Our Hurricanes were fitted with four 20-mm cannon, and our main tasks were ground strafing and escorting the Dakotas. Later the escort work diminished, and we were mainly used on strafing. At about the same time, we were fitted with bomb racks and became Hurribombers for army support, carrying two 250-pound bombs.

Owen Parry as a squadron leader after the war.

Private Peter Hazelhurst
Commando Platoon, 9th Battalion, The Border Regiment
The Commando Platoon was commanded by a lieutenant and the sergeant was an ex-gamekeeper. A lot of the platoon were poachers or employees of large landed estates. The first week we were at Imphal we were alongside 3rd Carabiniers, and they had wirelesses in their tanks. We heard Tokyo Rose, she was saying how they had wiped out the 17th Indian Division the 'Black Cats', and how they had finished what they had started in 1942.

It was a very personal war. We did it better than the Japs. They would dig a pit in the track with pangyis in the bottom. On each side would be another pit to catch you if you walked round the pit in the middle. They would smear excrement on the pangyis. So we did that too, and put them in front of our positions. They would booby trap their wounded.

Trooper Malcolm Connolly
7 Troop, C Squadron, 3rd Carabiniers
On 13 April 1944, Lion Box round the big ordnance supply base at Kanglatongbi was attacked, and held for three days and nights, defended by the non-combatants and an Indian battalion. We were sent with the 1st West Yorkshires to evacuate the Indian non-combatants. Number 7 Troop was in reserve initially, but eventually summoned forward and the place was ablaze. The Jap guns were firing down from the tops of the mountains. Jap soldiers came so close we couldn't depress the guns to engage them. We relied on the infantry lads to keep them off the tanks.

Corporal Arthur Freer
Squadron Leader's driver/operator, B Squadron, 3rd Carabiniers
We had a battle on 13 April to remove the Japs from Nunshigum, a hill about one thousand feet above the plain, with two false peaks and one main peak.

The whole of B Squadron was involved. Two troops were to mount the ridge, climbing from two different places. Half of B Squadron HQ and the squadron leader would go up as well. The squadron leader, Major Sandford, was twenty-seven years old, the 37-mm gunner was 'Sherley' Holmes, after Sherlock Holmes, the loader was Joe Nussey, I was the driver/operator, the driver was Paddy Ryan, a London bus driver, the 75-mm gunner Ginger Whitely, plus the 75-mm gun loader, whose name I can't remember.

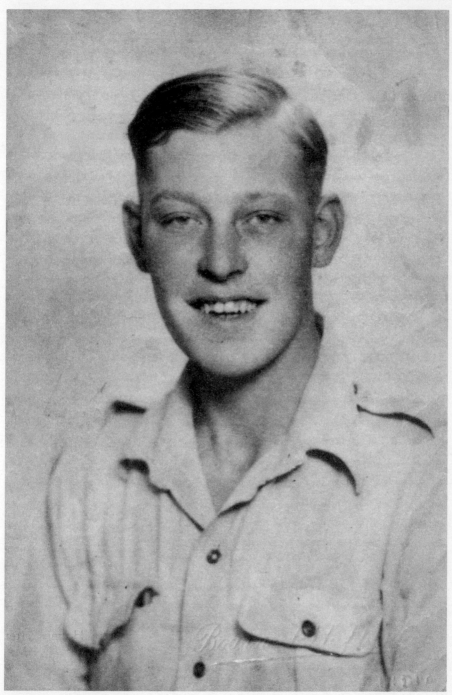

Private Peter Hazelhurst.

We got to the foot of the hill very soon, driving across the paddy fields with infantry walking on either side, two companies of the 1st Dogras: A Company up the left-hand spur and B Company up the right-hand spur, each with a troop of tanks. The squadron leader's tank and the squadron sergeant major's tank went up the left-hand spur. A sapper officer guided the tanks to the position to start climbing; it suddenly became very steep. He walked ahead of the tanks giving signals to the drivers who couldn't see very much. He walked backwards looking over his shoulder guiding the tanks till the Japs saw him and started firing. This told us where they were. We fired a few rounds and we thought they had run away.

As we got closer some of them ran out of the bunkers, and ran up to the sides of the tanks carrying sticky bombs attached to a bamboo rod, they stuck the bomb on the side of the tank and as they ran off they pulled the pin and the theory was it would blow the tank to pieces. We managed to deter them from sticking them on by firing machine guns along the side of the tank, one tank covering another. I fired the front Browning which could not traverse but only elevate or depress. If I could have traversed it I could have killed a lot more Japanese.

Over the squadron net we started hearing of people being killed, 'number nine hit in head'. They were the tank commanders with their heads out of the turret looking for the way forward. As they instructed the drivers over the intercom, they were firing their pistols and throwing grenades at the Japanese. They were exposed to rifle fire and were shot in the head. I heard a thump at the side of me, and called up to Sherley Holmes, 'What's happened?' He said, 'Dizzy's been hit in the head,' the nickname for our squadron leader. I looked into the turret, my head was on the level of the feet of anyone standing in the turret, and I could see the squadron leader lying down on the floor. I asked, 'How badly is he hurt?' Sherley Holmes said, 'It's gone into his head, and he won't survive.' I passed two morphine tubes back and Sherley injected him with both in case he was in pain.

Paddy Ryan was still driving forward and by now we were in the lead. We had left this bunker, still occupied by Japs. He was asking the gunner on his right, 'Can you see the bunker in front, have a go at it?' We had no tank commander now. I told Sherley Holmes to close the lid, we didn't want any grenades in the tank. The gunner fired a few rounds, I fired my machine gun at them. We went right over the top of the bunker.

I told them to stop: we must report what was happening, I reported to the CO on the radio that number nine was hit. He said, 'What do you mean by number nine?'

I said, 'Our number nine.'

He asked, 'Is he alive?'

I said, 'He's still got a pulse, but he's not in pain.'

He told us to try to get down. We could hear the reports over the radio of the others being killed. So Paddy Ryan went over the peak, and down to the far tip, and it was a sheer drop. So I told him to reverse. I told Sherley to turn the turret round and guide him back. He had forgotten the tank was going back and saying, 'Left a bit, left a bit,' when he meant right a bit. The tank ended up on the ridge, rocking on its tracks with a sheer drop in front and behind. Paddy Ryan, a brilliant driver, put enough power on each track to get back on the ridge, and we moved back past the other tanks. We got away and got down. By that time all the officers were killed, and four men who had replaced the tank commanders. The squadron sergeant major was left in charge.

There was a subedar major commanding the Dogras; all their officers were casualties as well. So Squadron Sergeant Major Craddock was left with the job of finishing the battle, which he did very efficiently. The tanks fired into the bunker slits, and we learned afterwards that there were about two hundred and fifty Japanese bodies found later that afternoon when the position was taken.

Trooper Malcolm Connolly
7 Troop, C Squadron, 3rd Carabiniers

We were green, and suddenly in the fray with one of the most efficient armies in the world. We were pulled on to the side of the road, and I opened my driver's hatch, and saw the infantry, who had been digging in, run like the hammers. Enemy artillery fire came down. A shell hit the right-hand sponson. Someone shouted, 'Get out of here.' I engaged reverse and backed out of it. The gunner got out to look and about six track connectors had been blown out. I knew we couldn't go very far, the troop leader had gone off somewhere, so I said to the wireless operator, 'Tell squadron we've got, to get out.'

The squadron leader, Dimsdale, didn't trust us, and came to look. He said, 'Get out of here as fast as you can.'

We laid the track out, and the LAD appeared in a scout car and we repaired the track in about twenty minutes. Meanwhile thousands of non-combatants poured out of the depot.

Corporal Arthur Freer
Squadron Leader's driver/operator, B Squadron, 3rd Carabiniers
The squadron leader was hit by a bullet under the chin, it came out of the top of his steel helmet. Under his body we found a grenade, which he had been about to throw, without a handle. We had had it in the tank with us amongst all that ammo, 120 rounds of HE, and couldn't understand why it hadn't exploded. Paddy Ryan started to unscrew the base plate to look inside. I told him to get outside the tank while he did it. So he walked off into the paddy, took the base plate off, the cap had been struck, and the fuse burnt all the way round to the detonator, and burnt out. Fortunately for us it was a dud fuse.

We left two tanks up on the mountain, one which had slipped down the ridge, and another one – both recovered. The only casualties were to tank commanders or men who took over. One tank lost three men. At the time I thought why did they stick their heads out? The reason was because the drivers couldn't see where they were going, the slope was so steep that the tank was up at an angle.

From my position in the tank I could look through a porthole on the left-hand side, about three by four inches, by raising the plate, which I didn't do. I also had a periscope to aim the Browning. The Japanese on Nunshigum were not little chaps, as we had been told, they were strapping big six-footers, formidable foes.

My first reaction on coming down was relief; instead of the rattling of rounds hitting the armour on the side of the tank, and noise of the guns going off, it was quiet. The Lee-Grant tank was a superb tank in these conditions, with tremendous fire power. The only weakness was that being a riveted tank, if a shell blew off the head of the rivet, it could fly off inside the tank and kill or wound the crew. I had friends killed in this way. We were using the tanks as mobile artillery pieces.

That night Colonel Younger came round to our tank, bubbling with the success. Although he had lost some of his bright young men, he looked upon this as one of the risks of war. I was new to it. He had fought with the 7th Hussars in North Africa and in Burma in the retreat. I wrote in my diary 'I have had my first taste of action and I don't like it'. The others felt the same. But from then on everything was better. The next day we had a lot of work cleaning up the tanks, and cleaning and oiling guns, and replenishment of ammunition. The tracks were clogged with bits of Japanese uniforms, bones and bits of meat.

Trooper Malcolm Connolly
7 Troop, C Squadron, 3rd Carabiniers

We returned to the box and were ordered to rejoin the squadron on the perimeter. Next day the RAF attacked the perimeter of the box, causing a lot of casualties to our own side. We were then moved to defensive positions at Sengmai. Our job was to hold there and ensure that the Japs did not get closer to Imphal.

On a sortie, we ran straight into three Jap 47-mm anti-tank guns. The troop sergeant in front had his tracks blown off and his gunner killed. They were a sitting target, unable to move. We came up: the troop leader, and troop corporal. The troop corporal realised that he'd better scarper, which he did, which left me in the troop leader's tank; we took the full brunt of three guns, at a hundred yards. They put out of action all our guns except one machine gun. One 47 projectile came through our 37-mm gun periscope, and lifted the scalp right off the gunner's head. You could see his brains, but it didn't kill him. A round came through and knocked the 75-mm gun's actuating shaft out, which took the back off my seat. So we had a 75-mm gun with a 47-mm AP projectile stuck in it. That gun was useless. The 37 gunner above was mortally wounded. They had hit the armour on the outside and pin-punched the two sides of armour together, jamming the 37 gun. When we got out we counted that we had been hit nine times, penetrating the tank five times. It was an act of God that we got away with it. My troop officer was in a panic. I shouted into my mike, 'For God's sake get us out of here.'

Fortunately the infantry, the West Yorks, were fighting hand-to-hand with Japs surrounding us trying to get at us. If you ever go to war, go with a Yorkshireman.

We were told to return to Oyster Box. We took out our wounded, and they were bringing out West Yorkshires by the drove. We turned round and beat it for Imphal. The battle was at its height. Tanks could not be replaced. The tanks we had had to see us through. The REME chaps said the tank was

A Lee-Grant tank of the 3rd Carabiniers supporting the 1st Battalion the West Yorkshire Regiment at Imphal.

beyond repair. She was called Clacton, because all C Squadron tanks had names beginning with C. They were bringing in tanks from other battles and there were some tanks there that had engines destroyed and not their guns, and others guns destroyed and not their engines; they cannibalised one to make another. They replaced our guns from a tank with a destroyed engine at Nungshigum. Some tanks still had dead in them. We were there for a week. They repaired the holes. Lucky the shells were AP solid shot, not AP/HE which would have penetrated and then exploded. We lived to fight another day.

Flight Lieutenant Owen Parry
11 Squadron, RAF
As well as being on hand to support the army, we harassed the Japanese line of communication doing low-level 'rhubarbs' by day and night. Strafing was dangerous at night. It was OK flying over the road with one's canopy open looking over the side for vehicles on the road, but once you closed the canopy to attack, and dived in at low-level head-on, the thick bullet-proof windscreen reduced visibility considerably. As soon as you fired your cannon, you were temporarily blinded by the muzzle flashes. There was a grave danger of flying straight into the ground, and we lost a number of pilots on night operations.

Night operations were very fruitful, even when we didn't destroy trucks, because the presence of aircraft slowed down the progress of Japanese road convoys. When we came overhead they would usually park. Furthermore, once you spotted a road convoy and reported its location, the chaps going out at dawn would be able to work out where it had laid up for the day – they hardly ever risked moving by day.

On one occasion, I was out on an intruder raid armed with bombs, and saw a large Jap convoy on a road crossing an open plain – a good place to attack. I dropped one bomb on the road ahead of the convoy, hoping this would be difficult to get round, and another behind them. I kept a patrol over the area, until another intruder pilot arrived. I told him where I was, and he took over the standing patrol until dawn, when more aircraft appeared and dealt with the convoy. Some Japs got away, but most were caught.

Private Peter Hazelhurst
Commando Platoon, 9th Battalion, Border Regiment
We had only been at Imphal for about two weeks when I got wounded on Black Ridge at Palel, the Commando Platoon was with the Gurkha Commando Platoon. We had to stop the Japs from getting the airfield. We went up one side and were to stop the enemy escaping, while the battalion attacked on the other side. I was in a hole with two others, and I saw a Jap, the sergeant said, 'Shoot him,' but he threw a grenade first. I threw myself sideways out of the hole as did the other lads. But the sergeant threw himself in the bottom, and the grenade landed on him; he copped it. Things went hazy after that. I got shrapnel in my back and in my leg. A kid called Fisher got a big piece in his ankle. I managed to get round to where the rest of the platoon were. I was put on a stretcher between two mules. One in the front and one behind. One was nibbling your ear hole and the other defecating over your feet. At the bottom of the hill was the American ambulance, conscientious objectors. They were fantastic, the bravest people you could wish to meet.

Private Ray Dunn
1st Battalion, Devonshire Regiment
My first experience of facing the Japs was on Crete East when Japs put in a night attack. On some features we fought on, we did not have wire or mines. The majority of Jap attacks were night attacks. The first thing you were aware of was when the Japs were almost on us, well within grenade-throwing distance.

On occasions on Crete East the fighting was hand-to-hand. On one night Japs got to within ten yards of our bunker. I woke up to shouting and firing, from another man in our bunker, followed by the Brens and tommy guns firing, and 3-inch mortars. I was the 'bomber', with a grenade-projector on my rifle. The others got out their grenades. We also used phosphorus grenades. The bunker I was in exploded. They were roofed over with timber and earth. The other two men were very badly wounded. Our rifles were on the floor, under earth. The firing stopped and I didn't know if the Japs had taken the position. But we held it. It was a long night. I wasn't sure whether to stay there or not, or get off and be bayoneted to death. I knew the Japs bayoneted the wounded, and I didn't want to leave them. My best friends were in the other side of the bunker, and one was killed, the other severely wounded. This was the first time I had been under attack. I was ill-prepared for the ferocity of the Jap attacks. We had been told to fight to the last man and last round. The OC eventually gave the order to what was left of us to evacuate the position, contrary to what we had been told. The CO was not best pleased. But if this order had not been given, I would not be here today.

Corporal Stanley May
Stretcher-Bearer, 1st Battalion, Devonshire Regiment
Nippon Hill was at right angles to the Shenam Saddle. The Japs had taken Nippon Hill. We had orders to take it. It was a tough nut to crack, with steep sides and very little cover because it was rocky.

The road was so steep that at Dead Mule Gulch there was a two-way track. Nippon Hill was in advance of that. That morning we established the RAP in Dead Mule Gulch. D company and B Company went down the valley bottom and climbed up the north face of Nippon Hill, C Company went on the other side. We had the Commando Platoon in carriers. Our mortars put smoke rounds on top of the hill, then three Hurribombers came in and dropped 250-pound bombs and raked the hill with cannon fire, meanwhile the men were advancing up the slopes. When the Hurris moved off, the artillery opened up. During the final assault, the Commando Platoon with carriers belted in, and by 1200 the battalion was on top. The Japs were in deep bunkers. The CO had carrier-loads of barbed wire rushed up and he wired the hill all round, leaving gaps where tracks were. He put a fresh company, A, up there and withdrew the others. Japs attacked and came through gaps in the wire. In the morning there were forty or so hanging on the wire.

Private William Savage
1st Battalion, Devonshire Regiment
We left our positions at 0900 hours for the march to Nippon Hill. The hill was in stark contrast to everything else around. It was brown and stripped of vegetation. We felt apprehensive, as it was pretty certain someone was going to get hurt. The attack started with three Hurricanes coming over to drop two bombs each on the hill, followed by strafing. This was the signal for us to be on our way. We were making quite good progress. Mortar bombs were dropping round us. There was a huge bang, and I was disorientated, hit by

Soldiers of the 1st Battalion the Devonshire Regiment after capturing Nippon Hill at Imphal. L-R: Private Williams, Corporal Treasure, Private Willoughby (shaving), and Lance-Corporal Willis.

shrapnel on my left leg, breaking it. Our orders were that no one was to stop to assist the wounded. Lieutenant Atkinson, my platoon commander, just stopped and asked if I was all right. I said, 'Yes.' He pushed on.

My next thought was to get back on the track where I might get some help. I had to push myself down a gully and on to the track. I was worried that our own troops following up behind us would shoot me by mistake when I put my head above the ridge. I made my way down the track using my rifle as a crutch, and got patched up at the RAP.

Corporal Stanley May
Stretcher-Bearer, 1st Battalion, Devonshire Regiment

I stayed in the gulch all night as more wounded came in. We had thirty-one killed, and eight officer casualties – four killed and four wounded – and over a hundred wounded in the gulch. We cleared the gulch by late afternoon.

They brought Sergeant Major Jimmy Garvey of D Company into us, dying, he charged in front of the men with a bayonet. He said, 'Don't waste time on me.'

We went back to the Shenam the next day, and the Frontier Force Rifles were driven off Nippon Hill. Our CO named the crests of the hills, Scraggy and Gibraltar.

Private William Palmer
6 Platoon, B Company, 1st Battalion, Devonshire Regiment

On one of the attacks on Crete East, the Japs attacked in daytime, and I could see one of them carrying a flag attached to his bayonet. Three or four of us shot at him. Every one of us claimed him. We decided that the one that got to him first would claim the flag. When the fighting died down, I went over the top and collected the flag off the Jap. I had to go about twenty yards. I got roasted by my platoon commander for going.

Major Dinesh Chandra Misra
Second-in-Command, 5th/6th Rajputana Rifles

The Japanese had outflanked and penetrated a place we called Lone Tree Hill, and there were no troops between divisional HQ and the hill. The CO sent for me and said, 'I will take two companies and you stay in the rear.' I asked him to let me take the two companies. He let me take them. I chose a frontal attack, I thought speed was of the utmost importance, as the Japs were in the middle of preparing positions. We got to within thirty yards of the objective and were grenaded back. We withdrew, took up a defensive position, and spent all night there.

Next morning, the RAF liaison officer arrived and asked what he could do to help. We were so close to the target that any shorts from artillery would drop on us. During the shelling the Japs would withdraw on to the reverse slope, and come back when the artillery stopped. I said to the RAF LO, 'You bring in strikes from north–south. When your aircraft are flying north to south, drop bombs but then don't let them go away. Turn round and attack in dummy runs while we advance.'

During the dummy runs, we got on to the top without any firing. I told the company commanders to get their LMGs out in front, facing the direction that the enemy would come from. After about ten minutes, the Japs appeared chatting away. We let them come within thirty yards and opened up with everything. They dropped like flies. The survivors withdrew. I replenished with ammunition, got everything ready.

By then it was getting dark. I told the company commanders, 'Expect a counter-attack about two hours after dark. It's 4.15 now and they will come at seven o'clock.' And sure enough it came at that time. Everything opened up. We had taken a few casualties.

I knew that in the early morning there would be a final counter-attack. It came and in the hand-to-hand fighting we had casualties. I felt detached, but hatred for the Japanese, and determined to kill them; I became a demon. I was swearing and screaming. We were shouting our battle cries, and the Japs shouting 'Banzai', the officers had swords. We fought with bayonets. I had a Sten gun. The Japs withdrew and I knew we had won. There was a tremendous feeling of joy and relief. In daylight we counted one hundred and fifty Jap dead. The hill is now known as Rajputana Hill. In battle you reach an extreme state of hatred, but it goes away. You feel sad. How insane war is, but if you don't kill the enemy, he will kill you.

Pilot Officer Roger Cobley
20 Squadron, RAF
At Palel airstrip, the Japs attacked one night, and some of them holed up around a hillock near the airfield, and come daylight the Gurkhas sorted them out. We had the RAF Regiment to defend us but they were not very effective when it came to counter-attacking.

Sergeant Douglas Williams
Wireless Operator, 194 Squadron, RAF

We flew a load of bombs into Palel for the Hurribombers. This was followed by evacuating the RAF ground crew of one of the Hurricane squadrons. Having loaded up, started a normal take-off and about to get airborne, a cross-wind gusted, the wing dipped dangerously, the pilot thumped the throttles back, but both oleo legs collapsed. Everyone got out OK, but sitting on the ground we were very shaken. Our beloved C Charlie was now a write-off – it was like losing our home. We felt insecure and lost. Having to fly other Dakotas as and when they were available was not the same.

Lieutenant Mahesh Sharma
70th Independent Field Company, Bengal Sappers and Miners

At the Torbung block, I was ordered to go as soon as it was dusk and lay some mines on the road; we had heard some Jap tanks. As soon as it became dusk we moved on to the road in a defile. We were ambushed, and lost two mules with mines on their backs. But we picked up the mines and went on. We laid the mines, were coming back about one or two o'clock in the morning, and on the way back, there was a river crossed by a bamboo trestle bridge, one bamboo wide which you crossed by shuffling across. All in the day's work. Coming back I thought it prudent to stop by the riverbank to see if the Japs were about, before crossing. One of my sappers asked my permission to move away to answer a call of nature. I told him to do it here. But out of respect he wouldn't and moved about six feet away. There was a big bang and he started screaming.

You are in unknown territory. How did that mine or booby trap get there? The Japs must have been setting booby traps for us. The morphine didn't work. So I rushed back across the bridge and reported to the company commander. I had hid the man under a bush, and asked for a stretcher. I went back with four fresh men and recovered him, it was difficult to cross the single bamboo bridge. His leg was horrible, the knee was there, but his foot was held on by skin, but no bone. He died in the morning.

Flight Lieutenant Owen Parry
11 Squadron, RAF

The Japs were very good at camouflage. About an hour before dawn they would pull off the road under the trees on the sides. If there was insufficient

A Hurribomber attacking a bridge on the Tiddim Road.

cover, they would cover their vehicles with branches cut from further in. After a while we realised that the vegetation by the road was light coloured because of the covering of dust, whereas the branches brought from some way in was dark green. So we flew along the road looking for what looked like new growth, standing out fresh green against the khaki-coloured vegetation.

The Japs also took advantage of areas used by our army during the retreat of 1942, where we had set up refuelling points at intervals along the main road. Here vehicles had collected and been struck by the Japanese air force, or perhaps had been immobilised and abandoned. From time to time the Japs artfully parked some of their own vehicles among these trucks during the day. So we learned the pattern of the layout of these parks, and were able to spot when new trucks had been popped in. It used to annoy new pilots when they excitedly reported a concentration of vehicles, only to be told, 'Don't bother with those, they are our own left behind in 1942.' Then perhaps a couple of days later, we would attack one or two of these parks where we had spotted some additional trucks, and the new pilots couldn't work out how we knew.

Sometimes smoke from cooking fires would betray the position of a parked-up Jap convoy. Even so, it could be frustrating, because although you could make out the vehicles from dead overhead, when you come in on an attack heading from say half a mile out, at an angle of dive, the trees covered the target and it was hard to spot exactly where they were. Just occasionally you would catch them in the open in daylight. Once I saw a Jap staff car on a winding road in the mountains. I strafed it, and saw it go over the edge down the hillside. I assume all the occupants were killed. On another occasion my flight was returning from a 'rhubarb', when we spotted a truck on a bare hillside. Only my tail-end-charlie had any ammo left and he asked permission to break off and attack. I said, 'Yes', so in he went. I don't know whether he hit the truck or not, but the whole hillside behind it went up in an enormous ball of flame. I assume the truck was refuelling and he hit a fuel dump.

Lieutenant Junichi Misana
33rd Mountain Artillery Regiment, 33rd Japanese Division
I had to go back. Of course, my wound hadn't healed yet. I self-discharged myself from the hospital, although I wasn't scheduled to be discharged yet. The hospital was unwilling but I forcefully checked myself out. So still with crutches, I got myself a ride on several trucks. The division commander had

changed, and the new division commander became Lieutenant General Nobuo Tanaka. When the division commander changed, they said there would be a truck that would take him directly to the front line, so I asked to ride the same one. So I went in the car that took General Tanaka to his new post.

Captain John Randle
Adjutant, 7th/10th Baluch Regiment

The battalion was sent to the Silchar Track: it was rather like the Western Front, dug-in wired positions and the Japs only about fifty-sixty yards away. Everyone mixed up. For about three weeks there was very intensive fighting. Scrub thicker than in the Chin Hills, very wet. It was a very hard infantry slog. The Japs attacked, then we counter-attacked. Positions changed hands several times. I was the controller of the fire support, guns, mortars, 25-pounders, and 5.5s, also some AA guns in direct-fire role. We shared a CP with the 5th Gurkhas.

The features had names like Water Picket and Mortar Bluff, these were pimples or hills occupied by companies or platoons, and mostly mutually supporting. Subedar Netrabahudur Thapa on Water Picket called for fire through me. He spoke in Gurkhali, but switched to Urdu when realised he was not talking to a Gurkha officer. He was overrun. Got a VC.

Next day the 5th Gurkhas got another VC, Agansing Rai, only time I've seen Gurkhas go in with the kukri; an awe-inspiring sight. They were counter-attacking the position and took it back. It was the closest fighting I ever saw in Burma. There were four VCs won in a week in an area about a mile square.

Japanese attacks tended to come up and close the last few yards with bayonets. We gave enemy positions a really good pasting, then fought our way in. We cleared enemy positions with grenades, tommy guns, Gurkhas with kukris. Our chaps used a bayonet.

We had no morale problems. We had good officers, and were experienced. We thought we were winning. We had far more artillery, and the RAF were in evidence. Rations came up. Wounded were taken out by American Field Service. There were none of the uncertainties of the retreat.

Naik Agansing Rai of the 2nd/5th Royal Gurkha Rifles, awarded the Victoria Cross for his actions at the recapture of Water Point and Mortar Bluff on the Silchar Track at Imphal.

Lieutenant Arthur 'Mac' McCrystal
Officer Commanding 14 Platoon, C Company, 9th Battalion, Border Regiment

We were switched to finish off the 33 Div. South of Imphal was a place called Bishenpur, and the next village was Potsangbam, which was known as 'Pots and Pans'. This was one of the villages that crossed the road. On the eastern side of the road, it was held by the Japs. They had guns in the foothills a mile away. B and C Company put in an attack. We had a couple of Lee-Grant Tanks in support. It was very hot day. It was half-past one in the afternoon of Sunday 14 May.

We crossed the road with C Company on the left and B Company on the right. We moved in with two platoons up, mine and another, and one behind. We moved through sporadic bursts of fire. A soldier on my left saw a Japanese in a hole shooting out of it, and he too excitedly leapt up and fired at him and was shot by a sniper from forty yards away. All the time the tank was on the fringe, out in the open, firing in. The Jap artillery could see us, and never worried about hitting their own troops. You could hear the boom, and we lay down. At one point a shell landed near, and I was hit by shrapnel in the hand and arm. John Petty picked me up and my batman, Private Hunt from Norfolk, took me back across the road through part of the village we already held. Someone put on a first-aid dressing, and later I got a jab of morphine. I was walking wounded, and was taken to an ambulance jeep, and sat in front. We were being shelled all the time.

Corporal Les Griffiths
9th Battalion, Border Regiment

Before the battle at Potsangbam, we lay up all night on the edge of the paddy. At dawn the whole place was covered in mist. We were all tapped on the shoulder, 'Come on up.' Once up on our feet we moved forward through a line of gunners. One said, 'Good luck,' and we moved on to the paddy and lined up, on one side the Gurkhas, and further along another battalion.

We got the signal to advance, and we started to walk, just a stroll. And we had walked for quite a while and then the Jap guns began to open up. One chap fell alongside me, and the Colonel said, 'Stay by him.' So I did. He had shrapnel all over him. He was yelling, I slapped his face.

I stayed there with him as the troops moved forward. I felt very lonely.

Corporal Les Griffiths.

Eventually the stretcher-bearers came up and took him away. I was on my own. There was no one else around. Eventually I got quite close to the jungle fringes, and I jumped into a shell hole. And on the other side were two chaps who I thought at first were Japs. I threw my tommy gun forward, and they grinned and laughed, they were Gurkhas. Eventually I found the battalion.

Private Fred McCloud
12 Platoon, B Company, 9th Battalion, Border Regiment
They said this is your last 'duffy', in Potsangbam. We went across the road into a paddy field, and two Jap machine guns at each end of Potsangbam hit us. I went down on the floor. An air strike came in and hit the Japs in the wood, the road ran through it. You could hear them screaming and see them running on the road.

Corporal Arthur Freer
Squadron Leader's driver/operator, B Squadron, 3rd Carabiniers
A Squadron in Bishenpur and Potsangbam were having a rough time, so B Squadron was sent down to help. We were in action every day. It was paddy on both sides of road, on one side was the Logtak Lake. The Japs would fortify the villages with bunkers and use the bunds as defensive positions. At night, having half-cleared a village, we would remain guarded by the Bombay Grenadiers.

There were three of us with the 'runs' at the time and I was the worst. To sleep in the tank you sit in your sleep. To crap, the 75-mm gunner, who was standing on the escape hatch in the floor of the tank on the other side of the tank, moved to your seat, and you lifted the hatch, and crapped on the ground a few feet below. You then got the driver to move the tank a bit away from the stench, and put the lid back again. Nobody slept. We all stank to high heaven, we were all unwashed and sick. There was always a revolting stench in the tank. At dawn you stood to, the infantry tank guard would move away, and we would go into action again. It could go on for three days and nights at a time.

Private Fred McCloud
12 Platoon, B Company, 9th Battalion, Border Regiment
We were marched down the road and there were marquees, and we went in

there and went through a delousing centre, where they looked in our crotches for crabs. We had a bath, were shaved by barbers and given a haircut. Our rifles and ammunition were taken off us, and new rifles and bayonets, and brand-new uniforms, were given to us, everything new. We went in like rag men and came out like bloody princes. We couldn't recognise each other.

When we came out we fell in, and were ordered to slope arms. Somebody in the middle started singing 'D'ye ken John Peel', the regimental march.

BREAKING OUT AND BACK TO BURMA

Yuwaichi Fujiwara
Japanese Soldier
By the end of May the monsoon had started and our campaign had already failed. But GHQ Burma Area Army and Southern Area Army did not give orders to withdraw until July. Almost all Japanese soldiers were suffering from malaria and starvation. Many soldiers died on the retreat to the Chindwin, we called the road to Sittaung the 'death road'.

Lieutenant Junichi Misana
33rd Mountain Artillery Regiment, 33rd Japanese Division
They called it battlefront realignment. Yes, that's how it was. And we went all the way down that mountain, the same way we came up. By then we were hurt everywhere. We only had one cannon each.

Lieutenant Mahesh Sharma
70th Independent Field Company, Bengal Sappers and Miners
The Japanese were very tough. They stored their rice in old socks tied to their belts. I have seen a Japanese officer with part of his arm missing and maggots crawling over him still fighting. They are very brave. They had no idea of preserving human life. They lived off the land a lot of the time, which was hard on the villagers. They had few medical facilities.

Private Jim Wilks
11 Platoon, B Company, 2nd Battalion, West Yorkshire Regiment
On the Imphal–Kohima Road we broke out, each side of the road was jungle

and steep khuds. Every now and then there was a roadblock, where the Japs had felled massive trees across the road. You had to go round it or through it. We got to this roadblock on the Imphal–Kohima Road and our colonel, Colonel Cree, could see we couldn't get past this roadblock, the Japs were dug in both sides. So Colonel Cree sent D Company round the left of the roadblock to go right round and come in on the rear of the Japs. B Company, my company, went round the right-hand side to come in behind the Japs. Unfortunately D Company didn't go far enough to get behind the Japs, ran smack into them, and lost twenty-six men, including all the officers. We heard the fighting going on. The roadblock was plastered by artillery and the next day we went in. We were lucky and by the time we got there the Japs had scarpered.

We found the bodies of the D Company chaps who were killed. We buried them there.

Major Alexander Wilson
Brigade Major, 6th Brigade
Coming south from Kohima, we were clearing roadblocks quicker than the Japs thought we could. The Japs would blow the little culverts between two ridges, and sit on the other side, they could be anything up to battalion strength. There were no bunkers, but foxholes, and they fought hard. The technique was to fix them in the front and climb above them, and outflank them. The Japs were getting short of men, their artillery was very sparse, they were an army in disarray, but that didn't mean they didn't fight.

We went through and met the Imphal garrison coming north.

Trooper Malcolm Connolly
7 Troop, C Squadron, 3rd Carabiniers
During the clearing of the Imphal Road we were sent to bury the crew of a tank that had been hit, caught fire, and exploded a few days earlier. There was only one complete body: 'Chick' Henderson had managed to get out of the side door, and crawled to the back, possibly to cover the retreat of his crew. But the Japs must have killed him. He was pretty badly burned by the exploding tank. We had the job of bringing him down and finding the pieces of the crew. The inside was derelict; we crawled inside and managed to find a foot here and a hand there. Then the job was getting them down. Chick's

body was rotting, we rolled him into a blanket and put it on a stretcher. As for the bits and pieces of the others, nobody had an idea of which bit belonged to who.

Private William Palmer
6 Platoon, B Company, 1st Battalion, Devonshire Regiment
During the monsoon we went to the Ukhrul Valley to ambush Japs retreating from Imphal. On one ambush in the early morning, the Japs were using bullocks to carry their equipment. First of all came troops, then the bullocks, then more troops, about sixty of them. The signal to open fire was a grenade thrown at the far end of the ambush, at which we threw grenades, and fired using Sten guns and Brens. We had two wounded. Most of the Japs ran off into the jungle. We counted eighteen dead Japs, and buried them.

Lieutenant Junichi Misana
33rd Mountain Artillery Regiment, 33rd Japanese Division
They came and came and came. So we would do it little by little. Every five mile or maybe a few mile, or ten mile or so, we would take a good mountain that we can use to our benefit, and we would do this for a few days. That's how we proceeded.

The plane was the enemy. I thought that by the time we reach the Manipur River we would get caught. If they pursued us in the way that the Japanese army would have done it, they would have already caught up with us. Yes, so I thought to myself, that we would probably get caught before we reach Manipur. But I would never say this out loud.

But we were able to gradually retreat, and managed to reach the Manipur without getting caught.

Private Jim Wilks
11 Platoon, B Company, 2nd Battalion, West Yorkshire Regiment
We started going along the Tiddim Road, crossed the Manipur River – there was a dead elephant in the water – up the Chocolate Staircase, to Tiddim, then Kennedy Peak and on to the Chindwin.

Trooper Malcolm Connolly
7 Troop, C Squadron, 3rd Carabiniers
The Tiddim Road was like a shooting gallery in a fun fair, as the tanks drove along one behind each other they were targets for the Japs. If you panicked you risked driving over the edge and falling hundreds of feet.

Captain Peter Noakes
Number 4 Company, 1st Battalion, Northamptonshire Regiment
I was now second-in-command of Number 4 company to Mike Hazelhurst. We got ready to go back to Burma, assembled and marched along the Mombi Track. The Mombi Track is a well-known track between Burma and India, only fit for mule or horse transport, across the Naga Hills. It rises to six thousand feet and when you get to Mombi you overlook Burma and the Kabaw Valley. Some Nagas came to meet us. They hated the Japanese.

We got to the Kabaw Valley, crossed it and there our problems started. On the maps it said 'Path follows the chaung'. We followed the chaung and struggled for days, in water. It was forty-five miles long, and took us five or six days to get to where the chaung finished. Every night you were wet, you put a clean pair of socks on, you had kept in your pack, and left the others out to dry. Eventually we came to the end, it was a hard slog with mules.

We sent out patrols, found the enemy had decamped and made our way towards Monywa.

Trooper Malcolm Connolly
7 Troop, C Squadron, 3rd Carabiniers
My troop had to take out a 105-mm gun that was holding up the division. That might seem strange that one gun could hold up a division. The infantry they sent out to find and destroy it couldn't find it; the Jap camouflage was so good. But they did locate approximately where it might possibly be. They used us as 'stooges', making us go forward hoping the Jap would open up.

We were able to leave the road, which was unusual. The first tank, the troop corporal's, was mined just after leaving the road. I was driving the troop officer and we climbed past the tank which had had its track blown off, nobody hurt. We headed for the top of the mountain where we had been ordered to sit, hoping the gun would fire at us. The troop sergeant coming up behind us had difficulty climbing. As soon as we got on to the skyline, this gun opened up and plastered all round us. We couldn't go back and had to continue on up, the firing went on. The troop officer's face was bleeding, but he was OK.

Eventually it was decided to back out the way we had come, and the 'Nips' let us go. We went back down the hill, and harboured in a nullah with the troop sergeant. After my troop officer and I had crawled up on to the ridge with binos to see if we could spot this gun, we got the order to leave. A matter of minutes later the troop sergeant reported that he had thrown a track. The troop officer got out to see if he could help. He was standing in front of the troop sergeant's tank when a shell burst killed him: blew his belly open. A lump of shrapnel went straight through the visor. It took the driver's head off, the arm muscle off the 37 gunner, and stunned the troop sergeant. The young operator was out of his head as he had all the driver's brains all over him, and we had a hell of a job to persuade them to open up. Eventually over the wireless we persuaded them to open up. I got in touch with the squadron by wireless and asked, 'What do we do?'

We were told that a Jap counter-attack was imminent, we were to leave the tanks, and go. All fit members of my crew helped all unfit members of the other crew, and they scarpered. I decided I wouldn't go, and I stayed. Nobody knew I was there. I decided they weren't going to have my tank. I was there, two dead men, two tanks and me.

I don't know what made me do it. Late in the afternoon, Captain Law, a Canadian officer attached to the regiment, was sent to find me. He asked me what I was going to do, and I said that I would take the tank down. He left to tell the squadron what was happening.

I brought the tank down and the squadron met me on the road.

Corporal Arthur Freer
Squadron Leader's driver/operator, B Squadron, 3rd Carabiniers
In the autumn of 1944, we headed down the Kabaw valley. It was typical wet jungle. Disease was rife: tick typhus, dengue fever, and malaria. B Squadron was allocated to supporting the leading battalion whoever it was. Whichever troop was leading, the squadron leader was up with them. This was a bit of a strain. We arrived at the southern end of Kabaw Valley at Kalewa, where the Bailey bridge across the Chindwin had just been completed. Mountbatten came to inspect it, and I was walking down the track to check up on some of

the other wireless operators in the squadron. I had my Sten without a butt, and no hat. My trousers were torn at the knee. Coming towards me I saw an immaculate admiral's uniform covered with medals, and six red-tabbed officers behind him. I didn't know what to do, I couldn't salute him, but at that moment a Jap Zero flew over, spotted this target, and came down machine-gunning. I threw myself into the ditch by the road, but Mountbatten beat me to it. I landed about two yards from him. I looked at him thinking I had an excuse for looking scruffy now. He laughed and walked off.

Trooper Malcolm Connolly
7 Troop, C Squadron, 3rd Carabiniers
That evening Major Morgan said, 'Have you seen Captain Law?'

'No,' I replied.

So they said they wanted me to go up with some of them and find him. I went to the cookhouse to get a cup of tea before we set off, and lo and behold, Captain Law was there. He had been found by a patrol of the West Kents who had found him hiding in the jungle.

He had gone off and a matter of fifty to a hundred yards away from us, two Japs took him prisoner. They were marching him away and our artillery started to shell the area. One shell landed close and the Jap in front of Captain Law scarpered, and slipped running down the hill. Law turned and hit the Jap behind him and dived down the bank and down the hill.

He said he had enough and wanted to go back to his own army.

Captain Peter Noakes
Number 4 Company, 1st Battalion, Northamptonshire Regiment
Before Monywa we had a battle, at Budalin, quite a battle. I commanded the company as Mike had been repatriated. We were on the right flank, and by the time we got there we had marched about two hundred and fifty miles from Wangjing, and had to put in an attack. Here there was a railway, the first we'd seen for a long time; it ran from Rangoon to Mandalay. The line was built on an embankment, which we had to cross in full view of the enemy. The idea was to rush the Japanese positions, and secure the main road between Monywa and Shwebo. We never got there. We were met by heavy machine gun and mortar fire, and my company had to withdraw. We dug in that night.

Corporal Arthur Freer
Squadron Leader's driver/operator, B Squadron, 3rd Carabiniers
We crossed the Chindwin on Bailey pontoon sections towed by DUKWs. There were no Japs on the other side. The advance to Shwebo was through teak forest and jungle. Travelled for about three days like this. Nothing happened until we started to get into thicker jungle. When there were signs that we were catching up on the Japs, such as food left behind, I told Major Huntley-Wright, the squadron leader, and asked, 'Shouldn't we net in on the sets to talk to the infantry?' He didn't do anything about it. On 23 December 1944, we came upon a Jap roadblock, and came under small-arms fire. He couldn't speak to the infantry CO on the wireless, and got out of the tank to do so.

About an hour later there was no sign of him. A troop leader, Captain Swann, called us eventually, telling us that the squadron leader was badly wounded and dying. I was sitting next to the driver, I took off my headset, and climbed into the turret to take command of the tank. I put my head out, and I felt a heavy bang on my head, and woke up on the floor of the turret. My head was hurting, no blood, but there was a lump the size of an egg. The sniper's bullet had hit the turret outside chipping off something, which hit me, but I got away with it.

I ordered the turret gunner to spray the trees above us and around. Captain Swann came on the air and said he was taking command of the squadron, and asked why I was firing. I told him I was trying to spray the sniper. He told me to leave him alone, the infantry would sort him out. We were told to bypass the Japs and press on.

The next day we burst through a Jap cookhouse, smashing a huge pot of boiling rice, which burst all over the tank. We were hungry and the rice smelt delicious, but we couldn't stop. By now we were out of the jungle and smashed through the Jap roadblocks. Each day another battalion from 2 Div took over the lead.

Captain Peter Noakes
Number 4 Company, 1st Battalion, Northamptonshire Regiment
B Company on the left flank of the battalion commanded by Peter Cherrington managed after a couple of days to get the Japs out of Budalin. It had a railway station and police HQ. Peter was awarded an immediate DSO.

SE 3173

A Lee-Grant tank of the 3rd Carabiniers on a pontoon constructed from a Bailey Bridge section crossing the Chindwin.

SE 1883

Soldiers of the 9th Battalion, Border Regiment cross the Chindwin at Kalewa.

Flight Lieutenant Owen Parry
11 Squadron, RAF

We had very little opposition from enemy fighters, the Spitfires dealt with them pretty easily. The majority of sorties by Jap fighters seemed to be sneak raids on airfields or ground targets, and they were a nuisance only. Flak was more of a problem for us. They would defend key points like bridges with Bofors-type guns. Impossible to spot were their heavy machine guns, you just saw the bullet holes when you returned, or an aircraft shot down.

You were always conscious that you might have to walk back if you were unlucky enough to be shot down. In our squadron we flew in long trousers and long-sleeved shirts, wearing army boots and short puttees, so we were well equipped to walk if we had to. You tried not to think too much about what would happen if you fell into Jap hands, but concentrated on how you would get away into the jungle and survive.

Ursula Graham-Bower
Naga Watch and Ward and Women's Auxiliary Corps (India) (WACI)

After the Imphal Plain had been clear for some time, it was arranged for a team of Nagas and me to train RAF personnel in jungle survival. They were faintly surprised at my teaching them survival and ambush techniques. The clearing where the camp was was right on top of an elephant trail. We used to take the men out into the jungle and practise stalking and hunting techniques. One day we found a large bull elephant in the middle of our class. We tiptoed away.

At the end of the course the air crew were taken out by jeep and dropped off in the jungle about twenty miles away with a compass and emergency rations. They were taught that if you happen to meet a tiger he is probably not hostile. He wants to be left alone. If you hear a deep growl in a thicket, turn round and creep away. He won't interfere with you. One of a party of two walked in on a tiger, there was a growl in the thicket, and they did creep away. It worked. After that the reputation of the instruction went up a lot.

Corporal Arthur Freer
Squadron Leader's driver/operator, B Squadron, 3rd Carabiniers

Two days after Huntley-Wright was killed we got a new squadron leader, Major E.S.P. Dorman. He was an Irishman. We had an Irish driver and they used to curse each other with Irish curses, nothing serious, just fun.

To get to Shwebo we had to cross the Mu River. It was shallow, and slow flowing. We crossed using a ford. We encountered continual sniping, and mines on the road, covered by machine guns. The few Japs we saw were dead or dying and emaciated. I didn't feel sorry for them in those days.

We entered Shwebo from the north. We took a war correspondent in our tank. We came to the gateway where there was a dry moat crossed by a bridge. There was no sign of life, but there were Jap bunkers on the other side of the moat. The leading tank crossed and others behind him noticed wires from the bridge over the moat to bunkers. Everybody was told to halt, and our sapper officer went forward and found some 500-kg bombs set for setting off by men in bunkers, but they had been abandoned because we had sprayed the bunkers first. We went into the town, it was dead, with a few chickens running around: no Burmese or Japs.

The war correspondent produced a report, which he showed me, and the only thing I could recognise was the names and addresses of the tank crew. The rest of the report was his imagination.

Captain Peter Noakes
Number 4 Company, 1st Battalion, Northamptonshire Regiment
When we came to Monywa I was still commanding Number 4 Company, but then it was taken over by Major Donald Eales-White who had been wounded in action some months before. I became 2i/c again.

We attacked through a mango grove, the Japs were up in the trees and in foxholes. Poor old Donald got wounded again, and I took over. We cleared the area. The rest of the battalion cleared an area known as the rifle butts, used by police. The Japs retired post haste to defend the passages over the Irrawaddy. Peter Cherrington was killed in this battle.

Corporal Arthur Freer
Squadron Leader's driver/operator, B Squadron, 3rd Carabiniers
After Shwebo, we had a few more actions in villages in the area between the Irrawaddy and Chindwin. The tanks were wearing out. New tracks were dropped to us by parachute and we fitted them within hours. Food was also dropped by air. In mid-January 1945 it was announced on squadron orders that Christmas Day 1944 would be on 15 January 1945. The cooks produced some chickens and we had Christmas pudding.

After that it was back to sorting out roadblocks again.

Captain Peter Noakes
Number 4 Company, 1st Battalion, Northamptonshire Regiment
We advanced over open country. It was very strange at first, advancing in extended line; two platoons up, one back. We saw Japanese running out of a village, and I sent in patrols. They reported Japs there. I said, 'Dig in.' The next day they had gone.

Corporal Arthur Freer
Squadron Leader's driver/operator, B Squadron, 3rd Carabiniers
We were clearing a village with a company of the Royal Scots, with tanks in the lead. The squadron leader was to the rear with the infantry. I saw two Japs jump into a slit trench just ahead. The squadron leader told me to guide the driver to it. I opened my little port, and a grenade landed beside the trench, about five feet away from my port. It was the squadron leader who had thrown the grenade. It killed the Japanese. Splinter from the grenade had cut wires under the tank wing leading to the aerial. The set wouldn't work, so the squadron leader ordered me out to repair it. I asked him to turn the tank sideways to give me cover. I climbed out with a pair of pliers and jack knife. I looked under, found the two wires, repaired them, but not before I got a tremendous shock: the squadron leader was transmitting, using me as an aerial. Fighting continued and we had tiffin on the move, eating cold baked beans out of the tin.

We then went back to the slit we had attacked earlier. We lifted up the Jap bodies and took the papers out of their pockets. Just then machine guns opened up and rounds cut up the ground around us. I recognised the sound of a tank Browning. We all threw ourselves to the ground. I said, 'It's one of our tanks, sir.'

He said, 'Well, go and stop it.'

That's when the hundred-yard record was broken for the first time. I jumped into our tank, picked up my headset to hear a troop leader say, 'I still think there's some movement there, give them another burst or two.'

I said over the radio, 'Able 5, were you firing your Maggie?'

He said, 'Yes, I'm engaging some Japanese, over.'

I said, 'Cease firing.'

'Why, over?'

'You are firing on number 9 and his crew, over.'

There was a horrible hush, then, 'Wilco out.'

Next day followed the same routine. During that second day, one of our troop leaders wirelessed back to the squadron leader, 'There are some boats crossing the Irrawaddy.'

He replied, 'Sink them then.'

They were laden with troops, and they were sunk.

That was the end of that phase. We relaxed, swam, fished with grenades to improve our diet. Then we were told we were going to cross the Irrawaddy, and go to Mandalay.

On to Rangoon

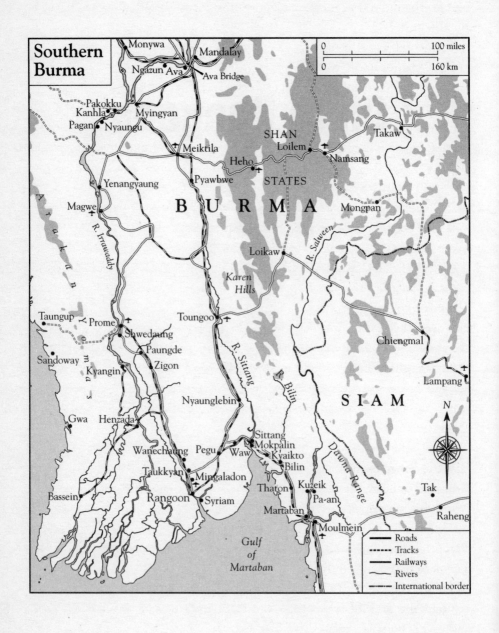

Southern Burma

Monywa
Mandalay
Ngazun Ava
Ava Bridge

0   100 miles
0   160 km

Pakokku
Kanhla
Pagan Nyaungu
Myingyan

SHAN
Loilem
Takaw

Meiktila
Heho Namsang
Pyawbwe
STATES

Yenangyaung
B U R M A
Mongpan

Magwe

R. Irrawaddy

Loikaw

R. Salween

Karen Hills

Taungup Prome
Toungoo
Chiengmai

Shwedaung
Paungde

Sandoway
Zigon
Lampang

Kyangin

R. Sittang
R. Bilin

Nyaunglebin
S I A M

N

Gwa Henzada

Sittang
Mokpalin
Wanechaung Pegu Kyaikto
Waw Bilin
Dawna Range

Taukkyan
Mingaladon
Thaton Kuzeik
Tak
Bassein
Rangoon Syriam
Pa-an

Martaban
Raheng

Moulmein

Gulf of Martaban

Roads
Tracks
Railways
Rivers
International border

We were moving about twenty to thirty miles per day. We had to get to
Rangoon if only to get proper rations. The monsoon was not far away,
air supply would be unreliable in monsoon.
The whip was out.

After the defeat of the Japanese in Assam and before the subsequent advance by the British, Slim was told by Mountbatten to limit his objective to securing Mandalay. Rangoon, he was informed, was to be captured by Operation Dracula, an airborne and amphibious force consisting of formations released from the Arakan after that area had been cleared of the enemy. Mountbatten considered that it was pointless to push further south into central Burma, and was concerned that by driving the Japanese closer to Rangoon, they would be in a better position to oppose Operation Dracula.

Slim, believing that his great victory should be fully exploited, ordered that the Fourteenth Army would take Rangoon overland. In order to do so, he aimed to bring the Japanese army to battle as early as possible, in a place where his superiority in armour and in the air could be employed to best advantage. To begin with, he thought that this would be on the Shwebo Plain on the approach to the Irrawaddy. But he discovered that the Japanese had changed their plans.

Lieutenant General Kawabe, commanding Burma Area Army, had aimed to hold the area between the Chindwin and the Irrawaddy in strength. However, he was replaced by Lieutenant General Hyotaro Kimura, who changed the plan to one which involved allowing Slim to start crossing the Irrawaddy, and, as he was committed, finishing him off.

Slim, therefore, also changed his plan, to destroying the Japanese east of the Irrawaddy instead of west of it, by getting across their line of communication to Mandalay in the region of Meiktila. In essence, he would cross the Irrawaddy north of Mandalay, which is where he identified that Kimura expected him to cross, but his main effort would be well south of the city. Having smashed the Japanese army, Slim would head for Rangoon.

Concurrent with operations in central Burma, the efforts of Christison's XV Corps in Arakan were aimed at helping the Fourteenth Army by holding down the maximum number of Japanese in the Arakan. In addition, if the XV Corps captured air bases on the Arakan littoral at Akyab, Cheduba and Ramree, this would hugely reduce the range that aircraft flying to support Fourteenth Army would have to cover.

Although Christison had pulled back to easily defended localities in the Arakan in mid-1944, British troops were kept busy with local attacks, aggressive patrolling and intelligence gathering. Even while the great battles in Assam were underway, the British, with their command of the sea, were able to raid down the Arakan coast. Later, more amphibious operations were mounted, and these, combined with a series of limited offensives, kept the Japanese from reinforcing their troops facing the main effort in Assam and the advance to the Irrawaddy, Mandalay and Meiktila, and eventually to Rangoon.

The Japanese, on their part, fought hard to prevent the British breaking into the Irrawaddy Valley through the Arakan Yomas.

In early 1945 the pro-Japanese Burmese National Army of around nine battalions, led by Aung San, decided to change sides. The Burmese people, in contrast to the Karens, Chins, and Shans, had initially welcomed the Japanese as liberators from British rule. Eventually they became thoroughly disillusioned by their new masters' conduct, culminating in systematic looting of Burmese towns and villages as the Japanese retreated. From the end of the British retreat in May 1942 until they advanced across the Chindwin at the end of 1944, the Burmese in the central plains were hardly touched by the war. But they suffered casualties and extensive damage to their homes as the fighting moved out of the Assamese and Arakan hills and jungles into the more heavily populated terrain in the Irrawaddy valley.

THE ARAKAN

Lieutenant Richard Acton
Support Troop, 44 (Royal Marine) Commando
We embarked in Z lighters, and went down the Naf River to a small village on the west side of the Naf River, to carry out an operation at Alethangyaw. The idea was to interrupt the Japanese communications leading up to where 25 Div were fighting. We were told that Alethangyaw was very lightly defended and wouldn't cause much problem. Unfortunately the information was out of date. There was a battalion of Japs at Alethangyaw, so we landed at night into a bit more than we anticipated from LCP(L)s. These were funny craft with gangways let down each side of the bow, manned by RIN people. They were keen we got off the craft quickly, and dumped us in deep water. My chaps were carrying about a hundred pounds on their backs, parts of Vickers machine guns or mortars, and ammunition. We were reluctant to jump into deep water as our lifejackets would not keep us afloat with all that weight. So there was a little bit of a palaver. The Rifle troops had gone in before us.

Sergeant John Webber
B Troop, 44 (Royal Marine) Commando
B Troop was the reserve troop at Alethangyaw. With a heavy surf running, the crews were reluctant to push the boats in; we kept going in and being washed back out again. Finally when we got in again I said to Lieutenant Ryder, 'For God's sake jump,' gave him a push, and jumped in after him. I landed in water up to my chest. We staggered ashore where there was a state of complete confusion. C Troop were tangled up in a battle in Alethangyaw, and eventually we finished up among a collection of huts. By morning we had dug ourselves in near a bamboo fence looking towards Alethangyaw. There was sniping coming from there. I was with our sniper, George Deacon.

Eventually, I said to George Deacon, 'I'm sure that's the sniper up in that tree.' He raised his sniper rifle, with a telescopic sight, and fired a round at the tree. There was no more sniping from that tree.

Colour Sergeant 'Dinger' Bell
B Troop, 44 (Royal Marine) Commando
We went into the foothills and could look back and see the village. I had a

sniper in my section with a telescopic sight on his rifle, and from a hill, we saw six Japanese washing in a water hole, about six hundred yards away. He got one, and wounded another in the leg. After half an hour they sent out a patrol. Our TSM was sent out to capture these blokes. They laid an ambush for them. The TSM went forward to take them prisoner, and his tommy gun jammed so the Bren gunners opened up and killed all the Japs.

Sergeant John Webber
B Troop, 44 (Royal Marine) Commando

The next night we were given orders to withdraw down a chaung. My section was due to go first, followed by Sergeant Grant's; somehow he got in front of us. He never made it, and was missing presumed killed, in the darkness. We went to the West African base at Nahkaungdo, we called it 'No can do'.

We then went back for Operation Screwdriver Two, where troops were based on villages. We patrolled at night, by day the Japs could spot our movements. Captain Sturges would always take me with him, because I was the only single sergeant; a dubious honour.

On one patrol, which we did from 'No can do', we had quite a scrap with the Japanese in a village. We got into the village and could look through and see the Japanese in their pits. Sturges wouldn't let us fire on them, but as we were withdrawing, the Japs opened fire on us from another position; our machine gunners were firing back to cover our withdrawal.

We had a marine with us, the bane of my life, who was always doing things wrong. He got up from a depression in the ground to run, and as he ran the Japanese machine-gun bullets were nearly catching him up. Suddenly his trousers fell down, he went headlong into a dip, and the bullets went over his head.

Lieutenant Dominic Neill
Intelligence Officer, 3rd/2nd Gurkha Rifles

I would often go out with patrols. On one occasion we were tasked with seizing a prisoner from behind Japanese lines. The plan was to board a small coastal steamer at Maungdaw, steam down the Naf River by night, towing three large country boats to a point about five miles south of the river entrance, where we were to get into the country boats, and row ashore. Having left a section to hold the beach, with the heavy radio to brigade HQ, we were to advance about a thousand yards to set up an advance patrol base.

At about midnight, in an ominous swell, we climbed, heavily laden, into the country boats, which were about the size of a fairly large rowing boat. The mens' faces in the moonlight were studies – if I was afraid, how much more must the men have been, in fear of their lives as not a single one could swim. After a nightmare five-hundred-yard journey in the boats, we all landed safely and spent the rest of the night on the beach.

We were taking up a position overlooking a strip of paddy between the two halves of a village, when three Japs stood up from behind a small mound about three-quarters of the way between us and the far side of the paddy. After a few minutes, perhaps they were suspicious, they took up fire positions behind the mound, but still clearly in sight. We watched fascinated for another minute, as they lay exposed about seventy-five yards away.

We had never had the chance in 1943 to study Japs at leisure, at short range. We made the most of this opportunity and then killed them. I fired first with my Thompson SMG, and my Bren gunner shot the other two.

The next day while ambushing a track, a Japanese patrol approached. We watched like cats watching mice, but these mice were dangerous. A long burst of Bren shattered the silence.

The Japs took cover behind a bund like lightning. A Jap tried to crawl away, I fired quickly two or three times, seeing hits on the wet shirt on his back. A wet rump poked up for a moment, and I fired three quick shots, one hit and flung the Jap back into the flooded paddy. As I hit him with another shot, I remembered that our mission was to take a prisoner, and if I didn't act soon, all candidates for the POW cage would be dead. I screamed above the din to the left-hand section to give me covering fire, ordered the section with me to cease fire, fix swords, draw kukris and charge.

Two enemy broke cover and tried to make a dash for it. One stopped and flung up his hands in surrender. I was not gaining on the other man, my chest was heaving, my tommy gun muzzle was going up and down, my eyes full of sweat. I fired three bursts and could see the rounds hitting the man's back, flicking away pieces of shirt and flesh. I had not realised the hitting power of a .45 bullet before. The Jap shot forward like a rag doll hit with a sledge hammer.

I walked back to where the prisoner was standing among the dead and the reddening rice water. We had shot them to ribbons. I told my men to check the remaining seven bodies for signs of life, and search each for documents. Our prisoner was a JIF.

Lieutenant James Sherwood
C *Group*, 2 *SBS*

Shortly after I arrived at Teknaf with my group, I took the place of a sick chap in A Group on an operation. We were taken in an MGB run by the Indian Navy, a tremendous bunch of blokes running those things. We motored down the Naf River into the Bay of Bengal. By nightfall we were some miles from where we were supposed to land. There was only a slight swell, which can be very big by the time it reaches the beach. We got our canoes over the side, there was no moon, and set off to the beach.

By this time A group had developed a technique for dealing with surf on a beach, which no one had thought of before. Not to plane into the beach, but turn and face the swell, watch for the moment when the horizon went black, which it did when the wave built up, and paddle like hell into it; bash through it before it broke, or as it was breaking, and you had enough speed on to go straight through it, shipping the minimum amount of water, and remain upright. Once that had passed, you paddled astern as fast as you could, waited until the same thing happened. With successive waves you got on to the beach dry-shod and upright. This we did.

We pulled the canoes up just above the water line. A bloke was left to guard the canoes; we could hear drums inland. We crept inland, the object being to glean information, not stir up a hornet's nest. We heard whistling and spotted a figure ambling along the beach. We lay in the sand. I had alongside me a great big hulking bloke who had been a member of the Manchester City Police before the war. I said to him, 'You grab him.'

He did. He was no Jap, only a young Burmese, a coast watcher appointed by the Japanese to look out for people like us. He was terrified and thought he would be killed. He spoke a little English. We reassured him we would not kill him, and asked him to lead us to the nearest village. He agreed to do so. He said there was a Japanese sergeant living in a basha. He would take us there, but only if we took him with us. You could always stuff a passenger in the bow section of the canoe, with his head in the lap of the front paddler.

He led us up the beach along a track and we could see flames from a fire. The officer in charge, Holden Wright, allocated people to tasks, covering

James Sherwood as a captain in the Royal Ulster rifles after the war.

approaches and so forth. As we approached we could see light through the split bamboo of the basha. The local would go to the door and tap on it to get the Jap to come out at which point he would be grabbed or shot, whichever seemed appropriate.

There must have been about eight of us, all armed with tommy guns or pistols. The chap knocked, the door opened, a figure appeared and came outside, and must have realised that something wasn't quite right or something, because he took to his heels pursued by a fusillade of shots, none of which got him. He escaped, astonishing, but that sort of thing happens in war. But the hut was full of all sorts of valuable intelligence information.

The coast watcher told us that there was a Jap platoon just down the track who must have heard the firing, so we returned to our canoes, tucked the coast watcher into the bows of one of them, and got back to the MGB without further problems. The intelligence was of value to the corps commander, we subsequently learned. But it was typical of so many SBS operations: somehow they went off half-cock very often. I don't think we thought far enough ahead.

Pilot Officer Roger Cobley
20 Squadron, RAF

We had been sent to attack Akyab, where a Japanese general was supposed to be visiting. There was no aircraft there. I was leading, and was hit by flak. The others peeled off. My engine kept stopping then picking up, and glycol smoke was coming out. I had eighty miles to go, and wasn't going to make it. I told the others to go home. I headed for the Kaladan Valley where I knew there were some relatively bare hillsides, and the West Africans were still about. I landed wheels up on a barer patch, and it was right by a West African forward patrol. The West Africans arranged for an L-5 to come into a strip they had prepared and fly me out. I was back in the squadron before nightfall that day. I was very lucky, I didn't get a scratch.

Lieutenant Stamford Weatherall
C Group, 2 SBS

We penetrated the chaungs in our canoes. We went as far as the Kaladan River and were able to watch the Jap sentries on a jetty. We had with us two Burmese interpreters. Major Livingstone and Lieutenant Sherwood went across in two canoes at night with the two interpreters to see a village headman. While they were gone, a rowboat pulled up not far from us, and out of it got a woman, a man and three children. We grabbed them, the man was escaping from the Japanese and returning home. He could speak English and read a map, so I took a lot of notes off him. I captured a young Burmese fishing and hauled him into our den. He was the first man's brother-in-law, and was suffering from horrible sores, and we bandaged him up. When Livingstone came back he got him to come with him with a map and pinpoint all the Japanese positions. We took him and his brother-in-law to Chittagong for interrogation. They were taken to Calcutta from there, were feted and given money.

Havildar Umrao Singh
33 Mountain Battery

I volunteered to attack a hill near the sea in the Arakan, this hill was proving very difficult to take, so I took my troop down a path which we had made. Unfortunately the Japanese had discovered that we had made this path and we ran into a party of them. It was very difficult terrain, the bamboo was so thick you couldn't see anyone. All the main troops who were accompanying me ran away or were killed. But my troop stayed with me. I was with one troop and I had two howitzers with me and we started firing on the Japanese, and eventually we ran out of ammunition for our howitzers. We suddenly found ourselves surrounded. So I told my troop to withdraw. They said they would not go without me, so I started to withdraw with them. Suddenly I thought to myself a gunner never leaves his gun, so I went back again, and started firing at them with my Bren gun, which was all I had. This went on for five hours, firing when someone came within five yards of me. Eventually I ran out of ammunition, so I picked up a hammer from my howitzer and attacked the Japanese with this, and I managed to kill quite a few of them. Until some aeroplanes flew overhead, this frightened the Japanese, and they ran away. I collapsed senseless because I had several wounds.

When I was eventually rescued I was told that there were thirty to thirty-five Japanese dead in the small area near where we had been fighting. Of course I did not kill them all, many of them were killed by my colleagues in my troop.

Lieutenant Richard Acton
Support Troop, 44 (Royal Marine) Commando

Soon after Christmas 1944 we mounted an operation on Akyab, but had an unopposed landing, just a few Japanese booby traps. Bit of a damp squib.

Sergeant John Webber
B Troop, 44 (Royal Marine) Commando

After the unopposed landing at Akyab, we were bombed by Zeros. A Dakota came to land at the airfield and the Indian AA gunners opened up on it. They stopped when it fired a red Very light.

Havildar Umrao Singh
33 Mountain Battery

When I got back after hospital, it was announced that I had the VC. I did not know what it was. I thought that it meant I was going to get a Viceroy's Commission. So I was taken to the commandant who told me that I was Bahadur, a brave man, and I was being rewarded for bravery. I thought to myself I don't know what bravery is. I joined the artillery to fight, and I fought, that was my job.

Sergeant Frank Allison
A Troop, 42 (Royal Marine) Commando

After Akyab we landed at Myebon. The air strikes had gone in. We landed in deep mud. As we were getting off, the chap sitting four rows in front of me had his head taken off by a shell. Jed Allen, just to my left, put his hand to his head and said, 'I've been hit.' Blood was coming from between his fingers. But he hadn't been hit, this chap who'd had his head blown off had sprayed him with blood.

We charged ashore. I took my section just off the beach, in front of us was a Jap bunker. I took my section round the back. I charged in, it was all in darkness, you couldn't see a thing. I pressed the trigger of my tommy gun. Nothing happened. I rushed out. The magazine was jammed with mud. I put on a fresh magazine, and this time threw a grenade before I went into the bunker.

From there my section had to go up to establish a radio on a hill. Before we set off an officer came up and asked, 'Who cleared the bunker?'

'Me and my section.'

'Anything to declare?' says he.

'No, if there was there wouldn't be anything left of them.'

He said, 'There was a 2-pounder gun in there.'

'Well, I couldn't see because it was dark.'

We went on about two hundred yards. My first thought was to make a cup of tea. But my water bottle was full of salt water.

Sergeant John Webber
B Troop, 44 (Royal Marine) Commando

Landing at Myebon, we were the reserve commando. It was late afternoon and we were put ashore on a receding tide on a mangrove swamp, mud up to our midriffs. The longer the landing lasted, the more the tide went out. Once we got ashore we weren't fit to fight – weapons and equipment covered in mud. I took off all my clothes in a shell hole full of water, washed my clothes and myself, and the sun dried it all out. Luckily the other commandos had landed ahead and pushed the Japanese back. There was some Japanese mortar fire, but the bombs exploded in the mud and didn't do any damage. We spent the night in some old Japanese defensive positions, cleaning all our clips of ammunition.

Private Victor Ralph
4 Troop, 1 Commando

Having cleared the Myebon peninsula it was decided that the next landing should be at Kangaw. The Japs were pulling out down through the Arakan and had used the Daingbon Chaung and Myebon river as an escape route. We had virtually cut them off by taking Myebon, but there was a road that led over the mountains. Kangaw was a key point that overlooked the road; they would have to use it to complete their withdrawal. It was not far from Myebon, but impossible to get to overland, so another landing was needed, by sailing up the Daingbon Chaung in landing craft.

We were first ashore, having negotiated the mangrove swamp, which wasn't easy, we got to the paddy, and we could see Hill 170 in front of us. The Japs opened up on us. But we took the hill fairly easily. About halfway up the hill there was a young Burmese girl, about seventeen or eighteen, and her baby a few months old, lying in a pool of blood, her stomach torn open.

Sergeant John Webber.

I thought, was it our shelling of the hill that did that or was it when we were attacking, when the Japs mortared us? And it occurred to me that it didn't matter very much, she was in her homeland and here were two foreign powers fighting each other and she and her baby had died because of that.

Sergeant Jack Salter
4 Troop, 1 Commando
We dug in around the hill top, with firing positions all within a few yards of each other. I was the demolition man for laying booby traps at night. I went out and laid Bangalore torpedoes and grenades in tins with trip wires. Every morning I would go out and disarm them.

Sergeant John Webber
B Troop, 44 (Royal Marine) Commando
We landed on the beach and moved up behind Hill 170 which had already been taken, and moved on to take the next hill called Milford, and on again to Pinner, the hill nearest the track which led into central Burma. We started to dig in on Pinner. We hit rock not far down. We were told to stop digging because we were due to move on to the next hill called Duns that night. We stood to and waited for orders to move. It was a beautiful moonlit night. The Japs had a gun dug in on the hill opposite us and no sooner did you hear the gunfire than the shell exploded in amongst us.

The hill was heavily tree-covered, and some of the shells exploded in the trees and shredded the trees into sharp bits of wood, and these showered down on us. Then they put in attacks, one after another supported by mortar fire; it was a very long night. I never saw them, but heard them. Corporal Fleming was killed close to me. 'Ack-Ack' Marshall, another of my corporals, was hit. We carried him down the hill, getting hold of his shoulders was like catching hold of pulp, because he had been hit by showers of wood. He kept on shouting, 'Come on Number 1 Section, at 'em,' which was bad, because it pinpointed the position. But he died during the night.

Acting RSM 'Dinger' Bell
44 (Royal Marine) Commando
Pinner was right up alongside the track the Japs were using to withdraw down the Kaladan Valley. I was standing in for the RSM, and had a lance corporal

with me as an orderly. The signals officer had his back blown off by a tree burst. He was dying. My orderly had a big hole in his back from a tree burst. Why he got out of the trench I'll never know.

Japs came in with sandbags with corners pushed out over their heads as camouflage. They crawled up and tried to throw grenades into our trenches, but most of our casualties were from tree bursts. We ran out of HE grenades, and instead threw phosphorus grenades, which burnt them, especially their eyes.

My job as RSM was to organise the burials, get the discs off them, and make a note of where they were buried. I went to get the details off a chap who had been a BBC pianist before the war. He was so badly blown to bits, I had to leave everything in his trench, and put a wooden cross on it. I burnt his name on it with a blackened nail. The rest were buried down below the hill.

We lost twenty-seven killed and nearly one hundred wounded, some badly, that night. We went into action well below strength at about 320 and when I did my muster the next morning there were about 180 left to fight, out of a commando that should have been 450. Behind us we had fourteen Indian stretcher-bearers. The Japs got in behind us, we heard screaming, it was the Japs kicking their heads in. We found them the next morning.

I thought the Japanese were very brave. Once the Japanese started attacking in a place and they were failing, they went on without any sort of manoeuvre, or looking for another place. You knew that once they started attacking in one place they went on doing so in that place.

Captain Richard Acton
Officer Commanding Support Troop, 44 (Royal Marine) Commando
I was dug in between commando HQ and C Troop. When darkness came the Japs started to attack. Their method was always to try and make us reveal ourselves, by coming close and trying to taunt you. The response was to throw grenades. They retaliated with grenades. One chap in a slit trench near me got a foot blown off by a grenade. The TSM went to him, and I went to commando HQ to get the doctor, a marvellous chap. Eventually we managed to evacuate him.

All night we were shelled by the Japanese, and we directed return fire from the RIN sloops *Nerbudda* and *Jumna*.

Sergeant John Webber
B Troop, 44 (Royal Marine) Commando

Brigadier Hardy came up the next morning, and I think was surprised that we held it. Later in the day we were relieved by the Hyderabad Regiment, and withdrew behind Hill 170 to defend the beach, codename Hove.

Sergeant Frank Allison
A Troop, 42 (Royal Marine) Commando

In the night on Hill 170, reinforcing Number 1 Commando, the Japs were shouting, 'Come out and fight, you marines.' They knew we were there. You couldn't shout back. Except one chap did shout back and told the Japs where to go, using an obscene word. He was put on a charge.

A Troop was on the end of the hill. We were relieved by another troop. But the Japs took that part of the hill. A Troop was about to go in to take it back, but being under strength, two other troops were put in. They took it back with heavy casualties. One troop was wiped out completely. We had to go in and dig the bodies out of the trenches and bury them at the bottom of the hill. As we were burying them the Japanese were sniping at us.

Sergeant Jack Salter
4 Troop, 1 Commando

I was given orders not to put the booby traps out because Indian troops were relieving us the next day and they wouldn't know where they were. The next morning, at about four o'clock, a terrific barrage of artillery and mortar fire hit us. They blew up the three tanks we had at the foot of the hill with pole charges and the attacks lasted all day. The OP for the artillery was knocked out in the early stages, so messages were passed back by shouting to troop HQ.

I lost a lot of friends there. One of them, 'Snipe' Lander, I had known for years. He came up to rejoin us as a reinforcement wearing a bush hat instead of his beret. I said, 'Hey Snipe, take that off. They'll think you're the brigadier.'

Next minute he was shot through the head.

Private Victor Ralph
4 Troop, 1 Commando

Hand-to-hand fighting took place all day. The Bren gunners in the Bren pit were being wiped out one after the other. One of our officers, Lieutenant

Nolan, I don't know if he was mad, or very brave, but he was walking about in the open with a 2-inch mortar which he fired from the hip, with a Bren gun, a tommy gun, a rifle, anything he could lay his hands on. He took out an awful lot of Japanese. Eventually he was killed.

Number 4 Troop took the brunt of the attacks, but as we lost a lot of men, various sections of other troops, troops of Number 5 Commando came and troops of 42 Commando as the day went on. Parts of the whole brigade were involved all day. It was like Rorke's Drift. The hill was quite overgrown and this was a problem, you couldn't see people approaching until they were quite close. One, a Japanese warrant officer, came charging waving his sword. Everyone on the hill seemed to fire at him, and he went down. Some idiot ran out to grab his sword, and waved it over his head, shouting, 'I've got it. I've got it.' He went down, shot by the Japanese. But he had only leg wounds and was dragged back in.

A Japanese left by himself by an abortive attack and likely to be taken prisoner pulled out one of his grenades and, lying face down, put it under his stomach and blew himself to pieces.

Sergeant Jack Salter
4 Troop, 1 Commando
When the evening came the attack had been pushed back. We counted about four hundred dead Japanese. We had fighter planes in support, and gunfire from ships, and from artillery on pontoons off the beach.

Private Victor Ralph
4 Troop, 1 Commando
I was too busy to be frightened at the time. I don't think any of us expected to come out of it. It was not a question of bravery, but you had too much to do to think about it. After the battle was over and we were relieved, the next day, the thought of what might have happened overtook you.

Lieutenant James Sherwood
C Group, 2 SBS
Before the landing on Ramree we did a recce, involving eight Folboats. We embarked in an MGB and put our canoes over the side, not far from Ramree Island at the entrance to Kyaukpyau Harbour, which is a huge bay,

25-pounder guns on a Z-lighter pontoon supporting the landings and battle at Kangaw.

there is no harbour. It is dotted with tree-clad islands. We paddled to the RV on one of these islands to establish a small base from which we would carry out recces of the surrounding area, of Kyaukpyau Harbour and Ramree Island generally.

It was dark when we landed on a rocky little beach there, established our base and waited for daylight. No sooner had it come than we saw a group of Burmese come along the beach, they were living on the island. They were wholly cooperative and were delighted to see the British coming back.

Livingstone decided to lead the first recce of Ramree, and one of the Burmese volunteered to go with him. He saw a Japanese patrol on a road running south out of the town, without being spotted, and returned to the island but did not discover anything.

The next night we all went back, guided by a Burmese who said he would take us to a village about a mile inland. This was quite a long way. We landed, and crossed dried-out paddy fields. Our chief fear was being caught by Japs. We arrived in the village and while we waited outside, the Burmese went to the headman of the village, and discovered that there were no Japs there. We spoke to the headman. We got all the information we wanted and where the Japs were. He got one of his chaps to go back with us to the island, the aim being to take him to Div HQ at Chittagong so he could be debriefed there.

Livingstone was staying on a day or two longer. He said, 'You take three canoes, take this bloke back, and RV with the MGB.'

It was a long paddle of about six miles to the prearranged RV. I had this chap in my bow with his head in my lap. The bow was low in the water and it was a hell of an effort paddling. The MGB got us back to Teknaf by daybreak next morning. I took the Burmese up to Chittagong for debriefing with General Lomax, 26th Indian Division. The Burmese was taken home with the invasion fleet a few days later.

Major Dominic Neill
Officer Commanding B Company, 3rd/2nd Gurkha Rifles
At first light, the CO passed through my position and warned me to take Snowdon East. He reminded me that the position was to be taken regardless of cost. Rumours that 25 Div was about to be pulled out for retraining and refitting, were among the thousand and one thoughts that range through an

infantryman's mind as he prepares himself to cross a start line, glancing so frequently at the minute hand of his watch as it moves towards H-Hour. There were many of us in B Company that hot afternoon that wondered if this was to be our last attack, and which of us would remain behind forever on the hill that rose in front of us. At 1428 the troop of 25-pounders and medium guns boomed out from behind us, and the shells whistled over our heads to burst on Snowdon East. For a moment we forgot our own thoughts as we watched the shells burst. Then the bombardment ceased: it was H-Hour. At 1430 both assault platoons fixed swords and advanced.

The leading sections came through the bamboo and into the primary jungle. The trees had been splintered and shattered by our artillery fire, many felled in a criss-cross fashion making an obstacle to us that no Jap working party could have equalled had they toiled for days. On the right flank, in the path of 5 Platoon the dry jungle had started to burn. It was while the assault platoons were struggling through this tangle of broken trees that the Japs first hit us with every weapon they possessed. Then they rolled grenades taped to mines down on us. The leading soldiers started to fall, tumbling over like shot rabbits. So far the assault did not falter, individual soldiers gave covering fire to others as groups leapfrogged up the hill.

Then they hit us again, from Whistle, where Japs had a rifle company dug in. They hit us with MMGs on fixed lines. The stream of bullets came at hip height, mowing like scythes through the timber. As the Jap fire started from our left flank so it intensified from the dug-in position ahead. With numbers of soldiers going down, we began to waver and finally halted, cover was sought, and the long fire-fight, which was to use up so much of our precious ammunition, started.

The guns on Whistle never ceased firing until the very end of the battle. The momentum of our attack was failing. I wondered then if the rumours about the division coming out of the line were having a subconscious effect on our actions.

Content to remain where we were, I was doing no leading. I went forward and as the platoon commander was badly wounded, told the havildar to take command. I crawled to 5 Platoon, then asked for artillery fire on to Whistle. But, because the gunner was further back and couldn't see the target, all the ranging rounds for Whistle fell among my forward platoons, causing casualties, and effecting morale. A rifleman just in front of me was hit in the face by a large piece of shrapnel, reducing it to pulp and showering everybody in the vicinity with blood. If the FOO had been beside me at that moment I would probably have killed him. I crawled back and shouted at the gunner in Anglo-Saxon and told him the result of his ranging. He shouted back his apologies and said the guns could not clear the crest and hit Whistle. There was nothing for it but to accept that the Jap machine-gunners on Whistle would continue to fire at us for as long as they pleased, or ran out of ammo. Our prospects looked bleak.

Then the unexpected happened. Lance Naik Chamar Singh Gurung rose to his feet and, yelling obscenities to the Japs above him, started clambering through the broken tree trunks and up the hill. In the face of showers of grenades and heavy rifle and machine-gun fire, and urged on by the screams of encouragement from the men of his platoon, he ran on up the hill spraying the hill with his tommy gun. He was hit by goodness knows how many enemy bullets as he reached the first enemy trench. But he stumbled on, squeezing the trigger of his tommy gun, falling dead across the lip of the Jap trench. Chamar Singh Gurung was the first man on Snowdon East that afternoon. His gallant conduct and inspiration turned what might have been defeat into victory. His action triggered off a series of other actions, which resulted in the Japs being flung off Snowdon.

Rifleman Bhanbhagta Gurung stood up and, inspired by Chamar Singh's bravery, yelled to those near him to follow, and started to run towards the top of the hill. Others rose and charged with a tremendous roar. The Japs met this attack with showers of grenades and rapid fire. The MMGs on Whistle cut down soldiers, and once again they wavered in the face of this murderous fire, and went to ground this time only twenty yards from Jap forward trenches. This, however, was no repeat of the first time. Without waiting for orders, Bhanbhagta Gurung dashed forward alone, attacked the nearest enemy foxhole just above him, and throwing two grenades he killed the two occupants. Without hesitation, he rushed to the next trench and bayoneted the Jap in it to death.

The leading platoons rose and fell upon the Jap defenders of Snowdon East, and the battle lasted until the last Jap soldier had been killed or run off. Bhanbhagta Gurung then attacked a lone machine gun in a bunker. Now, out of HE grenades, he flung in two white phosphorus grenades, two Jap soldiers came out with their clothes on fire, to be cut down by him with his kukri. A remaining Jap, despite grievous wounds from burning phosphorus, continued to fire, whereupon Bhanbhagta Gurung crawled inside the bunker, where he beat out the Jap gunner's brains with a rock, capturing the machine gun.

Seven Japs with fixed bayonets counter-attacked, and were repulsed by a naik with grenades and a bayonet charge, killing two and putting the rest to flight. Enemy positions bypassed started firing and holding up the reserve section and were taken out by the section commander.

There were eleven men left in the right-hand platoon. The left-hand platoon was still under fire when the platoon commander, screaming with rage, killed Japanese with his bayonet red with blood. He had six men left. One NCO attacked the enemy using his TG as a club when out of ammo. Then, drawing his kukri, charged the position, hacking to death one enemy: two others fled.

The reserve platoon now came up as the assault platoons were pitching in to the enemy, and I told the platoon commander to take over the ground from the assault platoons. As they advanced they came under fire from the guns on Whistle, killing and wounding soldiers. As they reached the top the machine-gun fire from Whistle stopped momentarily, and twelve Japs appeared with fixed bayonets and attacked the rear of 4 Platoon. Seeing them, the reserve platoon left-hand section killed them. They then beat off a counter-attack from Whistle.

It was chaos on the top of the objective. The first of the organised counter-attack Banzai charges was beaten off with heavy losses. Snowdon East was now ours. My two assault platoons were smaller than one weak platoon. The part of Snowdon East held by enemy was eighty yards long by thirty yards wide, the whole area pockmarked by trenches. All over the objective lay bodies.

After three further Japanese counter-attacks there was silence. More than sixty per cent of B Company had gone. I was very proud of them. They had captured Snowdon East, regardless of cost.

Corporal Jim Dunning
15 Platoon, C Company, 2nd Battalion, Green Howards
We were the first company wave ashore at Letpan. There was very little opposition. Going up the narrow chaungs in landing craft I thought how vulnerable we were. On our way in we passed a hospital ship and the nurses

Corporal Jim Dunning.

waved to us. I thought how nice it would be to be on board with all those nurses.

We were supposed to advance down the road to Taungup, the roadhead for the Japanese route from Prome in Central Burma. It took us quite a long time to get to Taungup. Along the road there were lots of small hills, covered in secondary jungle, bushy and small trees. All places where the Japs could defend and delay us. All the time we leapfrogged companies taking these hills. You were advancing up very narrow tracks and had quite a few casualties taking these hills. It was so enclosed you couldn't see very far.

Fifteen or twenty people could put up a lot of opposition. Our battalion never took a prisoner. Each engagement happened so quickly. You would bump into the Japanese on the hill, there would be a fire-fight, and they would melt away, usually taking their wounded with them. It was nerve-wracking, fighting in constricted spaces.

I was a section commander until our platoon sergeant went sick and I took over. We were on top of a hill, you had the sea on one side and hills on the other, and through our binoculars we could see a warship with sailors on the deck sunbathing. I thought I'd swap places with you any day. A few minutes after that the platoon commander was killed. He was a lovely chap. I started the morning as a section commander and ended up as the platoon commander.

Then the two battalions we were with were pulled out of the brigade to take part in the capture of Rangoon. We got to the outskirts of Taungup, and the Japs just melted away.

ACROSS THE IRRAWADDY

Major Frederick Rowley
Officer Commanding A Company, 5th/10th Baluch Regiment
Crossing the Irrawaddy was the longest swim I ever had. I was charged by my divisional commander to take my company across the river, four miles higher than where the main crossing was to be, and we had to swim it. I had some Indian Sappers who helped us build bamboo rafts to carry our weapons and kit. We also took our eighteen mules. The Irrawaddy is quite a fast-flowing river, so we had to work out how far we had to start upstream to hit the bank

on the other side where we wanted to be. I took one platoon to start with, and I got across reasonably all right. I was able to signal the rest of the company to come over plus the mules. Mules are very good swimmers, we crossed dressed, except for our boots. All mules got across. I was very relieved; a mule swept away down the Irrawaddy would have given away the fact that we were there to the Japs. In fact they did not know we were there for several hours. I moved downstream to where the main crossing was to be, and we joined the main bridgehead.

Gunner James Baker
134 Medium Regiment, Royal Artillery

We were firing on a Japanese division on the other side of the Irrawaddy with our 6-inch howitzers. Guarding our guns were Sikhs. I was told to report to an officer with my Bren gun, to lay line from guns to where the Gurkhas were being held up in a village. I didn't have a wireless. That night the Japs came charging in to within about fifteen yards. The Jap mortars set the village huts alight. I had to call fire from the guns, but the Japs had cut the wire. I couldn't see the Japs but could hear them. I was firing my Bren gun into the dark. Then everything was lit up by village huts on fire. The Japs sniped at us. The Gurkhas got rid of the snipers, we traced the wire back, found it booby-trapped, but got back to the regiment.

Major Frederick Rowley
Officer Commanding A Company, 5th/10th Baluch Regiment

The Japs still had occupation of a hill called Pear Hill. They were bombarding our crossing. The crossing had to stop. I was having a few hours' rest, having rejoined the battalion, when I was summoned to divisional HQ, to our magnificent commander Pete Rees, who said to me, 'I want you to get Pear Hill, and hold it.' When you are told by your general that's what you've got to do, you say, 'OK sir, I'll do it.'

I went back, sorted out my company, and we left the bridgehead. This was quite risky because the Japs had surrounded us and were potting at us; I didn't want to get too close to where they were. We went out in single file along the riverbank. Several hundred yards along, we got to the bottom of Pear Hill. I left my company at the bottom, and climbed with my subedar major, my orderly and my signaller. I wanted to recce and see what was up there. It was very rugged, and I was trying to keep as quiet as possible. It was quite lightly wooded. I got on top, and there was no sign of the enemy. I turned to my subedar major and told him to bring the rest of the company up. Like an idiot I had taken my equipment off with my revolver; to my horror I found myself looking straight at a Jap OP close by. I turned to shout at my men, the subedar shouted 'Sahib'. There was a Japanese officer rushing towards me with sword raised to knock my head off. He got to within three yards of me. My subedar major shot him. We killed the OP party, all of them.

We could hear the gun position calling up the OP on the telephone. We didn't know what they were saying, but we could hear them calling up. I told the subedar major to get the company up as fast as possible, and I laid them out ready for an onslaught, which we knew would come without question.

As I sat on a rock I felt the most appalling anguish. I was not religious at that time. But I sat saying, 'Lord Jesus, what is wrong?' And I listened, the most important thing when you pray is to listen, and this is what staggered me. I got a message, not a voice, but a message, and it said, 'You're not on the top of the hill.'

I thought oh my God. I walked forward. We were short of the top by about eighty yards, and the Jap emplacements were totally empty. I shouted to my chaps, 'Get up, advance at once.' We secured that place. And in due course the Japs belted us. But it would have been a massacre if we had been in the original place. We held the hill. In the OP there were maps of the Jap positions. I asked for a gunner to be sent up. The following morning a captain and subedar of Indian gunners came up. As I was explaining the position to this captain, he was hit by a huge piece of shrapnel.

Another company joined us the following day. I was up there for four nights, the rest of the battalion for more. But the battle of Pear Hill was fundamentally the opening of the big drive for Mandalay.

Pilot Officer Harry Morrell
211 Squadron, RAF

I did my first op sortie as one of a pair attacking river craft on the Irrawaddy. We lost touch with the other aircraft in cloud, but got there OK. I had done lots of navigation using rivers, roads, railways etc. Pagodas were especially useful, you could see the Shwe Dagon's gold dome forty miles off in daytime.

We were highwaymen, anything that moved we hit. The big prize was a train. If there were no trains about, we attacked the stations, or the engine sheds. The Beaufighter was a formidable aircraft and had four 20-mm cannon, six machine guns, eight 60-pounder HE rockets or eight 25-pounder AP rounds. We always used HE on river craft.

Captain Peter Noakes
Officer Commanding 4 Company, 1st Battalion, Northamptonshire Regiment

We eventually found ourselves on the banks of the Irrawaddy. It was hot. A couple of nights before we crossed a young officer called Thomas was sent out with two or three signallers in a rubber dinghy to cross the river and set up an Aldis lamp on the far bank as a guide to us. He was told to put a red filter in the lamp, and it would be a beacon for us to home on. The Irrawaddy flows very fast. You have to head well upstream in order to land up where you want to finish up. This red lamp was a brilliant idea. The RAF were asked to fly their loudest planes to fly up and down to mask the noise of our outboard motors.

My company was reserve for the crossing. The crossing, at night, was to be carried out by 1 and 3 Companies. When 3 Company got in their boats to go, their boats promptly sank. Major Norman Vita, the company commander, ordered his men out of the boats and on shore. The CO was fed up about it because it meant our plans were awry. He ordered me to take over from 3 Company and get my boys into other boats that were available and we set forth in a crocodile of rubber dinghies, with an outboard on the one in front, which kept on conking out. As we crossed the river we were met with rather inaccurate machine-gun and mortar fire from the Japs who didn't know where we were and fired at random.

We landed after some mishaps and alarms. When we got out of our craft, we found ourselves in four feet of water; the sand banks had shifted, but it didn't matter, we were on the other side. We immediately dug in. The other companies got across. The next morning battalion HQ got across with supplies. The Japs shelled the far bank, and our side, using their infantry guns, we called whiz-bangs. They were quite small calibre, and were manhandled up into the front line, with a very flat trajectory. You heard the gunfire as the shell was exploding. They caused quite a few casualties.

Captain William Rhodes-James
Officer Commanding B Company, 1st/6th Gurkha Rifles
Having crossed, we advanced south following up the Japs as they withdrew. We had Grants in support. We formed up on the start line and were shelled by Japs, which was disconcerting. I rode on the tank until the bullets started to bounce off the armour. We found the Japs dug in, the tanks seemed to hypnotise and cow them. My men sorted them out, while the tanks stopped. My left platoon found two battalion guns dug in ahead. My right-hand platoon commander rushed forward and captured both.

There were a lot of Jap bullets flying about. A Jap grenade landed in the road, the shrapnel hit my forehead, and filled my eyes with blood. It was not serious.

Private Tom Cattle
17 Platoon, D Company, 2nd Battalion, Dorsetshire Regiment
The next obstacle was the Irrawaddy. On the way towards the river, we bumped the Japs at a place called 'Gun Copse', a very arid area with bits of jungle and villages, and we couldn't move as we were caught in the open. All we could do was bury our noses in the ground and hope for the best. They called in an air strike to help us. Instead of dive-bombing the village they dive-bombed us. We could see the bombs falling and exploding, the earth opening up in front of us. Luckily it was just in front of us. After a while they realised they were bombing the wrong place, and started bombing the village. We put in a flanking movement and got the Japs out of it. The Japs were dug in, in foxholes, letting us go past and shooting people in the back. We had quite a few casualties shot in the back.

The Irrawaddy is a mile wide. I was a bit apprehensive: I couldn't swim. We could see the Japs on the other side and knew it would not be an easy crossing. We were at a village on the west bank and dug in. We were patrolling across the river and so were they. One night the Japs managed to get in amongst us. It was hand-to-hand fighting, and hope for the best. We were so close to each other you couldn't even use grenades, just bayonets. Eventually they left. There were not many of them.

Some fold-up canvas boats operated by Royal Engineers with an outboard engine were produced by the division and brought up. These boats weren't very stable and the engines were not reliable. Some people had to paddle to get across or back to where they started. It was a steep bank on the other side, and immediately we were into high elephant grass. We were being shelled and machine-gunned, but managed to enlarge the bridgehead.

Captain Peter Noakes
Officer Commanding 4 Company, 1st Battalion, Northamptonshire Regiment

After a few days it was decided to extend the bridgehead and my company was sent to occupy the North Chaung, a big chaung running from the Irrawaddy leading eastwards inland. It was used as an OP for Japanese artillery. When we advanced into it there were two or three Japs lurking around, we got rid of those. We occupied it, dug ourselves in, and we got shelled. It was an impossible defensive position because the area round was elephant grass, about eight to ten feet high. The Japs attacked us one night, not through the elephant grass, which crackles and gives you away, but up the chaung. Fortunately we heard them; the Japs are great chatterers, they talk a lot. I put up parachute flares from our 2-inch mortars, and we beat off the attack.

Then some barbed wire came up for us. We had plenty of trees round our perimeter; we managed to erect a two-strand fence of wire round our position, which was a godsend. We also had a section of Vickers MMG from the 9th Jats, a machine-gun battalion. We had a very big attack two nights later. The Japs got fed up with our parachute flares, because they illuminated them and we could pick them off. So they employed smoke with smoke canisters. For a while we thought it was gas; our anti-gas respirators were back in India. But it was smoke.

Our Royal Artillery 4.2-inch mortars and the MMGs put down defensive fire in our support, this curtailed the Jap advance to the wire. The Japs brought up Bangalore torpedoes, but we never allowed them to get close enough to put the Bangalores through the wire and blow gaps. The Japs eventually withdrew. We found a lot of Japs on our wire, and nearby in the morning. I can't remember how many dead, but there was certainly one officer, whose sword I took. His name was Second Lieutenant Yamamoto. He was dead and beautifully dressed.

Lieutenant Michael Marshall
Officer Commanding Mortar Platoon, 4th/5th Royal Gurkha Rifles
Our objective on the way to the Irrawaddy was the town of Pakokku. Within four or five miles of Pakokku our patrols found a heavily defended position at Kanhla. Here we had the biggest battle the battalion had experienced so far. The battle took all day. We overran the position at about 1600. Many Japs were finished off in their holes as they refused to surrender. During the morning of the battle, our new CO, Lieutenant Colonel John Turner, was giving his orders in middle morning, and was hit by sniper in the stomach. I was one of those taking orders from him and was about three feet away from him. He died that evening.

Lieutenant Colonel Hugh Pettigrew
GSO 1, HQ, 17th Indian Division
I flew with 'Punch' Cowan, the divisional commander to Slim's headquarters, to plan our part in the campaign. 7 Div had already got to Pakokku on the Irrawaddy and was in contact with the Japanese. We had to advance secretly to Pakokku; 7 Div would seize the bridgehead, then the whole of our division, less one brigade, would cross, and make for Meiktila. We would block the Japs in Mandalay from getting out.

Lieutenant Michael Marshall
Officer Commanding Mortar Platoon, 4th/5th Royal Gurkha Rifles
Shortly after, we crossed the Irrawaddy. Our crossing was relatively straightforward. We landed at Nyaungu and had a battalion position close to Pagan.

Sergeant Stanley Wood
Platoon Commander, 2nd Battalion, Durham Light Infantry
We got across with very little trouble, and dug in ready to advance. When we moved out, we were moving up a dried up riverbank with tanks. In the middle of the riverbed we saw a pile of fresh straw. I contacted the tank commander through the tank telephone, and suggested he gave the heap a short burst with his machine gun. Luckily, because no sooner had he blasted away the straw, than a little Japanese jumped out of the hole. I don't know what he was going to do, but was caught by another burst of fire. When we got there, he was

A Japanese soldier shot sitting in a hole with a shell between his knees waiting to detonate it when a tank passes over him.

sitting, dead, cross-legged in the hole, with a huge shell between his legs, and with a stone to hit the detonator, waiting for a tank to go over.

After moving up the riverbed we were held up by fire, by now it was getting dark, so we laagered up with the tank. We were in a crescent shape round the tank. The tank commander fired the gun without checking his barrel clearance for branches: the shell burst, and wounded three of my men.

Private Tom Cattle
17 Platoon, D Company, 2nd Battalion, Dorsetshire Regiment
Our objective now was Mandalay. We were in open ground and from Ngazun we headed for Ava. At one place we found ourselves in a huge area of tomatoes. And as we were walking along, we were picking them and eating them. I had never come across anything like it. The CO, Colonel White, behind us, thought we were taking casualties as people were bending down to pick tomatoes and asked what was going on.

We reached Ava Bridge without much opposition. It started getting dark. The Worcesters were in front, and we were on both sides of the road. At this point it was rocky and hilly, and the Worcesters halted, for some reason. The Dorsets took the lead and advanced at night on to a hilly position. Why I don't know. We went through the Worcesters, they were in a nullah. It was a pitch-black night. We got to a bit of a hill with a black pagoda on it. There was no one there and we advanced through and C Company went over the top to the other side of the hill. We went to the top and to the left. Battalion HQ were in the area of the pagoda, and the other companies at the back of the hill. We got to our positions without any opposition, and started to dig in. It was quiet, but the clanking of our entrenching tools hitting hard rock made a noise you could hear for miles. I thought my God, this is a bit precarious.

A patrol came back and said there were no Japs. We couldn't dig down far and had to build up to get protection. At daybreak, all of a sudden a hell of a machine-gun barrage started to sweep the hill, and from where C Company was we could hear shrieks and screams and shouts; we knew they were taking casualties. Bullets were sweeping over the hill and our positions and we were taking casualties, as was everyone else. Jimmy Wells, our platoon commander, was badly shot in the legs. There were about two Japanese machine guns doing the damage. They seemed to know exactly where we were going to be.

We had to pull back, we couldn't sustain the casualties we were taking.

Soldiers of the 2nd Battalion The Dorsetshire Regiment about to cross the Irrawaddy at Ngazun.

There was no cover. My friend I joined up with was killed. After causing all the casualties the Japs withdrew. It was a stupid attack that we had to do.

Lieutenant Harpratab Singh
A Squadron, 7th Light Cavalry
On the Mandalay bridge we shot them where they were on the bridge structure, sniping. We shot them, but admired them; one man could hold up a company, and he would not give in. One Japanese attacked my tank on his own with an explosive charge, and for a moment I wondered if I should shoot him, but had to in order to stop him.

Lieutenant Colonel Hugh Pettigrew
GSO 1, HQ, 17th Indian Division
Next day, started to move. 'Punch' Cowan had a real rush of blood to the head, because he cut straight across country with the whole of Divisional HQ. It was highly exhilarating, the whole lot in jeeps, signalling trucks etc, over fields, leaping over the bunds. Flat and dry, went all right, across the short side of the triangle.

Major John Randle
Officer Commanding B (Pathan) Company, 7th/10th Baluch Regiment
At Meiktila we surprised the Japs by our advance, and caught them. I came across a Jap field hospital on fire. It was like a scene from hell. There were wounded, there were sick, it smelt ghastly, chaps were screaming. It had been about one hundred miles behind the Japanese lines.

I pushed on at dawn next morning on a company sweep, with one tank and a FOO. We ran into a main Jap position. The leading platoon commander was killed. The FOO was killed. The enemy was widely deployed. I couldn't get on. I stayed where I was, and another company put in an attack with a whole squadron of tanks, very successfully. The tanks just fired point-blank into the slits of the bunkers.

Lieutenant Colonel Hugh Pettigrew
GSO 1, HQ, 17th Indian Division
One bit of shrapnel took the toes off a gunner officer alongside me and hit the general's caravan. We captured Meiktila, but it took a long time to root out

the Japs. Every night there was a battle as brigades sortied to catch Japs on the move. We were on air supply. We were stuck there quite a long time.

Gunner James Baker
134 Medium Regiment, Royal Artillery

Then we had a headlong rush to the outskirts of Mandalay and could see Mandalay Hill right in front and sighted our guns and fired on Mandalay Hill. The infantry could not get the Japs out of the caves, so they drilled holes and poured in oil and set fire to it. Most Japs stayed in the caves; others, in full view of us, jumped from the caves all alight. I saw about eight or nine. We had captured the hill but the Japs were still inside.

Major Frank Brodrick
Second-in-Command, 9th Battalion, Border Regiment

We crossed the Irrawaddy at Pakokku and on the way across from there the armour came with us. They were very efficient and made the move to Meiktila so much easier. There were quite a number of Japanese there, hidden behind trees. The chap doing the attack was a friend of mine and I thought he could do with help, so I went forward, and heard somebody groaning. I got two people to cover me to see if I could see this wounded person, in an old paddy field without water, so I went and stood behind a palm tree and looked to see where the noise was coming from. A Jap fired at me with a rifle, which hit me on the lip. It felt like being hit by a sledge-hammer. I dropped down behind the bund, and these two I had brought to cover me, they dealt with the Japanese who had fired at me.

I went back to report, I picked up a Japanese flag on the way. Often the Jap would keep a flag folded inside his tin helmet, which is where I found it. I met my CO on the way back, I explained what I had done, gave him the flag and went off to the RAP to be treated. They stitched me up and I waited there to be flown out next day.

Corporal Les Griffiths
Battalion HQ, 9th Battalion, Border Regiment

The battle for Meiktila was fierce, each village had to be fought for. We went for three days without water supply. We had tanks with us; some of us were on the tanks and some walking alongside. The Japs were firing at us, I was alongside the CO, waiting to go in, and out came 'Smudge' being carried out, grimacing and holding his stomach, and just as I looked at him, a figure ran across in my vision, running like the clappers. Chaps started shouting, and I ran too, shouldn't have done, I was supposed to be looking after the CO. We ran on a converging course. I was going like the clappers, then he appeared to fall over. I caught him up and pointed my tommy gun at him. I didn't know what to do. I hadn't the heart to shoot him. An officer came up and said, 'Shoot him, corporal.' I still couldn't shoot him. The officer went off, and another officer came up, a tank officer, and he stood there, and said, 'Shoot him, corporal, now!'

I did. I went off, didn't bother to look round, I knew I'd shot him. I went back to the CO and where 'Smudge' was waiting for a small aeroplane to come in, and he had all his fingers blown off. The butt of his rifle was smashed, and his fingers with it, he had a little finger and thumb on each hand. I felt justified in shooting the Jap.

Private Jim Wilks
11 Platoon, B Company, 2nd Battalion, West Yorkshire Regiment
They decided to fly our battalion in Dakotas into an airstrip at Meiktila, some troops had taken it, but it was still under Jap attack. The snag was, as we were landing, the Japs were shelling the strip. So the American crew said, 'We are not stopping, as we taxi along you lot jump out. And as soon as you lot jump out, we are taking off at the other end.'

This is what happened. The plane landed, taxied, it was a bit of a shambles: men and packs all over the airstrip.

Private Peter Hazelhurst
B Company, 9th Battalion, Border Regiment
The fighting on the plains was different. I rejoined B Company. The commando platoon had been disbanded. Our company commander was 'Long John' Petty, he was a classic soldier, a good fighting man.

The advance was great: we had trucks to ride in. At Meiktila a couple of companies of us were sent out to liven up the Japs. We were in trucks and drove straight into the attack of a Jap camp, 'Long John' Petty bayoneted a Jap. The bayonet went straight through, bent when it hit the ground, and he couldn't get the bayonet out.

Private Jim Wilks.

Private Jim Wilks
11 Platoon, B Company, 2nd Battalion, West Yorkshire Regiment
When we got sorted out we went into a defensive box. The Japs shelled the airstrip and shelled us. Then it quietened down. I've been frightened before, but this was one of the worst. Our job was to go out and clear that airstrip before the next lot of planes could land. The Japs were in the jungle on each side of the airstrip; up in the trees sniping at us. You never knew who was going to get hit next. That was our job for about eight or nine days.

They used to tie themselves in the trees. We could not see them. We advanced down the airstrip, about five yards apart, spread out. We walked along spraying the trees with bursts. Eventually we got them. Of course we lost one or two of ours at the same time. After we cleared the strip, the planes came in.

When we shot a Jap we had to search them for diaries and letters etc, to hand in for intelligence. We kept things like watches. I have a Jap silk flag. The Jap was a brave man. We only ever took one prisoner. He didn't know what day it was, he was wandering about in a coma. We gave him a cigarette, and bandaged him up. If it had been one of us they would have used us for bayonet practice. Another we went to pick up, when he saw us coming, he took the pin out of his grenade and blew himself up.

Private Peter Hazelhurst
B Company, 9th Battalion, Border Regiment
The next action was south of Meiktila. That was one of the hardest fights we had. We went in on tanks. The Kittyhawk fighter-bombers came in and strafed and bombed the village, but only half the bombs went off. When they fired their cannons people were hit by the empty shell cases falling out of the planes. We went to the edge of the village and the snipers were having a go at us, some lads were knocked over.

We got to the edge of the trees and things were getting really warm, and I was tired and thirsty. I was sitting on an unexploded bomb, I was that exhausted – if it goes up, it goes up. There was a great big bunker in the centre of the village, a tank came up and put a 75-mm shell in it. Sam Wilson was the wireless operator with the company commander. He was sitting on a tree trunk with a wireless on his back when a Jap shot out of the bunker with a sword in one hand and a grenade in the other shouting, 'Banzai!' He set out

343

Soldiers of the 9th Battalion the Border Regiment clearing a village on the outskirts of Meiktila.

A Bren gun team of the 1st Battalion the West Yorkshire Regiment clearing Japanese positions at Meiktila.

for Sam who jumped up off the log, and vaulted over another log. The Jap threw the grenade at him, which did not explode, and then turned and ran back, waving his sword. Of course everybody started shooting at him. He went down. An officer jumped up and finished him off.

Major Frederick Rowley
Officer Commanding A Company, 5th/10th Baluch Regiment

We surrounded Fort Dufferin in the centre of Mandalay. My battalion, with the 2nd Worcesters, were charged with attacking across the moat. As we were preparing ourselves to go, our aircraft bombed in support, but unfortunately killed twenty-seven of the Worcesters by mistake.

Gunner James Baker
134 Medium Regiment, Royal Artillery

At Fort Dufferin, we had to fire the guns over open sights to breach the wall. We fired at the bottom but didn't make any difference – no breach. Then we fired at the top of the wall, and slowly made a breach with our 120-pound shells. US bombers came over and bombed.

Major Frederick Rowley
Officer Commanding A Company, 5th/10th Baluch Regiment

The Japanese departed: we were told by people coming out with white flags that the Japs had left. We went in all ready because we didn't trust the Japs. We crossed the moat, climbed up over the rubble, and into what had been the prison courtyard. We knew there was a prison in there, but not that the doors were locked from outside so we could not get out. I had to use machine guns to blow the locks off. The fort was deserted except for one person. We were gingerly going along, when we heard and saw a figure about fifty yards away. As it got closer it didn't look like a Japanese. I shouted out at him, and challenged him. He turned out to be an American from Shwebo, who had just driven in to look for souvenirs in his jeep. He said, 'The gates were open. I'm on holiday, on leave.'

Gunner James Baker
134 Medium Regiment, Royal Artillery

A Signal Sergeant Williams decided to climb and look in. Inside there were

Fort Dufferin Mandalay under air attack before the British take the city.

A 6-in howitzer of 134 Medium Regiment Royal Artillery firing point-blank to breach the walls at Fort Dufferin.

some Indian civilians with white flags who told him the Japs had left. This Sergeant kicked a bag which he thought was rice, and he got peppered: it was a booby trap. So don't touch anything, not a single thing. Not even a flag, especially flags.

Private Tom Cattle
17 Platoon, D Company, 2nd Battalion, Dorsetshire Regiment
By the time we got into Mandalay the 19th Division had taken the place. We saw General Rees hauling up the British flag in the centre of town.

Corporal Arthur Freer
Squadron Leader's Driver/Operator, B Squadron, 3rd Carabiniers
B Squadron commander was told that his squadron was not required for the attack on Mandalay, it would be A Squadron. He lost his temper and said it was only right for B Squadron to go to Mandalay. The Brigadier told him to calm down. We couldn't care less. We wanted to get home to England.

However, he was told that one tank of B Squadron could enter Mandalay. He chose his own tank, so we set off for Mandalay next morning. We had no infantry with us. No one wanted to know us. We drove in alone, until we reached the Jap detention centre, mostly women, detained there for two or so years. The Japs were not willing to open the gates when demanded by the infantry who had appeared, but the squadron leader volunteered to charge the gate with the tank. The Japs opened the gates, and internees wandered out, mostly young women, some with babies.

Captain Peter Noakes
Officer Commanding 4 Company, 1st Battalion, Northamptonshire Regiment
Eventually we got behind Mandalay, astride the road. The Japs were evacuating Mandalay; we ambushed a party that walked into one of my positions. One turned out to be a Jap warrant officer who was the head clerk of the Japanese Army HQ at Mandalay; we shot him, and as we heard him moaning, I said to one of my platoon commanders, 'Put him out of his misery,' but before he could, this warrant officer shot himself. He carried a briefcase full of documents, which were immediately sent back to division. They were translated, and they were very important intelligence.

Major General 'Pete' Rees GOC 19th Indian Division entering Fort Dufferin on 19 March 1945.

Major Harry Smith
4th Battalion, Queen's Own Royal West Kent Regiment
We went up the road to 7 Division's bridgehead and cleared the road to Meiktila as the Japs had taken the road between the town and the Irrawaddy. I was sent to occupy a hill top which was under heavy fire. The next day we advanced again like a partridge drive against scattered Jap forces. Our jovial colonel, together with the signals corporal and the OC HQ Company, were blown up in a jeep by a mine. The CO and OC HQ Company were grievously wounded and the signals corporal killed. So the 2i/c became acting CO and I was dug out from a rifle company to become battalion 2i/c.

I commanded the advance down the road to Meiktila where we met odd Japanese positions. We had tanks with us and tanks could operate in the open country in the Burmese plain. We also had two Typhoons circling overhead, and an RAF officer in a jeep behind me to contact the Typhoons to attack the Japanese positions with rockets. With tanks and Typhoons in support we made splendid progress, and covered forty miles in a day and linked up with the 17 Div who were already in occupation of Meiktila. Japanese dead were everywhere.

Major John Randle
Officer Commanding B (Pathan) Company, 7th/10th Baluch Regiment
I was nearly put under close arrest after a para drop. I was putting a parachute in my jeep, when a major from the military police said he was going to put me under close arrest. I said, 'Look around at my one hundred and twenty Pathans, they won't take it kindly if you manhandle me.'

He looked round, and said, 'You'll hear more of this.'

I heard nothing more for a bit, then had a note from the assistant adjutant general of the division, saying, 'John don't be a bloody fool, if you're going to nick things don't do it with the assistant provost marshal around.'

Major Harry Smith
4th Battalion, Queen's Own Royal West Kent Regiment
Very soon after this, our two divisions 17th and 5th started the advance down the road and railway to capture Rangoon before the monsoon broke. The orders were to go as quickly as possible and not be held up by Jap positions on the flanks. We began our drive to Rangoon, three hundred and twenty miles away.

THE RANGOON ROAD

Captain Michael Marshall
Officer Commanding A Company, 4th/5th Royal Gurkha Rifles
In March I took over A Company as a captain. The general advance started and we were told to capture the oilfields at Yenangyaung and Minbu. At all these places we came across telltale signs of the 1942 retreat: old British vehicles, burnt-out light tanks, and oil wells demolished and set alight.

The Japs fought a rearguard action throughout. We were supported by the Carabiniers tanks. They were excellent. I saw a young tank commander receive a direct hit while we were advancing at Minbu. At the moment he was hit, he was standing up giving instructions, the whole tank burning in front of our eyes.

Trooper Malcolm Connolly
7 Troop, C Squadron, 3rd Carabiniers
We crossed the Irrawaddy at Magwe to Minbu. Our job was to cut the Japanese off and stop their retreat from the Arakan. We had plenty of crews, but were running out of tanks. The infantry was held up by a Japanese gun, and they said the tanks could take them out. They'd lost two or three tanks the previous days. The tank advanced, the gun fired, and the tank went up with the loss of seven men. When the infantry overran the gun it was a British 25-pounder which we didn't have a hope against; one of the finest tank busters in the world. The Japanese had a lot of these which they had taken on the retreat.

Captain Peter Gadsdon
Officer Commanding A Company, 4th/14th Punjabis
In one village we came under machine-gun fire. We took cover quickly. There were Jap wounded all over the place. One in particular I hoped to capture. I shouted at him, 'Hands up,' in English, putting mine up to show what I wanted. All he held up was a grenade, so I hastily backed off and told my troops to lie down. Nothing happened, so I advanced again. The same thing happened, and the third time he banged the grenade to set the fuse, put it down his shirt front and blew himself up. No prisoner.

Major John Randle
Officer Commanding B (Pathan) Company, 7th/10th Baluch Regiment
We had heavy fighting down the main axis south to Pyawbwe, which was held strongly by Japs. Our brigade did a right flanking movement, and a squadron of tanks reported a strong force of Japs on Point 900 were in the mood to surrender, so they said. The CO deployed the battalion in attack formation, my company on the left. It was a bare hill. We were engaged by Jap MMGs on the left. We dealt with that, got to the top, and all the Japs were up there. The tanks had pushed off, they seemed to have a habit of doing this. Then, as we went over a little crest, a soldier just in front of me was shot by a Jap. On that my soldiers went mad, and we killed 124 Japs with bayonet, grenades and tommy guns, the men were screaming and had a wolfish look with bare teeth. I tried to take a few prisoners, but my subedar said, 'It's no good, you're wasting your breath.' It was unusual, we saw the Jap company commander running away, my boys put a burst in him. They gave me his sword. We were on a high, adrenalin running, all steamed up. My chaps were in a bloodlust.

Private Peter Hazelhurst
B Company, 9th Battalion, Border Regiment
At Pyawbwe, we lined up on the paddy fields and were told we were going to have to move on foot, there was a big railway embankment about a mile in front of us. We were told we had to take the railway station. They were shelling us. We fought our way to the embankment and lost a few lads crossing the paddy fields, and we killed about four hundred or five hundred Japs that day. There were big railway sidings in the town. The Japs retreated out of the town and left it to us. That was our last big battle.

Lieutenant James Sherwood
C Group, 2 SBS
By now the monsoon was approaching. We then heard that an amphibious operation was to be mounted against Rangoon from Kyaukpyau. We were to accompany this force. This fleet ambled out of Kyaukpyau harbour just as we heard news about the war with Germany coming to an end. This cheered everybody enormously.

Private Peter Hazelhurst
B Company, 9th Battalion, Border Regiment
We got to Pegu and were all lined up ready to go in and the word came that the war in Europe was over. And we shouted, 'What the bloody hell use is that to us? When's our war going to be over?'

Sergeant Stanley Wood
Platoon Commander, 2nd Battalion, Durham Light Infantry
We were then pulled out and told that we were being taken out of Burma by air to Chittagong, by train to Calcutta, and then assault Rangoon from the sea. We had a very pleasant two weeks' rest on convalescent rations and had beer etc. As we were going down the Arakan coast in a trooper, tank landing craft and LCAs were launched to allow us to go ashore at Cheduba to swim. At that time we learned that the war in Europe had finished. The general remark was 'the lucky sods'. The pleasure of the good news was tempered by the prospect of an assault landing at Rangoon.

Lieutenant Colonel Hugh Pettigrew
GSO 1, HQ, 17th Indian Division
A sergeant despatch rider came up and handed me a message, which read, 'The war in Europe is over.' I called out to the sergeant, 'I've got a message here. The war in Europe is over.' He said, 'Very good, sir,' saluted, turned to some men nearby, and said, 'The war in Europe is over. Five-minute break.'

Major John Randle
Officer Commanding B (Pathan) Company, 7th/10th Baluch Regiment
We were moving about twenty to thirty miles per day. We had to get to Rangoon, if only to get proper rations. The monsoon was not far away, air supply would be unreliable in monsoon. The whip was out.

We ran into quite stiff opposition at Pegu. We put in an attack with A Company on my right. I had a bad day there. We got on to the hill, in pretty thick stuff, but couldn't get on through, because the Japs had a MMG and a 75-mm dug in, in defilade. They also had quite a few mortars. My leading platoon commander was badly wounded. We had a stupid order that morphine could be held only by company commanders, so I had to administer the stuff instead of getting on with my own job.

We were mortared badly in company HQ, the FOO was killed. It was so steep, the 25-pounders couldn't get crest clearance and hit the Japs. The battalion mortars did quite a good job. I just couldn't get forward at all, it was a semi-reverse slope position, and I couldn't get tanks up, it was too thick. Every time we moved we got fired on from flank. Just over the crest the foliage was cleared so there was no cover. When we captured the position we found that the MMG was dug in with logs overhead with a small slit allowing a critical arc of fire.

At nightfall the Japs counter-attacked with a few tanks. I had the whole of the corps artillery firing on my company front, about four field regiments, a medium regiment, and a troop of 9.2-inch heavies, on a front of about two hundred yards. My God, it didn't half make a crump. It broke up the Japs' counter-attack. This convinced the Japs that they would never take the position back. The plan was that another company would push through me the next morning, and take the rest of the position. But at first light, my leading platoon patrolled forward and reported that the Japs had pushed off. That was that.

Major Harry Smith
4th Battalion, Queen's Own Royal West Kent Regiment
Just as we were about to continue our triumphant march, the monsoon broke overnight. All the ground became a lake.

Corporal Les Griffiths
Battalion HQ, 9th Battalion, Border Regiment
At Pegu the monsoon had just started and the bridge collapsed, the river rose so high. We were stuck on the north side of the bridge. The CO, Major Brodrick, and a jeep driver called 'Blackie' Blackett, and I went to have a look at the state of the river.

The driver took us to the bridge and parked on a hump, and we decided we would just walk along the bank and look at the river. It was very hot, so we took our weapons off and left them with 'Blackie' in the jeep, and walked along in the pouring rain. The river was coming round the bend, and a Burman came out of the grass and pointed at a hut and said, 'Japani Sahib.'

Major Frank Brodrick
Second-in-Command, 9th Battalion, Border Regiment

We had stupidly left our rifles in the jeep, and had no weapons. I was faced with a CO who I didn't want shot, I could not send an NCO, so I walked to this house, it had outside stairs, I walked up, nothing happened. I opened the door at the top of the stairs and as I did so I heard a loud creaking of a door opening on the other side of the house. I thought you silly so-and-so. Out from this door came a miserable little Japanese about five feet high, knees knocking, he came downstairs with me.

The Japanese signed that he would like a drink. The CO was a blood and thunder man who used to tell everybody what he would do if he came across a Jap. He got his water bottle out and gave it to the Jap. We looked on with our mouths open.

Corporal Les Griffiths
Battalion HQ, 9th Battalion, Border Regiment

I tied his hands behind his back and took his knife off him. I gave him a cigarette. When we took him back everyone thought it was very funny, the CO and us two getting a prisoner, very rare.

Pilot Officer Henry Morrell
211 Squadron, RAF

Our Beaufighter squadron was operating from a tarmac strip in the Chittagong area, when the monsoon arrived early. We had to take off in the rain, sheets of spray flew up. As you flew across the paddy fields, flocks of birds would fly up and hit the aircraft, hitting the windscreen and engines. The blood and feathers would soon blow off.

We covered the landings at Rangoon. Wing Commander Montague Brown, our CO, flew over Rangoon Jail and took the photo 'Japs Gone'.

Lieutenant James Sherwood
C Group, 2 SBS

We joined the convoy, rounded the mouth of the Irrawaddy, and sailed up the mouth of the river in a landing craft, and were told that the Japs had gone, and withdrawn eastwards to Siam.

Sergeant Stanley Wood
Platoon Commander, 2nd Battalion, Durham Light Infantry
So we were able to sail upriver and land in the docks. We landed at Pyongi Street Docks. We had very detailed maps showing every Jap position. There was not much damage in Rangoon.

ROUNDUP

Major Harry Smith
4th Battalion, Queen's Own Royal West Kent Regiment
The Japs still had divisions cut off in the Arakan, and they tried to fight their way into Siam. We found ourselves positioned along the road and railway and as the Japanese emerged from the Pegu Yomas they were met by tanks and artillery and were massacred.

Private Peter Hazelhurst
B Company, 9th Battalion, Border Regiment
We were thirty-eight miles from Rangoon, but never got in because of the landings that took place. So we went north again to the Sittang river. We were lined up on the roads to stop the Japs from getting to Thailand. We took about three prisoners in over two years of fighting. We started taking more towards the end. But they fought back on the Sittang. They were in a bad state. I saw one with his kneecap gone and he was on a crutch. He begged us to shoot him.

Major John Randle
Officer Commanding B (Pathan) Company, 7th/10th Baluch Regiment
We stayed in Pegu for a while, then we went to Nyaunglebin. The division was strung along from Nyaunglebin to the north like guns in a partridge shoot, the whole of Jap 28 Army stuck in Arakan and west of Pegu trying to break out. We were well dug in, with massive artillery support. I had a platoon of six MMGs supporting my company. We killed countless Japs, but they did start to surrender then. I had taken a prisoner in Pegu, who just walked in. He seemed quite well nourished.

In the battle of the breakthrough the Japs were in appalling conditions, their attacks were pretty half-hearted; it was a pretty uneven contest. Their attacks were not to capture our positions but to divert our attention and get men across to the Sittang and across to Jap-held Burma. Some did get through in small parties. They had heavy casualties from disease. On one patrol we found a dying Jap, we gave him the *coup de grâce* with the bayonet. By this time the Burmese had changed sides again, and Aung San's chaps were harrying the Japanese.

Private Peter Hazelhurst
B Company, 9th Battalion, Border Regiment
We did a fourteen-day patrol by the Sittang River and counted the Japanese bodies floating down, dozens and dozens of them. George MacDonald Fraser was my section commander. I shot a vulture out of a tree there, because I was bored stiff. I looked at the vulture and thought, 'I bet you think you are going to eat me later. You're not, mate.' Fraser said, 'You could have alerted the Japanese for miles around.'

Major John Randle
Officer Commanding B (Pathan) Company, 7th/10th Baluch Regiment
We thought we would go on and on. We were wearing a bit thin by then. I had been in Burma from the beginning. If my CO had said, 'You have earned a rest,' even before we went back in early '45, I would have taken it. But I would never have asked for it; couldn't put your hand up and say. 'I've had enough.' One other officer had been in the battalion for the same period of time, but he had missed Imphal. We had a very aggressive brigade commander, from Probyn's Horse, who wanted aggressive patrolling. Neither our brigadier nor our CO ever came to see the companies, so we ignored this. The prospect of fighting on across the rest of Burma, Siam and China didn't appeal.

Major Harry Smith
4th Battalion, Queen's Own Royal West Kent Regiment
The battalion suffered ten men killed in one last effort, against Japanese marines of whom we killed forty. That was our last battle. I was told that I would be flown home and missed VJ Day.

Corporal Les Griffiths
Battalion HQ, 9th Battalion, Border Regiment
Then the bomb was dropped; nobody would believe it. Most chaps said, 'What's an atom bomb?' We'd never heard of it. The Japs didn't believe it either, there were lots of Japs killed after the bomb was dropped. They fought on.

Major John Randle
Officer Commanding B (Pathan) Company, 7th/10th Baluch Regiment
I heard of the bomb while my company was defending a gun box. I went into the gunner officers' mess, and heard about it there. The full significance did not sink in at once. All we heard was that the Japs were thinking of surrendering. About a week later, the division moved south, we were dug in and patrolling. We began to take a bit of a 'couldn't care less' attitude.

When the Japs surrendered, we were in line on the banks of the Sittang, the rain was pissing down. We put up a terrific *feu de joie*, with some captured Jap MGs. The gunners were firing star shell. Brigade HQ asked, 'What are you firing at?'

Major Frank Brodrick
Second-in-Command, 9th Battalion, Border Regiment
At the surrender I was given the job of meeting the Japs between Pegu and Bilin. I had to wait to meet this Jap officer with a jeep to take him back to our lines to arrange the surrender. He appeared, he was a major, in a beautiful uniform; I was scruffy.

Major John Randle
Officer Commanding B (Pathan) Company, 7th/10th Baluch Regiment
We were ordered to cross the Sittang by ferry, by the bridge, which we had been about the last unit to cross in 1942; a poignant moment. Then to Kyaikyto, where we were ordered to arrange the surrender of 18 Jap Division, and disarm them. The CO was on leave, I was acting 2i/c. When we arrived a whole crowd of Japs with fixed bayonets rushed up, and I thought we were going to be killed. It turned out to be a quarter guard. There was only one chap who could speak English, an oily Chicago University-trained chap.

We took a view that this was not a time for arrogant behaviour, and we would teach the Japs how to treat defeated people. We told them to hand in all weapons in Kyaikyto railway station. Then they asked about their swords. They wanted to hand them in personally and not have them dumped with the rest of the weapons. We decided that to treat them in a civilised fashion over their swords would mean they might cooperate over other weapons. So we told them that, provided all the other equipment was handed in, at the end each officer of the division was to hand in his sword individually to officers and the divisional commander to hand his to the brigade commander. Each Jap officer came up and saluted, unsheathed his sword, and handed it over.

Final Words

On 6 August 1945 the first atomic bomb was dropped on the city of Hiroshima, and three days later Nagasaki suffered the same fate. On 14 August the Japanese surrendered unconditionally. Three years and eight months after the beginning of the Burma Campaign the Japanese signed the preliminary surrender arrangements at Rangoon, thus ending the longest campaign fought by the Commonwealth army on any front.

We will never know how many lost their lives in this bloody campaign. No two sources agree, even approximately, on the precise numbers of killed, wounded and missing on either side. The best estimate we have of casualties to the 530,000 British, Empire and Commonwealth troops in the Fourteenth Army is 9,400 killed in action, and 61,800 wounded, taken prisoner or missing. Despite the well-tried British casualty procedures, and partly due to the nature of this campaign, doubts still remain as to the exact numbers.

Japanese figures are even more problematic. Their Burma Area Army records were lost or destroyed during the final days of the fighting. The very lowest estimate of Japanese casualties is 106,100 of which it is thought that 46,700 were killed in action, out of a total strength of approximately 400,000; a figure which itself has never been confirmed. It is impossible to guess how many of their soldiers died unseen in the hills and jungles of Assam and the Arakan, or how many bodies floated down the monsoon-swelled rivers of Lower Burma during the Japanese attempts to reach Thailand in the final months of desperate and confused fighting.

The terrain and climate in Burma challenged both sides, particularly in the monsoon when the rain sheeted down almost incessantly: clothing, webbing equipment and boots rotted and fell apart and the men could be soaked for days on end. In Assam and western Burma, men and animals were tormented constantly by sand flies, ticks, mosquitoes and leeches. Dengue, typhus, malaria, cholera, scabies, yaws, sprue and dysentery were endemic. Soldiers in the Arakan encountered all these, but with mangrove swamps and muddy chaungs thrown in for good measure. It is not surprising that soldiers were glad to emerge on to the plains of central Burma after crossing the Chindwin, and to fight there during the dry season.

Nobody knows who coined the phrase 'Forgotten Army', but its soldiers were calling themselves that long before it was picked up by the press. But as Slim himself said, 'The people of Britain had perils and excitements enough on their own doorsteps and Burma was far away. Its place in the general strategy was not clear, nor did what happened there seem vital. Much more stirring news was coming out of Africa.' Although victories followed the initial setbacks, progress in this remote campaign was intially slow, and the courage and hardships of the Fourteenth Army I went largely unreported.

To this day many people know about the Chindits, but the rest of the Fourteenth Army remains forgotten. This was the outcome of a deliberate campaign to publicise the first Wingate expedition to demonstrate that an enemy who had seemed terrifyingly invincible could be beaten. In the end, the publicity about the Chindits endowed them with an aura out of all proportion to their actual importance in the scheme of things.

There were many reasons for the lack of a clear strategy for Burma, not least because it was seen by the western Allies as a distraction from the main Eastern conflict in the Pacific. For after the USA's entry into the war, the British could not decide the strategy to be followed anywhere without consulting their major American partner, who did not necessarily share the same views on how and where the main offensives should be carried out. Because Burma was always a low priority for equipment compared with other theatres of war, plans for seizing Rangoon – the planned base for the British amphibious assault on Malaya – by sea had to be postponed time and again for lack of landing craft. Not until December 1944 did Slim lose patience waiting for Rangoon to be captured by assault from the sea, and extended his scheme for taking just Mandalay to advancing to Rangoon.

When the war against Japan ended so unexpectedly, plans for Indian and Burmese independence were still undecided. The end of colonial rule was seen as inevitable, but no one knew when, or how. No date had been fixed for the British to relinquish sovereignty, and the ultimate composition of an independent India had not been decided; including the vexed question of partition. Still economically crippled from the fierce fighting within its borders, Burma became the Independent Union of Burma on 4 January 1948. By this time Aung San was dead, having been assassinated. In 1962 a military oligarchy took control of Burma. Under international pressure an election was allowed in 1968. Aung San's daughter Aung San Suu Kyi won an unexpected landslide victory, which the military dictatorship immediately annulled, arresting and imprisoning Aung San Suu Kyi. At the time of writing she remains in house arrest. The Karens, Chins and Kachin hill tribes, who have no wish to be ruled by the Burmese, have been engaged in a guerrilla war ever since 1948.

As for the soldiers who returned home from Burma, many suffered after-effects for the rest of their lives. As with all conflicts, we will never know how many were mentally scarred by their experiences. Our ignorance especially applies to the Indian and African soldiers. Some of the Indian soldiers subsequently found themselves faced with the added trauma of fighting old comrades when the British Indian Army was divided up between the independent nations of Pakistan and India, who were soon at each other's throats over the disputed territory of Kashmir. Most old soldiers will talk only to one of their own, because they feel that anyone who has not been through the extremes of war could not possibly understand. This makes the Imperial War Museum's oral history records even more important. Fortunately, perhaps because of the official nature of the project, a number of survivors agreed to sharing their stories and we have on record experiences that might otherwise have been lost.

Private Henry Foster
Carrier Platoon, 2nd Battalion, West Yorkshire Regiment
I think it's good to talk about these things, although it affects me a bit. I talk to Burma Star people, that is when I talk. I never mentioned the war until about twelve years ago, aged 65. Since demob, I often wished I had stayed in, although at the time I was glad to get away.

Major Dominic Neill
Officer Commanding B Company, 3rd/2nd Gurkha Rifles
As for the Japanese, their soldiers were some of the bravest and most effective fighting men in history.

Lieutenant Colonel Gordon Graham
1st Battalion, Queen's Own Cameron Highlanders
I immediately formed a very high opinion of the Japanese as soldiers, as it seemed they were enormously self-contained. They had this mythical reputation of invincibility because we didn't know what to expect. But they also intrigued me, because they didn't react as we did. They didn't seem to be afraid of dying. Others didn't seem interested in psychoanalysing them, but I thought it would help to understand the enemy. It was important to understand that their whole thought process and motivation was so different from ours, that we should recognise this if we were going to defeat them. We were not schooled at all in what the Japanese mores were; they were entirely based on subjective observation.

Some of the troops shot the Japanese as they lay sick on the ground, until I stopped them. There was one incident when one of the Jocks was knocking a Japanese prisoner about, and a medical officer said, 'Stop that. We've got to live with these people after the war.' So there were interludes of humanity. Mostly it was just hate and destruction. There was no chivalry involved in this war. There was a clarity about it. No one had any doubts. The Japanese had a terrible reputation of cruelty to prisoners. It sharpened the hatred and determination of those fighting against them. It became counter-productive and, in the campaign in the early months of 1945, the Japanese were ruthlessly exterminated by thousands and tens of thousands, and nobody gave it a second thought.

Trooper Malcolm Connolly
7 Troop, C Squadron, 3rd Carabiniers
There was no compassion between British, Indian, Gurkha and Japanese. Even if he put his hands up, you didn't trust him. Vast numbers of Japanese were killed in the last stages. They were just like targets in a fun fair. If you saw a dead Japanese lying there, you drove the tank over him, because you didn't trust him.

When I watched the infantry lads advancing, Indian and British, if they came across a Jap lying there, everyone stuck a bayonet in him. And the tanks coming behind would roll over him. If he had been given the opportunity he would have taken someone with him, so we didn't give him the opportunity. But in the British Army if you had done half of the things the Japanese did you would have got a VC. They wouldn't give up.

Lieutenant Colonel Gordon Graham
1st Battalion, Queen's Own Cameron Highlanders
And yet there was this thrill, that sense of reality, that here you are facing death in conditions of extreme risk and it was not all a negative experience. I guess that each person engaged in the sharp end of warfare is brought to confront himself, either consciously or subconsciously; you get almost in touch with a sense of reality which can be gained in no other way. One's senses become sharpened. And even if there is nothing pleasant or constructive about it, it still is a trial of the human spirit which has got a positive outcome for those who are ready to acknowledge it.

I don't regret any part of fighting in the war with the Cameron Highlanders. When one considers one's experiences against the background of the history of these times I felt that was the right place to be. I said to myself, aged nineteen, if there is to be a war the place to be is in the infantry, in the front, that is what wars are about. That may have been an innocent, misguided attitude, but looking back on it I think I was right. There is a sense of satisfaction of having been at the sharp end. There is also a sense of conscience about having survived. You feel very bad about your contemporaries who have not survived. Why were they killed and why was I not? These are questions that lead one into all kinds of philosophical and quasi-spiritual reflections which I think become an asset in one's subsequent life when one is no longer dedicated to destruction. I was not wounded. My batman was wounded next to me, twice.

Trooper Malcolm Connolly
7 Troop, C Squadron, 3rd Carabiniers
On the Tiddim Road, during shelling, I jumped into a slit trench by the road, and in it was an Indian IEME soldier. He was attached to us. He spoke English. I said, 'You have no need to be here.'

He replied, 'Sahib, you share my house. It is only right in time of trouble we help you. But when this is all over we are going to kick your butts out of India.'

Captain Kristen Tewari
Divisional Signals, 25th Indian Division, attached 51st Brigade
We had three battalions in our brigade, all different castes and races: Kumaonis, Punjabis, and Baluch. Kumaonis are very conservative hill people. The Baluch regiment consisted of Muslims and Hindus combined. Punjabis are Mussulmans. In Akyab, after the battle of Kangaw, we had a party with the commandos before setting sail for India. It was amazing: with our conservative Indian troops in a huge tent all together, sitting one commando, one Kumaoni, one Baluchi, one Punjabi, being given rum to drink and drinking rum from the same mug. These troops, who normally wouldn't touch anything touched by someone of a different caste or race, were doing this, there was such comradeship. As for the commandos, we had seen their gallantry and their toughness and were amazed that they could be so friendly.

Private Victor Ralph
4 Troop, 1 Commando
Lieutenant Nolan, who was awarded the VC, was a very recent member of our unit; he had joined us at Myebon as a reinforcement. We knew nothing about him. He seemed a good, keen, young Lieutenant. He was from the Norfolk Regiment. Men behave in that fashion for two reasons, either they are very stupid or very brave. I assume in his case it was the latter. To put that into perspective, there was a private who, previous to us going into action, bragged that he was going to win the VC, but when the action started he hid behind a tree all the time. A lot of bravery is done knowingly, for example when one sets out to rescue a wounded comrade. We had a medic and he went out on several occasions to bring men in and treat them. He got killed; he got nothing. War is a peculiar thing.

Captain Kristen Tewari
Divisional Signals 25th Indian Division, attached 51st Brigade
Have my war experiences changed me? Yes, you must surrender truly to your destiny.

Squadron Leader Arjun Singh
Commanding Officer, Number 1 Squadron, Royal Indian Air Force

You mature very fast in war. If a man takes ten years to mature in peace it will take only a few weeks in war.

Major Ian Lyall-Grant
Officer Commanding 70 Independent Field Company, Bengal Sappers and Miners

I don't think the Chindits achieved much. They were brave, but from a military point of view they were a very big diversion of effort. Although they blocked the road to where Stilwell was fighting, he was fighting only one Jap division. They made no difference to Kohima and Imphal. Wingate's head was in the air. He had never fought against any real opposition in his life.

Captain A. M. Vohra
14th/13th Frontier Force Rifles

The Chindits did good things for morale after so few battle successes. It was very good going behind enemy lines, but no follow-up or link-up was possible; strategically, the Chindits were a failure, as any airborne operation that does not end in a link-up is a failure.

Major John Randle
Officer Commanding B (Pathan) Company, 7th/10th Baluch Regiment

The Chindit Operation? It was an epic of human courage, but strategically it was a waste of time. It was a case of a very strange and mentally unbalanced man getting the ear of important people and being allowed to prove his own strategic visions. I don't think it achieved anything. At Imphal so much air effort was diverted to the Chindits. The battles of Kohima and Imphal won the war.

Lieutenant Richard Rhodes-James
Cypher Officer, HQ 111 Brigade

Now people ask, 'Were you in Burma, were you in the Chindits?' It continues to attract an enormous amount of interest. It was imaginative and romantic. When somebody said that they turned the tide in the campaign, I said, 'No, they didn't turn the tide.' The tide was turned when the Fourteenth Army held the Japanese at Imphal and Kohima.

Brigadier Bernard Fergusson
Commander, 16th Brigade, Chindits
Wingate had the ability to make us believe in ourselves and be confident that we could achieve what we had set out to do. One day he wanted to send a patrol into an area of jungle, which I knew was impenetrable and I said so. He rolled a contemptuous eye on me and added to his orders, 'No patrol will report any jungle impenetrable until it has penetrated it.'

Havildar Umrao Singh VC
33 Mountain Battery
When I went to London to receive my VC, I had a wonderful moustache in those days. And a lot of women came up and kissed me on my moustache, I didn't know what on earth was happening. So I went and looked in a mirror and saw I was covered in lipstick. So I washed it off quickly.

At first I was a bit afraid, but got to like it very much.

Glossary

2i/c – Second-in-Command

AA – anti-aircraft

Ack-Ack – slang for anti-aircraft, from the phonetic alphabet in which 'Ack' stood for 'A'. By 1943 replaced by 'Able', and now 'Alpha'

ADC – aide-de-camp, a general officer's personal assistant. Nearest civilian equivalent is a PA.

Adjutant – the CO's personal staff officer in a battalion or regiment in the British and Indian Armies. In the Second World War, and for several years thereafter, there was no operations officer at this level, so the adjutant was responsible for all operational staff work as well as discipline and all other personnel matters

Aldis Lamp – a hand-held lamp used for flashing Morse signals.

AP – armour piercing (ammunition) – see HE

Aung San – leader of the pro-Japanese Burma National Army (BNA). Aung San, along with the BNA, changed sides in March 1945, when they saw that Allied victory was inevitable. His daughter, Aung San Suu Kyi, is still, in 2009, kept under house arrest in Burma (Myanmar) by the regime there

Ayo Gurkhali – 'the Gurkhas are coming', battle cry of Gurkha troops

Bangalore torpedo – a length of piping filled with explosive, used for blowing a gap in barbed wire entanglements

Basha – the correct definition is: 'a wooden hut made from bamboo and roofed with jungle foliage.

Beaufighter Mk VI – British long-range fighter with crew of two. Armed with four 20-mm cannon, six .303-inch guns, and eight rockets

Bhisti – water carrier, like Kipling's Gunga Din

Bofors – a quick-firing 40-mm anti-aircraft gun of Swedish design

BORs – British Other Ranks, collective term for all British soldiers other than officers

Bose – Subhas Chandra, President of the Indian National Congress in 1939, who saw the Second World War as an opportunity to throw off British rule. Fled to Germany, and sought the assistance of Hitler. He was sent to Japan in 1943, where his government in exile was recognised by Germany, Italy, and the Irish Free State, whose President, Eamon de Valera, sent him a personal telegram of congratulations. He was in Singapore when the war with Japan ended, and was killed in an aircraft crash in Tawain while fleeing to Russia (See INA and *Netaji*)

Bren – the British light machine gun of the Second World War and until the late 1950s. Fired a standard .303-inch round from a thirty-round magazine (usually loaded with twenty-eight rounds)

Brigade – a formation of two or more infantry battalions or armoured regiments, commanded by a brigadier

Brigade Major (BM) – the senior operations officer of a brigade, *de facto* chief of staff

BTA – Burma Traitor Army, British name for Burmese who elected to join the Japanese side in the naïve expectation that the Japanese would grant Burma independence

Buffaloes – domesticated water buffalo

Bunds – earth banks built to contain paddy fields, or to hold back thecourse of a river to prevent flooding

Bushido – Japanese for the way of a warrior, a military code of honour

Carrier – a lightly armoured tracked vehicle, often called a Bren-gun carrier, although it was also used to carry the Vickers medium machine gun, and for many other tasks

Casevac – Casualty Evacuation

C-47 Dakota – the great workhorse aircraft of the Second World War and for years afterwards. Had one door, and could carry twenty paratroops or a few more troops in the air-landing role, and had a radius of action of 450 miles

(350 miles towing the US WACO glider). The C-46 Commando had two doors, carried forty paratroops, and had a radius of action of 500 miles. Twenty C-46s carried a lift equivalent to thirty C-47s

Chagul – a canvas water bag. Keeps water marvellously cool in hot weather through condensation

Chaplis – stout leather open-toed metal-studded sandals, worn by many troops of the Indian army on the North-West Frontier. Pronounced chupply

Chaung – Burmese for watercourse or minor river, could be as narrow as a ditch, or wide enough for small craft, particularly near the coast

C-in-C – Commander-in-Chief

CO – Commanding Officer

Commando – can refer to the individual commando soldier or marine, or to the unit. A commando unit was around 450 strong, divided into five rifle troops each of about sixty men, a support troop of Vickers medium machine guns and 3-inch mortars, and a headquarters troop. The 3rd Commando Brigade, which served in Burma, consisted of two Army Commandos, numbers 1 and 5 Commandos, and two Royal Marine Commandos, 42 (RM) and 44 (RM) Commando

Coolies – manual labourers.

Corps – a formation of at least two divisions commanded by a lieutenant general. Also a generic term for arms and services except armour, artillery and infantry, hence Corps of Royal Engineers, Royal Signals, Royal Army Service Corps, Indian Army Service Corps, Royal Army Medical Corps, Indian Army Medical Corps and so on

CP – Command Post

CRE – Chief Royal Engineer, the senior Royal Engineer in a Division

CSM – Company Sergeant Major

Cu-nim – cumulo-nimbus cloud, very dangerous cloud formation consisting of towering thunderheads containing very powerful up draughts and down draughts. Aircraft entering such cloud often crash after being borne up faster than an express lift, followed by hurtling earthwards, while the men inside are thrown around like peas in a pod. The aircraft might be completely inverted after having its wings torn off. Modern aircraft have weather avoidance radar to warn them to avoid such cloud. This was not available in the Second World War, and it was easy to fly into cu-nim by mistake, either in bad visibility or at night

Dah — Burmese equivalent of a machete

DC3 – the airliner on which the C-47 Dakota military transport aircraft was based (see C-47), but the name was still used by some to refer to the C-47

DCM – Distinguished Conduct Medal, a highly regarded decoration, instituted in 1854, the equivalent of the original DSO for Warrant Officers, NCOs and soldiers of the army (and Royal Marines when under army command). Awarded for gallantry in action. Now discontinued

Deccan Horse – an Indian cavalry regiment

DF – defensive fire, mortar, artillery, or machine-gun fire by troops in defensive positions against attacking troops or patrols. Usually pre-registered on a number of key places, and numbered, so a particular DF can be called down quickly by reference to its number. Guns and mortars will be laid on the DF SOS when not engaged on other tasks. As its name implies, the DF SOS is the target deemed to be the most dangerous to the defenders

Dhobi wallah – man who does the washing, literally the washing fellow

Direct fire – weapons that have to be aimed directly at the target as opposed to indirect fire weapons such as mortars and artillery

Division – a formation of two or more brigades, commanded by a major general

Doolies – hammock-like pieces of canvas suspended from two poles, carried by two or four people on their shoulders. Used for carrying wounded or sick

DSO – Distinguished Service Order, instituted in 1886, and until the awards system was changed in 1994, it was a dual-role decoration, recognising gallantry at a level just below that qualifying for the VC by junior officers, and exceptional leadership in battle by senior officers

DUKW – American six-wheeled amphibious truck. Initials from maker's code, pronounced 'duck'

DZ – dropping zone, the area chosen for landing by parachute troops, or on which supplies are to be dropped

EY rifle – a rifle fitted with a discharger cup on the muzzle for launching grenades

FFD – first field dressing, a packet containing a bandage impregnated with antiseptic, carried by every officer and soldier on active service

Flak – German slang for anti-aircraft fire, from the German for anti-aircraft gun *fliegerabwehrkanone*

Flit gun/Flit pump – a small hand-pumped device for spraying insecticide, known by its commercial name: Flit

Folboat – originally a two-man, collapsible canoe built for recreational purposes by the Folboat company. During the course of the Second World War, some eight marques of canoe were designed and built by the British to improve on the original design

FOO – Forward Observation Officer, an artillery officer who directs artillery fire. Normally one with each forward rifle company and provided by artillery battery supporting the infantry battalion

G1 ops – short for GSO 1 (Operations), see GSO

Galloper – a messenger on horseback

Gharry wallahs – a gharry is a horse-drawn carriage, or cab; see Wallah

GOC – General Officer Commanding

Goolie chit – was, and still is, airman's slang for a document carried for use by downed aircrew to show local tribespeople, guaranteeing a financial reward in return for the airman being handed over unharmed. Tribesmen on the North-West Frontier of India, where the practice of issuing goolie chits originated, commonly castrated the enemy, either before or after killing them

GSO – General Staff Officer, a staff officer who dealt with General (G) Staff matters (operations, intelligence, planning and staff duties), as opposed to personnel (A short for Adjutant General's Staff), or logistic matters (Q short for Quartermaster General's Staff). The grades were GSO 1 (Lieutenant Colonel), GSO 2 (Major), and GSO 3 (Captain). The GSO 1 in a division was the senior operations staff officer, effectively the chief of staff. The AAG, or Assistant Adjutant General in a division was the senior personnel staff officer, and the AQMG, or Assistant Quartermaster General, in a division was the senior logistics staff officer

Gun Box – an artillery gun position defended by infantry, and possibly armour

H-Hour – the time an attacking force crosses the start line

Havildar – see ranks

HE – high explosive

High Port – carrying a rifle across the body at an angle with the muzzle upwards

Howdah – a box-like arrangement on an elephant's back in which people sit

Howitzer 3.7 inch – a mountain gun, designed for operating in country impassable for wheeled vehicles, primarily the North-West Frontier of India. Dismantled into nine parts: breech, chase, cradle, split trail, carriage and two hard-rimmed wheels. Could be carried by eight mules. The gun could be modified to be towed by a jeep, by fitting pneumatic tyres and a smaller shield. The shell weighed twenty pounds, and the gun had a maximum range of seven thousand yards. (Compare with the 25-pounder which had a maximum range of 12,500 yards with a 25-pound shell)

Hurribomber – the fighter-bomber version of the Hurricane Mk II

Hurricane Mk II – single-engined monoplane, of Battle of Britain fame. Various sub marques, equipped with either twelve .303-inch machine guns, four 20-mm cannon, or two 40-mm cannon. Below ten thousand feet was less manoeuvrable than the Japanese Zero, but above twenty thousand feet proved superior. Also developed as a highly successful fighter-bomber (see Hurribomber)

IEME – Indian Electrical and Mechanical Engineer, see LAD

INA – Indian National Army, formed from Indian soldiers taken prisoner after the fall of Malaya and Hong Kong, who were persuaded to fight for the Japanese by a Japanese officer, Major Fujiwara, assisted by Captain Mohan Singh of the 14th Punjabis. Around twenty thousand out of the total of sixty thousand Indian soldiers taken prisoner joined the INA initially. When Subhas Chandra Bose arrived in Singapore about a year afterwards (see Bose) the INA was increased several thousandfold by recruiting civilian Indians living in Malaya, Hong Kong, Singapore, Thailand and Burma. Very few Gurkhas joined

Jemadar – see Ranks

JIF – Japanese Indian Forces (see INA)

Jitter Party – a party of soldiers sent to create noises near enemy positions at night in order to give them 'the jitters' and get them to fire their weapons thus revealing their positions. The Fourteenth Army was trained not to respond, the watchword was 'the answer to noise is silence'

Jocks – slang for soldiers in Scottish regiments

Khud – khud is Urdu for hillside, and a khud stick is a stick with a metal point to assist one when climbing or descending the khud

KOYLI —King's Own Yorkshire Light Infantry

LAD – light aid detachment, a small sub-unit of fitters and mechanics from the Royal Electrical and Mechanical Engineers (REME) or Indian Electrical and Mechanical Engineers (IEME), to provide immediate battlefield repairs to vehicles and equipment

Lance Naik – see Ranks

Lantana – a particularly thick scrub resembling raspberry canes. It is almost impossible to advance through without cutting, and offers good concealment to the defender. The Japanese made skilful use of it

LCA – landing craft assault, maximum load an infantry platoon. Designed to be carried at a ship's lifeboat davits, and to land infantry in a beach assault

LCP(L) – fast landing craft of American design and originally bought by the British for Commando raids. They had no ramp, and a spoon bow over which troops landed either by gangplank or jumped straight into the sea, the latter leading to a very wet landing

Lead pencil delay fuse – a metal tube containing a strong spring pulled out to its full extent. When the retaining pin was removed, the spring was held in tension by a lead wire. A combination of the thickness of the wire and the outside temperature determined how long it took for the lead wire to snap, thus allowing the spring to drive a firing pin on to the detonator which set off the primer and the explosive. The warmer the temperature the more malleable the lead wire, and the quicker it would break. Provided one could accurately forecast the temperature at the target, one could select the timer with the necessary thickness of lead wire to achieve the delay required

Lee-Grant – American-built, M3 tank. Had a 37-mm gun in the turret, and a 75-mm (main armament) gun in a sponson in the hull

Liberator Mk II – American B-24 four-engined heavy bomber with crew of eight

Lightning P.38 – twin-engined American fighter. Crew of one. Four .50-inch and one 20-mm cannon. Very effective low-level attack aircraft

LMG – light machine gun

LO – Liaison Officer

Longcloth – the codeword for Wingate's first expedition behind enemy lines

LZ – landing zone, in the Second World War an area chosen for glider landings

Martial Class – the British Indian Army was mainly recruited from what were known as the martial classes (sometimes known as Martial Races), such as Sikhs, Jats, Rajputs, Gurkhas, Garwhalis, Dogras, Kumaonis, Punjabi-Mussulmans (Punjabi Muslims) and Pathans

MC – Military Cross, instituted in 1914, and awarded to army officers of the rank of Major and below, and Warrant Officers, for gallantry in action. Now all ranks are eligible

MGB – motor gun boat, a small, fast vessel armed with small-calibre guns

Mitchell – B-25, twin-engined American medium bomber with crew of five. Good at attacking ground targets in support of ground troops

MM – Military Medal, instituted in 1916, and awarded to army NCOs and soldiers for gallantry in action. Now discontinued, see MC

MMG – medium machine gun (see Vickers)

MO – medical officer

Mahout – elephant driver, sits astride the elephant's neck.

MDS – Main Dressing Station, located in a rear area. the place to which casualties are taken from the RAP (see RAP), and where, if necessary, surgery can be undertaken to stabilize the casualty before further evacuation further back

MG – machine gun

Mohawk – single-engined American fighter, earlier version of the Tomahawk. Obsolete by 1941, but retained by RAF for use in India/Burma. Six .303-inch guns

Mosquito Mk IV – twin-engined light bomber, or high-level reconnaissance aircraft. Crew of two. Almost as fast as a Spitfire, and much faster than any other aircraft, Allied or enemy

MTB – motor torpedo boat, a small, fast vessel mainly armed with torpedoes

Naik – see Ranks

NCO – non-commissioned officer; lance corporal to colour sergeant

Netaji – Hindi for leader, equivalent of the German term *führer*. Subhas Chandra Bose, the figurehead of the INA, decreed that he was to be addressed by the title *Netaji*. He wore uniform although he had never been a soldier. See INA

Nullah or nala – a small watercourse, ditch or depression in the ground

OC – Officer Commanding, applicable to commander of sub-units below battalion/ regimental level: companies, batteries, squadrons, platoons etc

O Group – short for Orders Group, the group to which orders are given at any level of command from platoon to army. For example at platoon level the platoon commander briefing his section commanders, the battalion CO briefing his company commanders, and at brigade level, the brigade commander briefing his battalion and supporting arms COs, and other people who need to know the plan

OP – observation post

Panga(s) – the African equivalent to a machete or dah

Pangyi – a sharpened stake usually made out of bamboo and pronounced punji. The point can be hardened by scorching in a fire. Excellent for use in booby traps, or obstacle belts, and can be concealed in pits, covered with twigs and grass or leaves, and planted in the undergrowth. Once impaled on a bamboo stake, it is difficult to pull oneself off, because the bamboo fibres act like a barb

PIAT – Projector Infantry Anti-Tank. The hand-held anti-tank weapon of the British Second World War infantryman from about mid-1942 on. Consisted of a powerful spring mounted in a tube which threw a hollow-charge projectile. Effective up to one hundred yards

Pugree, puggaree – turban

RA – Royal Artillery

Radius of action – the distance an aircraft or ship carrying out a sortie can cover from base to target and back without stopping to refuel

RAF – Royal Air Force

RAP – Regimental Aid Post, the place where the Medical Officer (MO) of a battalion or equivalent-size unit sets up his aid post. Usually the requirement is to administer 'sophisticated first aid' to stabilize the casualty sufficiently to enable him to survive the next stage of evacuation; in 'conventional' warfare usually within hours. In Chindit columns casualties might spend days in the RAP before evacuation was possible, and the MO had to do far more

Range – the distance to a target, or the total distance an aircraft can fly or a ship can steam. See Radius of action

Ranks – Indian Army Ranks below 2nd Lieutenant were as follows:

Indian Army	Typical Job/	British Army Equivalent
Subedar Major	Senior VCO (see VCO)	None
Subedar	Company 2i/c or platoon commander	None
Jemadar	Platoon commander	None
Havildar Major	Company Sergeant Major (CSM)	CSM
Havildar	Platoon Sergeant	Sergeant
Naik	Section commander	Corporal
Lance Naik	Section 2i/c	Lance Corporal
Sepoy/Rifleman		Private/Rifleman

The word Sepoy is an eighteenth-century British misspelling of the Persian word *Sipāhi* from the Persian word, *Sipāh* meaning army

RAP – Regimental Aid Post, the place where the medical officer (MO) of a battalion, or equivalent-size unit, set up his aid post. Usually the requirement here was to administer 'sophisticated first aid' to stabilise the casualty sufficiently to enable him to survive the next stage of evacuation

RASC – Royal Army Service Corps

Regiment (British and Indian Army) – originally of horse, dragoons or foot, raised by command of monarch, and later Parliament, and named after its colonel, originally a royal appointee. The regiment became the basic organisation of the British Army and Indian Army, for armour, artillery, engineers, signals, and logistic units equivalent to battalions of those arms in other armies. In the case of the infantry, the British or Indian Army battalion belongs to a regiment, of which there may be one or more battalions and who may not serve together in the same area, or even in the same theatre of operations.

The Indian Army reorganisation of 1922 formed infantry regiments of up to six battalions each, and, on the outbreak of war, many more battalions. There were several regiments with the same title, depending on the origins of their soldiers, and these were numbered. Often an Indian Army battalion would contain mixed classes of soldiers (see Martial Class) divided into companies. Hence the 7th/10th Baluch Regiment is the 7th battalion of the 10th Baluch Regiment whose soldiers are Dogras, Punjabi Mussulmans (Muslims) and Pathans. The 3rd/2nd Gurkha Rifles, is the 3rd battalion of the 2nd Gurkha Rifles

Regiment (Japanese) – a formation of three infantry battalions, usually stronger than a British brigade

Regimental Sergeant Major (RSM) – it is one of the idiosyncrasies of the British Army that infantry battalions and regiments (artillery and armoured) all have a Warrant Officer Class 1 called the Regimental Sergeant Major. He is the commanding officer's right-hand man and adviser on many aspects of battalion/regiment daily life, especially matters involving the soldiers and NCOs. The CO and the RSM have very likely known each other since the former was a second lieutenant and the latter a young private or equivalent. There was no equivalent in the Indian Army of the time, the nearest being the Subedar Major (see VCO and Ranks)

'Rhubarb' – an RAF slang phrase for opportunistic strafing

RIN – Royal Indian Navy

RM – Royal Marines

RV – rendezvous

Sapper – the equivalent of private in the Royal Engineers, or a name for all engineers

SBS – there were two organisations with the acronym SBS in the Second World War. The first was founded as a Folboat Section in 1940 and was known as the Special Boat Section (SBS). The sections were numbered, and 2 SBS appears in this book. This was entirely separate from the Special Boat Squadron (also SBS) formed from a squadron of the Special Air Service in the Middle East, which did not serve in Burma

SEAC – South East Asia Command. The Supreme Allied Commander SEAC, Admiral Mountbatten, was responsible direct to the British Chiefs of Staff in London, and through them to the Combined British and US Chiefs of Staff for all operations by land, sea and air in Burma, Malaya, and

Sumatra, and for clandestine operations in Thailand and French Indo-China

SMG – Sub-machine gun, a short weapon, capable of firing automatic. (See Sten gun)

SpitfireMk VIII – single-engined fighter of Battle of Britain fame. Proved superior to Japanese Zero and Oscar fighters

Start Line – a line in the ground, usually a natural feature, stream, bank, or fence, preferably at ninety degrees to the axis of advance, which marks the start line for the attack and is crossed at H-Hour in attack formation. Can be marked by tape if there is no natural feature which lends itself to being used as a start line

Sten gun – a cheap, mass-produced sub-machine gun of British design. It fired 9-mm ammunition, and had a thirty-two-round magazine. Ineffective except at close quarters; it was inaccurate and the round had poor penetrating power. Because of its propensity to fire by mistake, it was sometimes more dangerous to its owner and those standing around, than to the enemy

Subedar, Subedar Major – see ranks

Syce — groom

Tac HQ – Tactical Headquarters, a small group including the CO, or brigade commander forward of the main HQ

TEWTS – Tactical Exercises Without Troops, theoretical exercises conducted on suitable terrain to test officers and non-commissioned officers in tactical problems, map reading, and giving orders, but not involving troops

Thursday – the codeword for Wingate's second expedition behind enemy lines

TG – short for Tommy Gun, or Thompson Sub-machine gun, favoured by American gangsters in the 1920s and 1930s

Tiffin – lunch

Tiger Moth — a light aircraft of pre-1939 design

Tokyo Rose – the name given to Iva Toguri D'Aquino, an American–Japanese citizen with an especially beguiling voice who broadcast propaganda in English to the Allies

TSM – Troop Sergeant Major

ULTRA – originally the British codeword for intelligence gained by decrypting German and Italian codes. When the war against Japan began, the British and Americans used this codeword to include all Japanese military communications broken by cryptoanalysis. (Neither the Soviets, the Chinese nor any other Allies were privy to the secret)

USAAF – United States Army Air Force; until 1947 the air force was part of the US Army

VC – Victoria Cross, the highest British award for bravery in the face of the enemy. To date, in the 145 years since its inception by Queen Victoria during the Crimean War of 1854–56, only 1,358 VCs have been awarded, including a handful of double VCs, and the one presented to the American Unknown Warrior at Arlington. This figure includes the many awarded to Imperial, Commonwealth and Dominion servicemen

VCO – Viceroy's Commissioned Officer. There were three kinds of commissioned officer in the Indian Army of the time. British and Indian officers with the King's Commission who, in peacetime, or when not in battle or on operations in wartime, lived in the Officer's Mess. VCOs were commissioned from the ranks of the regiment or battalion, had a Viceroy's Commission as the name implies, and were junior to all King's Commissioned officers of any rank. Their nearest equivalent in the British Army was Warrant Officer, but VCOs had much higher status, commanded platoons, were second-in-command of companies, and lived in their own mess. They were addressed as Subedar Sahib, or Jemadar Sahib, by all ranks including by King's Commissioned officers. The Subedar Major was the senior VCO in an Indian Army Battalion, and had probably joined as a young sepoy or rifleman at about the same time as the CO joined as a subaltern. He was the CO's right-hand man and adviser on all regimental matters such as customs, promotions, recruiting, religion, and how well, or otherwise, the British officers (especially the younger ones) were relating to their Indian soldiers

Very Pistol – a smooth-bore pistol for firing green, white or red Very signal cartridges. Hence Very lights

Vickers medium machine gun – First World War vintage, belt-fed, water-cooled machine gun, rate of fire five hundred rounds per minute. Maximum range with Mark VIIIZ ammunition, 4,500 yards. Last fired in action in 1962

Waco glider – so called because it was made by the Waco Aircraft Co, USA, a fifteen-seater, troop- and cargo-carrying high-wing monoplane glider; payload 1.7 tons. The nose of the glider, including the pilot's cockpit, could be raised up and locked into position, which allowed jeeps and small bulldozers to be loaded, and driven out, through the nose

Wadi – Arabic for valley, a term much used by British troops in the Middle East at the time, and by the British Army to this day

Wallah – an Anglo-Indian civilian and army slang expression meaning 'chap' of 'fellow' as in, 'tell that Wallah to go away.' Often associated with a profession, or someone in charge of a particular activity. For example, the 'amen Wallah' is the chaplain, the 'ghorry Wallah' is the driver, and the box wWallah' is a businessmen

Watch and Ward scheme – set up by an ex-Assam Rifles officer to use local tribespeople as intelligence scouts against the Japanese

Zero(s) – Mitsubishi A6M Zero-Sen, the most famous of all Japanese combat aircraft, fast, highly manoeuvrable, and with a long radius of action. To begin with it ruled the skies, but it was eventually outclassed as the Allies produced better fighter aircraft

Z-Lighters – flat-bottomed vessels, usually without engines, and towed by tugs, used for unlaoding cargos from merchant ships, or for transporting vehicles and stores to a beach. Can be beached and used as a pontoon or jetty

PRONUNCIATION OF BURMESE NAMES

The more unusual names are as follows:

Spelt	Pronounced
Buthidaung	Buthidong ('u' as in 'book')
Chaung	Chong
Daingbon Chaung	Danebonchong
Indawgyi Lake	Indoorji Lake
Kabaw	Korebore
Kyaukchaw	Chalkchore
Kyaukpyu	Chalkpew
Kyaukse	Chalksi
Kyauktaw	Chalktore
Maymyo	Maymeeoh
Meiktila	Miketiller or sometimes Mecktiller
Moulmein	Moolmain
Myebon	My-ee-bon
Myitkyina	Michina
Tuitum	Tweetum

Index of Contributors

Number in brackets denotes IWM Sound Archive catalogue number.
Page numbers in **bold** refer to photographs.

Acton, Lieutenant Richard [20482] 309, 316, 320

Aitchison, Captain George [18822] 257–8, 259, 260–1, 264–5, 266, 269

Allison, Sergeant Frank [18472] 316–17, 321

Anderson, Captain John [20124] 118, 120, 124, 126, 128, 130, 131, 134

Atkins, Colour Sergeant Harold [12440] 154, 156, 158, 159, 160, 162, 164–5, 166–7, 191

Aves, Private Charles [15486] 66, 68–9, 89–90, 94–5, 99, 103

Baker, Private Arthur [12294] 154, 162, 164, 165–6, 340

Baker, Gunner James [13857] 330, 345, 347

Bell, Lance Corporal Henry [16726] 223, **224**

Bell, Colour Sergeant 'Dinger' [20309] 170, 309–10, 319–20

Binnie, Lieutenant Arthur [14724]156, 173, 177, 183, 191, 200–1

Bootland, Mrs Margaret ('Beth') [19821] 8–9, 28–30, 32–4, 37–8

Boshell, Major Francis 'Frankie' [15578] 220–1

Braithwaite, Flying Officer Cecil [12288] 47

Brimah, Private Ali Haji Abdul Aziz [18429] 146

Brodrick, Major Frank [20058] 340, 354, 357

Calvert, Major/Brigadier Michael [9942] 24–5, 27–8, 30–2, 35–6, 39–40, 63, 65–6, 68, 69–70, 71, 79, 80–1, 82, 83, 84–5, 91, 92, 93, 94, 104, 106, 108, 153, **155**, 167, 176, 184, 185, 187, 188, 189, 200, 201, **202**

Carfrae, Major Charles [10467] 183–4, 185, 188–90

Cattle, Private Tom [20363] 219, 225, 227, 238–9, 230, 245–6, 333–4, 337, 339, 347

Cobley, Pilot Officer Roger [19106] 116, 284, 314

Connolly, Trooper Malcolm [19049] 269–70, 272, 275–6, 277, 279, 294–5, 296–7, 298, 350, 364–6

Cook, Sergeant William [17265] 239–40

Cornell, Private William [14981] 222–3

Cottier, Corporal Fred [10601] 50

Cree, Lieutenant Colonel Gerald [10469] 127, 131, 210–11, 294

Cron, Private William [15609] 245

Crouch, Private Leslie [21102]118, **119**, 212

Daunt, Private Ivan [20461] 121–2, 213

Davies, Captain Dickie [17936] 238

Dillon, Lieutenant Anthony [19907] 4, 6, **20**, 23, 25–7

Dunn, Private Ray [19771] 280–1

Dunning, Corporal Jim [19665] 327, **328**, 329

Fergusson, Brigadier Bernard [2586] **74**, 75, 81, 84, 85, 153, 156, 158–9, 160, 188, 368

Fiddament, Private Dick [17354] 232, 233, 236

Fitt, Sergeant Albert 'Winkie' [16970] 230, 233, 234, 235, 236–7, 238

Foster, Private Henry [19815] 130–1, 133–4, **135**, 363

Franses, Second Lieutenant Maurice [17353] 243, 245

Freer, Corporal Arthur [19822] 272, 274–5, 276–7, 292, 297–8, 301–2, 303–4, 347

Fujiwara, Yuwaichi [2862] 252, 254, 293

Gadsdon, Captain Peter [10430] 124, **125**, 126, 350

Galley, Corporal Ernest [18510] 48, 49–50, 54, 55–6, 58

Gilding, CSM Walter [17534] 243, **244**

Graham, Lieutenant Gordon [19673] 228, **229**, 230, 246, 364, 365

Graham-Bower, Ursula [8756] 209–10, 211–12, 246–7, 301

Griffiths, Corporal Les [19766] 261–2, 290, **291**, 292, 340–1, 353, 354, 357

Groocock, Flight Sergeant Deryck [12559] 46–7, 79, 170, 221–2

Gudgeon, Lieutenant Denis [12355] 66–7, 68, 71, 77, 81, 93, 107

Hamilton, Lieutenant John [18430] 142, 144, 146–7

Harper, Major/Lieutenant Colonel Alexander [16442] 170, 177–8, 184–5, 186–7, 195–6, 198–9, 200

Harrison, Sergeant Frank [16730] 56, **57**, 58–9

Harwood, CSM Herbert [20769] 136–7, 139, **140**, 211, 213–15

Hazelhurst, Private Peter [19062] 272, **273**, 280, 341, 343, 345, 351, 356

Hazell, Sergeant Fred [17229] 230, 231, 233, 236, 355

Highett, Lieutenant Trevor [15334] 219, 239, 241

Hogan, Private Neville [12342] 6, **7**, 9–10, 14, 15–16, 17–18, 19, 31, 37, 195, 196–7, 198

Horner, Lieutenant Sam [17230] 230–1, 232, 234, 235, 241

James, Lieutenant Harold [12403] 67–8, 73, 75, 77–8, 79–81, 82–5, 87, 91–2, 93–4, 98–9, 105

James, William-Rhodes [19816] 333

Jones, Sergeant Clifford [16603] 51

Leatheart, Major Percival [18209] 171, 173, 178, 196, 198, 199–200

Lyall-Grant, Major Ian [28826] 267, 268, 367

MacFetridge, Major Charles [21295] 9, 36, 38–9

Marshall, Lieutenant Michael [11069] 116–17, 120–1, 122, **123**, 124, 335, 350

Martin, Lieutenant M. [15335] 267, 268–9

Mattinson, Private John [12915] 168, 169, 171, 173–4, 176, 186, 187

May, Bugler Bert [17684] 232, 233, 246

May, Corporal Stanley [19901] 281, 283

McCloud, Private [19067] Fred 292–3

McCrystal, Lieutenant Arthur 'Mac' [19066] 262, 264, 290

McCutcheon, Captain Donald [16067] 169, 174, 201, 203–4

McLane, Company Sergeant Major Martin [10165] 51, **52**, 53–4

Merchant, Private William [11619] 168, 176, 185–6, 187, 188, 192

Misana, Lieutenant Junichi [23843] 265, 266, 287–8, 293, 295

Misra, Major Dinesh Chandra [18370] 283–4

Morrell, Pilot Officer Harry [17824] 331–2, 354

Morris, Trooper Robert [20468] 21, 23, 34–5, 36–7, 38

Nazawa, Second Lieutenant Satoru [24593] 55, 59, 134, 136

Neill, Lieutenant Dominic [13299] and [14148] 65, 70–1, 72–3, 75, 77, 81, 88–9, 90–1, 92, 96, 97, 100, 101, 102–4, 105–8, 310–12, 324–7, 364

Noakes, Lieutenant Peter [20474] 257,
259–60, 263, 265, 296, 298, 299, 302,
303, 332, 334, 347
Norman, Corporal William [19777] 6,
8, 10–11, 12, 16, 17, 18, 19, 27, 34

Palmer, Private William [20476] 283, 295
Parry, Flight Lieutenant Owen [11366]
270, **271**, 279, 285, 287, 301
Preston, Private Alexander [15718] 156
Pettigrew, Lieutenant Colonel Hugh
[14742] 335, 339–40, 352

Ralph, Private Victor [20614] 317, 319,
321–2, 366
Randle, Second Lieutenant/
Captain/Major John [20457] x–xi,
10, 11–12, **13**, 14, 16–17, 19, 41,
264, 267, 288, 339, 349, 351, 352–3,
355–6, 357–8, 367
Rhodes-James, Lieutenant Richard
[19593] 169, 179, 192, **193**, 195,
204, 333, 367
Robinson, Sergeant William [17667] 234
Rowley, Major Frederick [20520]
329–31, 345

Salter, Sergeant Jack [20957] 319, 321,
322
Savage, Private William [19063] 281,
283
Savin, Sergeant Sidney [10424] 47–8,
50, 51, 54–5
Scott, Major Walter 'Scottie' [12352]
66, 87–8, 95, 97, 101, 107, 167,
178–9, 197
Sharma, Lieutenant Mahesh [28829]
254–5, 256–7, 285, 293
Sherwood, Lieutenant James [9783]
312, **313**, 314, 322, 324, 351, 352,
354
Simpson, Pilot Officer Joe [12376] 176,
194
Singh, Squadron Leader Arjun [28836]
366–7
Singh, Lieutenant Harbans [28849] 254

Singh, Lieutenant Harpratab [28845]
339
Singh, Second Lieutenant Shiv [28849]
254
Singh, Havildar Umrao [28861] 315,
316, 368
Smith, Major Harry [19090] 118, 136,
137, 139, 141, 211, 212, 216–17,
219, 220, 349, 353, 355, 356
Smyth, Major General John 'Jackie'
[2812] 4, 15

Taylor, Lieutenant Peter [19929] 154,
156, 160, **161**, 162, 163, 188, 189,
190
Tewari, Captain Kristen [18396]
115–16, 141–2, 366
Thirlwell, Pilot Officer James [17567]
171, **172**
Thompson, Squadron Leader Robert
'Bobby' [2559] 77, 78, 94, 99

Varwell, Captain Peter [19903] 24, 26
Vohra Captain A. M. [28830] 256, 367

Weatherall, Lieutenant Stamford
[12281] 314–15
Webber, Sergeant John [20267] 309,
310, 316, 317, **318**, 319, 321
Wheeler, Private Bert [20897] 139, 141,
214, 216
Whyte RAMC, Major Desmond
[12570] ix, 179, 181, 183, 192, 194,
197–8
Wilkins, Gunner Bert [19902] 124,
126–7, 128, 130, 131, **132**, 133
Wilks, Private Jim [19935] 293–4, 295,
341, **342**, 343
Williams, Sergeant Douglas [10041]
78–9, 133, 285
Wilson, Captain/Major Alexander
[20456] 114–15, 227, 294
Winstanley, Major John [17955] 212,
213, 215, 217, 220
Wood, Sergeant Stanley [12251] 335,
337, 352, 355

General Index

Page numbers in **bold** refer to photographs.

Aberdeen 162, 163, 166, 170, 185, 191, 192

Agartala 77

Ahmednuggur 58

air raids/bombing 6, 10, 12, 21, 23, 26–7, 31, 35, 46–7, 116, 127, 178, 185, 203, 265, 270, 281, 285, **286**, 316, 345, **346**, 374, 381–2 *see also* RAF and USAAF

Akyab 45, 46, 47, 48, 308, 314, 316, 366

Alethangyaw 309

Alexander, Lieutenant Colonel 4, 30–1, 35, 75

Allanmyo 34

Allen, Jed 316

Allied forces:

  casualties, number of 361

  retreat from Burma 3–41, 276, 308, 350

  strategy for Burma vii, viii

Allison, Colonel **155**, 169

Allnut, Stan 94

Anglo American Conference, Quebec, 1943 151

Aradura Spur 241, 245

Arakan 45–51, **52**, 53–9, 111–47, 208, 210, 215, 308, 309–29, 355, 361, 362

Assam 4, 26, 34, 36, 46, 64, 111, 141, 152, 155, 156, 185, 191, 200, 207, 210, 211, 307, 361, 362

atom bomb 357, 361

Auktaw 164, 166

Australia 4, 15

Ava Bridge 29, 107, 337

Awlinbyn Village 117

Basha East 255

Baw 88

Bawli Bazaar 118

Bhamo 91, 95, 174

Bhamo–Myitkyina Road 174, 177

Big Tree Hill 245

Bilin 357

Bishenpur 269, 290, 292

Blackpool 170, 194, 195, 196

Bladen, Jerry 188

Blaine, CSM Bob 85, 87, 91, 153, 156, 173, 200

Blaker, Major Frank 200

Blenheim, Bristol 10, 47

Bongyaung Bridge 81

Booth, Lieutenant Colonel 263

Bootland, Alan 8, 28, 29, 33, 37, 38

Bootland, Ian 8, 29, 30, 33

Borrow, Captain **155**

Bose, Chandra 254, 370

Brahmaputra, River 33, 45, 71, 209

'Brighton' jungle airstrip 116

Briscoe, Lieutenant Tom 120

Bristol Beaufighter 107, 332, 354, 370

British Army:

  British Other Ranks (BORs) 72, 77, 88, 100

  Bush Warfare School, Maymyo 24–5, 27–8, 30–2, 35–6, 39–40, 63, 65–6

  casualties, number of 361

  communications 6, 14, 45, 64, 65, 80, 98, 108, 111, 114–15, 126, 147, 152, 162, 165, 192, 207–8,

209, 210, 279, 309

morale 9, 12, 45, 70, 75, 79, 100, 152, 160, 166, 174, 232, 252, 288, 325, 367

Naga Watch and Ward Scheme 209–10, 211–12, 231, 246–7, 301

rations 36, 37, 50, 68, 69, 72, 76, 77, 78, 79, 91, 92, 95, 96, 100, 101, 116, 126, 134, 160, 165, 173, 176, 177, 181, 183, 190, 198–9, 214, 262, 288, 301, 307, 352

retreat from Burma 3–41, 276, 308, 350

strategy for Burma vii, viii, 362

training for Burma campaign 6, 8, 9, 10, 11, 49, 58, 64, 65–73, 85, 89, 96, 108, 114, 115–16, 118, 151, 154–5, 156, 160, 164, 169, 181, 195, 196, 209, 227, 255, 256, 262, 324

weapons *see* weapons

British Land Forces British and Indian Army

Armies:
Eighth Army 112
Fourteenth Army 112, 113, 207, 307–8, 362, 367

Brigades:
3rd West African 153, 196
6th Infantry Brigade 45–6, 294
7th Armoured Brigade 19, 23
14th Indian Infantry Brigade 153
16th Infantry Brigade 153, 154–67, 368
23rd Infantry Brigade 153
33rd Indian Infantry Brigade 118, 124, 126, 128, 131, 134
77th Indian Infantry Brigade 63, 67, 71, 75, 151, 153, 188, 192, 201
111th Indian Infantry Brigade 151, 153, 169, 179, 181, 183, 192, 194, 195, 195–8, 204, 367
161st Indian Infantry Brigade 209, 210

Corps:
IV Corps 64, 104, 106, 111, 207–8, 251
XV Corps 111, 112, 146, 308
XXXIII Corps 209

Divisions:
1st Burma Division 3, 4
2nd (British) Division 45–6, 48, 58, 114–15, 209, 217, 219, 220, 227, 299
5th Indian Division 111–12, 209, 210, 211
7th Indian Division 112, 114, 118, 120, 122, 124, 126, 127, 128, 131, 134, 335, 349
17th Indian Division/Light Division 3, 4, 15, 23, 25, 39, 40, 207, 208, 251–2, **253**, 272, 335, 339–40, 352
19th Indian Division 347, **348**
20th Indian Division, 207
23rd Indian Division 207
25th Indian Division 115–16, 141–2, 324, 366
26th Indian Division 324
70th Division 111–12, 151–2
81st West African 112, **145**, 152, 153

Regiments, Battalions and Batteries:
Commandos:
1 Commando 317, 319, 321–2, 366
42 (Royal Marine) Commando 316–17, 321
44 (Royal Marine) Commando 309–10, 316, 317, 319–20

Engineers:
Bengal Sappers and Miners 176, 254–5, 256–7, 267, 268, 293, 367

Infantry (in alphabetical order):
Argyll & Sutherland Highlanders 114–15, 227
Assam Rifles 220, 246
5th/10th Baluch Regiment 329

7th/10th Baluch Regiment 10, 11–12, 14, 15–17, 19, 41, 264, 267, 288, 329–31, 339, 345, 349, 351, 352–3, 355–6, 357–8, 367

Border Regiment 261–2, 264, 272, 280, 290, 292–3, **300**, 340–1, 343, 345, 351, 352, 353, 354, 355, 356, 357, **344**

Burma Auxiliary Force 6

Burma Frontier Force 3

Burma Rifles 3, 6, 9–10, 12, 14, 19, 30, 31, 37, 64, 67, 71, 75, 84, 85, 93, 98, 104, 105, 153, 163, 197, 219

Devonshire Regiment 280–1, **282**, 283, 295

Dorsetshire Regiment 219, 225, 227, 238–41, 245–6, 333–4, 337, 338, 339, 347

Duke of Wellington's Regiment 6, 8, 10–11, 12, 16–18, 19, 27, 34

Durham Light Infantry 47–50, 51, 54–6, 58–9, 222–3, 334, 337, 352, 355

Frontier Force Rifles 15–16, 256, 259–60, 283, 367

Gambia Regiment 142, 144, 146–7

Gloucestershire Regiment 4–5, 23, 24, 25–7

Gold Coast Regiment 144, 146

Green Howards 327, 329

1st Gurkha Rifles 10, 14, 38, 39, 126, 257–8, 259, 260–1, 264–5, 266, 333

2nd Gurkha Rifles 64, 66–8, 70–3, 75, 77–8, 79–85, 88–9, 90–2, 93–4, 96, 98–9, 100, 101, 102–4, 105–8, 310–12, 324–7, 364

3rd Gurkha Rifles 38, 64, 66–8, 70–3, 75, 77–8, 79–85, 88–9, 90–2, 93–4, 96, 98–9, 100, 101, 102–4, 105–8, 169, 171, 173, 174, 178, 195–6, 198–9, 200,

201, 203–4, 255, 260, 267, 268, 269, 289, 310–12, 324–7, 364

4th Gurkha Rifles 16, 39, 116–17, 120–1, 122, 124, 126, 153, 169, 170, 174, 177–8, 184–5, 186, 201, 203–4, 257–8, 259, 260–1, 264–5, 266, 269, 335, 350

5th Royal Gurkha Rifles 116–17, 120–1, 122, 124, 255, 267, 268, 269, 288, 289, 335, 350

6th Gurkha Rifles 333

7th Gurkha Rifles 10, 14, 38

9th Gurkha Rifles 153, 170, 171, 173, 174, 177–8, 184–5, 186, 195–6, 198–9, 200

10th Gurkha Rifles 106, 259, 265

King's Own Yorkshire Light Infantry (KOYLI) 8–9, 16, 19, 28–30, 32–4, 374

King's Regiment (Liverpool) 66, 67, 68–9, 87–8, 89–90, 94–5, 99, 101, 103, 107, 167, 178–9, 197

Lancashire Fusiliers 168, 169, 171, 173–4, 176, 185–6, 187, 188, 192, 230

Leicestershire Regiment 154, 162, 163, 164, 165–6

Nigeria Regiment 183–4, 185, 188–90

Northamptonshire Regiment 257, 258, 259–60, 263, 265, 296, 298, 299, 301, 302, 303, 332, 334, 347

Queen's Own Cameron Highlanders 228, 230, **242**, 246, 364, 365

Queen's Own Royal West Kent Regiment 118, 121–2, 136–7, 139, 141, 211, 212, 213–15, 216–17, 219, 220, 298, 349, 353, 355, 356

Queen's Royal Regiment 154, 156, 158, 159, 160, 162, 164–5, 166–7, 191

1st Punjab Regiment 258, 259, 260
3rd Punjab Regiment 127
4th Punjab Regiment 124, 126, 350
9th Punjab Regiment 263
14th Punjab Regiment 124, 126, 127, 263, 350
16th Punjab Regiment 258, 259, 260
Rajputana Rifles 136, 283–4
Royal Berkshire Regiment 220–1
1st Royal Jats 38, 39
Royal Norfolk Regiment 230–8, 241, 243, 245, 246, 366
Royal Scots 47, 51, 303
Royal Welch Fusiliers 50, 51, 225
South Staffordshire Regiment 184
West Yorkshire Regiment 127, 130–1, 133–4, 210–11, 270, 277, **278**, 293–4, 295, 341, 343, **344**, 363
Royal Armoured Corps and Indian Armoured Corps (in order of seniority):
3rd Carabiniers, 269–70, 272, 274–7, **278**, 279, 292, 294–5, 296–8, 299, **300**, 301–2, 303–4, 350, 364–6
7th Queen's Own Hussars 21, 23, 34–5, 36–7, 38
7th Light Cavalry 339
25th Dragoons 120, 126, 128, **129**, 131
45th Reconnaissance Regiment 154, 160, 162, 163, 188, 189, 190
Royal Artillery and Indian Artillery (in numerical order):
3rd Indian Light Anti-Aircraft Battery 9, 36, 38–9
33 Mountain Battery 315, 316, 368
134 Medium Regiment 330, 340, 345, **346**, 347

284 Anti-Tank Battery, 24th Light Anti-Aircraft/Anti-Tank Regiment 124, 126–7, 128, 130, 131, **132**, 133
Chindits:
Blaine Detachment (Bladet) 153, 173, 177, 183, 191, 200–1
Chindits 367
across the Chindwin 73–87, **76**
air drops 77–8, 79, 81, 84, 87, 94, 101, 108, 144, 146, 152, 154, 159, 173–4, 179, 181, 183, 192, 194, 221
commanders *see under individual name*
creation of 63–5
disperse and return to India 87–108
first expedition 63–108, 252
organisation of 64
second expedition (Operation Thursday) 151–204
training 65–73, 108, 154, 156, 160
3 Column 66–9, 71, 73, 75, 77–8, 79–81, 82–5, 91–2, 93–4, 98–9, 104, 105, 106, 107, 108
5 Column 74, 75, 84
7 Column 66, 68–9, 75, 80, 81, 89–91, 94–5, 99, 103
8 Column 66, 70–1, 72–3, 75, 77, 81, 87–9, 90, 92, 95, 96, 98, 100, 101, 102–4, 105–8
20 Column 168, 169, 171, 173–4, 176, 185–6, 187, 188, 192
21 Column 154, 156, 158, 159, 160, 162, 164–5, 166–7, 191
22 Column 156
29 Column 183–4, 185, 188–90
35 Column 184
40 Column 169, 174
45 Column 154, 156, 160, 162, 163, 188, 189, 190
49 Column 170, 186
54 Column 154

71 Column 154, 162, 164, 165–6
81 Column 167, 178–9, 197
82 Column 167, 178–9, 197
94 Column 170, 177–8, 184–5,
    186–7
142nd Commando Company 64,
    67, 71
Dahforce 153
Other Forces:
    Royal Marines 24, 309–10, 316,
        317, 319–20, 321
    SBS 312, 314, 314–15, 322, 324,
        351, 354
    V Force 105, 106
    Women's Auxiliary Corps (India)
        (WACI) 209–10, 211–12,
        246–7, 301
Broadway landing zone 153, 167, 168,
    170, 171, 176, 178, 187, 190, 191,
    195
Brodrick, Major 353
Brown, Wing Commander Montague
    354
B-25 178
Budalin 298, 299
Burma:
    Independence 363
    Japanese invasion of vii, viii, 3–41, 5
    military dictatorship, modern 363
Burma Road vii, 6, 111, 152
Burma Traitor Army 103, 146
Buthidaung 59, 111, 112, 120, 134

Calcutta 30, 34, 37, 124, 228, 315, 352
Cane, Peter 170
Cheduba 308, 352
Cherrington, Peter 299, 302
Chin Hills 78–9, 133, 255, 264, 288
China vii, viii, x, 6, 21, 24, 25, 26, 30,
    31, 45, 64, 100, 111, 152, 356
    Chinese–American forces viii, 64,
        111, 156, 192, 195, 201, 203, 204
Chindwin River ix, 4, 29, 35, 36, 37,
    39–40, 45, 64, 66, 73–87, 76, 91, 94,
    95, 96, 98, 101, 102, 103, 104, 105,

107, 111, 156, 159, 160, 207, 252,
    255, 257, 295, 297, 299, 300, 307,
    308
Chins x, 3, 6, 64, 308, 363
Chittagong 47, 48, 58, 59, 118, 124,
    315, 324, 352, 354
Chocolate Staircase 261, 264, 295
cholera 32, 35, 40, 362
Chowringhee landing zone 153, 169,
    170
Christison, Lieutenant General A. F. P.
    112, 114, 308
Churchill, Winston vii, viii, 151
Clinch, Freddie 121, 122
Coates, Captain 32
Coath, Tom 213
Cochrane, Colonel 152, 167, 168
Cole, Lieutenant Colonel 127
Cook, Lieutenant Colonel 95
Cowan, Major General D. T. 'Punch'
    39, 40, 207, 335, 339
Cox's Bazaar 48, 56
Craddock, Sergeant Major 275
Crete East 280, 283

Dacca 54, 55, 58, 77
Daingbon Chaung 317
Dakota 26, 34, 77, 97, 101, 152, 153,
    160, 168, 169, 170, 171, 176, 184,
    191, 195, 200, 211, 270, 316, 341,
    370
Davies, Captain Dickie 236
de Witt, Lieutenant 168, 169, 174
Deacon, George 309
Dead Mule Gulch 281
Dimapur 30, 33, 71, 207, 209, 210, 211,
    212, 219, 228, 239, 241, 257, 269
disease ix, x, 14, 29, 32, 35, 38, 54–5,
    58, 68, 104, 141, 179, 181, 191, 192,
    204, 259, 293, 297, 356, 362 see also
    under individual disease name
Dogras 17, 257, 274, 275
Dohazari 54, 118, 211
Donbaik 45, 46, 48, 50, 55, 56
Donthami river 14

Dorman, Major E.S.P. 301
Dunlop, George 65, 104
Dunn, Pat 15
Duns 319
dysentery ix, x, 38, 68, 141

Eales-White, Major Donald 302
Elbow 48
ENSA 241

Fairgrieve, Major 266
Faithfull, Lieutenant Colonel 27
Fleming, Peter 32
Fort Dufferin 345, **346**, **348**
Fort Hertz ix
Fort White 258
Fort William 34
Foul Point 48
Fraser, George MacDonald 356
Frontier Hill 146

Garvey, Sergeant Major Jimmy 283
Gilkes, Major 69, 75
gliders 152, 167, 170, 173, 174, 204,
    381
Godley, Colonel 38, 39
Gokteik viaduct bridge 30–1, 84, 85, 87
Goppe Pass 118, 120
Goschen, Brigadier 232
Gowan, Tony 197
Gracey, Major General D. D. 207
Griffiths, Captain Taffy 93
Grover, General 227
Gul, Jemadar Pir 126
'Gun Copse' 333
Gurung, Bhanbhagta 326, 327
Gurung, Kumarsing 80
Gurung, Lance Naik Chamar Singh 326

Ha-Go 114
Hailakandi airfield **155**
Hazelhurst, Mike 296
Hedley, Lieutenant Colonel 268
Hendaza raid 65
Herring, 'Fish' 177

Hill 170 317, 319, 321
Hill 551 142
Hill 2171 200
Hill, 'Tosh' 121
Hinks, Stanley 258
Hiroshima 361
Hklak 159
Hogg, Tom 214
Holmes, 'Sherley' 272, 274, 275
Homalin 105, 152, 153
Hong Kong 3, 29, 254
Hopkins, John 258
'Hove' beach airstrip 116, 321
Hudson 78, 79
'Hump' 111
Hunter, Tommy 223
Huntley-Wright, Major 299, 301
Hurribomber 270, 271, 285, **286**, 374
Hurricane 12, 47, 116, 178, 265, 270,
    281, 285, **286**, 374
Hutton, Lieutenant General J. T. 4, 15
Hyde, George 14

Imphal vii, 30, 45, 71, 73, 74, 101, 103,
    104, 106, 112, 162, 173, 207, 208,
    209, 210, 211, 213, 225, 228, 230,
    245, 251–304, 356, 367
Imphal–Dimapur Road 269
Indaw 101, 153–67
Indawgyi Lake 198, 199
India vii, 6, 10, 26, 31, 32, 34, 36, 37,
    39, 45, 46, 51, 63, 64, 65, 66, 69, 70,
    77, 87, 88, 89, 90, 91, 92, 98, 99,
    101, 107, 114, 118, 126, 151, 168,
    170, 191, 192, 208, 209, 210, 215,
    251, 254, 255, 256, 257, 262, 296,
    334, 363, 366 see also under individual
    place name
Irrawaddy ix, 24, 26, 28, 32, 34, 35, 65,
    81, 82, 84, 87, 88, 89, 90, 91, 93, 95,
    108, 169, 170, 173, 174, 203, 302,
    307, 308, 329–49, **338**, 349, 350
Japanese forces:
  Armies:
    Fifteenth Army 3, 112, 207, 208

Twenty-eighth Army 112, 355
Divisions:
  2nd Division 114, 115
  18th Division 357
  28th Army 112, 355
  31st Division 209
  33rd Division 257, 264, 265, 266,
    287–8, 290, 293, 295
  54th Division 114
  55th Division 55, 59, 114, 134,
    136, 146
Indian National Army (INA) x–xi,
  3, 70, 104, 114, 115, 126, 208, 214,
  215, 254, 255–6, 257, 267, 374
Regiments:
  112th Regiment 134
  143rd Regiment 114
  213th Regiment 114, 146
  215th Regiment 10, 11, 12, 14
audacity and courage of viii, ix, 3,
  41, 178, 293, 364
casualties, numbers of viii, 361
invade Burma vii, viii, 3–41, 5
POWs viii, 14, 121, 122, 146, 178,
  190, 215, 241, 256, 311, 312, 322,
  329, 343, 350, 351, 354, 355, 364,
  365
POWs, treatment of Allied viii,
  14, 28, 84, 107, 146, 151, 215,
  235, 256, 298, 311, 350, 354,
  357–8, 361, 364, 365
surrender 357–8, 361
Jumna 320

Kabaw Valley 257, 259, 265, 296, 297
Kachin Hills 91
Kachins x, 3, 64, 102, 163, 177, 363
Kai-Shek, Chiang viii
Kaladan river 45, 112
Kaladan valley 112, 142–7, 314, 319–20
Kalapanzin River 114
Kalewa vii, 29–30, 36, 37, 207, 251,
  297, 300
Kangaw 317, 323
Kanglatongbi 252, 269, 272

Kanhla 335
Kanzauk–Hitzwe Road 112
Kaphi Lui River 266
Karens x, 3, 6, 64, 82, 83, 87, 91, 93,
  163, 198, 308, 363
Kaukkwe Chaung 96, 101
Kawabe, Lieutenant General 307
Keeble, Major 260
Kennedy Peak 258, 259, 260, 261, 262,
  295
Khan, Mehr 11
Khaso 91
Kilroy, Colonel 115
Kimura, Lieutenant General Hyotaro
  307, 308
King, Victor 213, 217
Kohima 112, 162, 207–47, 251, 254,
  257, 269, 367
  Daily Issue Store (DIS) Hill 209, 215
  DC's Bungalow 209, 212, 216, 218,
    238
  Field Supply Depot (FSD) Hill 209
  Garrison Hill 209, 212, 215, 217,
    219, 223, 225, 226
  General Purpose Transport (GPT)
    Ridge 209, 232, 234, 235
  Jail Hill 209, 213, 214, 240
  Kuki Picket 209, 213, 217, 225, 240
Kohima–Imphal Road 245, 293–4
Kra Isthmus 3
Kuzeik 10
Kwazon 122, 124
Kyaikyto 11, 358
Kyaukchaw 258, 259
Kyaukpyau Harbour 322, 324, 351
Kyauktaw 112, 146, 147

L-1 light aircraft 152, 187
L-5 light aircraft 124, 152, 182, 187,
  200, 314
Laurie, Keith 14
Ledo 64, 111
Ledo Road 152, 153, 156, 157, 195
Lee-Grant Tank 120, 238, 239, 276,
  278, 290, 300, 375

Lentaigne, Brigadier W. D. A. 'Joe' 151, 178, 179, 183
Letpan 327
Letwedet 112
Lion Box 269, 272
Livingstone, Major 314–15, 324
Lockett, Lieutenant Geoffrey 80
Logtak Lake 251, 252, 292
Lone Tree Hill 283–4
long-range penetration (LRP) 151, 152
Lumley, Major 202
Lynn, Vera 241

Maingna 203–4
malaria ix, x, 26, 28, 29, 47, 54–5, 58, 68, 103, 104, 141, 179, 181, 191, 192, 234, 259, 293, 297, 362
Malaya viii, xi, 3, 114, 126
Mandalay ix, 19, 23, 26, 28, 29, 31, 32, 34, 35, 80, 153, 298, 308, 331, 335, 337, 339, 340, 345, 347, 362
Mandalay–Myitkyina railway 153, 175, 177
Manekshaw, Sam 16
Manipur River 262, 295
Martaban 9, 10
Masters, Major Jack/John 179, 181, 192, 196, 197, 204
Maungdaw 55, 56, 59, 111, 112, 118, 134, 139, 310
Maungdaw–Buthidaung Road 111, 134, 139
Mawlu 176, 188, 191
Maymyo 26, 31, 34
Mayu Peninsula 45
Mayu Range 112, 118
Mayu River 45, 48, 112, 114, 120
McCleavy, Jock 56
McKenzie, David 265
Medally, Private 39, 40
Meiktila ix, 31, 308, 335, 339, 340–1, 343, 344, 349
Mekong Valley 4
Mergui 3
Merrill, Brigadier General Frank D. 152

Messervy, Major General F. W. 112
Meza Chaung 162
Meza River 100, 160
Milford hill 319
Minbu 350
Mingaladon airfield 4, 6, 9, 23
Mitchell bombers 136, 152, 375
Mogaung 192, 199, 200, 201, 202
Mokpalin 16
Mokso Sakan 198
Monywa 296, 298, 302
Mortar Bluff 288, 289
Moulmein ix, 9
Mountbatten, Lord Louis 111, 297, 298, 307
Mu River 302
Murray, Captain David 242
Musgrave, Colonel 27–8
Mustang fighter-bombers, P-51 152
Mutaguchi, Lieutenant General Renya 112, 207, 208, 254
Myainggale 11
Myene 105
Myebon 316, 317, 366
Myitkyina 26, 34, 65, 80, 111, 152, 153, 174, 196, 200, 201, 203, 204
Myitkyina–Rangoon railway 75, 100

Naf River 309, 310, 312
Naga hills 158, 265, 296
Nagasaki 361
Nahkaungdo 310
Nam Mit Chaung 84, 85
Namkwin Chaung 196
Nankan 80, 81
Nerbudda 320
Ngakyedauk Chuang 117
Ngakyedauk Pass 112, 114, 126
Ngazun 337, 338
Nippon Hill 281, 282, 283
North Chaung 334
Nunshigum 252, 272, 276, 279
Nussey, Joe 272
Nyaungu 335

'Okeydoke' Pass *see* Ngakyedauk Pass
Oktaung 122
Ormandy, William 72, 91
Oyster Box 269, 277

Pa-an 10
Pagan 335
Pago 85, 87
Pagoda Hill 15, 16, 147
Pakokku 335, 340
Palel 73, 285
Paungde 25–6, 27
Pear Hill 330
Pearl Harbor vii, 6, 8
Pegu 11, 17, 19, 352, 355, 357
Petersen, Eric 80
Petty, 'Long' John 290, 341
PIAT (Protector Infantry Anti-Tank)
    115, 190, 266, 377
Piccadilly landing zone 153, 167, 169
Pinner 319
Point 8198 257, 260
Potsangbam 290, 292
prisoners (POWs)
    Allied viii, 28, 84, 107, 146, 151,
       215, 235, 298, 357–8, 361, 364
    Japanese viii, 14, 121, 122, 146, 178,
       190, 215, 241, 256, 311, 312, 322,
       329, 343, 350, 351, 354, 355, 364,
       365
    numbers of 361
Probyn's Horse 356
Prome 26, 28, 112, 329
Pulebadze 225
Pyawbwe 351
Pyinmana 18
Pyongi Street Docks 355

RAF viii, 12, 78, 87, 88, 95, 126, 152,
       178, 181, 194, 277, 349
    11 Squadron 270, 279, 285, 287, 301
    20 Squadron 116, 284, 314
    60 Squadron 47
    99 Squadron 46–7
    194 Squadron 78–9, 133, 170, 171,

       176, 194, 221–2, 285
    211 squadron 331–2, 354
Rai, Agansing 288, **289**
Rajputana Hill 284
Ramree Island 308, 322, 324
Rangoon Road 350–5
Rangoon vii, ix, 4, 6, 9, 10, 15, 17, 19,
    21, **22**, 23, 24, 30, 45, 107, 166, 204,
    298, 307, 329, 349, 351, 352, 354,
    355, 361, 362
Ranking, Major General 210
Rathedaung 45
rations 36, 37, 50, 68, 69, 72, 76, 77, 78,
    79, 91, 92, 95, 96, 100, 101, 116,
    126, 134, 160, 165, 173, 176, 177,
    181, 183, 190, 198–9, 214, 262, 288,
    301, 307, 352
Razabil 112, 137, **139**
Reeman, Fred 200
Rees, Major General 'Pete' 330, 331,
    348
Richards, Colonel 210
Roosevelt, Theodore 151
Roy, Major Alan **242**
Royal Artillery 334
Royal Engineers 333
Royal Indian Air Force 367
Ryan, Paddy 272, 274, 275, 276

Saizang 264
Sakawng 267
Sakurai, Lieutenant General Shozo 112,
    114
Sakurai, Major General Tokutaro
    114
Salween River ix, 4, 9, 10, 11, 12, 64,
    65
San, Aung 308, 356, 363
San Suu Kyi, Aung 363
Sandford, Major 272
Saugor 66–7, 154
Scoones, Lieutenant General G. A. P.
    106, 207, 209, 251
Scott, Colonel Robert 230, 232, 234,
    235, 236, 238, 243, 245

Scott, Major Walter 72, 75, 89, 90, 91, 97, 100
Screwdriver Two, Operation 310
Seaforth Highlanders 103
Shaduzup 201
Shans x, 6, 308
Sharp, Richard 239
Shenam Pass 73
Shenam Saddle 281
Shepherd's Crook 48, 50
Sherwood, Lieutenant 314–15
Shillong 191
Shuganu 252
Shwebo 298, 299, 302, 307, 345
Shwedaung 26, 27, 34, 36, 65
Shwegu 92
Shwegyin 36
Shweli River 84, 87, 88, 91, 105
Silchar Track 288, 289
Silcock, George 67, 68, 80, 81, 82–3
Singaling Hkamti 153
Singapore 3, 4, 21, 29, 114, 255
Singh, General Mohan 254
Sinzweya 120, 128
Sittang Bridge 4, 10, 15, 17, 252
Sittang River ix, 4, 10, 11, 14, 15, 17, 19, 207, 251, 355, 356, 357
Sittaung 29–30, 207, 293
Slim, Lieutenant General Sir William 'Bill' 36, 112, **113**, 115, 151, 167, 207, 208, 209, 252, 307–8, 362
Smyth, Major General 'Jackie' 4, 16
Snowden East 324, 325, 326, 327
Souter, Lieutenant Colonel 146
Spitfire 116, 301, 379
Sprague, Lieutenant 'Tag' 72, 88, 91, 96, 98, 100, 102, 104
Stilwell, General 64, 111, 152, 192, 195, 201, 204, 367
Stoker, Bill 262
Stopford, Lieutenant General M. G. N. 209
Sugar 4 and 5 48
Sunderland flying boats 198
Syriam oil refinery 24

Tagap 159
Tagap Ga 153
Tamanathi 207
Tamu 30, 38, 73, 207, 251, 252, 259
Tamu–Palel Road 252
Tanaka, Lieutenant General Nobuo 288
Taukkyan 23, 24
Taung Bazaar 114, 117, 146
Taungup 112, 329
Taungup–Prome Road 112
Tavoy 3, **5**
Teknaf 312, 324
Templecombe landing zone 153
Tenassarim ix, 9
Tengnoupal 252
Thailand (Siam) 3, 254, 354, 355, 361
Thapa, Subedar Indrabir 117
Thapa, Subedar Netrabahudur 288
Thaton 10
Theobalds, Lieutenant Colonel 55
Thetkegyin 163, 190
Tibbetts, Bill 246
Tiddim 251, 257, 261
Tiddim Road 251, 252, **253**, 261, 264, **286**, 295, 296, 365
Tiger Moth 9
Tonforce 264
Tonhe 75, 105
Tonlon 168
Tonzang 264, 267
Torbung 252, 285
Tottenham, Loftus 126
Treasure, Corporal **282**
Tuitum Ridge 265, 266
Tun Tin 91, 92, 96, 98
Turner, Lieutenant Colonel John 335
Twin Knobs 48
Typhoon 349

Ukhrul Road 252
Ukhrul Valley 295
ULTRA 207, 380
Urquhart, John 191

United States viii, x, 6, 21, 152, 208, 280, 288
  Chinese–American forces viii, 64, 111, 156, 192, 195, 201, 203, 204
USAAF viii, x, 26, 34, 152, 181, 194, 345, 380

Vaughan, Peter 184, 188
Victoria Point ix, 3
Vita, Major Norman 332

Walford, Lance Corporal Des 225
Wangjing 252, 265, 298
Water Piquet 288, 289
Wavell, General Sir Archibald 4, 15, 32, 63, 64, 71, **74**
Waw 17
weapons:
  Bangalore torpedoes 188, 319
  Bofors 38–9, 195, 263, 301, 370
  Boyes anti-tank rifle 8
  Bren gun 17, 24, 45, 53–4, 56, 121, 124, 126, 127, 128, 134, 136, 168, 187, 189, 212, 213, 214, 217, 234, 235, 239, 240, 245, 263, 280, 295, 310, 311, 315, 321, 322, 330, 344, 370
  EY rifle 188, 372
  faulty 51, 53–4
  flame throwers 48, 158, 187, 200, 201
  grenades 14, 26, 53, 54, 55, 56, 85, 90, 111, 121, 122, 127, 130, 142, 164, 165, 166, 176, 186, 187, 188, 189, 197, 201, 203, 213, 215, 222, 223, 227, 230, 237, 238, 245, 266, 268, 274, 276, 280, 284, 288, 295, 303, 304, 316, 319, 320, 322, 325, 326–7, 333, 343
  howitzer 315, 330, **346**, 374
  LMG 375
  MMG 12, 14, 24, 25, 71, 309, 334, 370, 371, 376, 381
  mortars 6, 8, 10, 19, 25, 27, 35, 38, 49, 50, 54, 58, 71, 82, 83, 87, 89,

    114, 115, 122, 137, 139, 159, 163, 181, 184, 185, 186, 187, 196, 200, 213, 215, 217, 220, 222, 225, 227, 230, 255, 259, 268, 280, 281, 288, 298, 309, 317, 319, 321, 322, 330, 332, 334, 352, 353, 371, 372
  Sten gun 238, 243, 284, 295, 298, 380
  Thompson SMG 311
  Vickers medium machine gun 12, 14, 24, 25, 71, 309, 334, 370, 371, 376, 381
Wellington bomber 46–7
Wells, Jimmy 337
White, Captain Neil **242**
White City airstrip 170, 174, 184, 185, 187, 188, 189, 190, 191, 201
Whiteley, Ginger 272
William, Private **282**
Williams, Bill 73
Williams, Sergeant 213
Willis, Lance-Corporal **282**
Willoughby, Private **282**
Wilson, Sam 343, 345
Wingate, Major Orde (subsequently Brigadier and Major General) 67, 68, 70, 71, 72, 73, **74**, 114, 183, 184, 195, 198
  American forces and 152
  Anglo–American Conference, Quebec, 1943 151, 152
  Calvert and 80
  Churchill and 151
  creates Chindits 63, 108
  first Chindit expedition 75, 81, 82, 84, 87, 88, 89, 90, 103, 107, 108, 151, 173, 252, 362
  opinions on character of 65, 66, 67, 68, 69, 178–9, 367, 368
  second Chindit expedition 111, 152–3, **155**, 167, 173, 178–9
  Wavell and 63
wounded soldiers 9, 14, 16, 18, 23, 26, 27, 28, 31, 32, 34, 37, 39, 49, 53, 54, 58, 73, 75, 83, 84, 85, 87, 95,

99, 101, 108, 117, 121, 122, 127, 128, 130, 131, 133, 136, 139, 141, **145**, 152, 154, 163, 164, 174, 177, 179–80, **180**, 181, 188, 189, 191, 198, 199, 211, 212, 213, 214, 215, 216, 217, 220, 221, 222, 223, 227, 230, 241, 245, 246, 255, 256, 258, 260, 264, 266, 267, 268, 269, 272, 277, 280, 281, 283, 287, 288, 290, 295, 299, 302, 310, 315, 320, 322, 325, 327, 329, 337, 339, 340, 349, 350, 352, 361, 365, 366

Wright, Holden 312, 314

Yainganpokpi 252
Yenangyaung 36, 350
Yu river 258

Zero fighters 23, 26, 27, 31, 127, 185, 316, 381–2
Zibyu Taungdan 100
Zimbugon 92
Zubza 219, 241